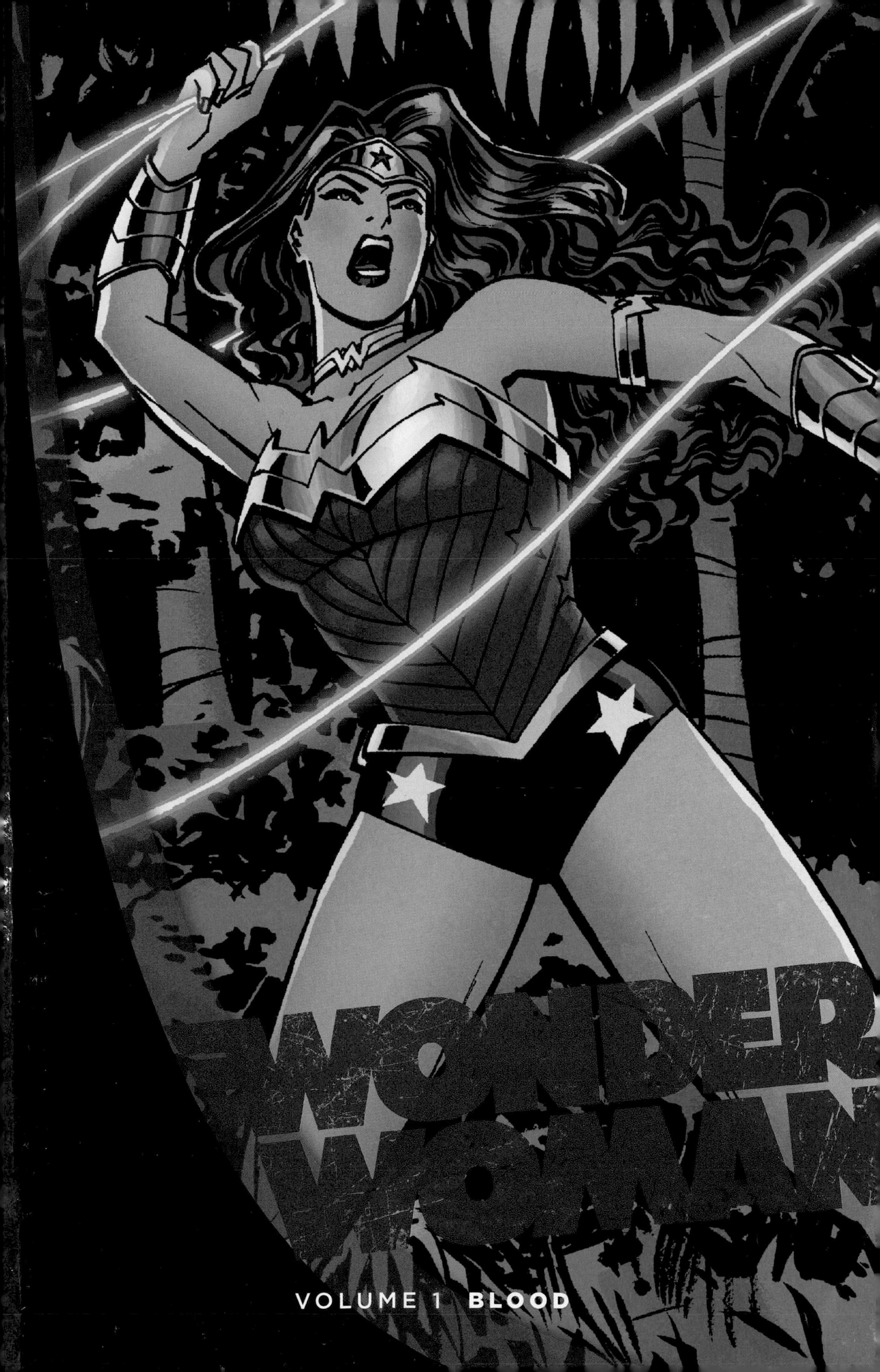
WONDER WOMAN
VOLUME 1 BLOOD

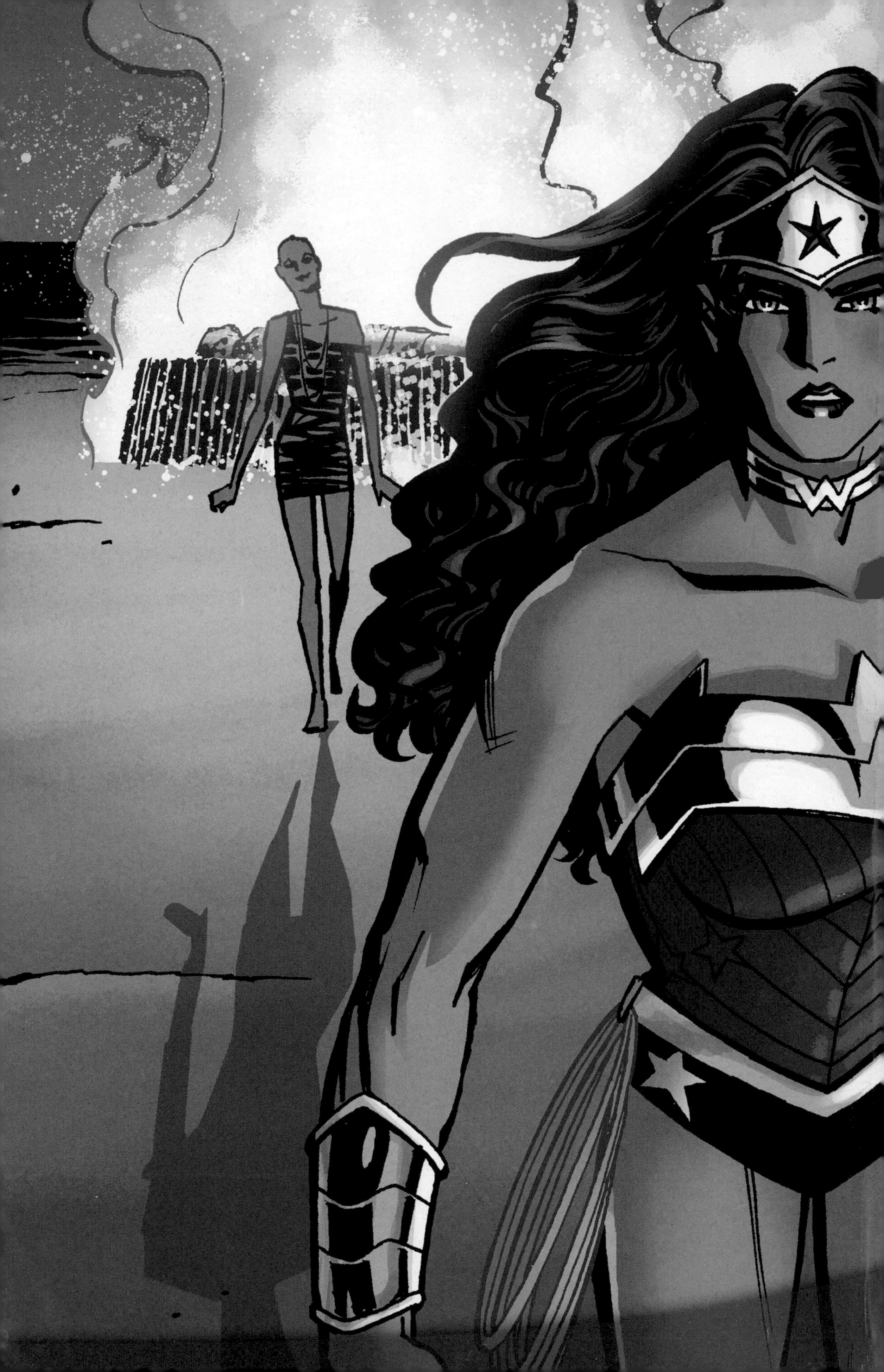

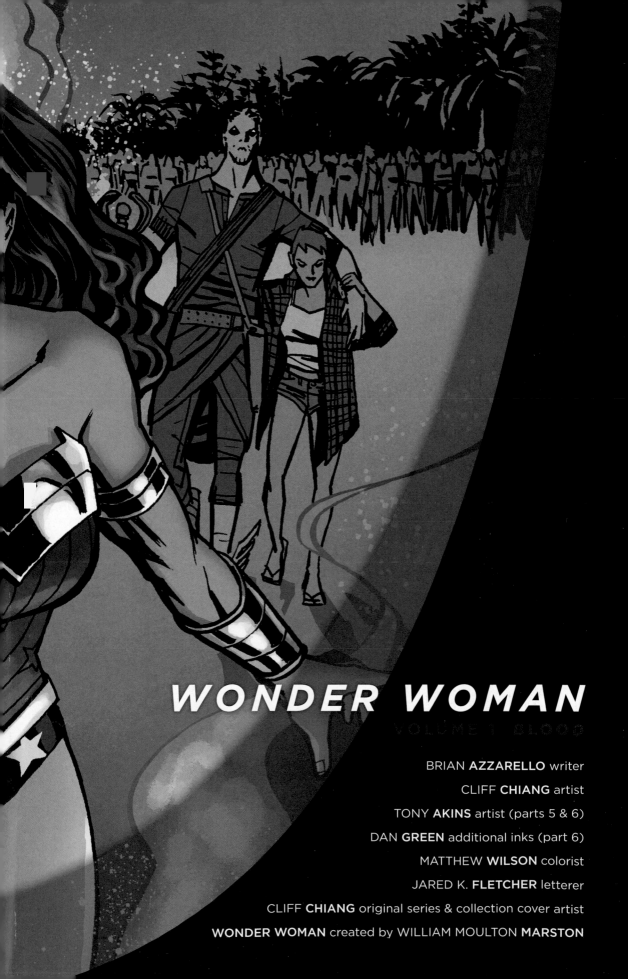

WONDER WOMAN
VOLUME 1 BLOOD

BRIAN **AZZARELLO** writer

CLIFF **CHIANG** artist

TONY **AKINS** artist (parts 5 & 6)

DAN **GREEN** additional inks (part 6)

MATTHEW **WILSON** colorist

JARED K. **FLETCHER** letterer

CLIFF **CHIANG** original series & collection cover artist

WONDER WOMAN created by WILLIAM MOULTON **MARSTON**

MATT IDELSON Editor – Original Series CHRIS CONROY Associate Editor – Original Series
PETER HAMBOUSSI Editor ROBBIN BROSTERMAN Design Director – Books
ROBBIE BIEDERMAN Publication Design

EDDIE BERGANZA Executive Editor
BOB HARRAS VP – Editor-in-Chief

DIANE NELSON President DAN DIDIO and JIM LEE Co-Publishers
GEOFF JOHNS Chief Creative Officer
JOHN ROOD Executive VP – Sales, Marketing and Business Development
AMY GENKINS Senior VP – Business and Legal Affairs NAIRI GARDINER Senior VP – Finance
JEFF BOISON VP – Publishing Operations MARK CHIARELLO VP – Art Direction and Design
JOHN CUNNINGHAM VP – Marketing TERRI CUNNINGHAM VP – Talent Relations and Services
ALISON GILL Senior VP – Manufacturing and Operations DAVID HYDE VP – Publicity
HANK KANALZ Senior VP – Digital JAY KOGAN VP – Business and Legal Affairs, Publishing
JACK MAHAN VP – Business Affairs, Talent NICK NAPOLITANO VP – Manufacturing Administration
SUE POHJA VP – Book Sales COURTNEY SIMMONS Senior VP – Publicity
BOB WAYNE Senior VP – Sales

DC Comics, 1700 Broadway, New York, NY 10019
A Warner Bros. Entertainment Company
Printed by RR Donnelley, Salem, VA, USA. 4/13/12. First Printing.
HC ISBN: 978-1-4012-3563-5
SC ISBN: 978-1-4012-3562-8

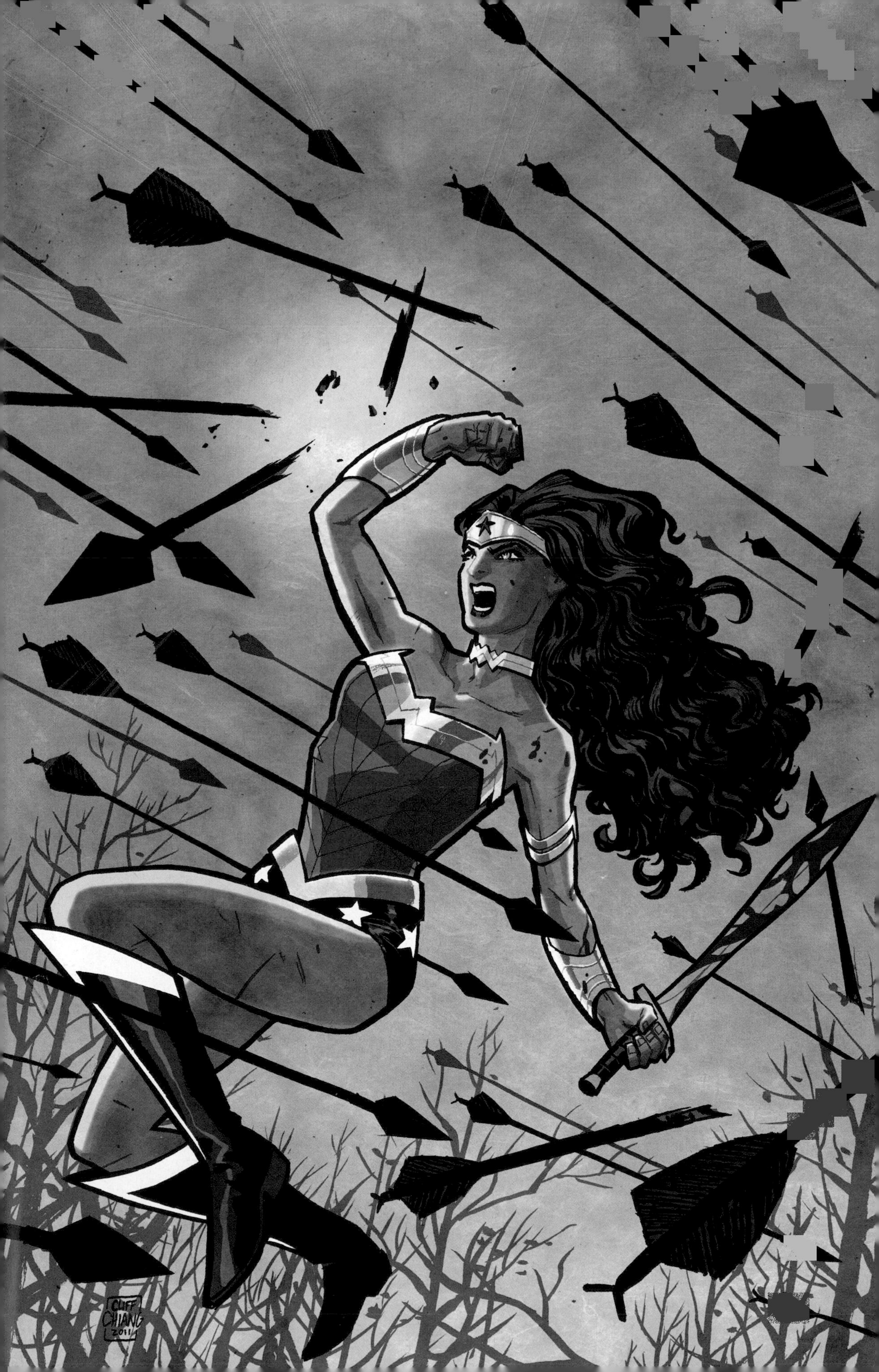
CLIFF CHIANG 2011

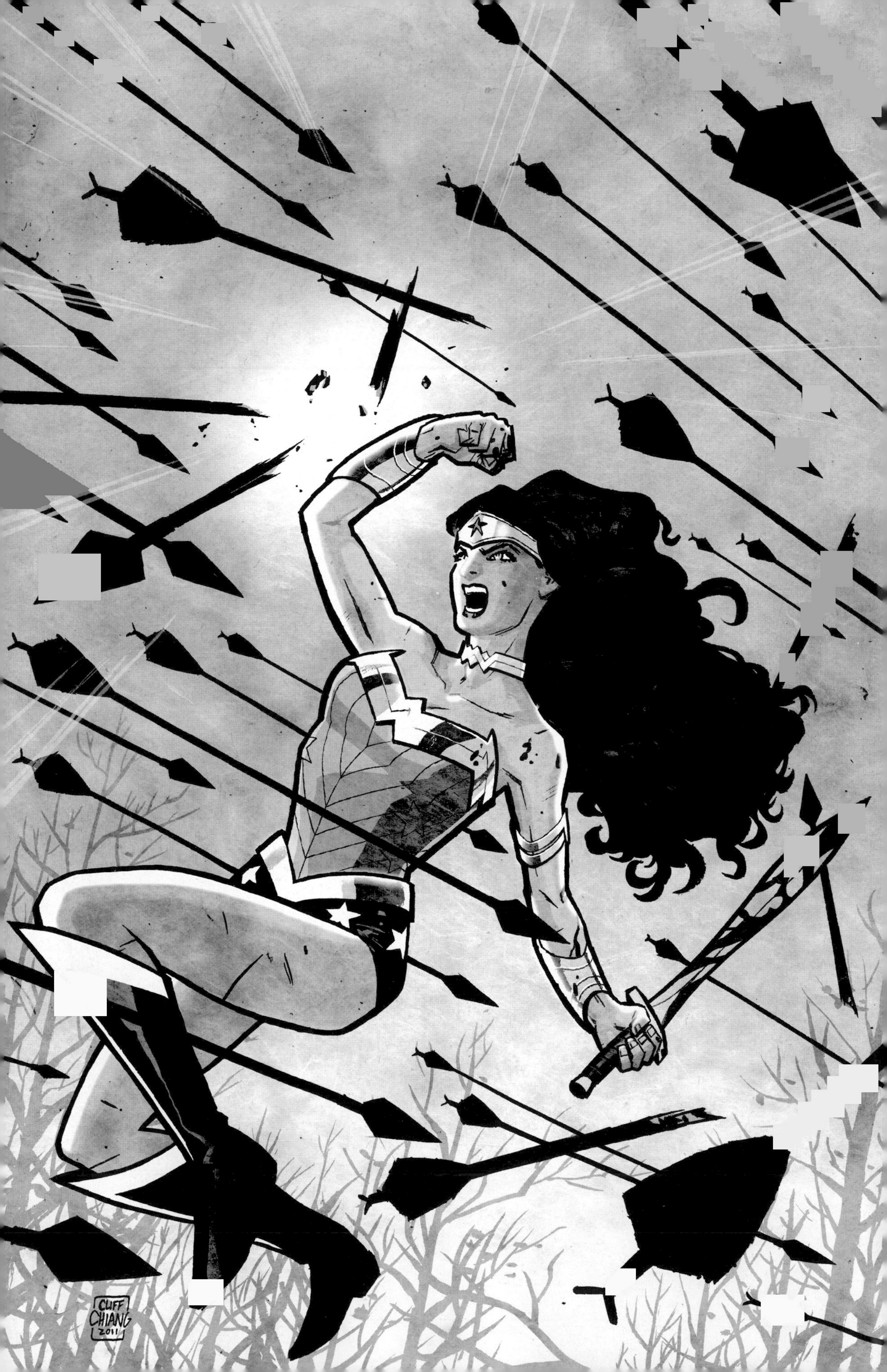
CLIFF CHIANG 2011

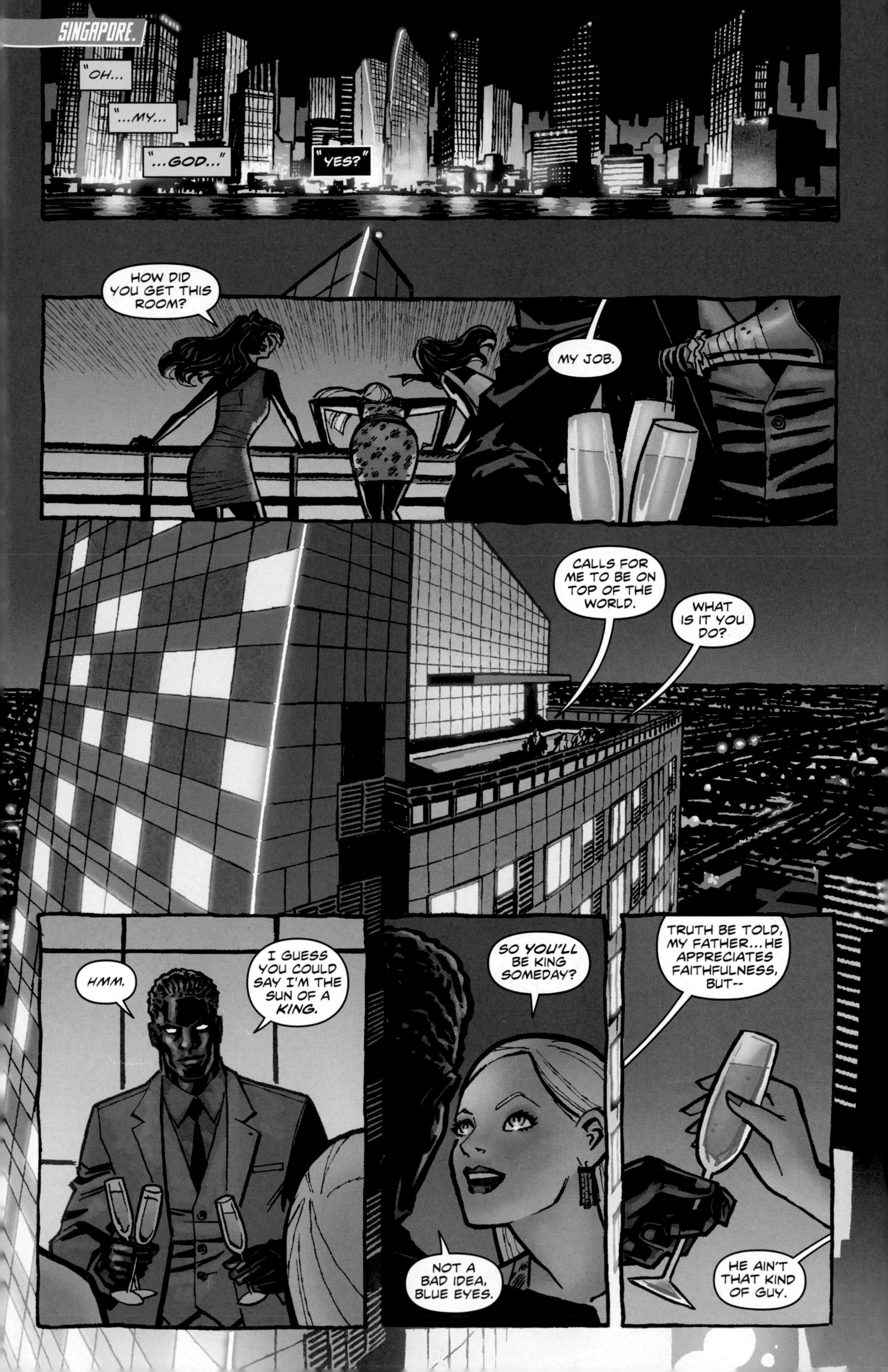
SINGAPORE.
"OH...
"...MY...
"...GOD..."
"YES?"
HOW DID YOU GET THIS ROOM?
MY JOB.
CALLS FOR ME TO BE ON TOP OF THE WORLD.
WHAT IS IT YOU DO?
HMM.
I GUESS YOU COULD SAY I'M THE SUN OF A KING.
SO YOU'LL BE KING SOMEDAY?
NOT A BAD IDEA, BLUE EYES.
TRUTH BE TOLD, MY FATHER...HE APPRECIATES FAITHFULNESS, BUT--
HE AIN'T THAT KIND OF GUY.

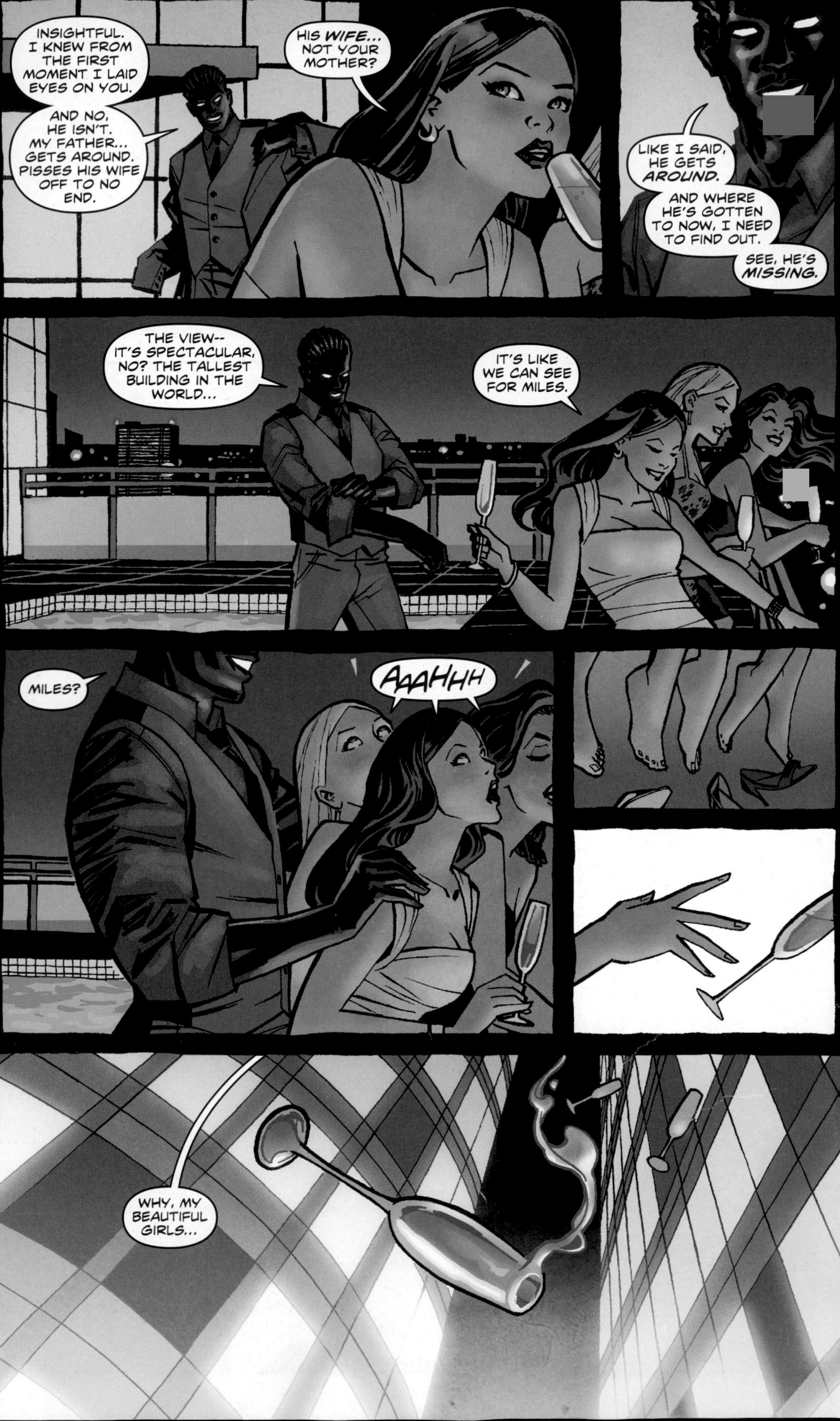
INSIGHTFUL. I KNEW FROM THE FIRST MOMENT I LAID EYES ON YOU.
HIS WIFE... NOT YOUR MOTHER?
AND NO, HE ISN'T. MY FATHER... GETS AROUND. PISSES HIS WIFE OFF TO NO END.
LIKE I SAID, HE GETS AROUND.
AND WHERE HE'S GOTTEN TO NOW, I NEED TO FIND OUT.
SEE, HE'S MISSING.
THE VIEW-- IT'S SPECTACULAR, NO? THE TALLEST BUILDING IN THE WORLD...
IT'S LIKE WE CAN SEE FOR MILES.
MILES?
AAAHHH
WHY, MY BEAUTIFUL GIRLS...

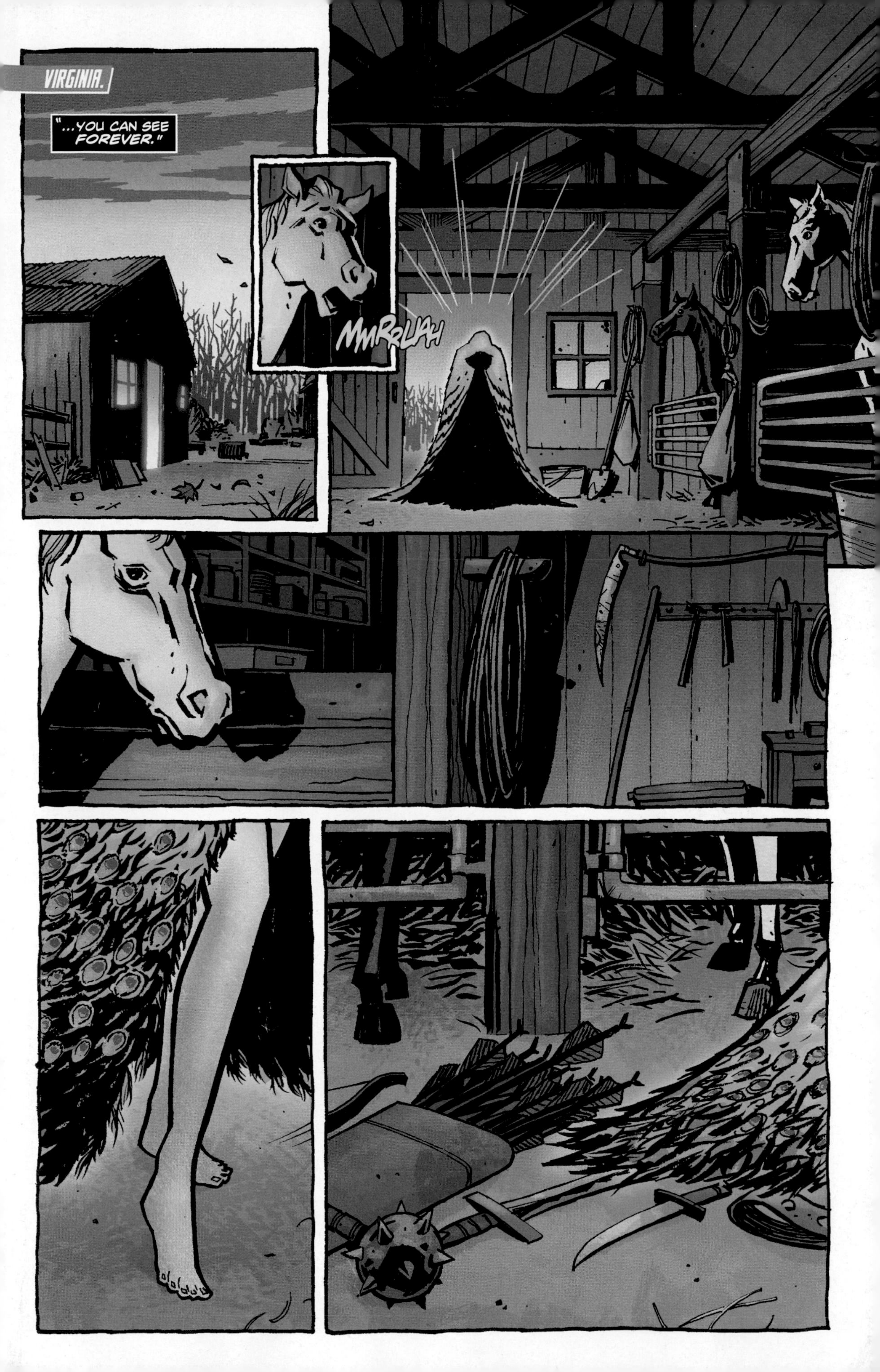
VIRGINIA.
"...YOU CAN SEE FOREVER."
MMRRUAH

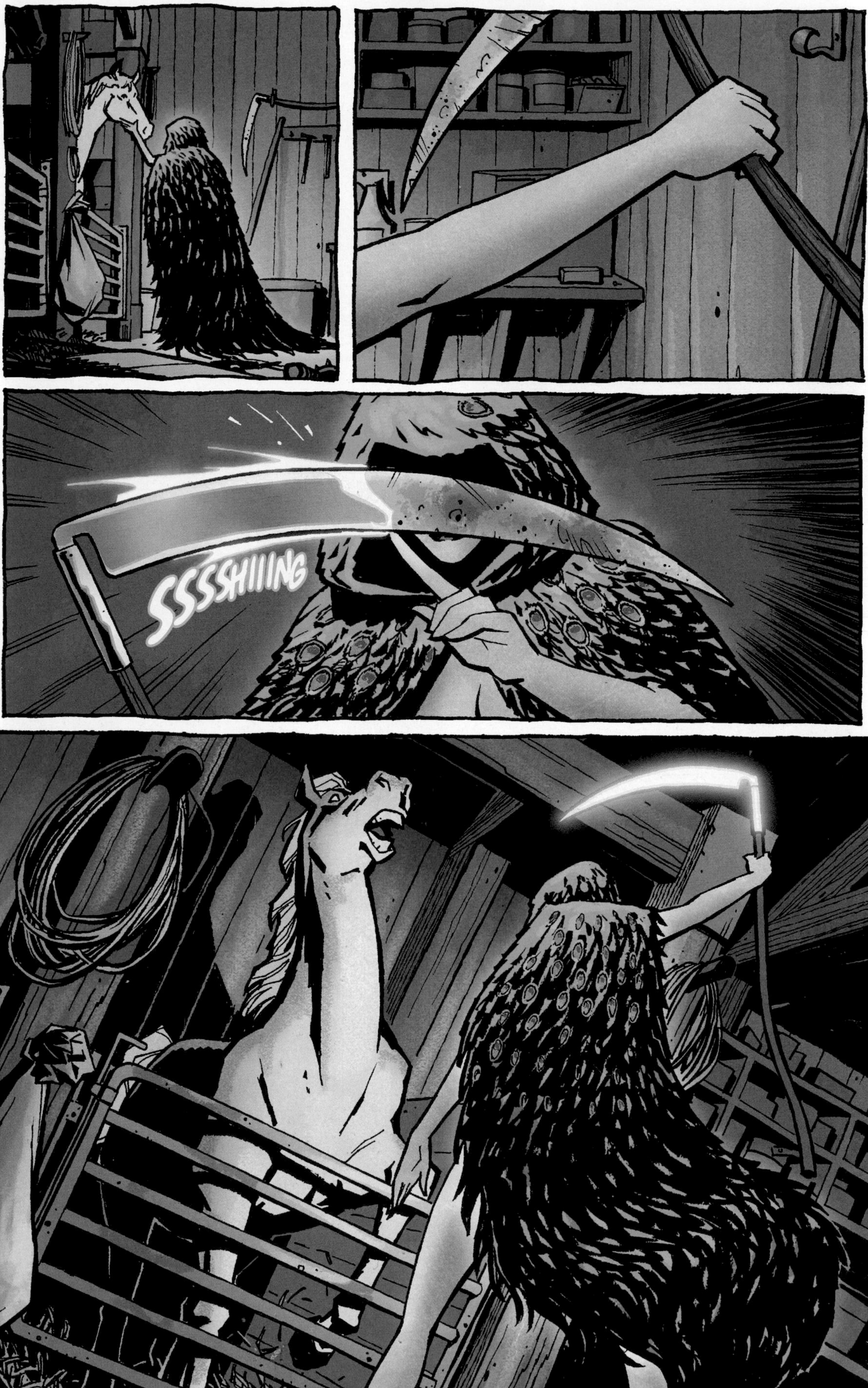
SSSSHIIING

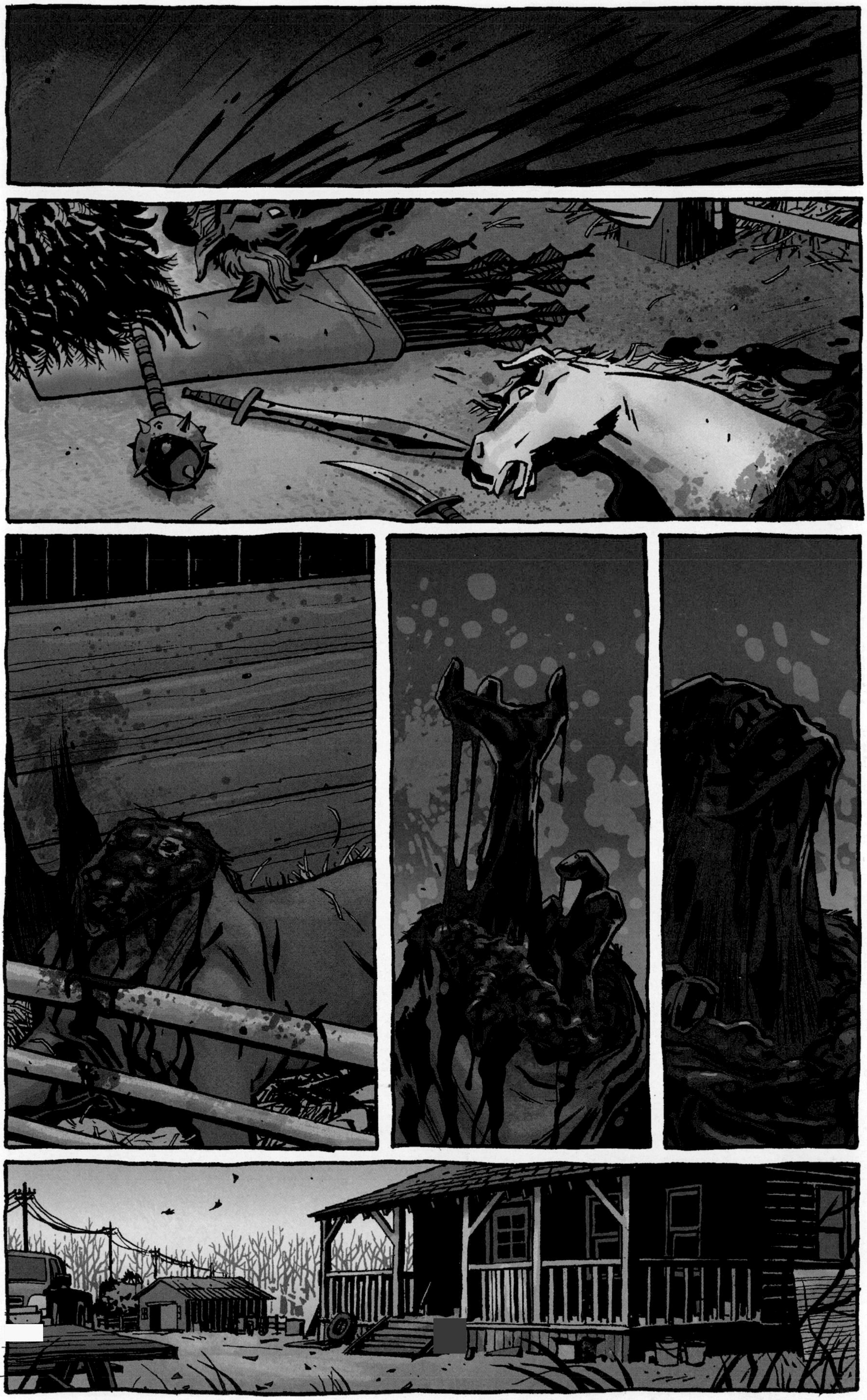

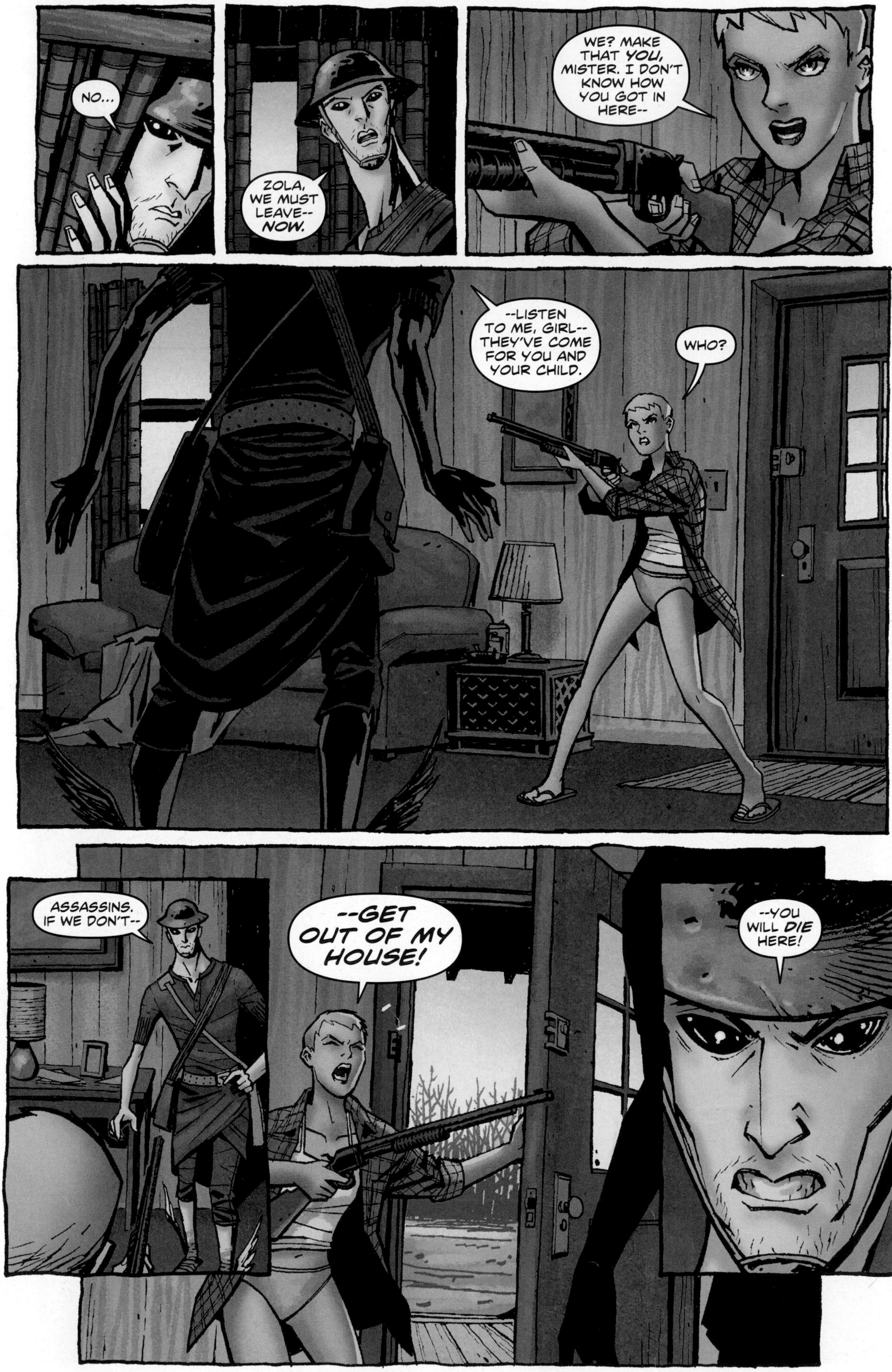
NO...
ZOLA, WE MUST LEAVE-- NOW.
WE? MAKE THAT YOU, MISTER. I DON'T KNOW HOW YOU GOT IN HERE--
--LISTEN TO ME, GIRL-- THEY'VE COME FOR YOU AND YOUR CHILD.
WHO?
ASSASSINS. IF WE DON'T--
--GET OUT OF MY HOUSE!
--YOU WILL DIE HERE!

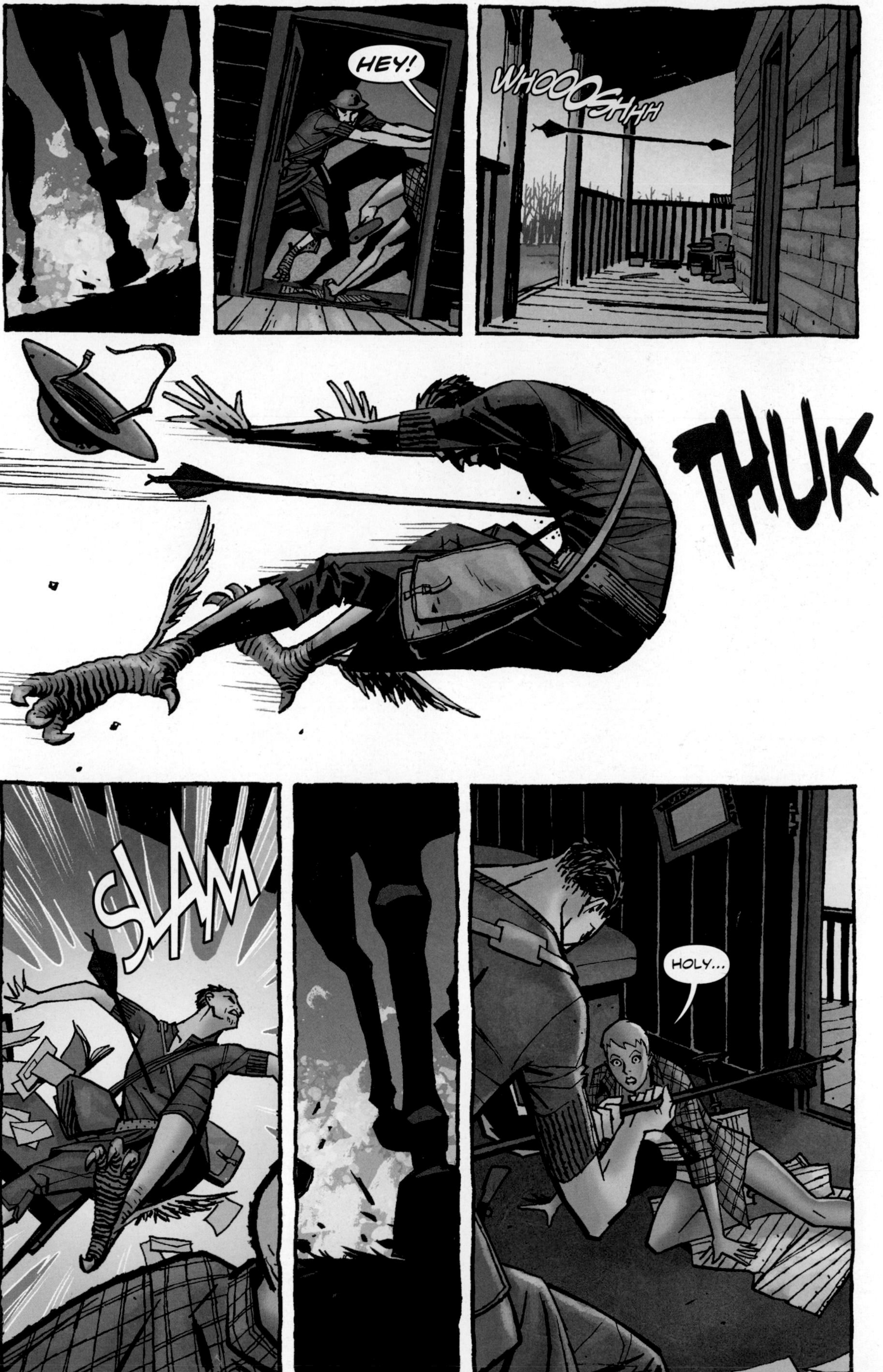
HEY!
WHOOOOSHHH
THUK
SLAM
HOLY...

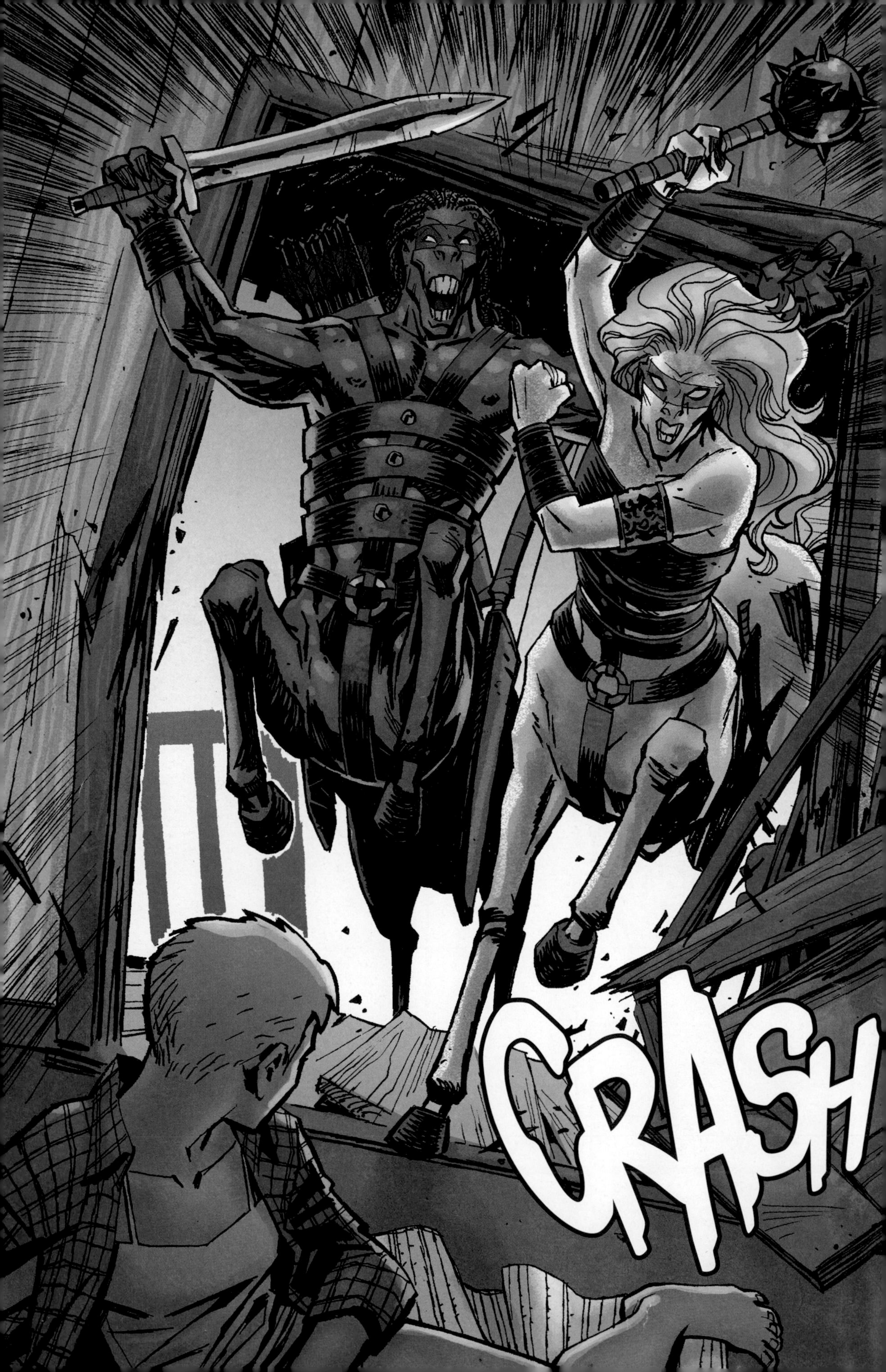
CRASH

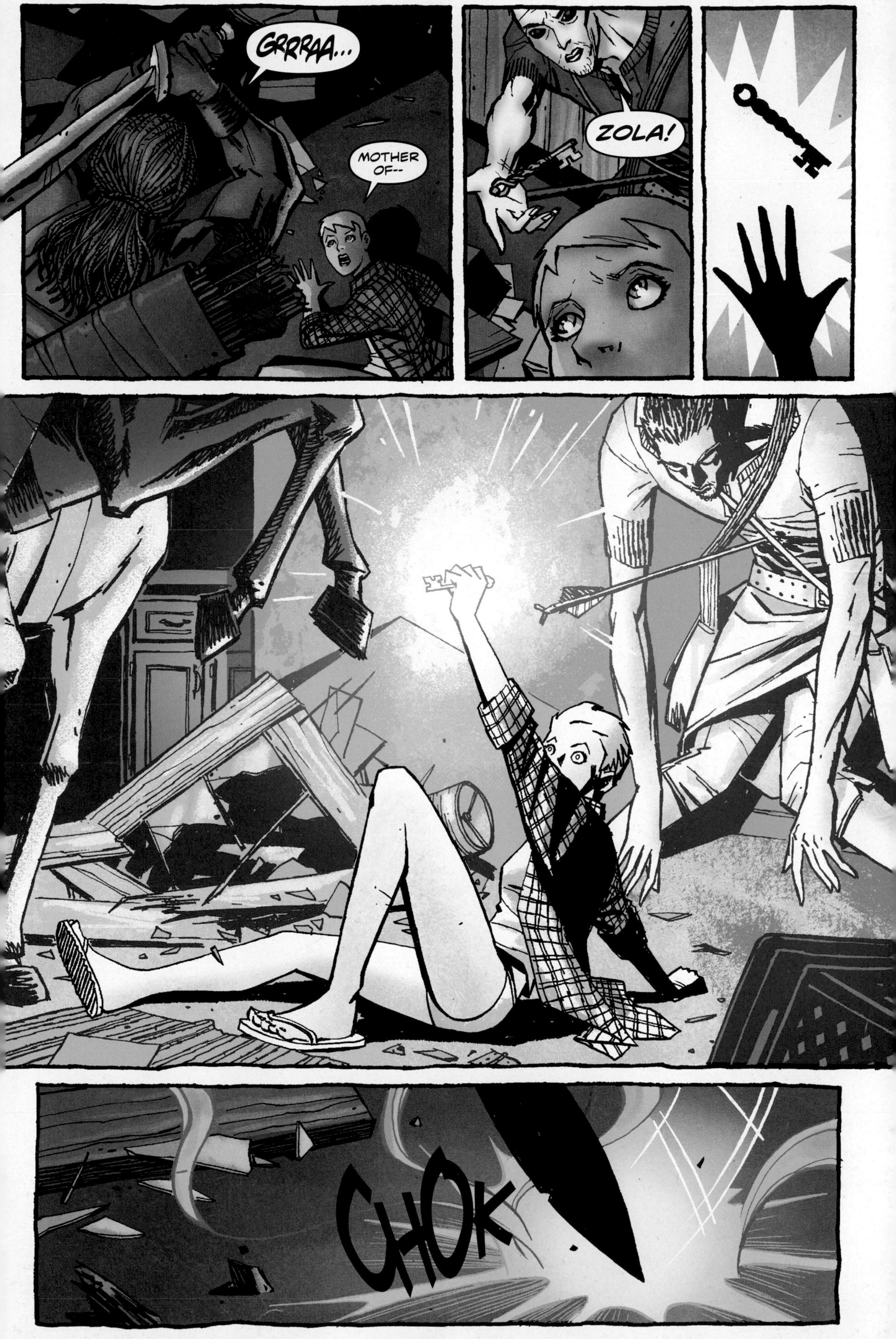
GRRRAA...
MOTHER OF--
ZOLA!
CHOK

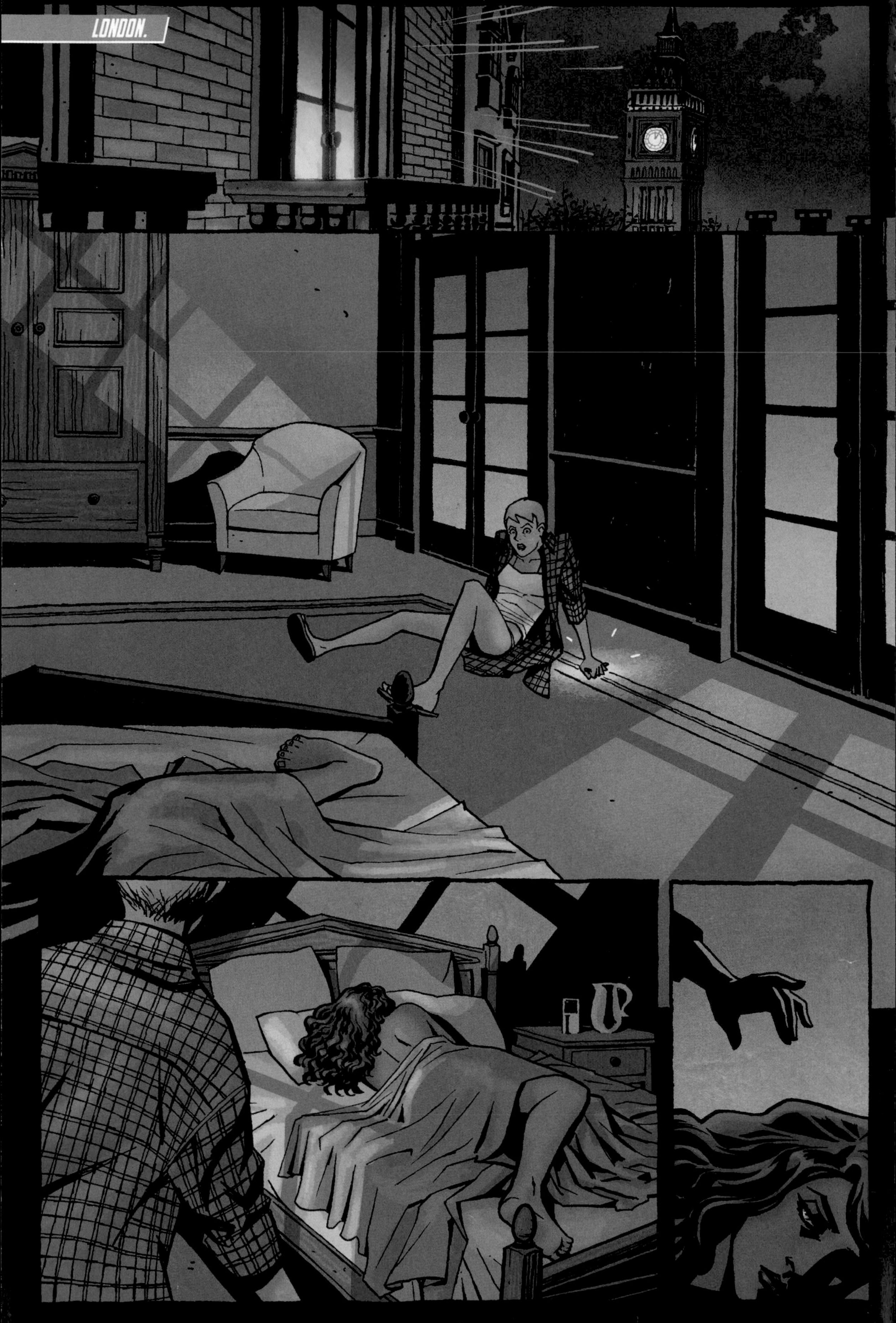
LONDON.

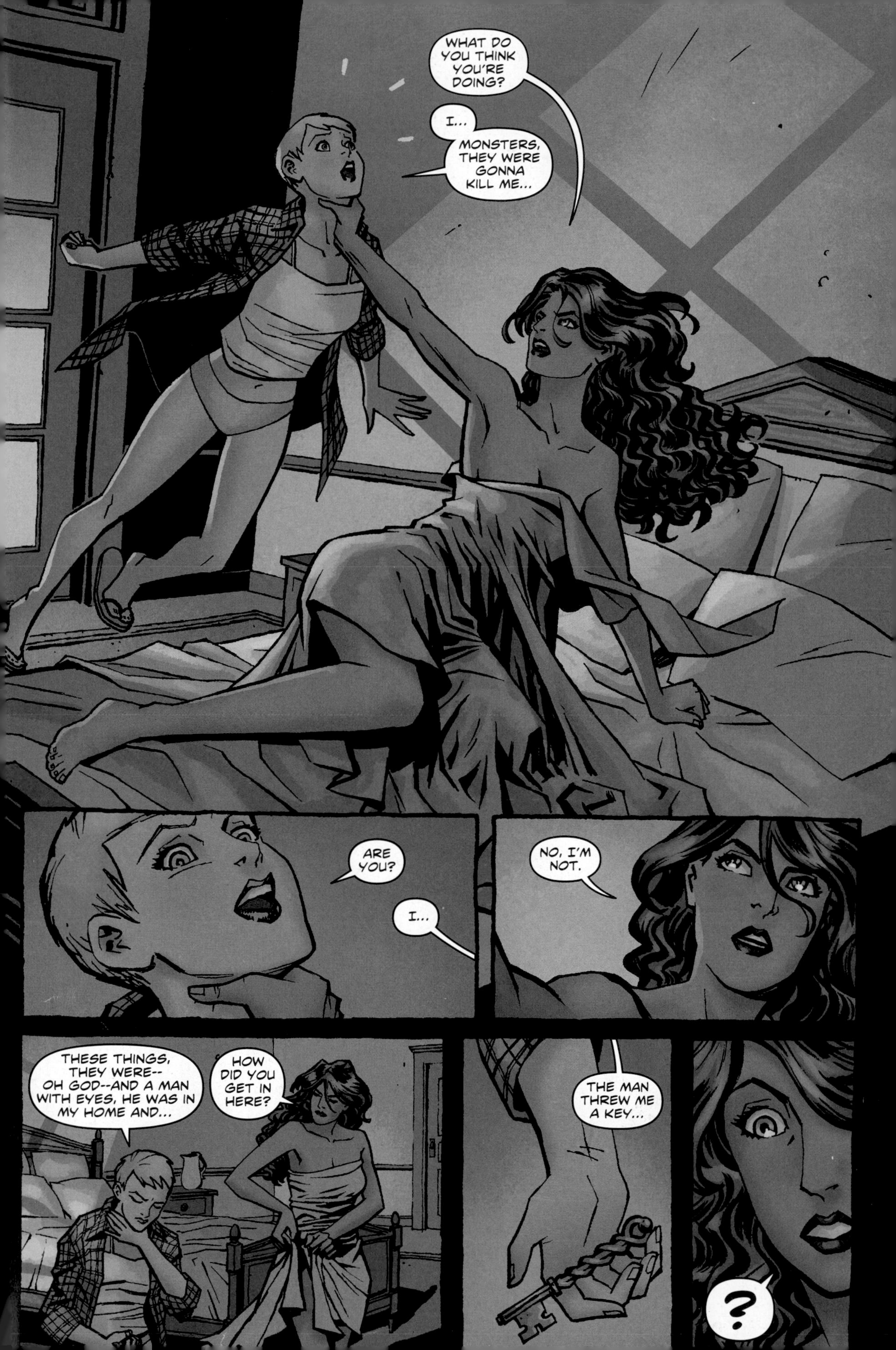
WHAT DO YOU THINK YOU'RE DOING?
I... MONSTERS, THEY WERE GONNA KILL ME...
ARE YOU?
I...
NO, I'M NOT.
THESE THINGS, THEY WERE-- OH GOD--AND A MAN WITH EYES, HE WAS IN MY HOME AND...
HOW DID YOU GET IN HERE?
THE MAN THREW ME A KEY...
?

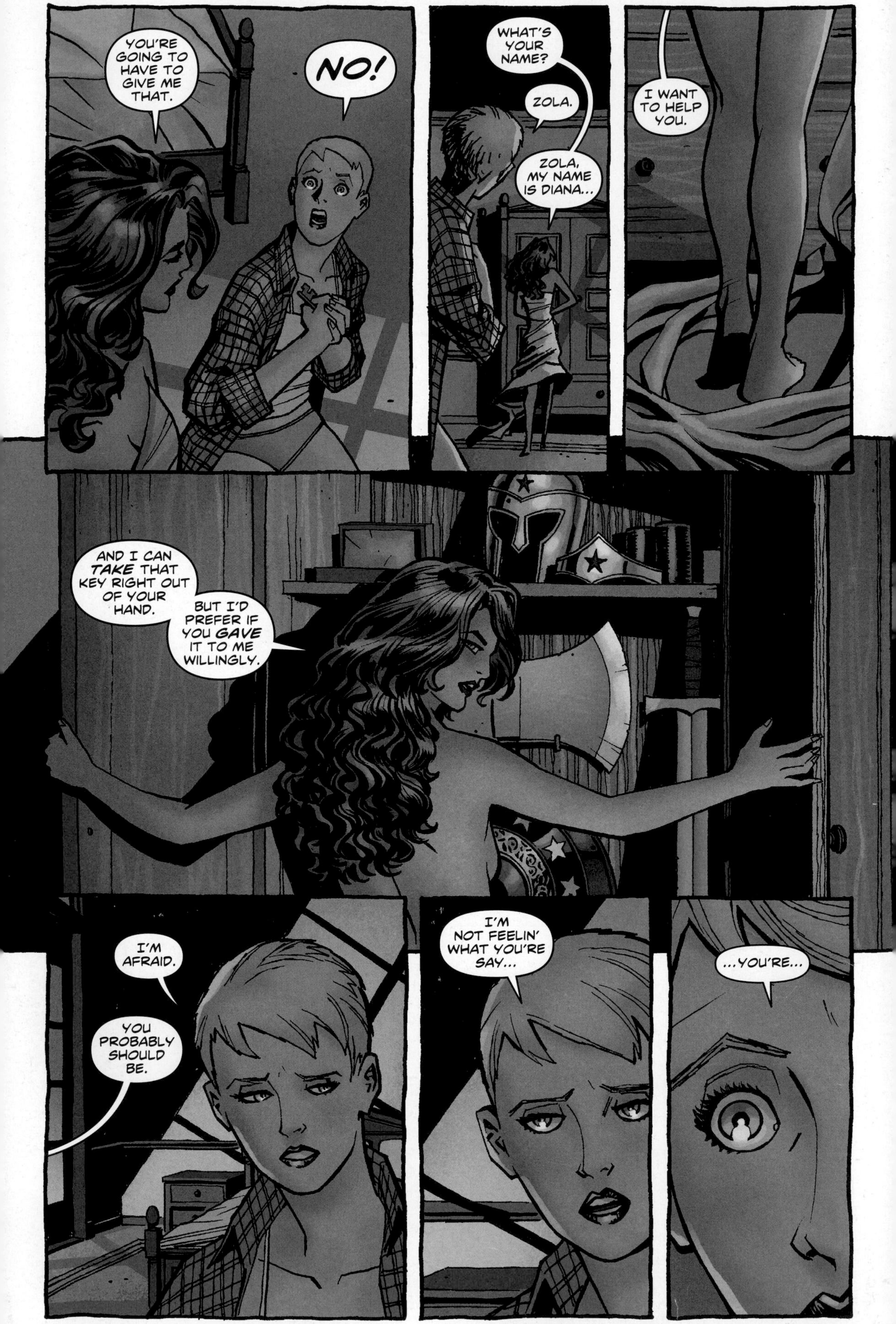
YOU'RE GOING TO HAVE TO GIVE ME THAT.
NO!
WHAT'S YOUR NAME?
ZOLA.
ZOLA, MY NAME IS DIANA...
I WANT TO HELP YOU.
AND I CAN TAKE THAT KEY RIGHT OUT OF YOUR HAND.
BUT I'D PREFER IF YOU GAVE IT TO ME WILLINGLY.
I'M AFRAID.
YOU PROBABLY SHOULD BE.
I'M NOT FEELIN' WHAT YOU'RE SAY...
...YOU'RE...

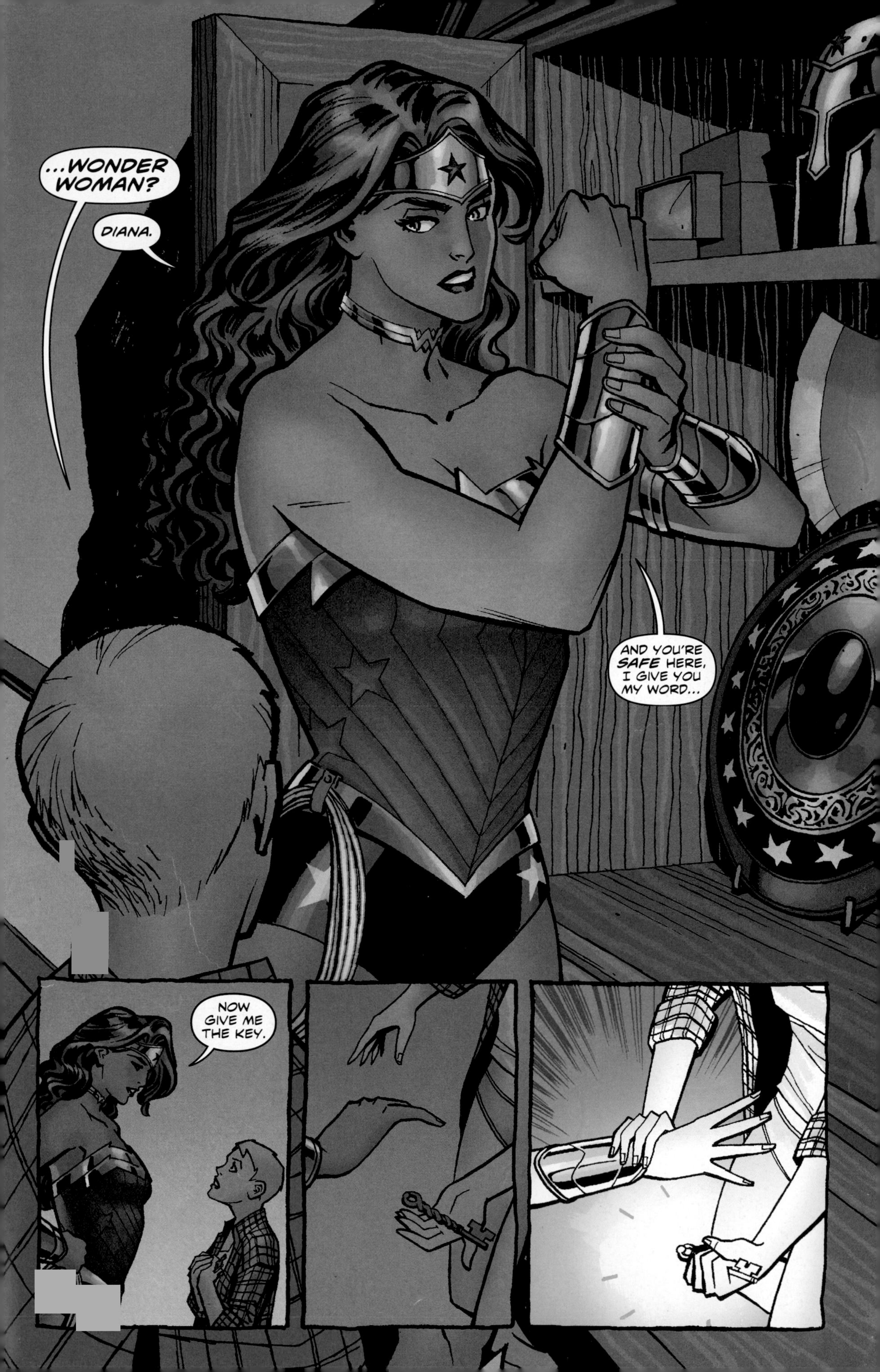
...WONDER WOMAN?
DIANA.
AND YOU'RE SAFE HERE, I GIVE YOU MY WORD...
NOW GIVE ME THE KEY.

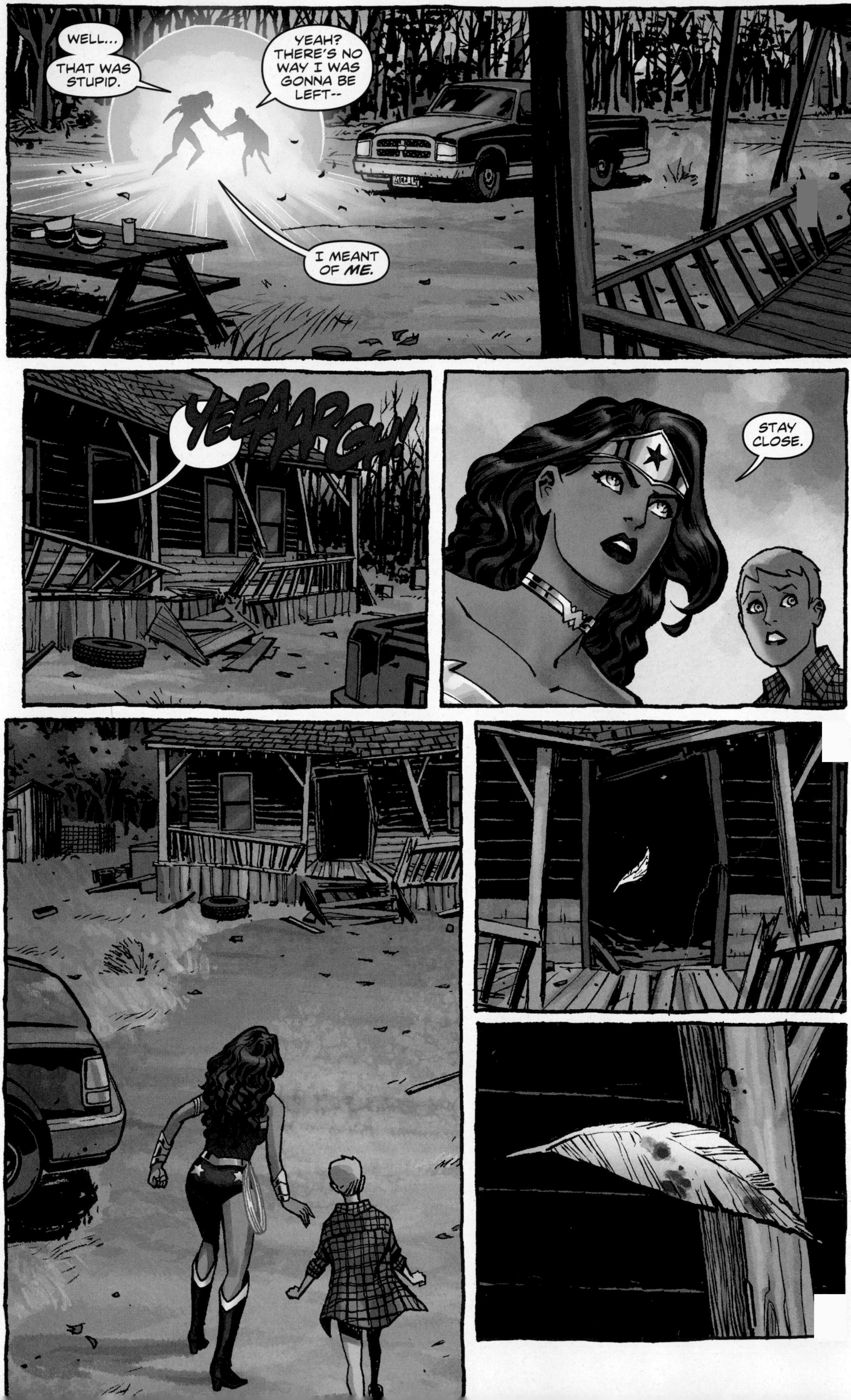
WELL...
THAT WAS STUPID.
YEAH? THERE'S NO WAY I WAS GONNA BE LEFT--
I MEANT OF ME.
YEEAARGH!
STAY CLOSE.

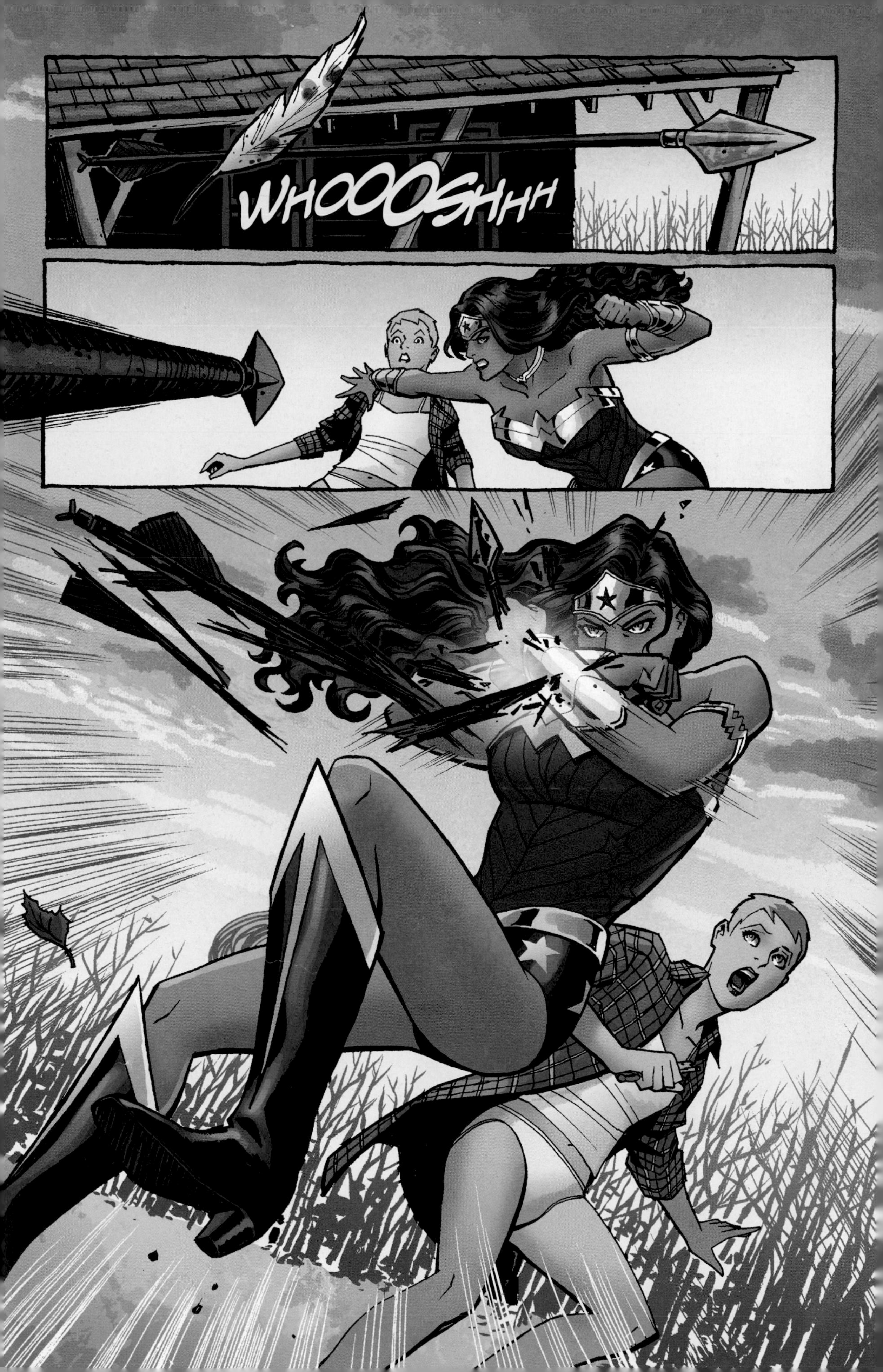
WHOOOOSHHH

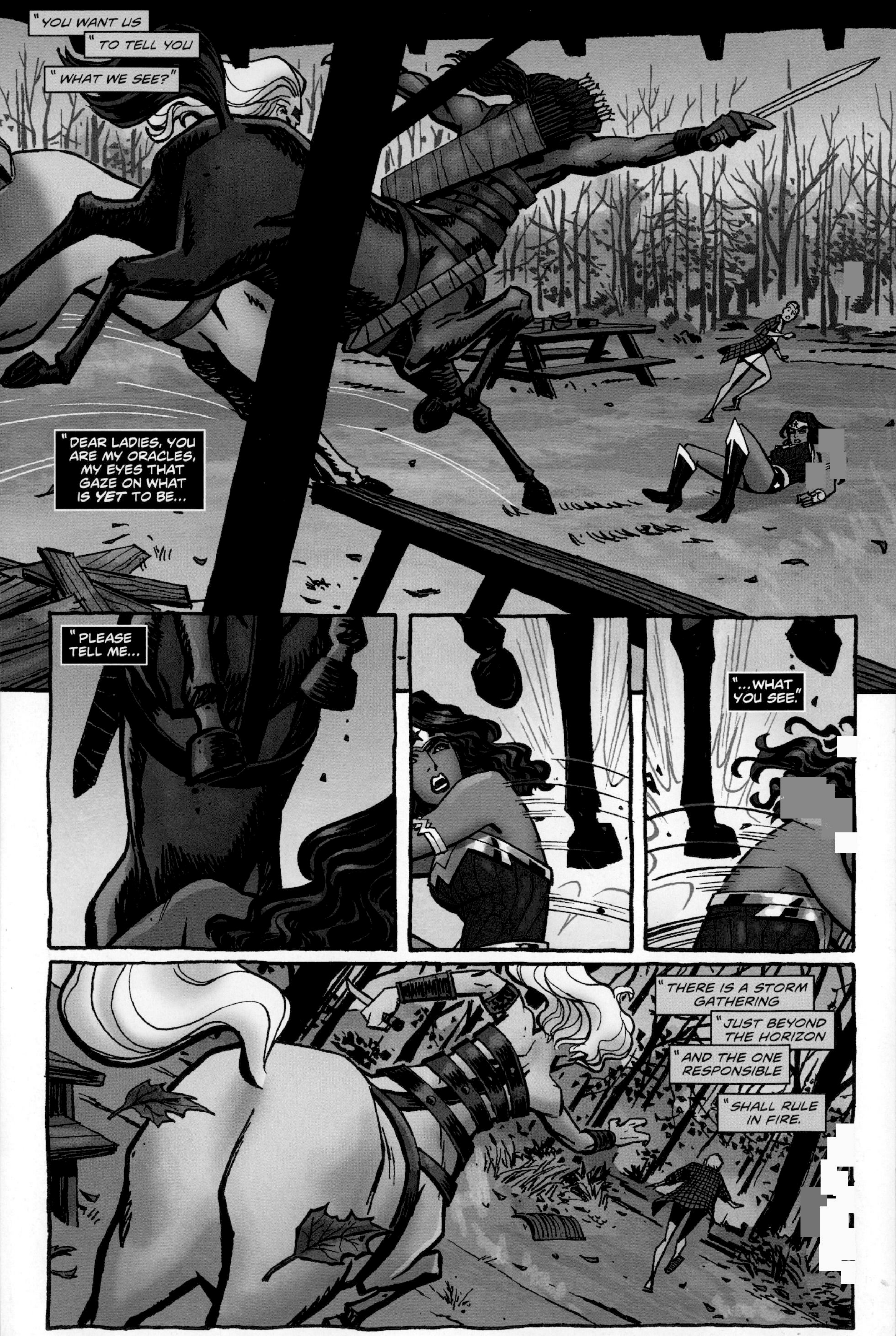
"YOU WANT US
"TO TELL YOU
"WHAT WE SEE?"
"DEAR LADIES, YOU ARE MY ORACLES, MY EYES THAT GAZE ON WHAT IS YET TO BE...
"PLEASE TELL ME...
"...WHAT YOU SEE."
"THERE IS A STORM GATHERING
"JUST BEYOND THE HORIZON
"AND THE ONE RESPONSIBLE
"SHALL RULE IN FIRE.

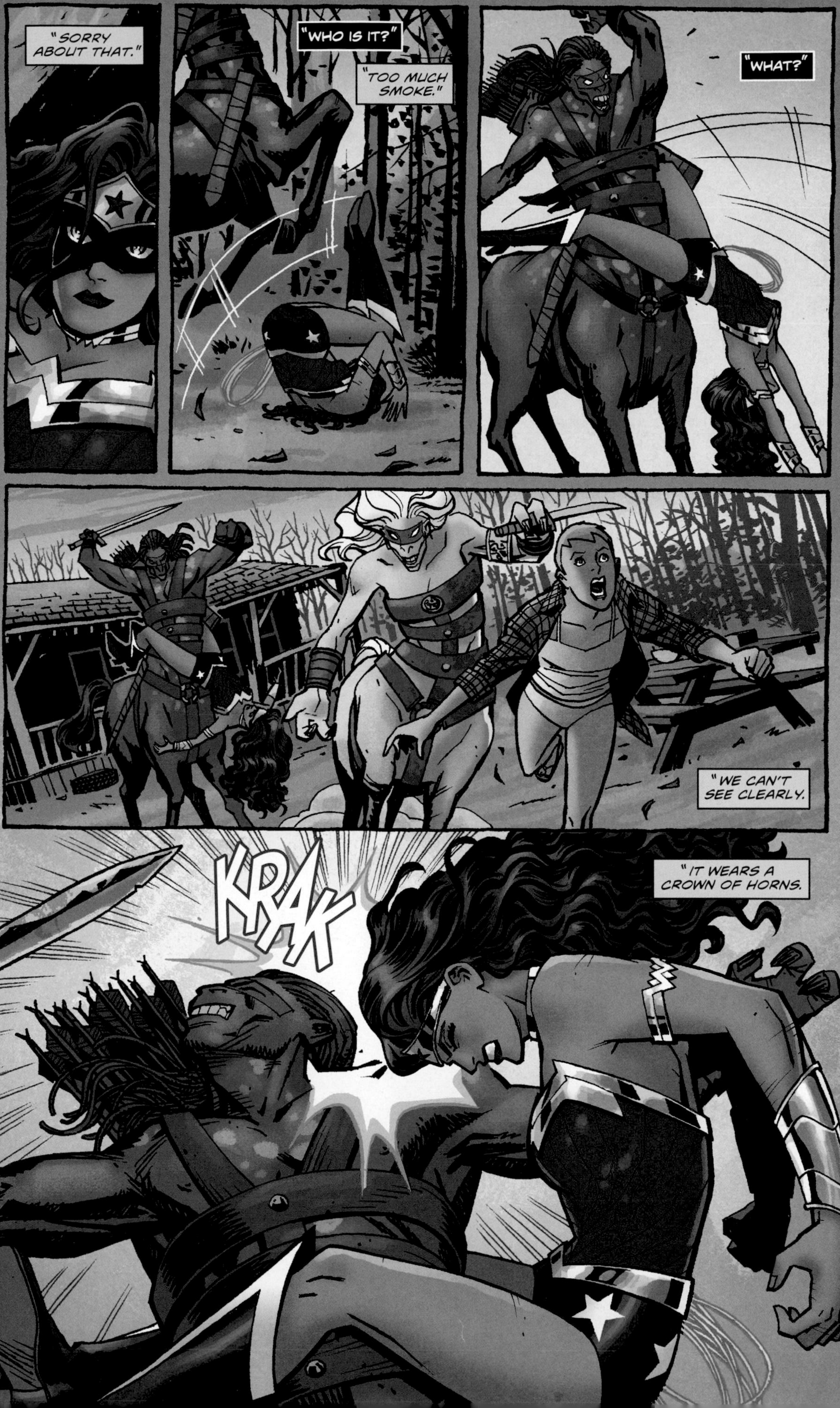
"SORRY ABOUT THAT."
"WHO IS IT?"
"TOO MUCH SMOKE."
"WHAT?"
"WE CAN'T SEE CLEARLY.
KRAK
"IT WEARS A CROWN OF HORNS.

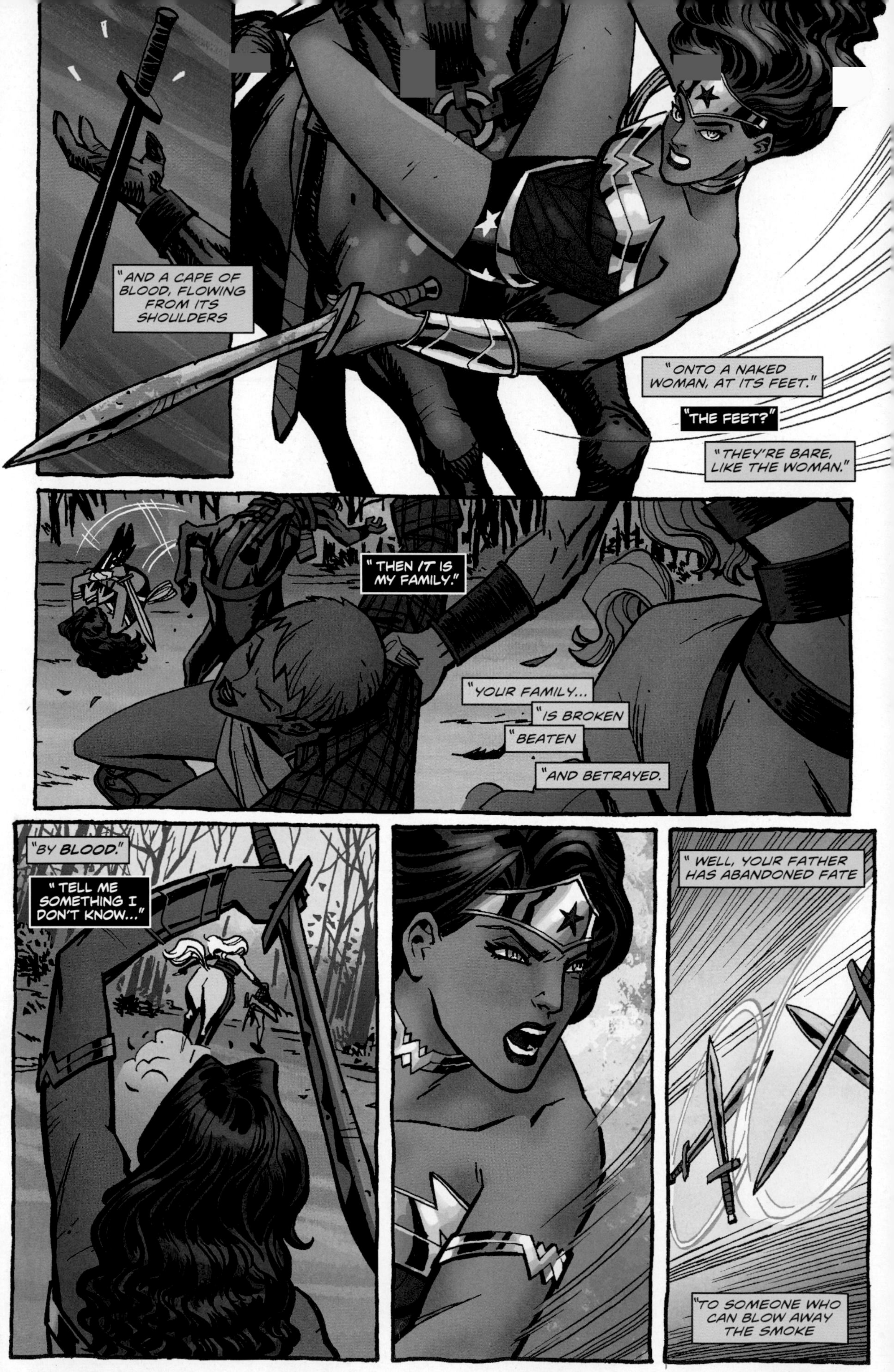
"AND A CAPE OF BLOOD, FLOWING FROM ITS SHOULDERS
"ONTO A NAKED WOMAN, AT ITS FEET."
"THE FEET?"
"THEY'RE BARE, LIKE THE WOMAN."
"THEN IT IS MY FAMILY."
"YOUR FAMILY...
"IS BROKEN
"BEATEN
"AND BETRAYED.
"BY BLOOD."
"TELL ME SOMETHING I DON'T KNOW..."
"WELL, YOUR FATHER HAS ABANDONED FATE
"TO SOMEONE WHO CAN BLOW AWAY THE SMOKE

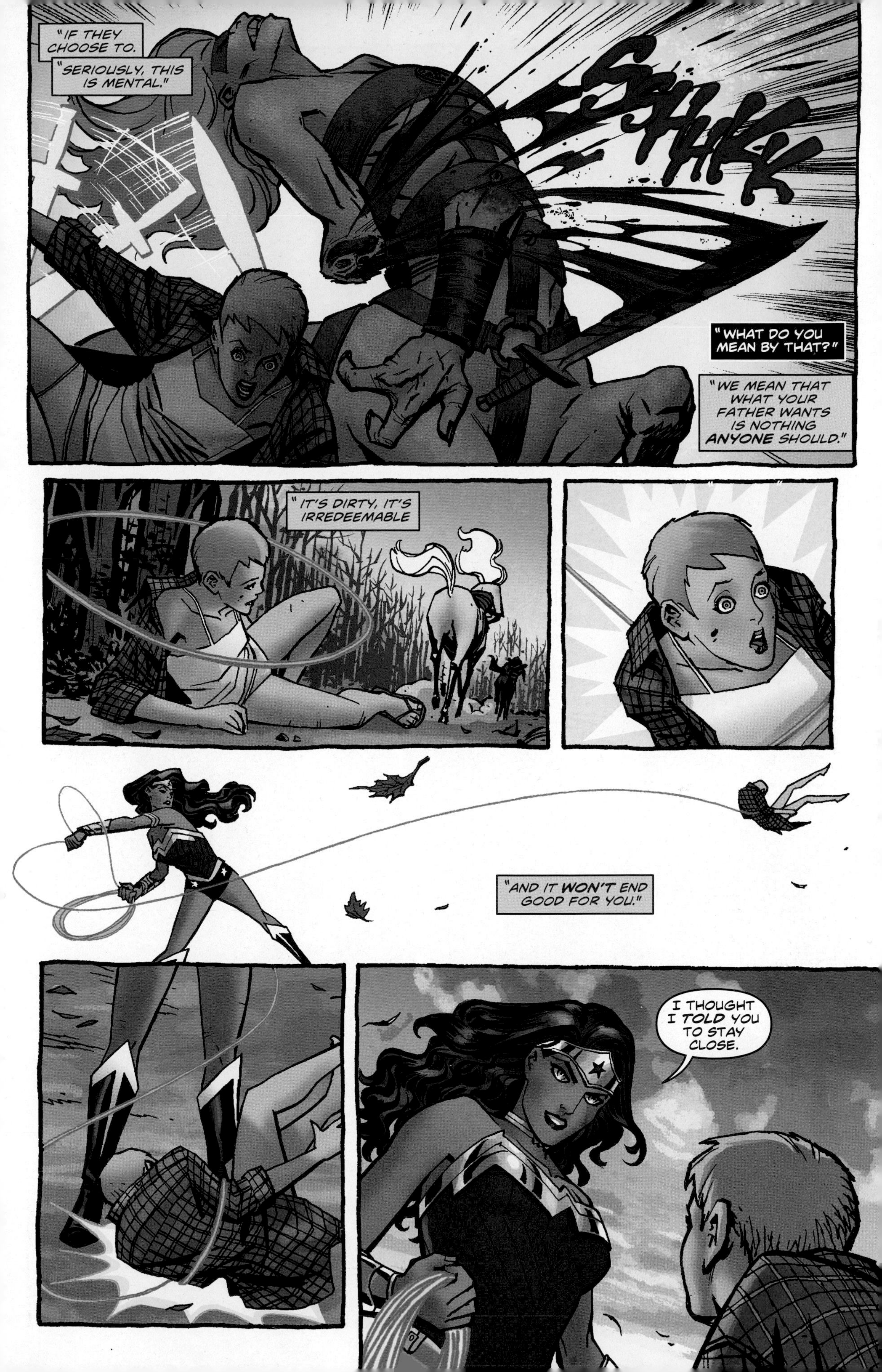
"IF THEY CHOOSE TO.
"SERIOUSLY, THIS IS MENTAL."
SCHHKK
"WHAT DO YOU MEAN BY THAT?"
"WE MEAN THAT WHAT YOUR FATHER WANTS IS NOTHING ANYONE SHOULD."
"IT'S DIRTY, IT'S IRREDEEMABLE
"AND IT WON'T END GOOD FOR YOU."
I THOUGHT I TOLD YOU TO STAY CLOSE.

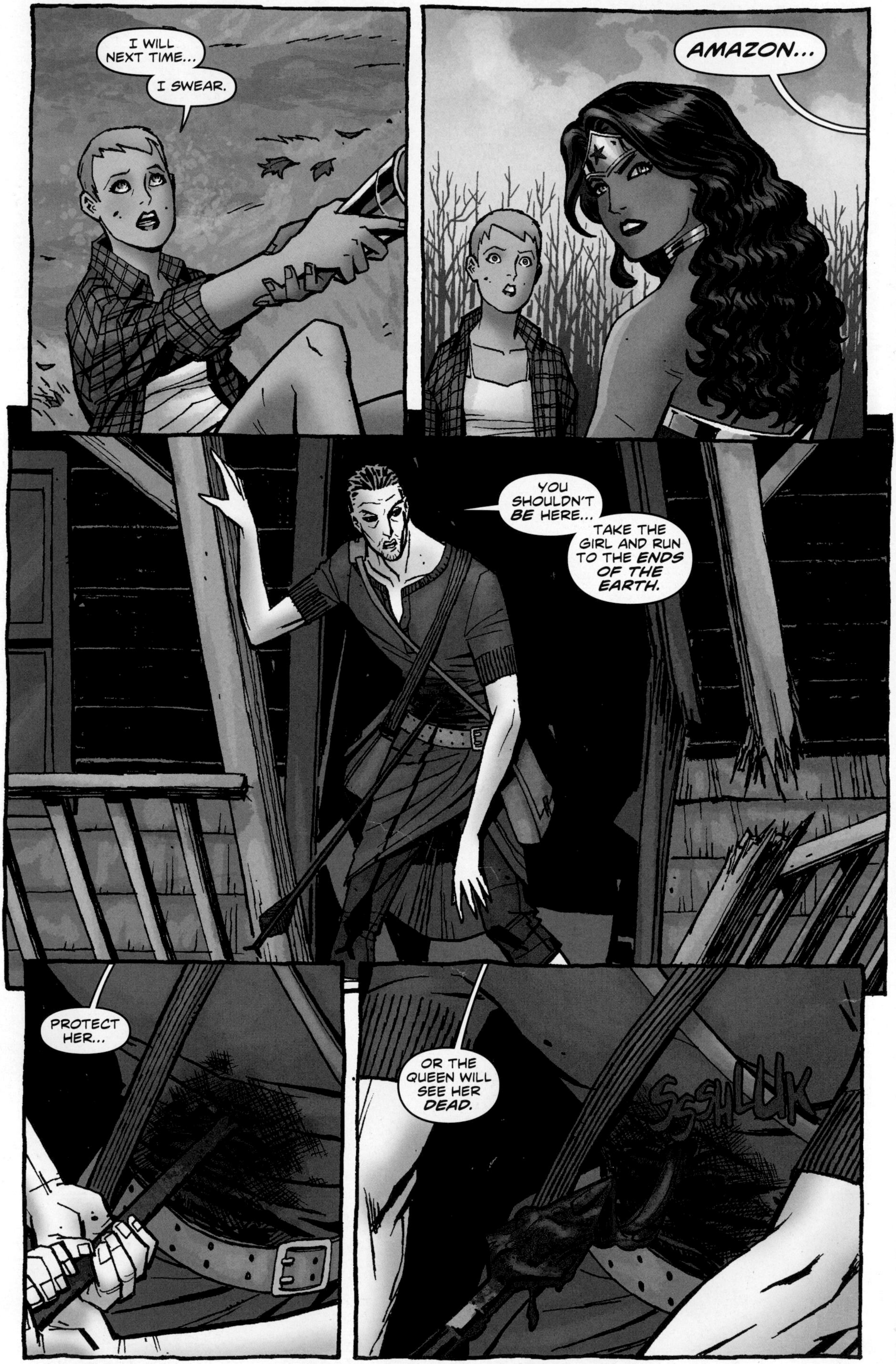
I WILL NEXT TIME...
I SWEAR.
AMAZON...
YOU SHOULDN'T *BE* HERE...
TAKE THE GIRL AND RUN TO THE *ENDS OF THE EARTH.*
PROTECT HER...
OR THE QUEEN WILL SEE HER *DEAD.*
SSSHLUK

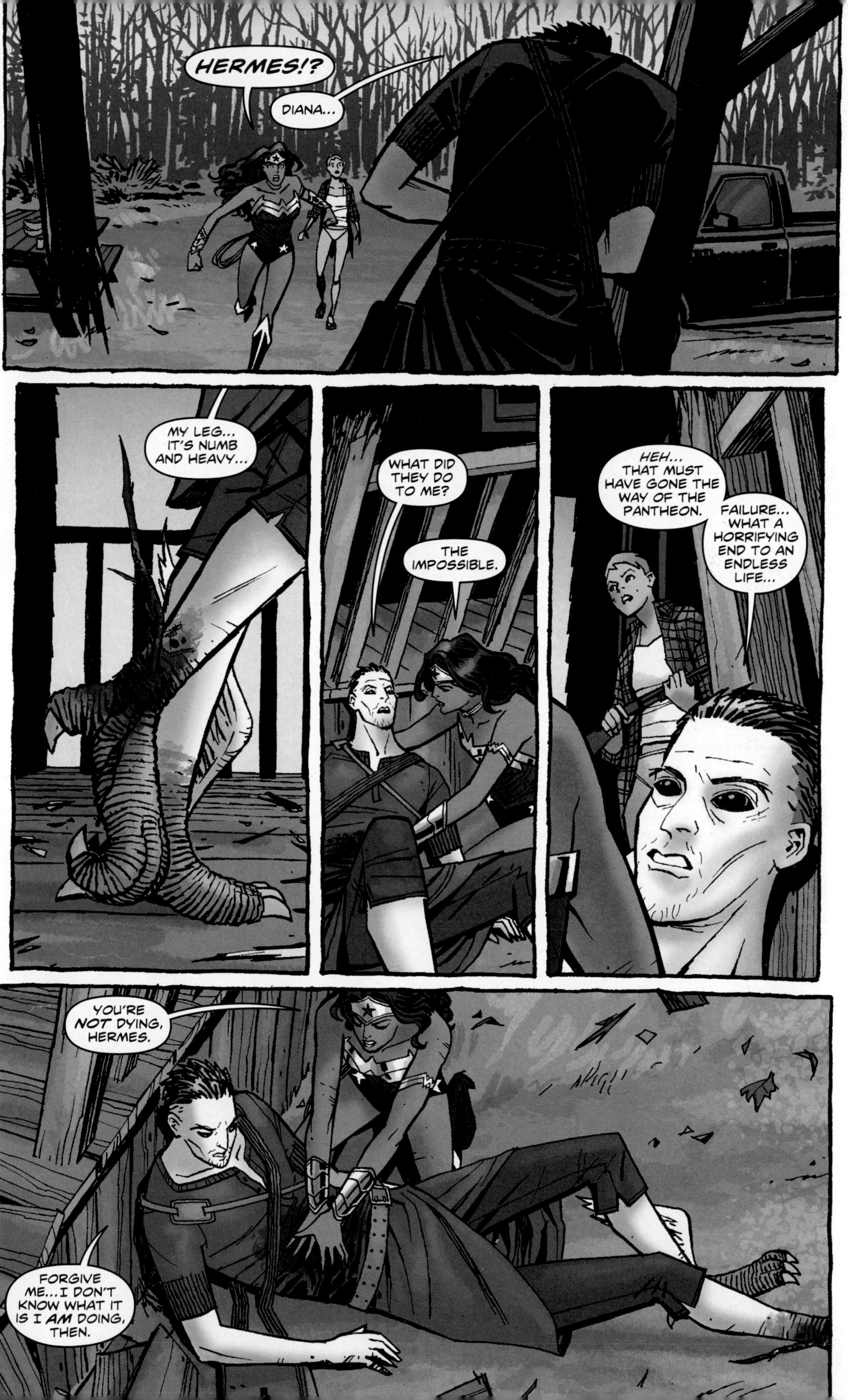
HERMES!?
DIANA...
MY LEG... IT'S NUMB AND HEAVY...
WHAT DID THEY DO TO ME?
THE IMPOSSIBLE.
HEH... THAT MUST HAVE GONE THE WAY OF THE PANTHEON.
FAILURE... WHAT A HORRIFYING END TO AN ENDLESS LIFE...
YOU'RE NOT DYING, HERMES.
FORGIVE ME... I DON'T KNOW WHAT IT IS I AM DOING, THEN.

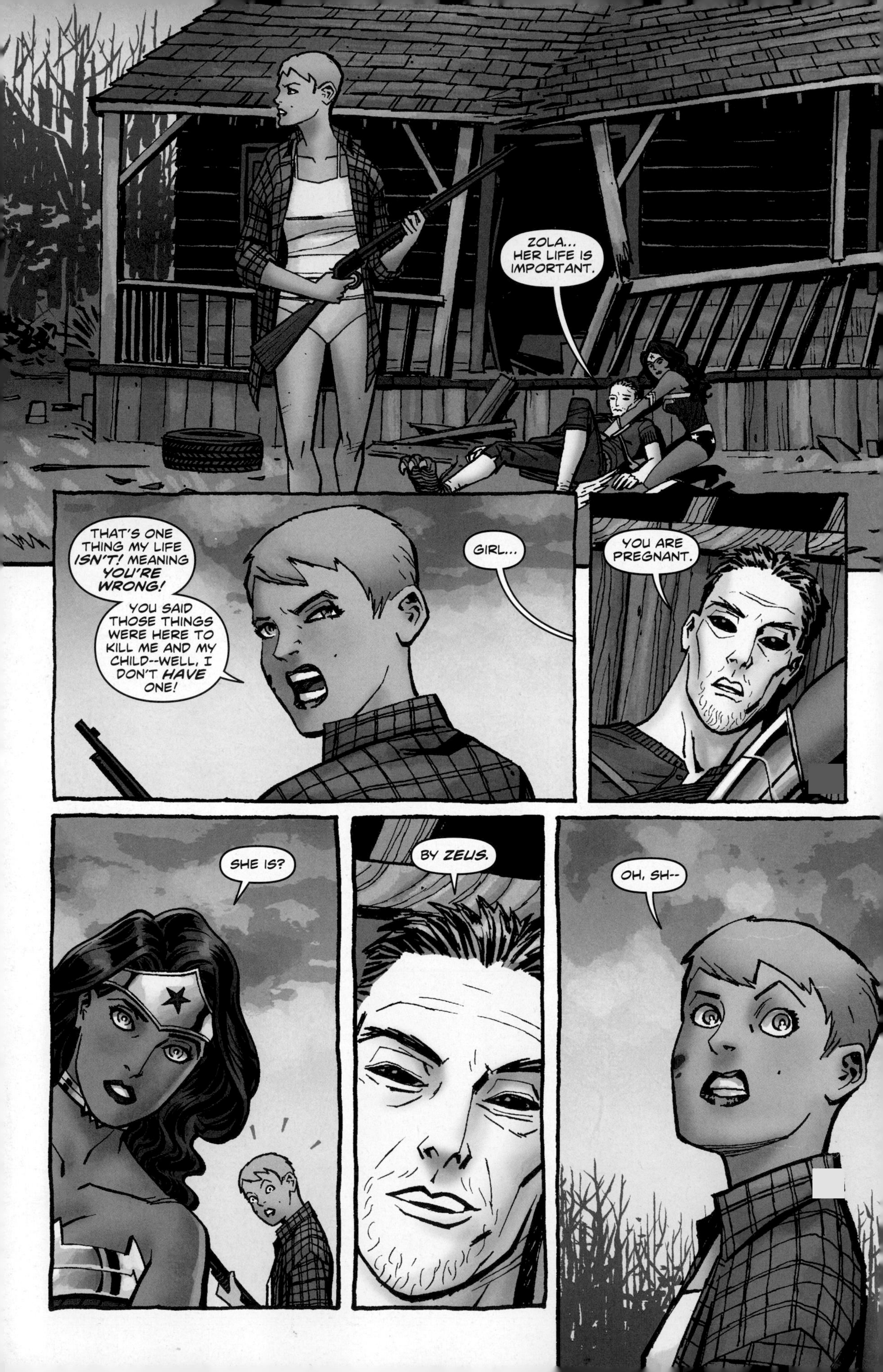
ZOLA... HER LIFE IS IMPORTANT.
THAT'S ONE THING MY LIFE ISN'T! MEANING YOU'RE WRONG!
YOU SAID THOSE THINGS WERE HERE TO KILL ME AND MY CHILD--WELL, I DON'T HAVE ONE!
GIRL...
YOU ARE PREGNANT.
SHE IS?
BY ZEUS.
OH, SH--

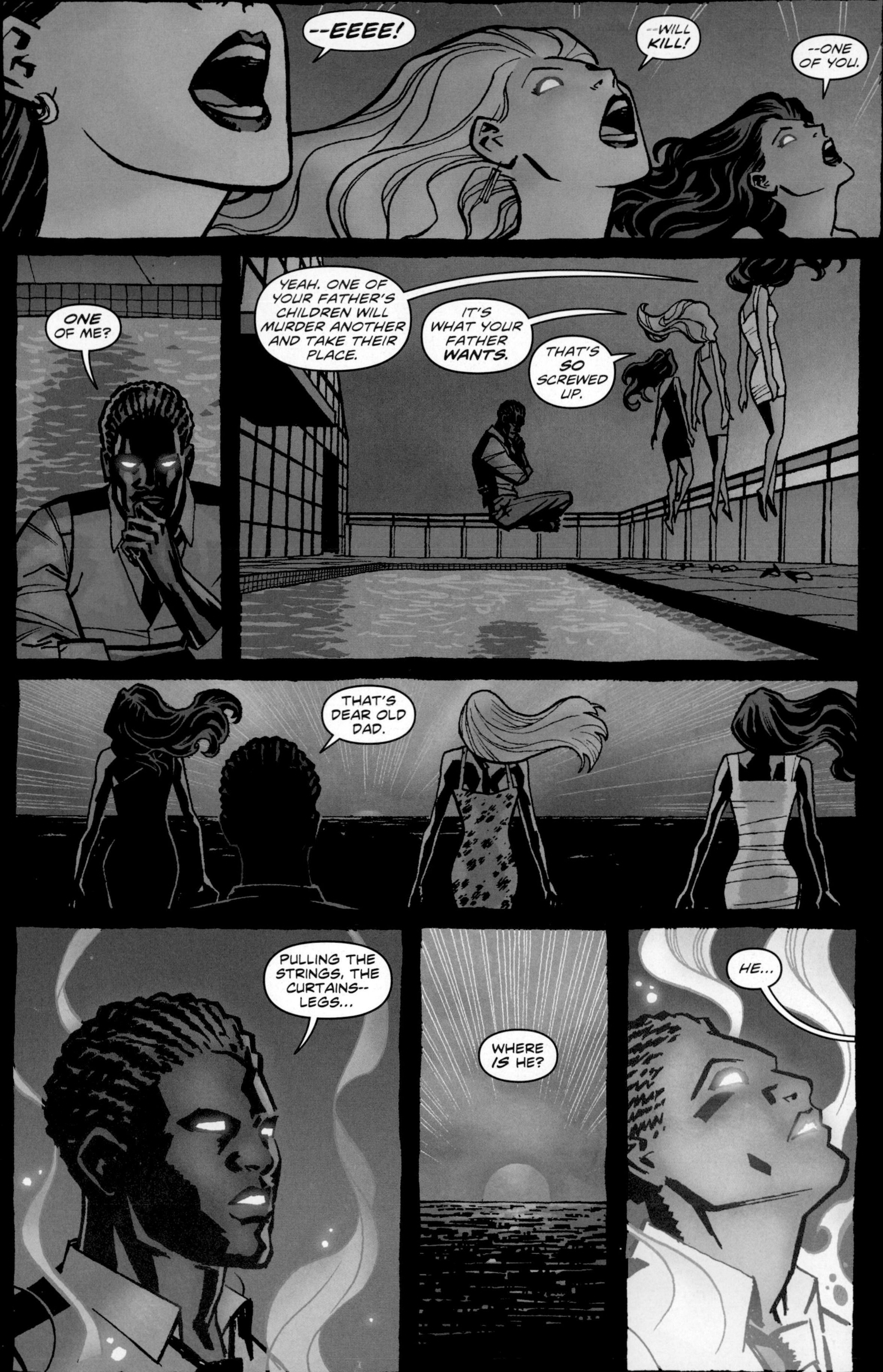
--EEEE!
--WILL KILL!
--ONE OF YOU.
ONE OF ME?
YEAH. ONE OF YOUR FATHER'S CHILDREN WILL MURDER ANOTHER AND TAKE THEIR PLACE.
IT'S WHAT YOUR FATHER WANTS.
THAT'S SO SCREWED UP.
THAT'S DEAR OLD DAD.
PULLING THE STRINGS, THE CURTAINS-- LEGS...
WHERE IS HE?
HE...

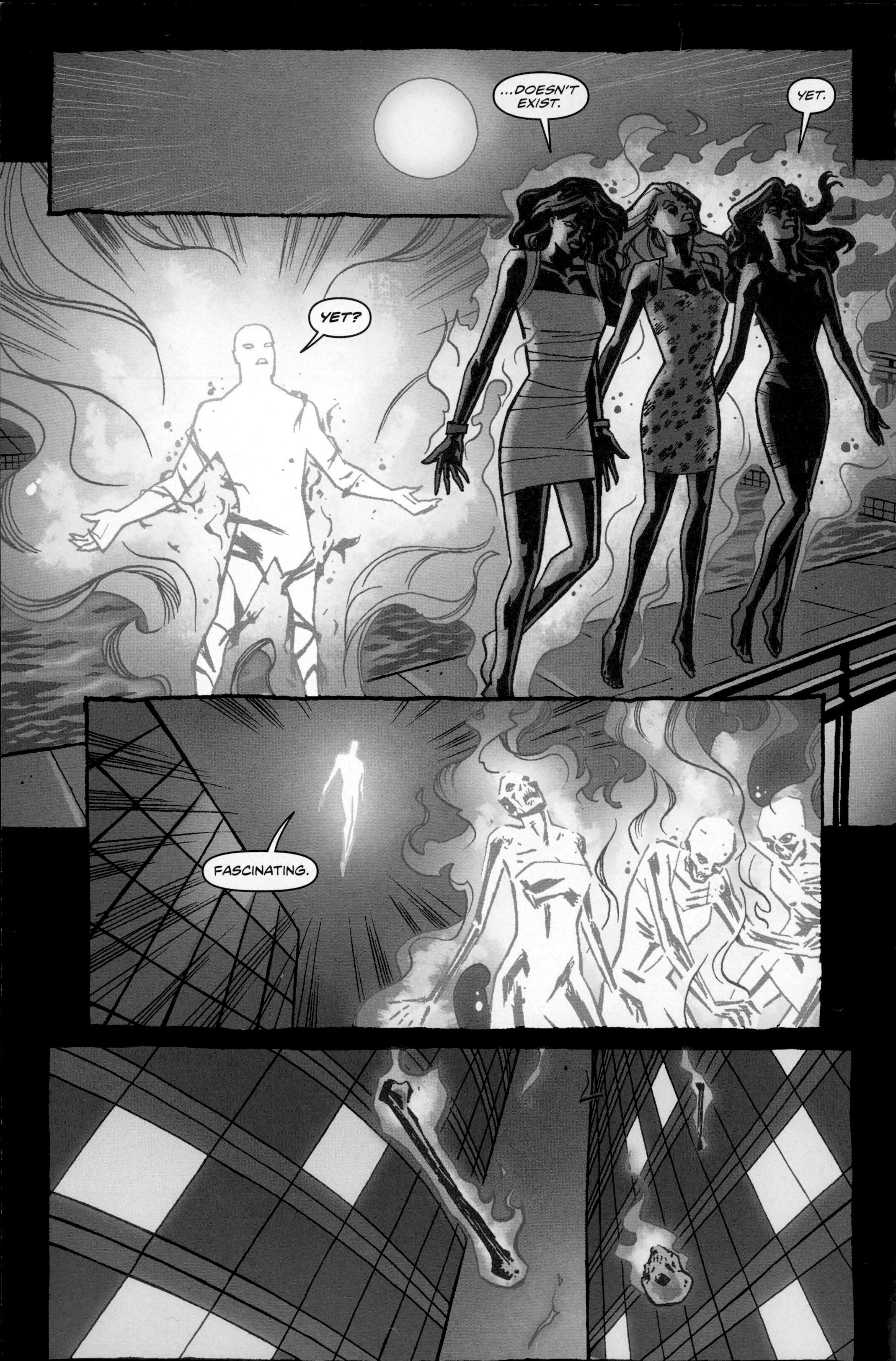
...DOESN'T EXIST.
YET.
YET?
FASCINATING.

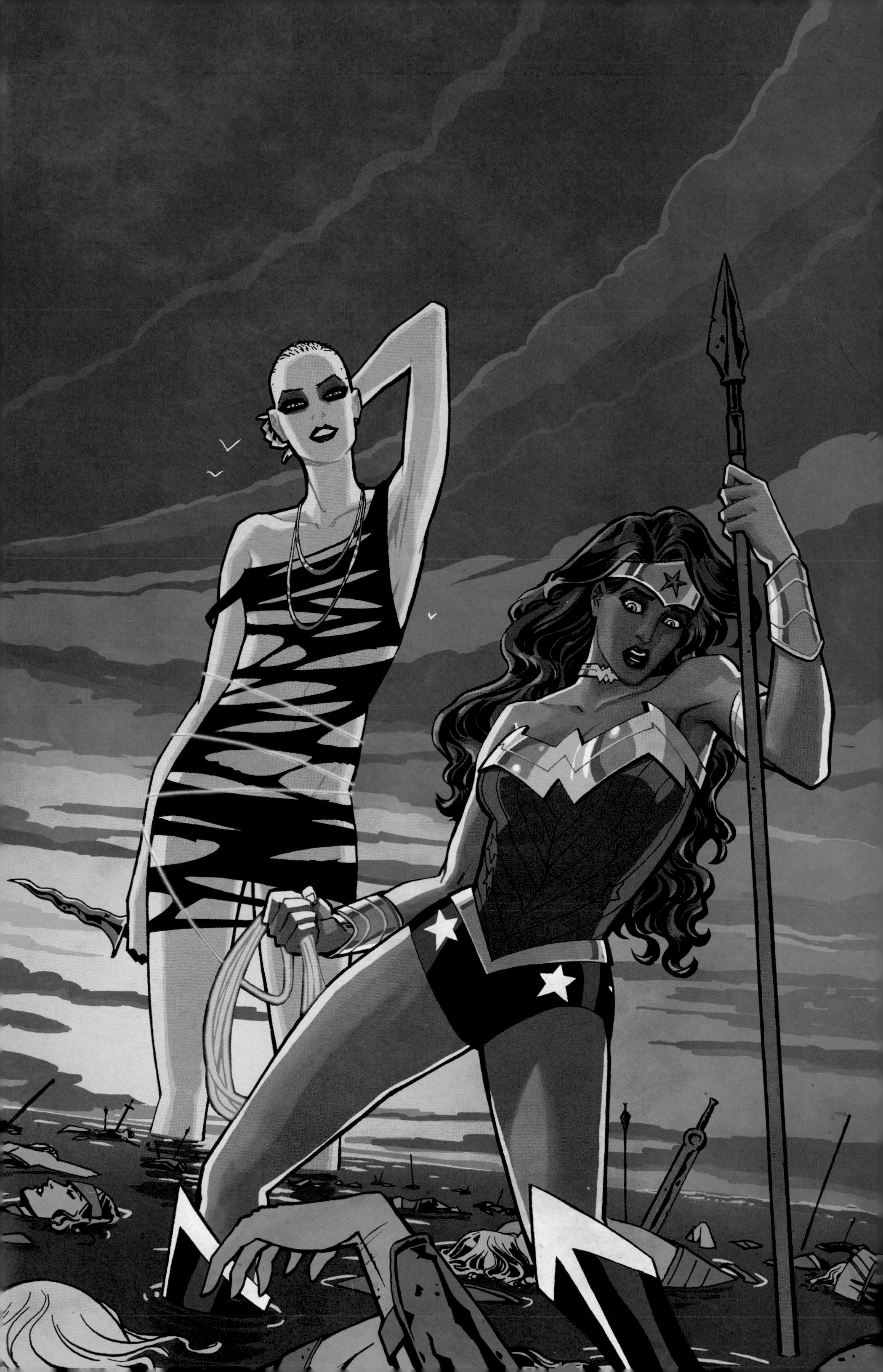

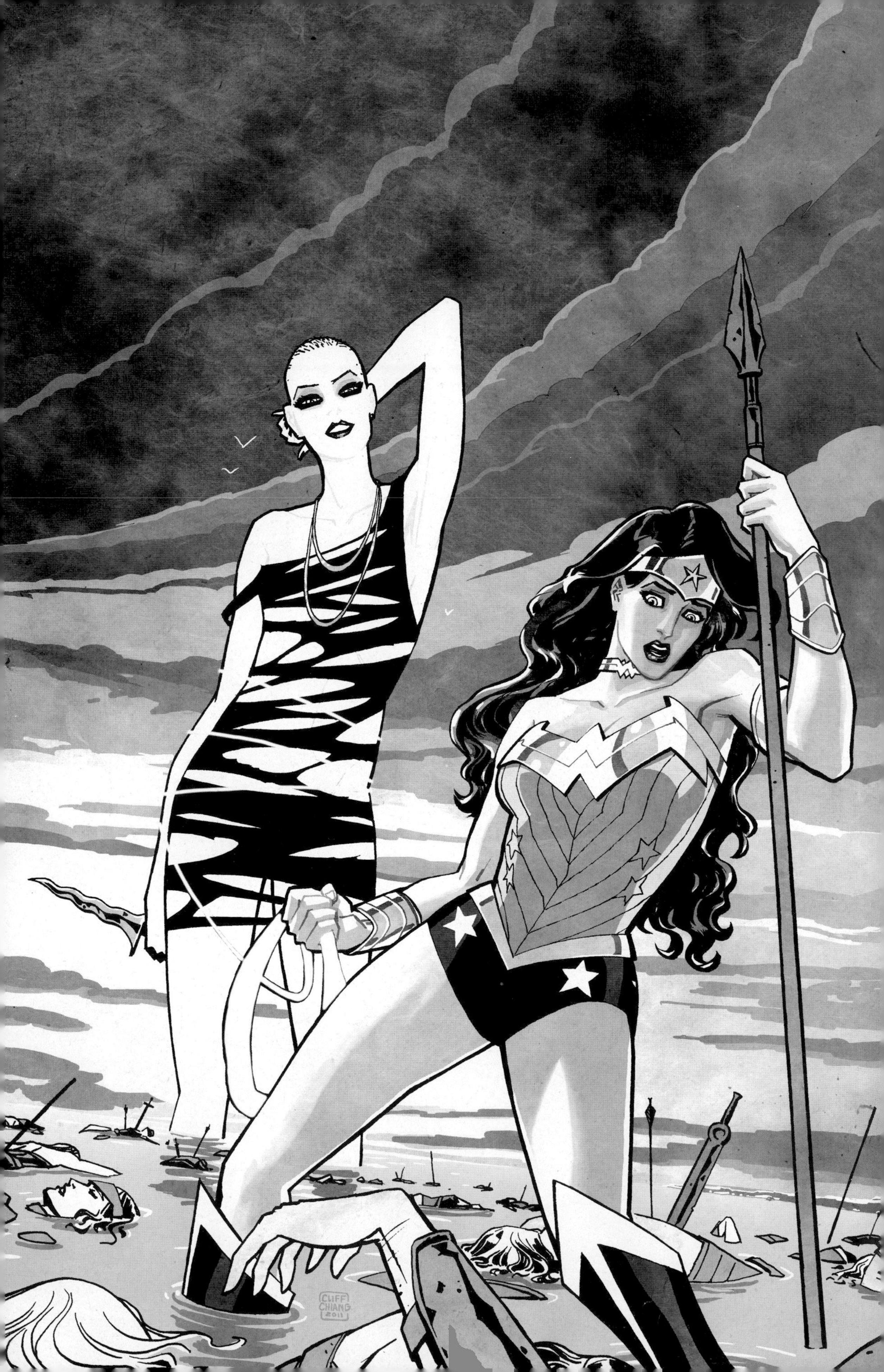
CLIFF
CHIANG
2011

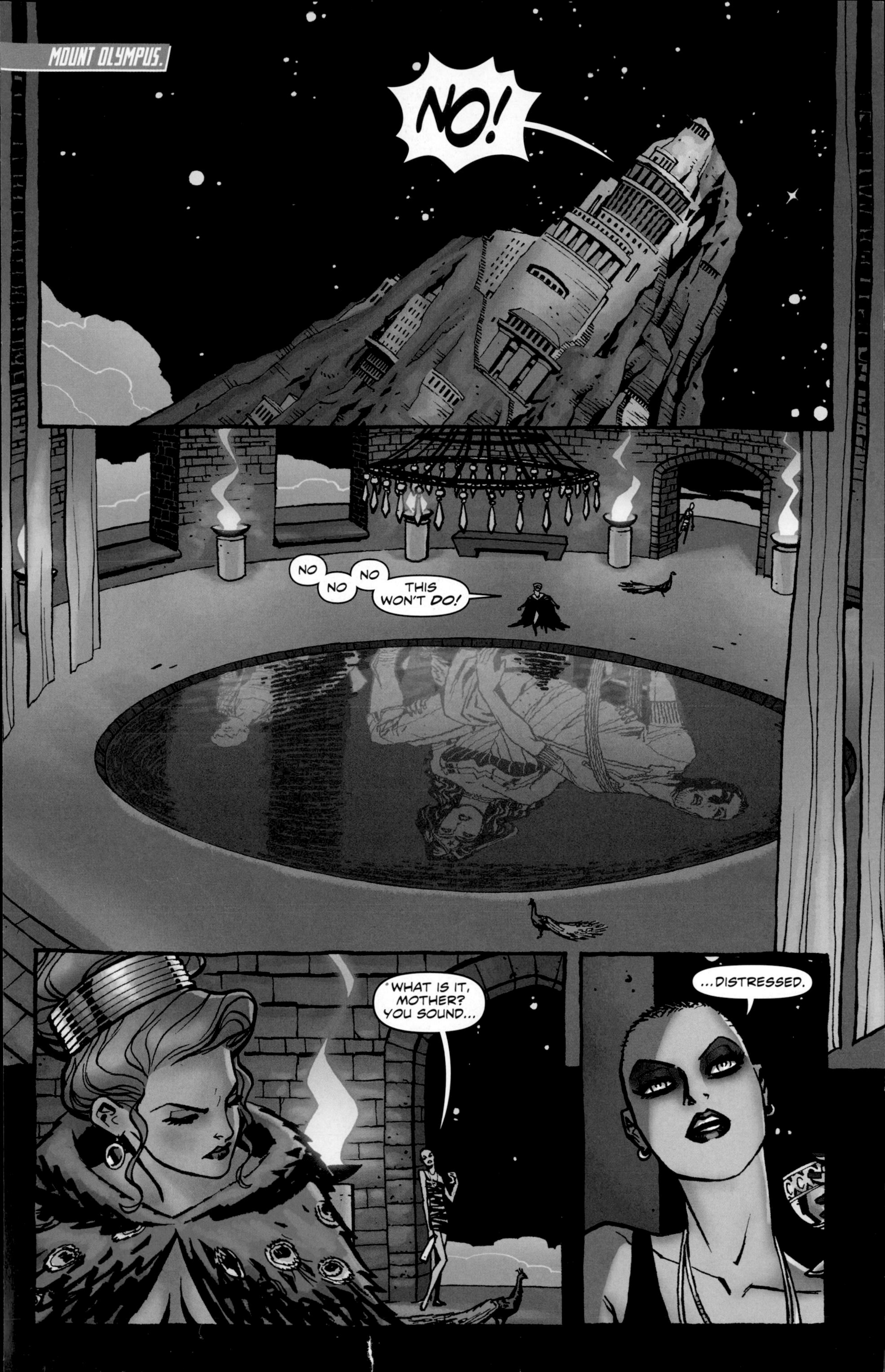
MOUNT OLYMPUS.
NO!
NO
NO
NO
THIS WON'T DO!
WHAT IS IT, MOTHER? YOU SOUND...
...DISTRESSED.

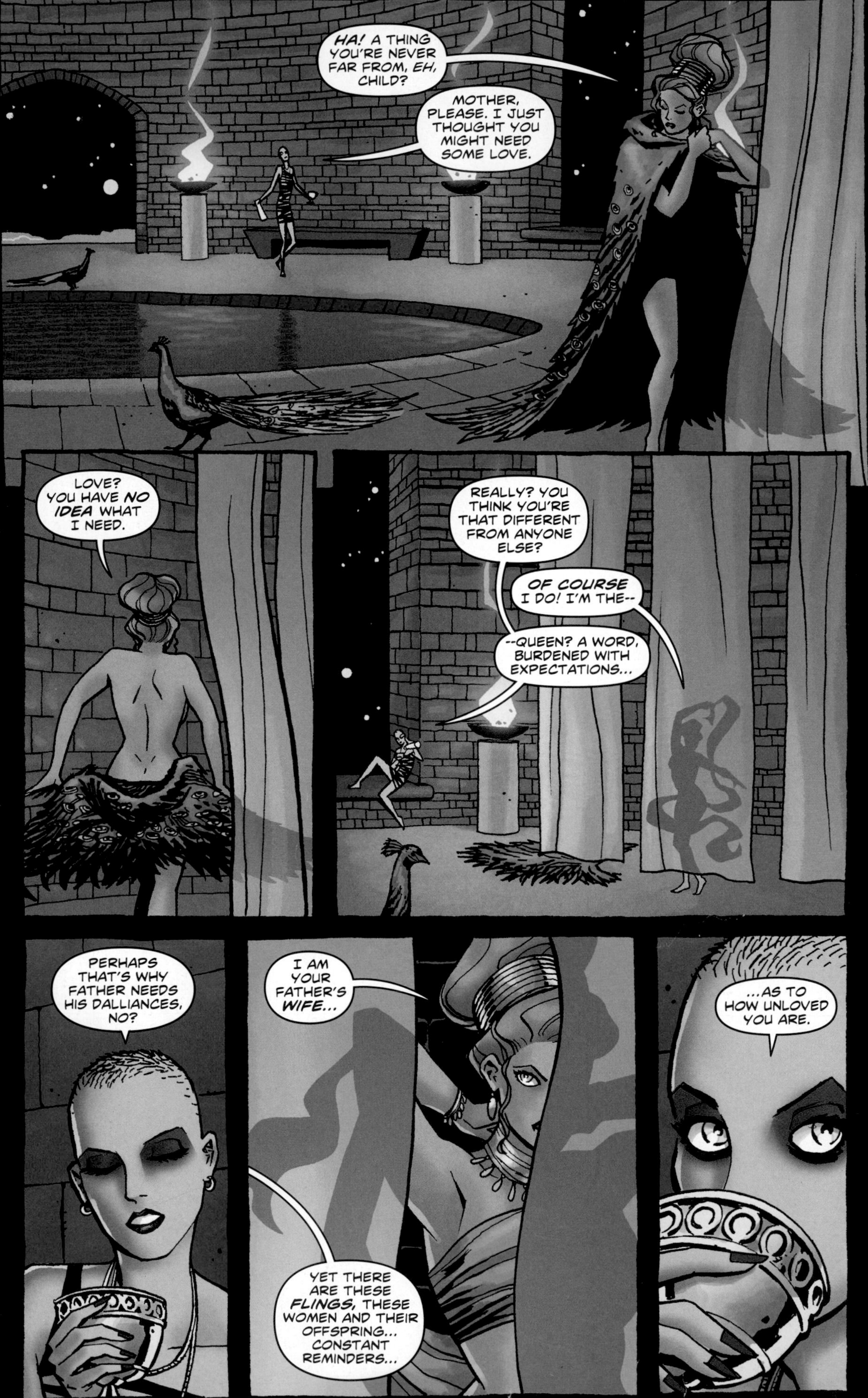
HA! A THING YOU'RE NEVER FAR FROM, EH, CHILD?
MOTHER, PLEASE. I JUST THOUGHT YOU MIGHT NEED SOME LOVE.
LOVE? YOU HAVE NO IDEA WHAT I NEED.
REALLY? YOU THINK YOU'RE THAT DIFFERENT FROM ANYONE ELSE?
OF COURSE I DO! I'M THE--
--QUEEN? A WORD, BURDENED WITH EXPECTATIONS...
PERHAPS THAT'S WHY FATHER NEEDS HIS DALLIANCES, NO?
I AM YOUR FATHER'S WIFE...
YET THERE ARE THESE FLINGS, THESE WOMEN AND THEIR OFFSPRING... CONSTANT REMINDERS...
...AS TO HOW UNLOVED YOU ARE.

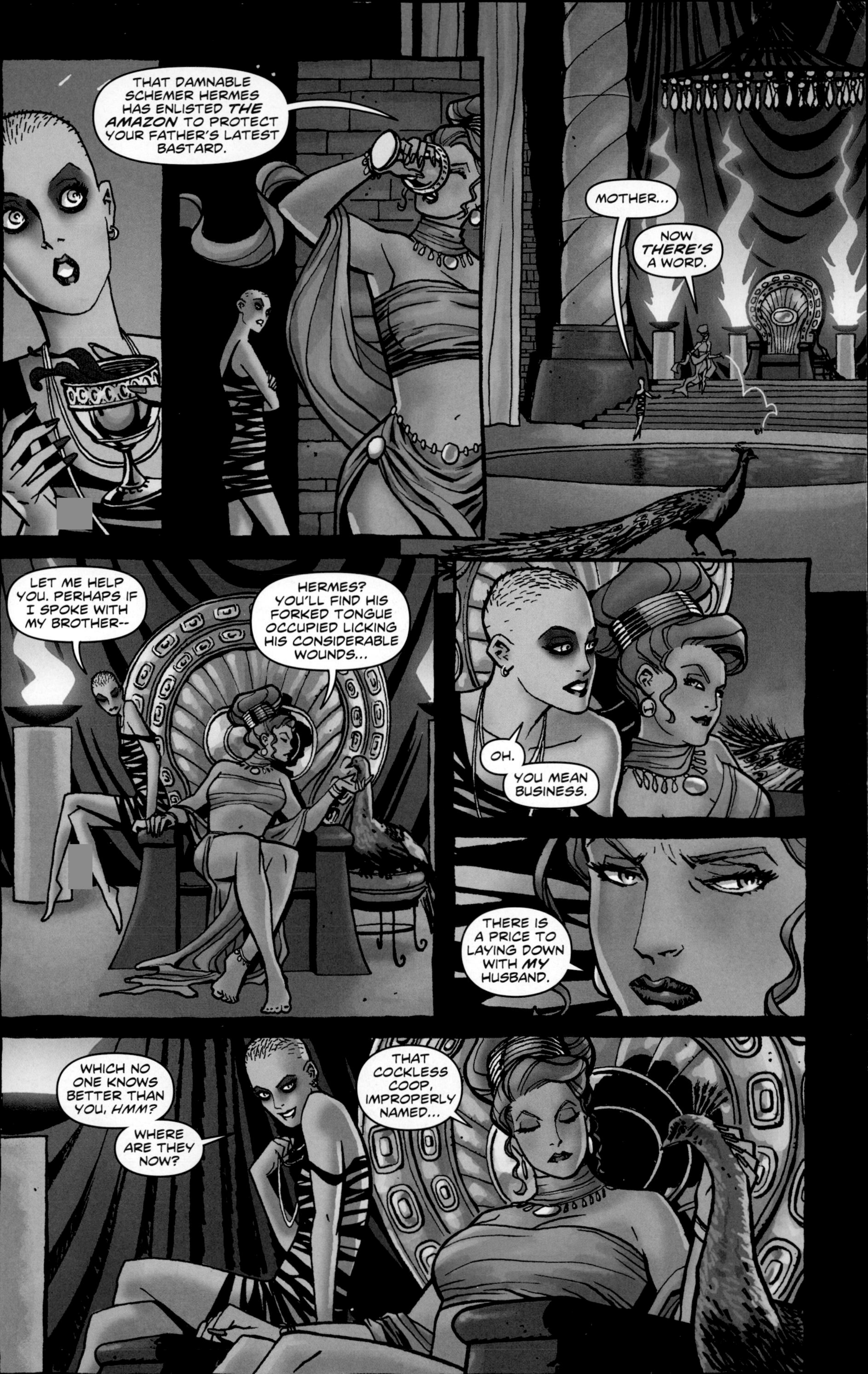
THAT DAMNABLE SCHEMER HERMES HAS ENLISTED THE AMAZON TO PROTECT YOUR FATHER'S LATEST BASTARD.
MOTHER...
NOW THERE'S A WORD.
LET ME HELP YOU. PERHAPS IF I SPOKE WITH MY BROTHER--
HERMES? YOU'LL FIND HIS FORKED TONGUE OCCUPIED LICKING HIS CONSIDERABLE WOUNDS...
OH.
YOU MEAN BUSINESS.
THERE IS A PRICE TO LAYING DOWN WITH MY HUSBAND.
WHICH NO ONE KNOWS BETTER THAN YOU, HMM?
WHERE ARE THEY NOW?
THAT COCKLESS COOP, IMPROPERLY NAMED...

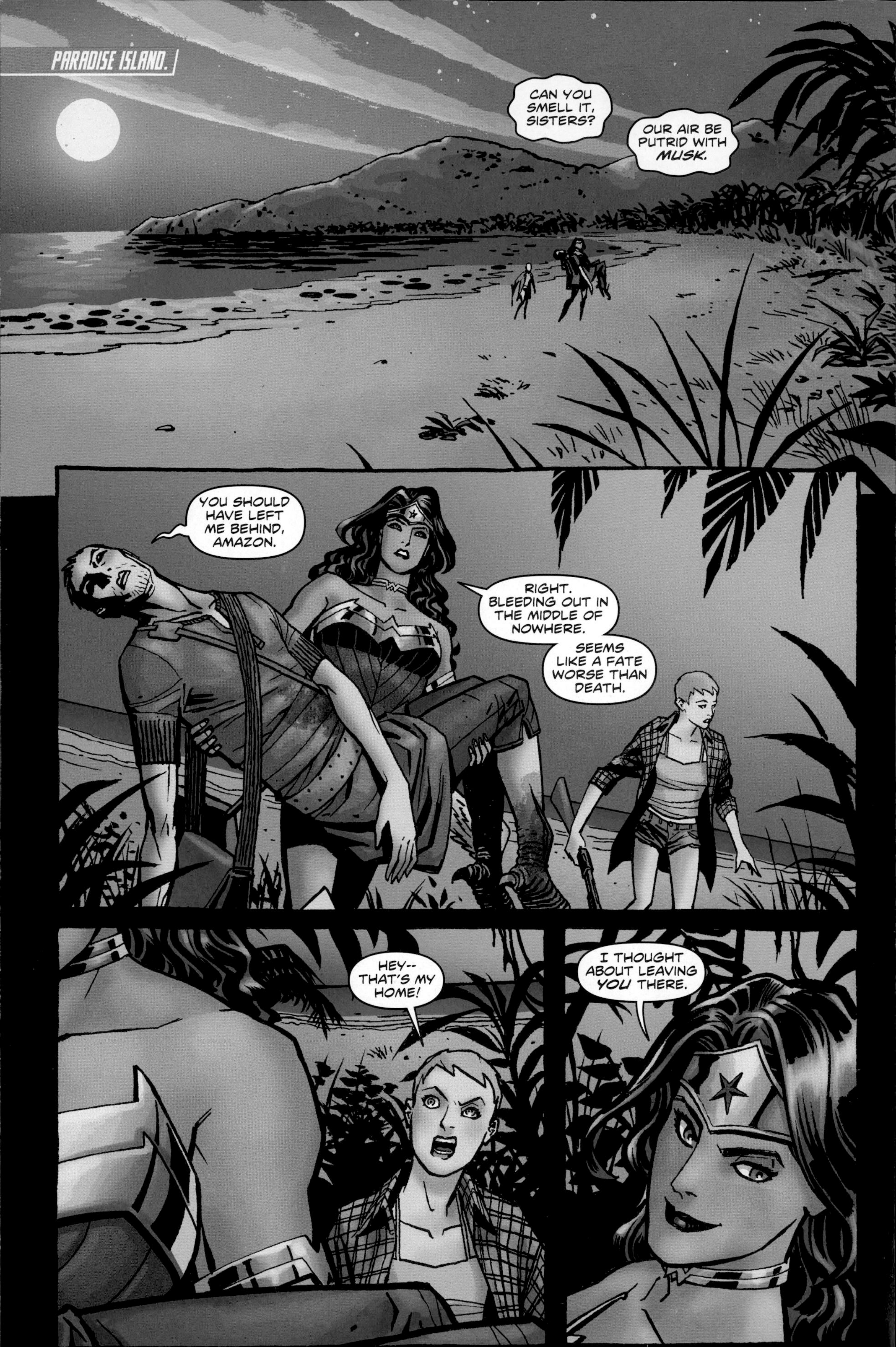
PARADISE ISLAND.
CAN YOU SMELL IT, SISTERS?
OUR AIR BE PUTRID WITH MUSK.
YOU SHOULD HAVE LEFT ME BEHIND, AMAZON.
RIGHT. BLEEDING OUT IN THE MIDDLE OF NOWHERE.
SEEMS LIKE A FATE WORSE THAN DEATH.
HEY-- THAT'S MY HOME!
I THOUGHT ABOUT LEAVING YOU THERE.

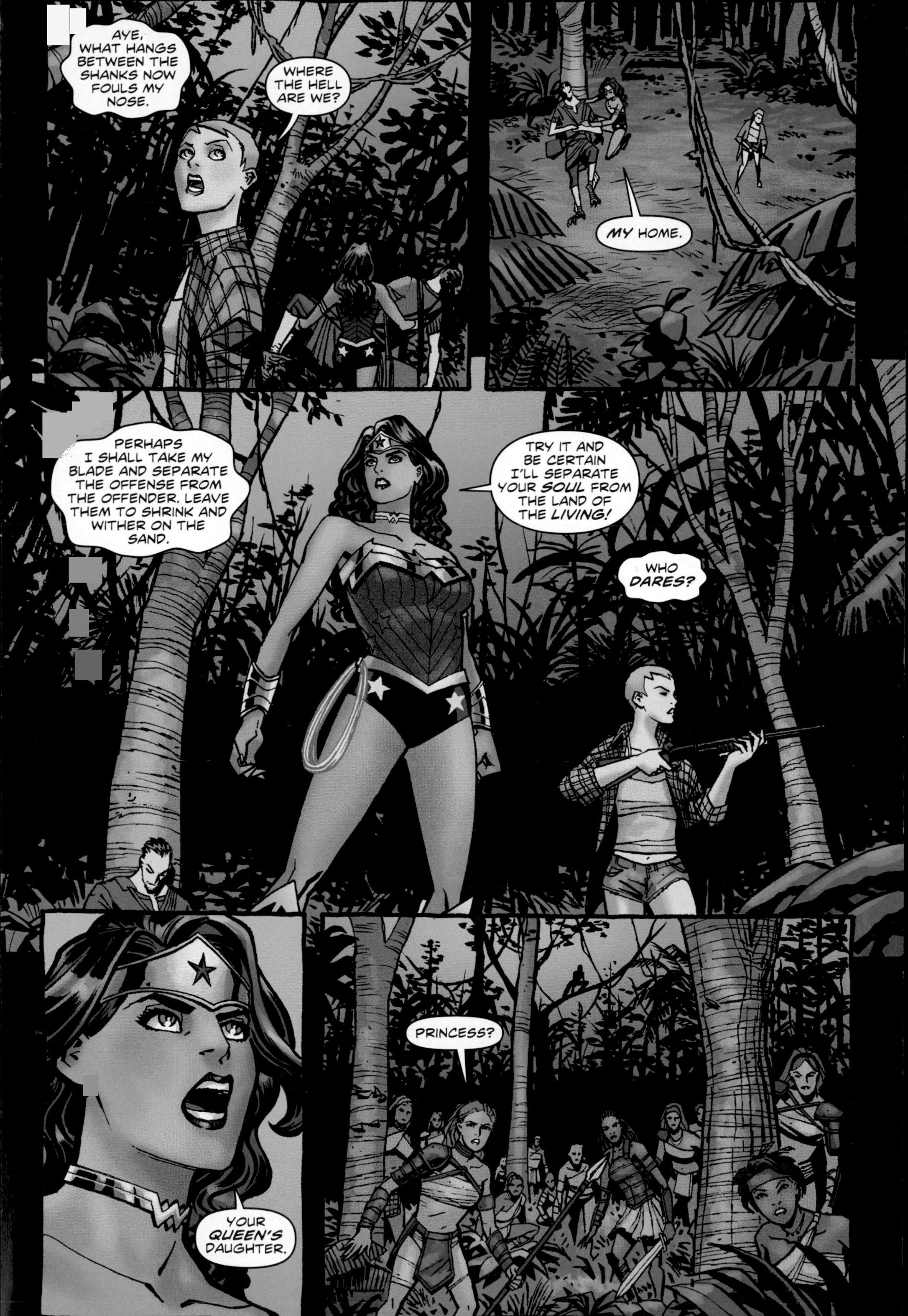
AYE, WHAT HANGS BETWEEN THE SHANKS NOW FOULS MY NOSE.
WHERE THE HELL ARE WE?
MY HOME.
PERHAPS I SHALL TAKE MY BLADE AND SEPARATE THE OFFENSE FROM THE OFFENDER. LEAVE THEM TO SHRINK AND WITHER ON THE SAND.
TRY IT AND BE CERTAIN I'LL SEPARATE YOUR SOUL FROM THE LAND OF THE LIVING!
WHO DARES?
YOUR QUEEN'S DAUGHTER.
PRINCESS?

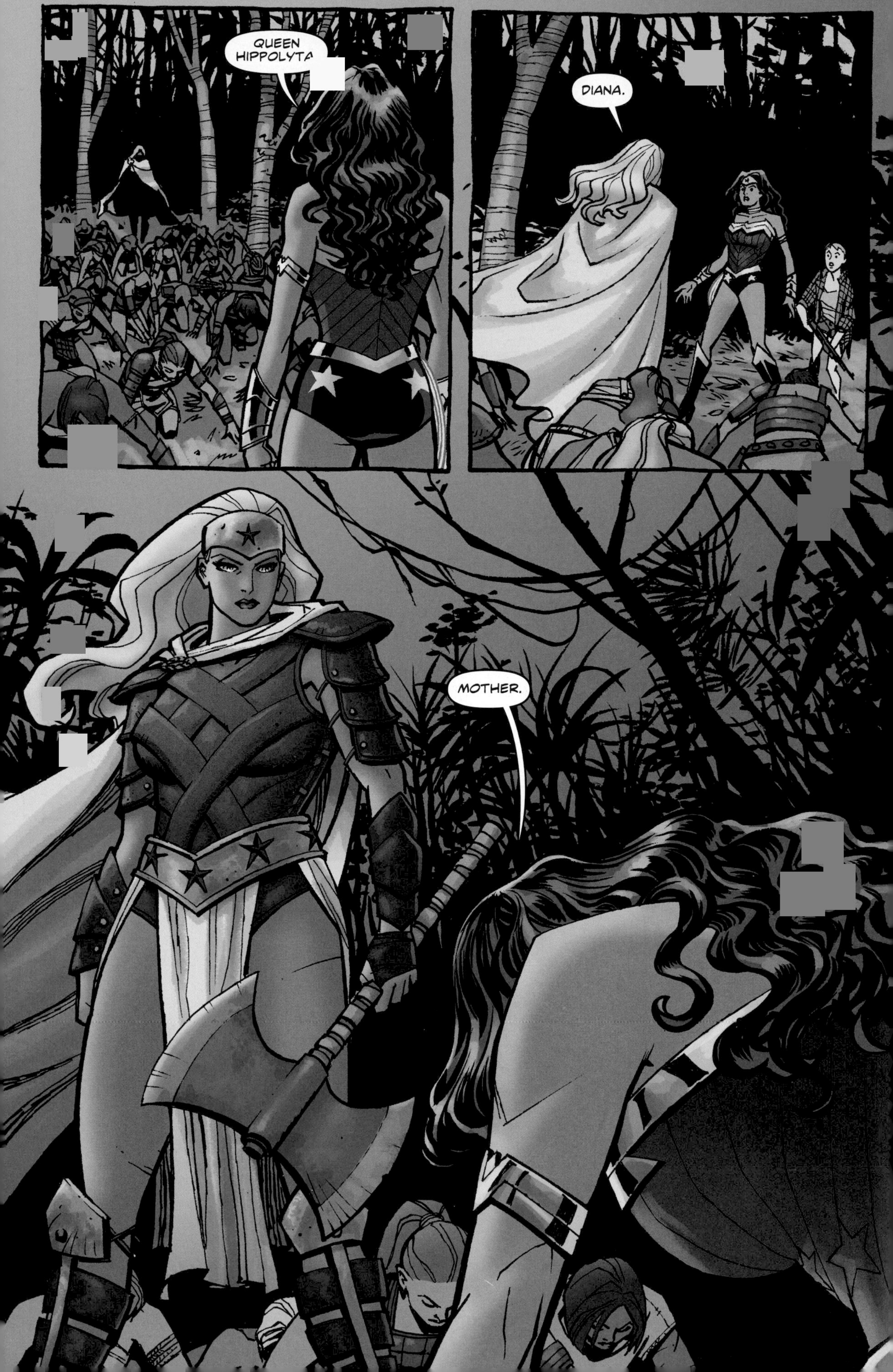
QUEEN HIPPOLYTA
DIANA.
MOTHER.

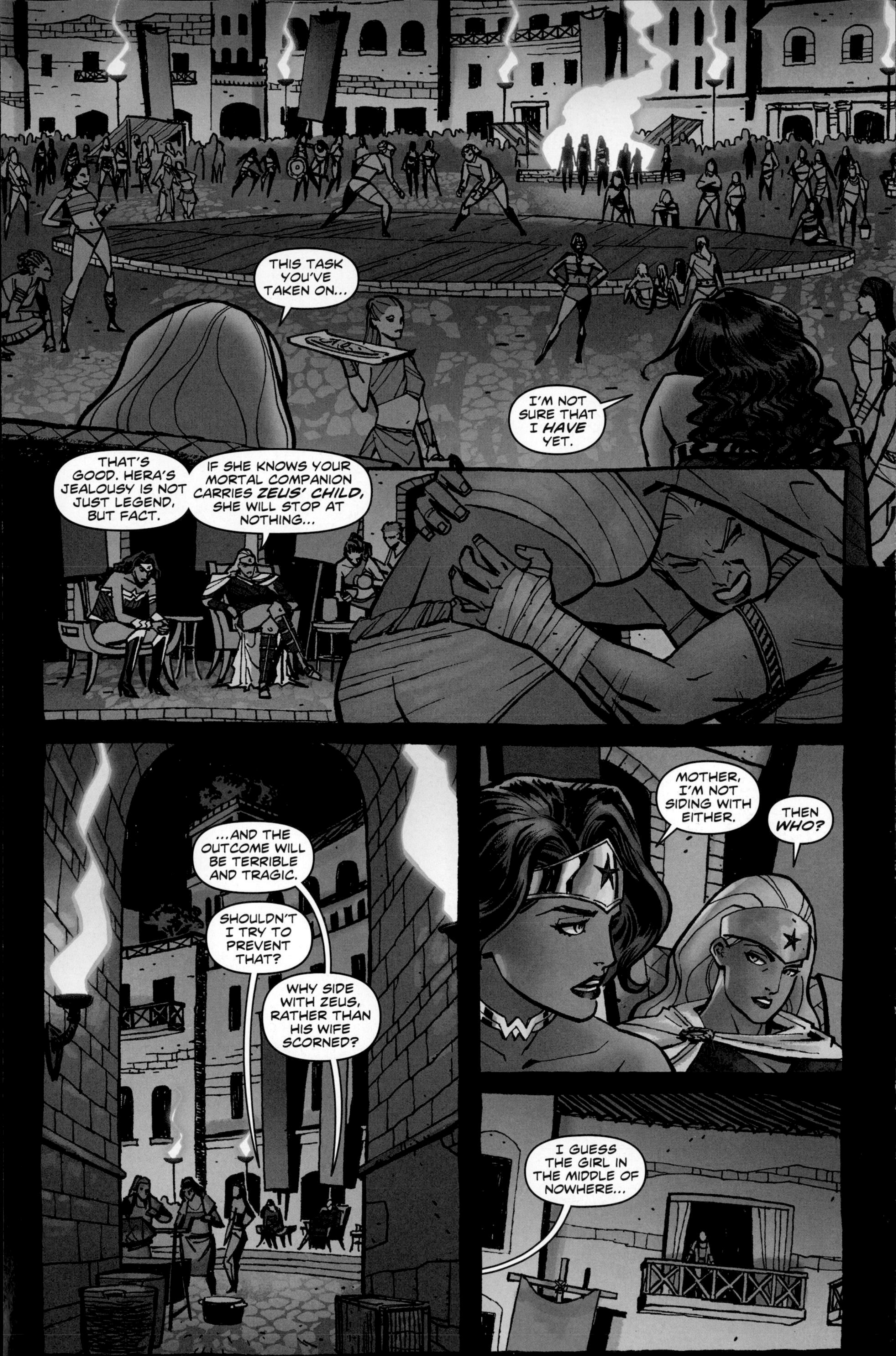

THIS TASK YOU'VE TAKEN ON...
I'M NOT SURE THAT I HAVE YET.
THAT'S GOOD. HERA'S JEALOUSY IS NOT JUST LEGEND, BUT FACT.
IF SHE KNOWS YOUR MORTAL COMPANION CARRIES ZEUS' CHILD, SHE WILL STOP AT NOTHING...
...AND THE OUTCOME WILL BE TERRIBLE AND TRAGIC.
SHOULDN'T I TRY TO PREVENT THAT?
WHY SIDE WITH ZEUS, RATHER THAN HIS WIFE SCORNED?
MOTHER, I'M NOT SIDING WITH EITHER.
THEN WHO?
I GUESS THE GIRL IN THE MIDDLE OF NOWHERE...

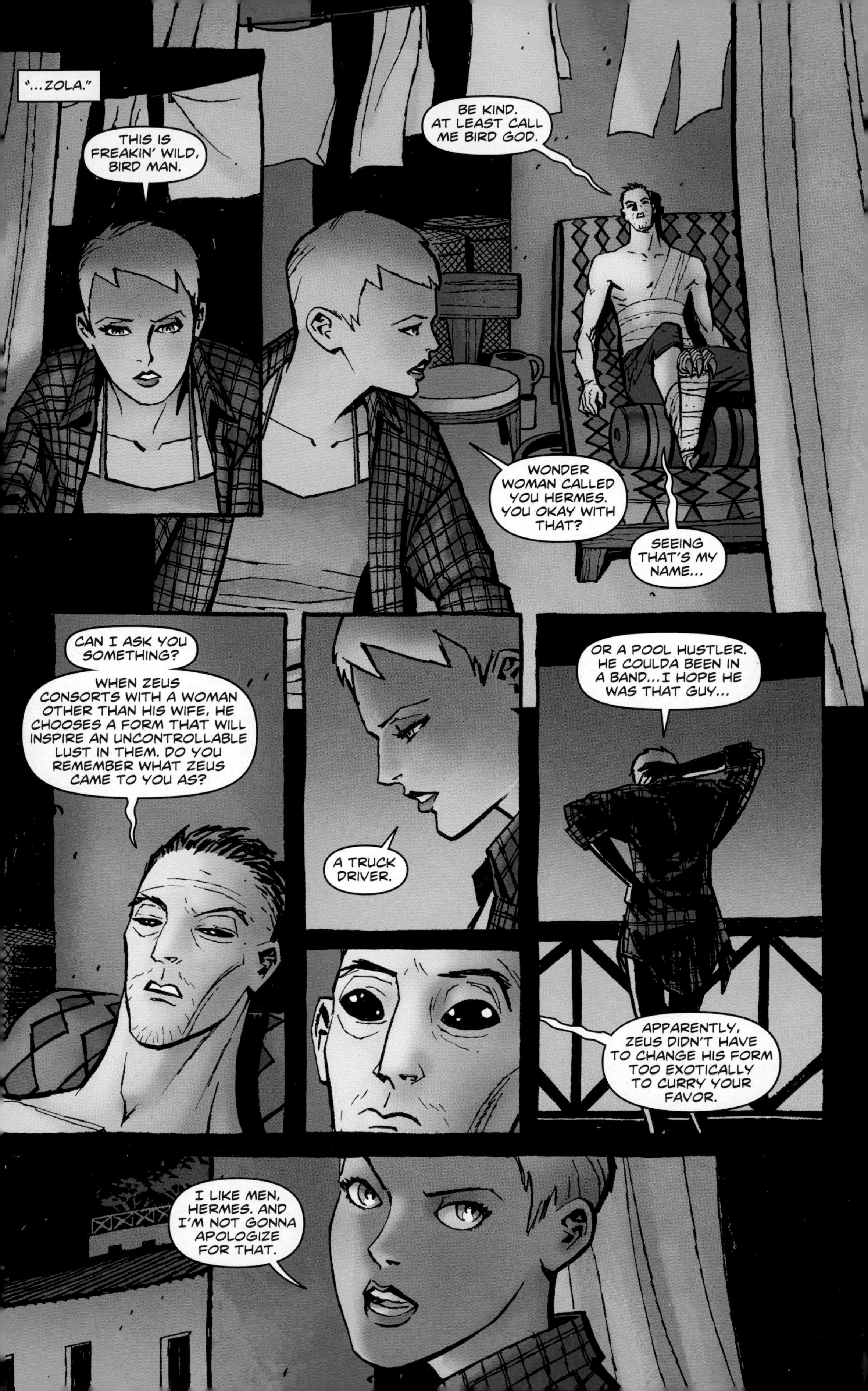
"...ZOLA."
THIS IS FREAKIN' WILD, BIRD MAN.
BE KIND. AT LEAST CALL ME BIRD GOD.
WONDER WOMAN CALLED YOU HERMES. YOU OKAY WITH THAT?
SEEING THAT'S MY NAME...
CAN I ASK YOU SOMETHING?
WHEN ZEUS CONSORTS WITH A WOMAN OTHER THAN HIS WIFE, HE CHOOSES A FORM THAT WILL INSPIRE AN UNCONTROLLABLE LUST IN THEM. DO YOU REMEMBER WHAT ZEUS CAME TO YOU AS?
A TRUCK DRIVER.
OR A POOL HUSTLER. HE COULDA BEEN IN A BAND... I HOPE HE WAS THAT GUY...
APPARENTLY, ZEUS DIDN'T HAVE TO CHANGE HIS FORM TOO EXOTICALLY TO CURRY YOUR FAVOR.
I LIKE MEN, HERMES. AND I'M NOT GONNA APOLOGIZE FOR THAT.

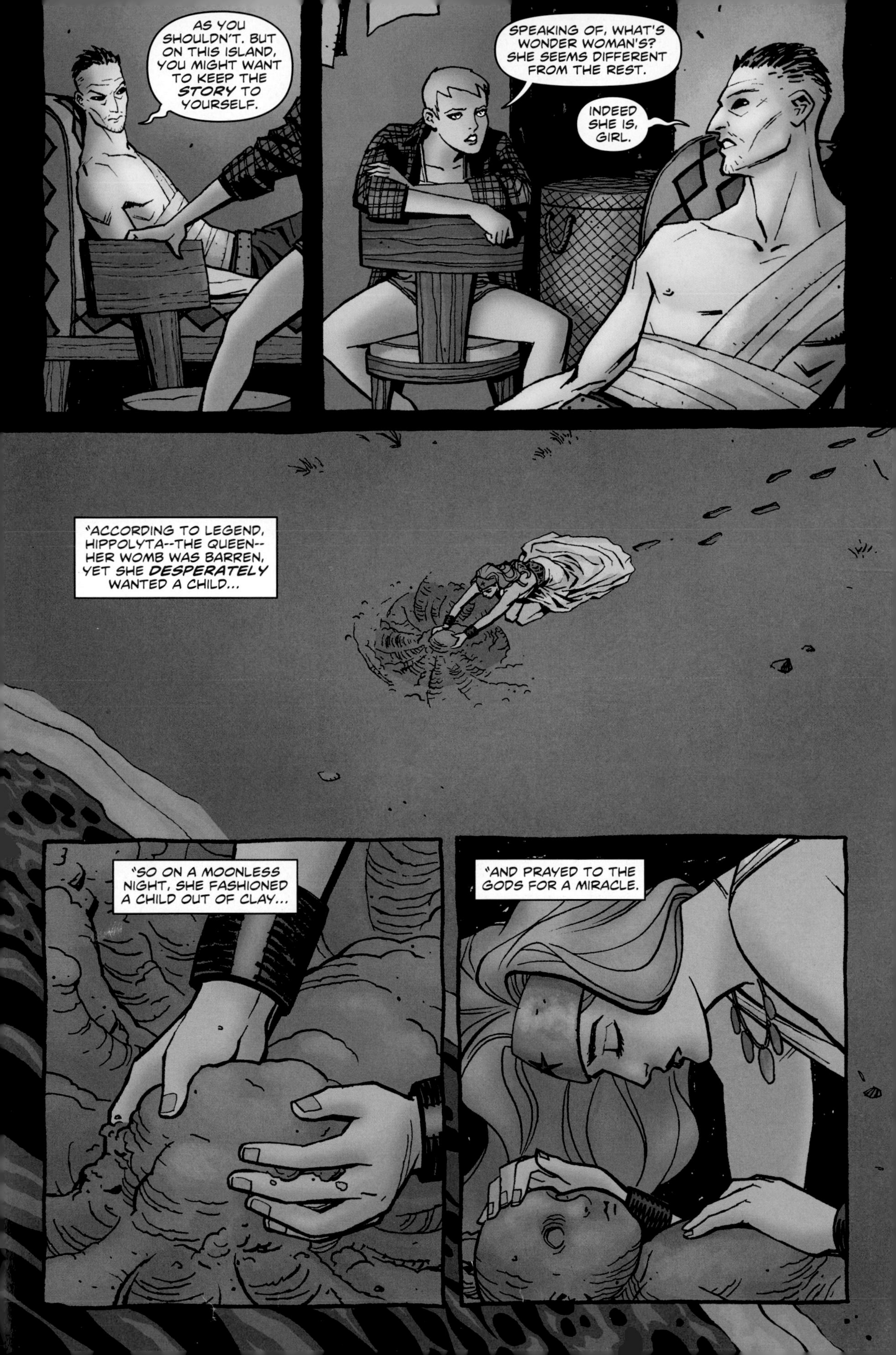
AS YOU SHOULDN'T. BUT ON THIS ISLAND, YOU MIGHT WANT TO KEEP THE STORY TO YOURSELF.
SPEAKING OF, WHAT'S WONDER WOMAN'S? SHE SEEMS DIFFERENT FROM THE REST.
INDEED SHE IS, GIRL.
"ACCORDING TO LEGEND, HIPPOLYTA--THE QUEEN--HER WOMB WAS BARREN, YET SHE DESPERATELY WANTED A CHILD...
"SO ON A MOONLESS NIGHT, SHE FASHIONED A CHILD OUT OF CLAY...
"AND PRAYED TO THE GODS FOR A MIRACLE.

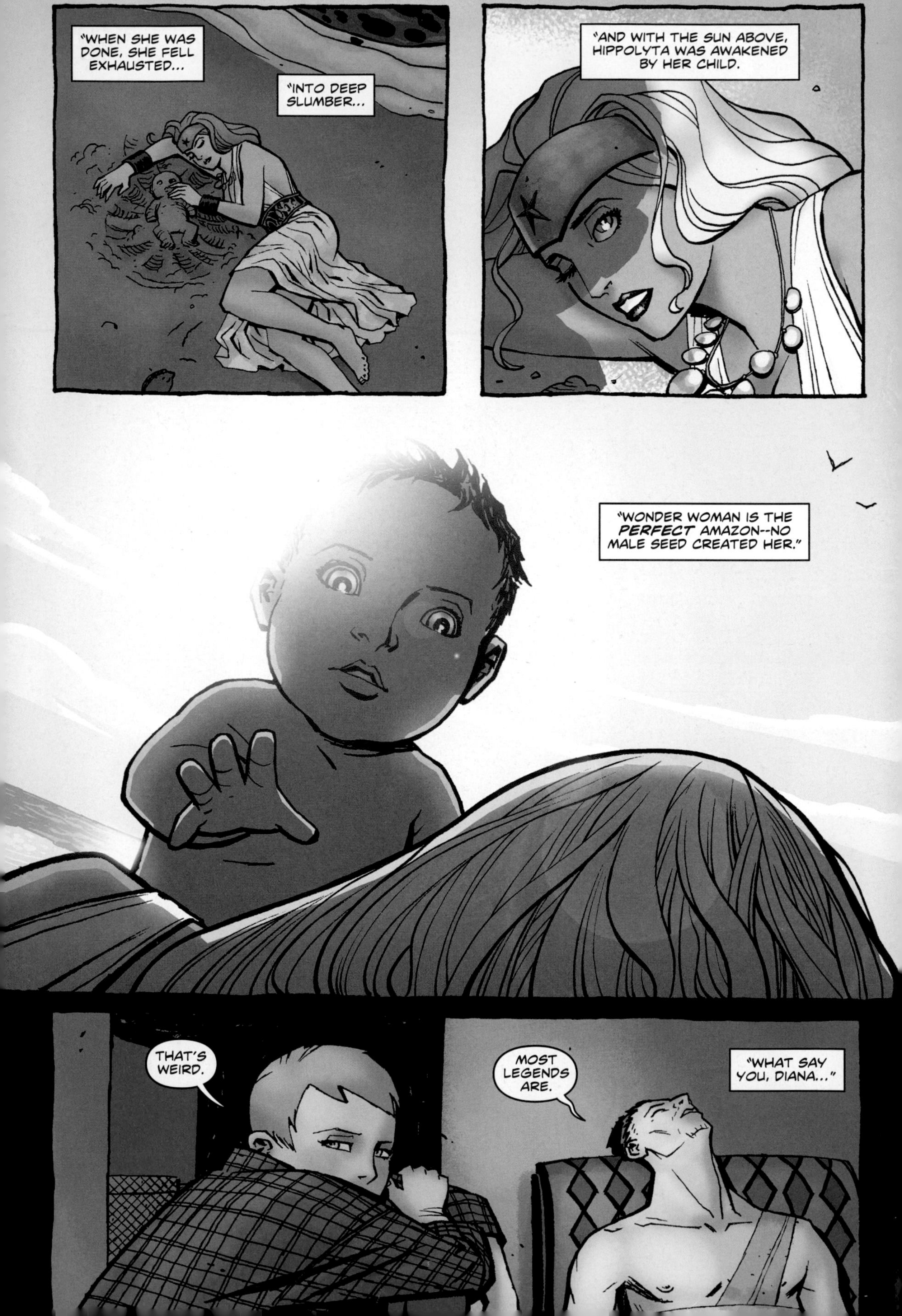
"WHEN SHE WAS DONE, SHE FELL EXHAUSTED...
"INTO DEEP SLUMBER...
"AND WITH THE SUN ABOVE, HIPPOLYTA WAS AWAKENED BY HER CHILD.
"WONDER WOMAN IS THE *PERFECT* AMAZON--NO MALE SEED CREATED HER."
THAT'S WEIRD.
MOST LEGENDS ARE.
"WHAT SAY YOU, DIANA..."

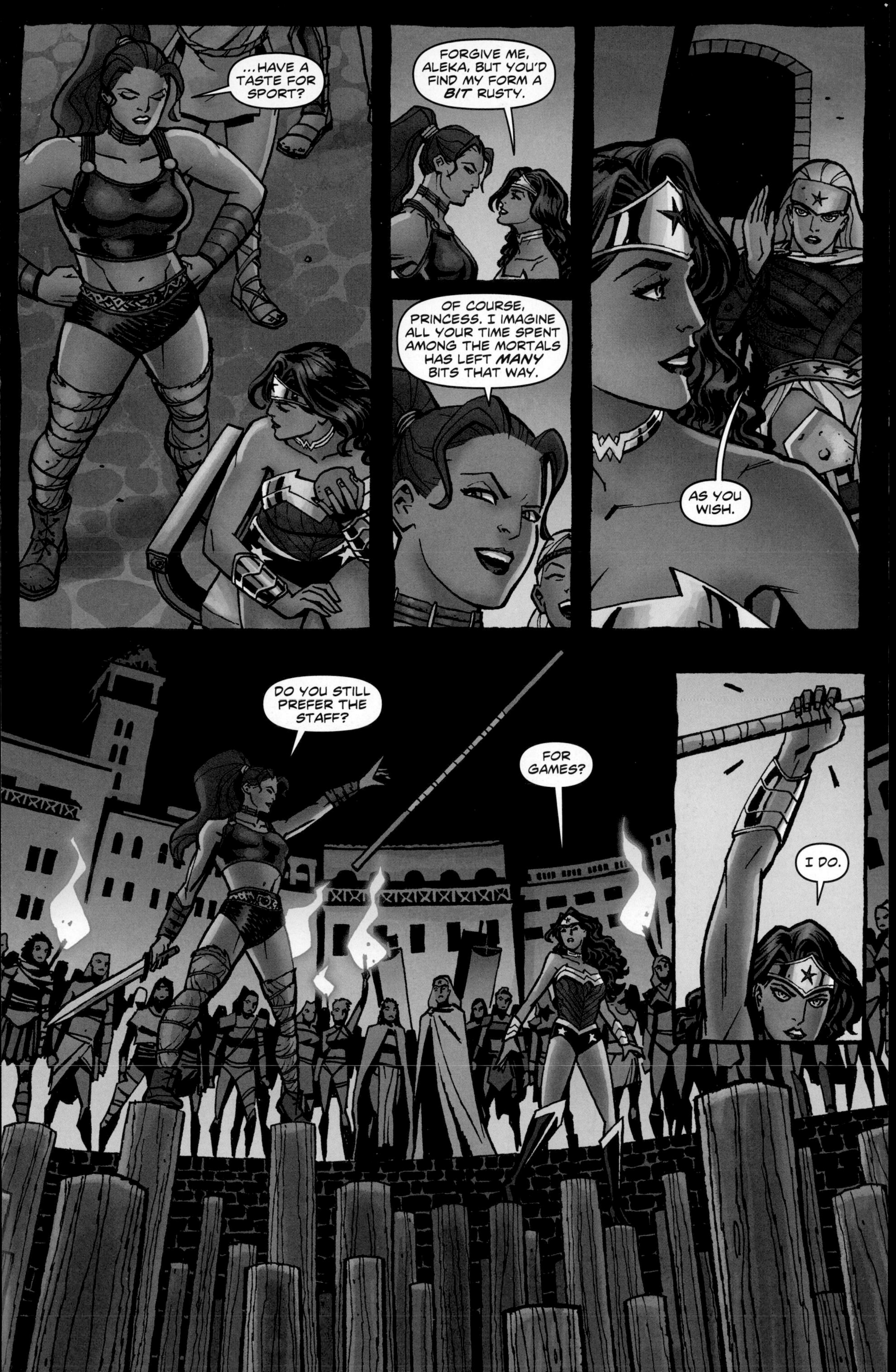
...HAVE A TASTE FOR SPORT?
FORGIVE ME, ALEKA, BUT YOU'D FIND MY FORM A *BIT* RUSTY.
OF COURSE, PRINCESS. I IMAGINE ALL YOUR TIME SPENT AMONG THE MORTALS HAS LEFT *MANY* BITS THAT WAY.
AS YOU WISH.
DO YOU STILL PREFER THE STAFF?
FOR GAMES?
I DO.

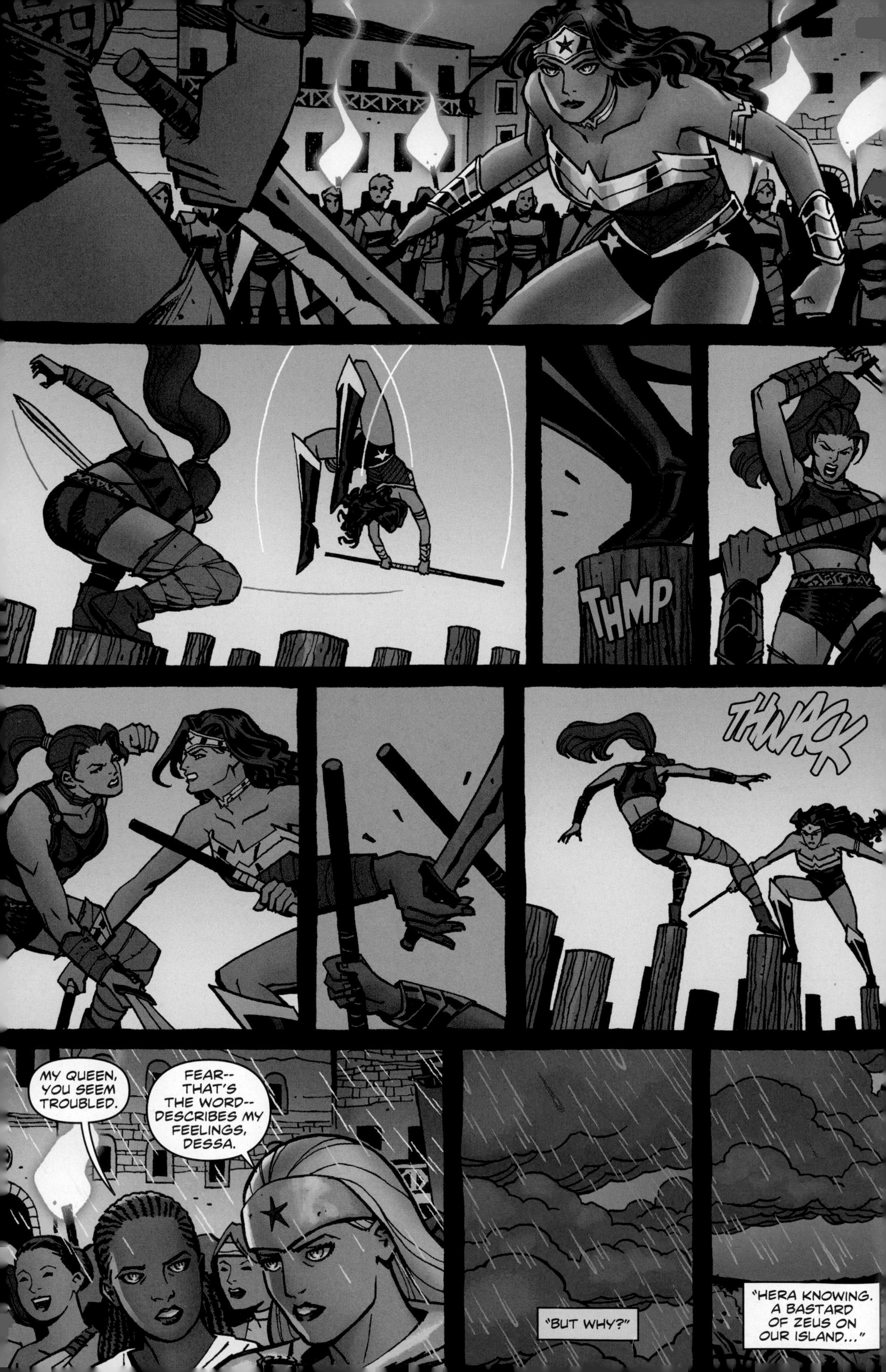
THMP
THWACK
MY QUEEN, YOU SEEM TROUBLED.
FEAR-- THAT'S THE WORD-- DESCRIBES MY FEELINGS, DESSA.
"BUT WHY?"
"HERA KNOWING. A BASTARD OF ZEUS ON OUR ISLAND..."

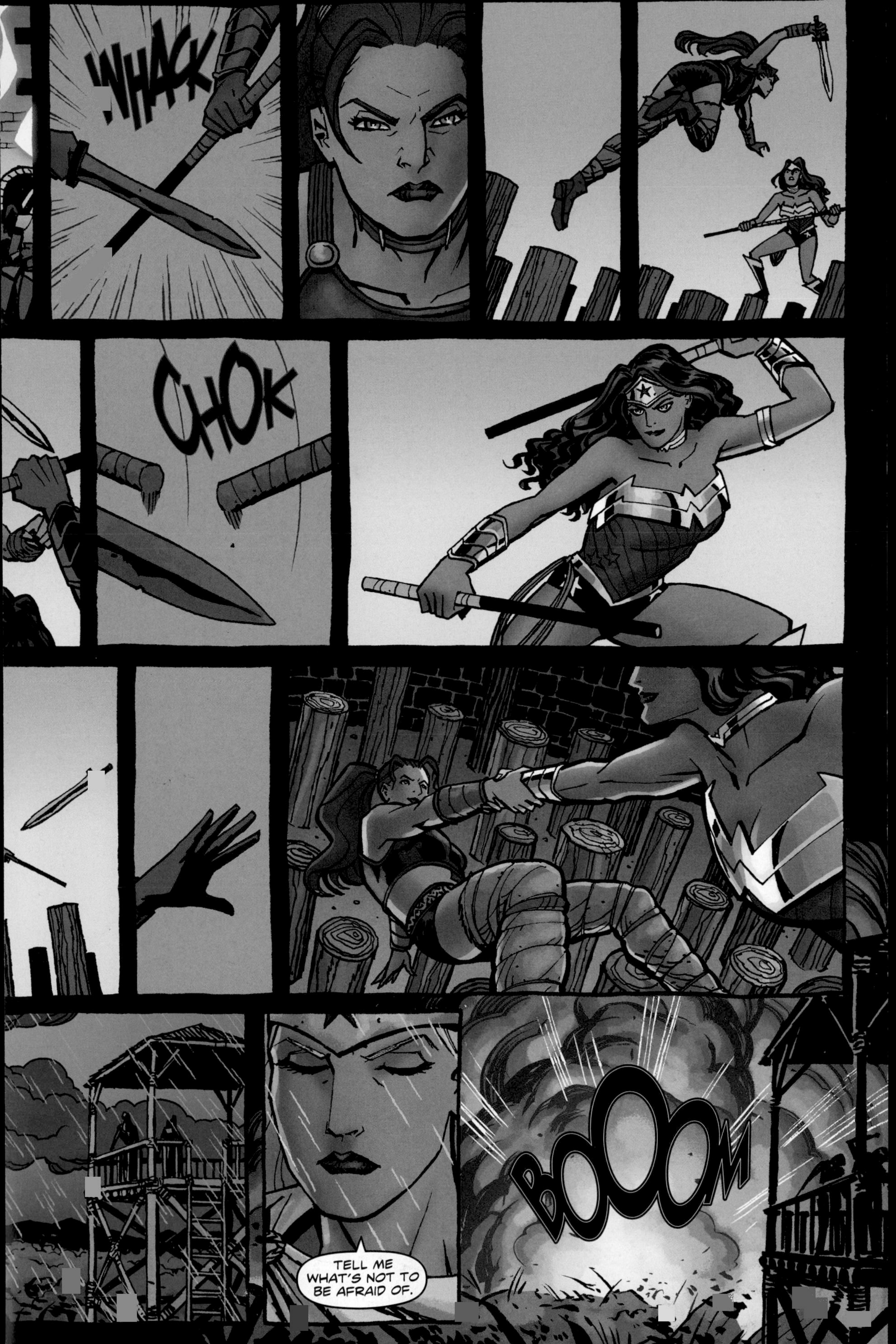
WHACK
CHOK
TELL ME WHAT'S NOT TO BE AFRAID OF.
BOOOOM

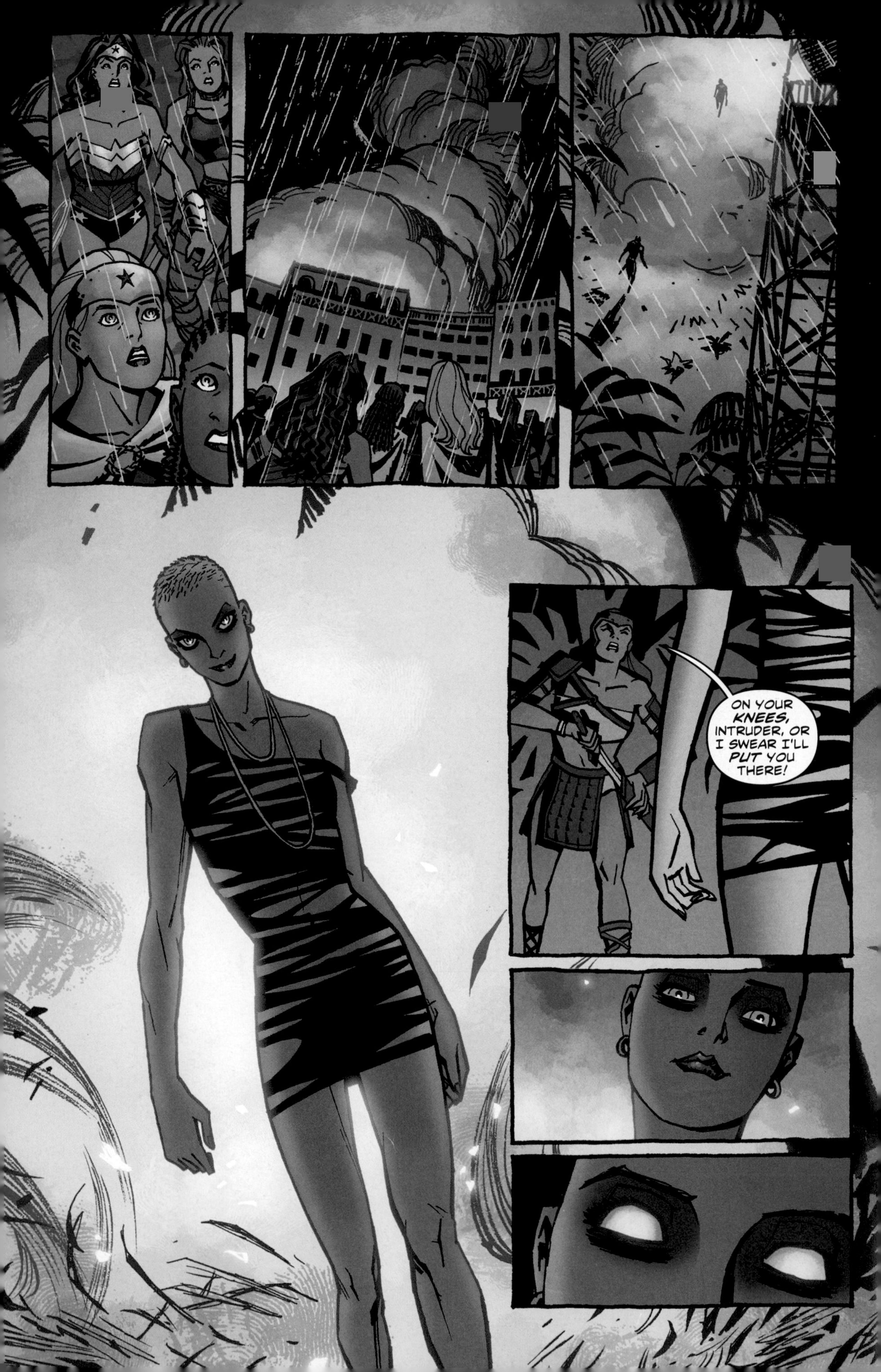
ON YOUR KNEES, INTRUDER, OR I SWEAR I'LL PUT YOU THERE!

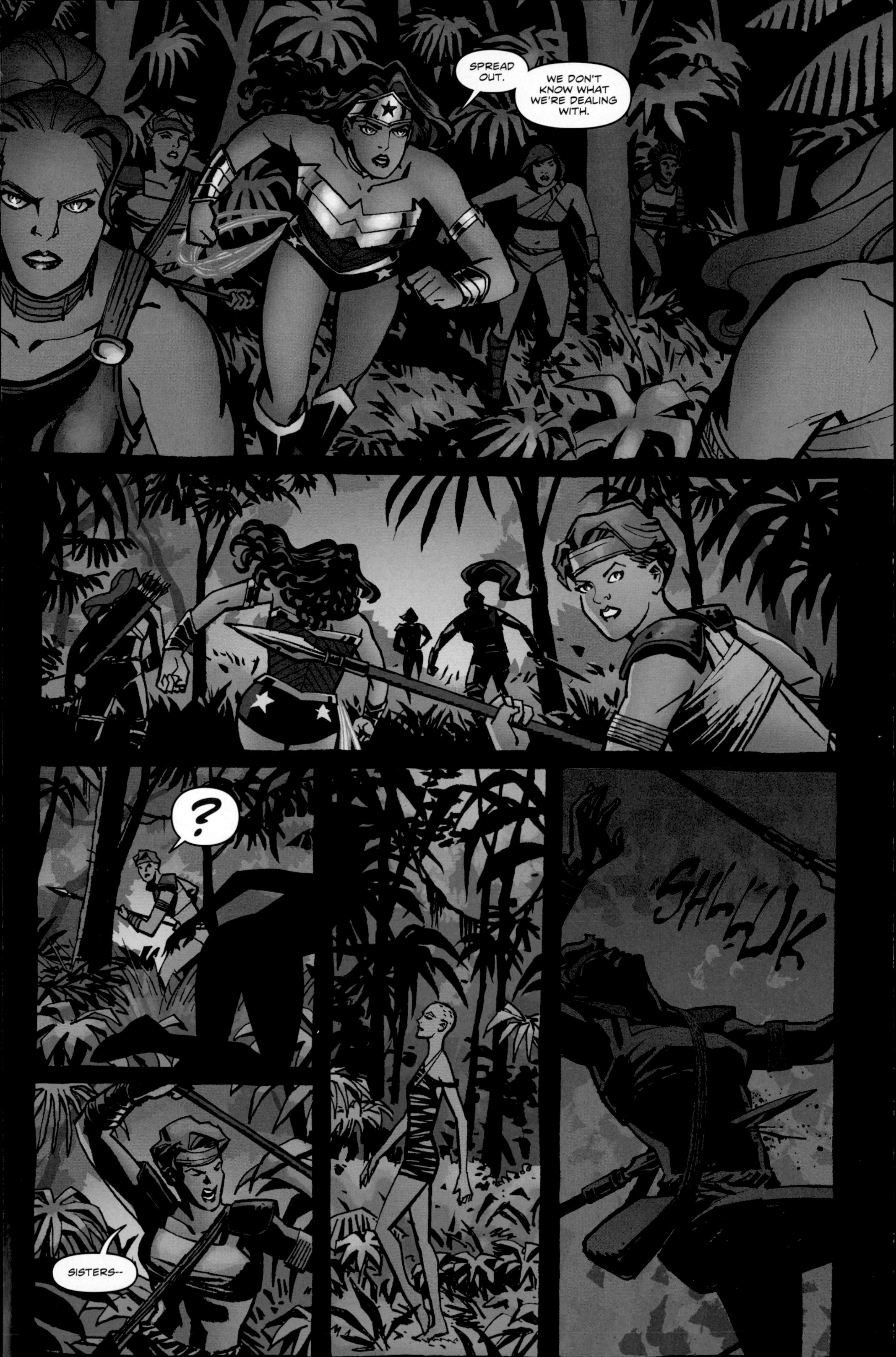
SPREAD OUT.
WE DON'T KNOW WHAT WE'RE DEALING WITH.
?
SHLLLK
SISTERS--

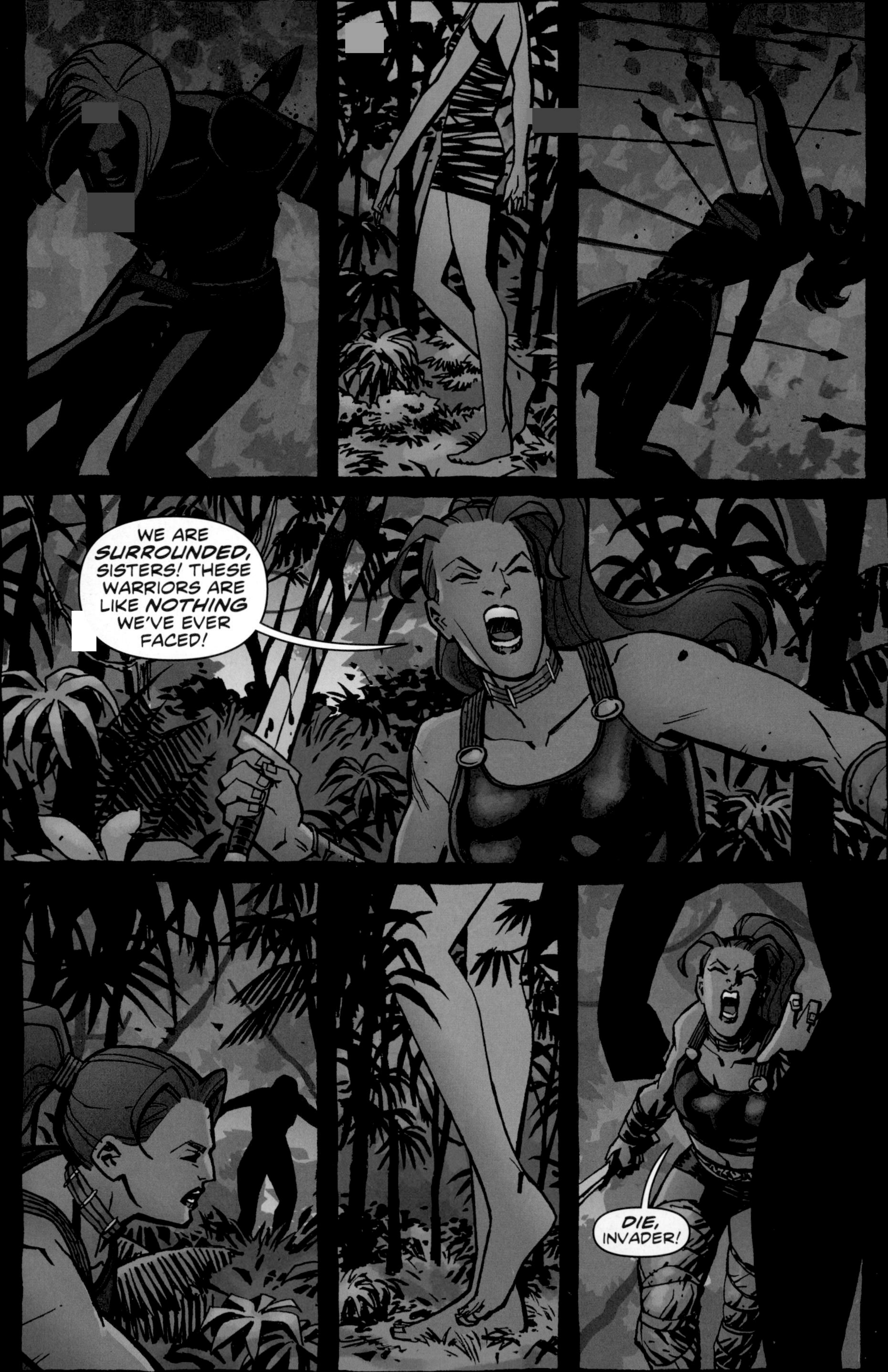
WE ARE SURROUNDED, SISTERS! THESE WARRIORS ARE LIKE NOTHING WE'VE EVER FACED!
DIE, INVADER!

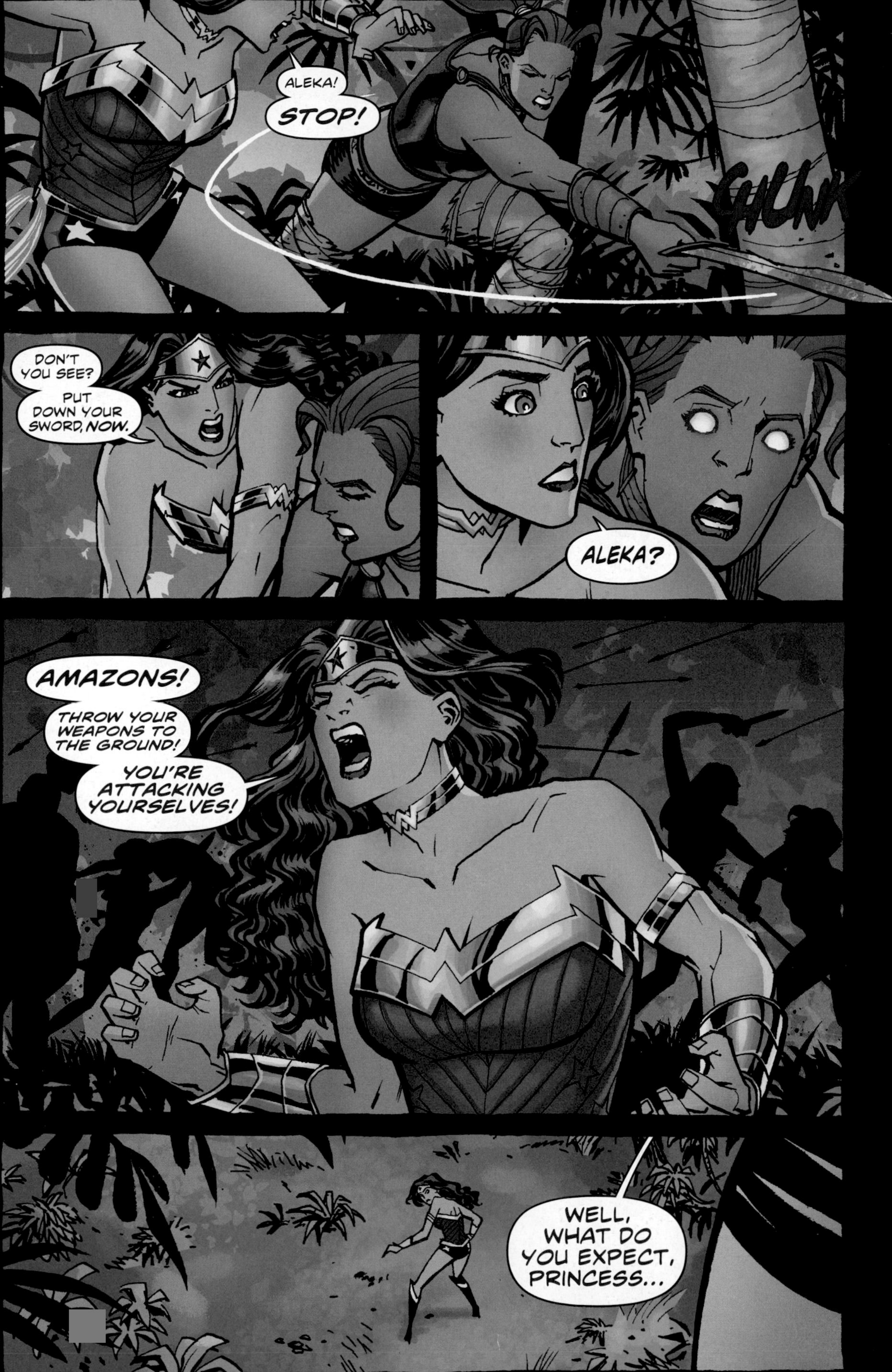
ALEKA!
STOP!
CHUNK
DON'T YOU SEE?
PUT DOWN YOUR SWORD, NOW.
ALEKA?
AMAZONS!
THROW YOUR WEAPONS TO THE GROUND!
YOU'RE ATTACKING YOURSELVES!
WELL, WHAT DO YOU EXPECT, PRINCESS...

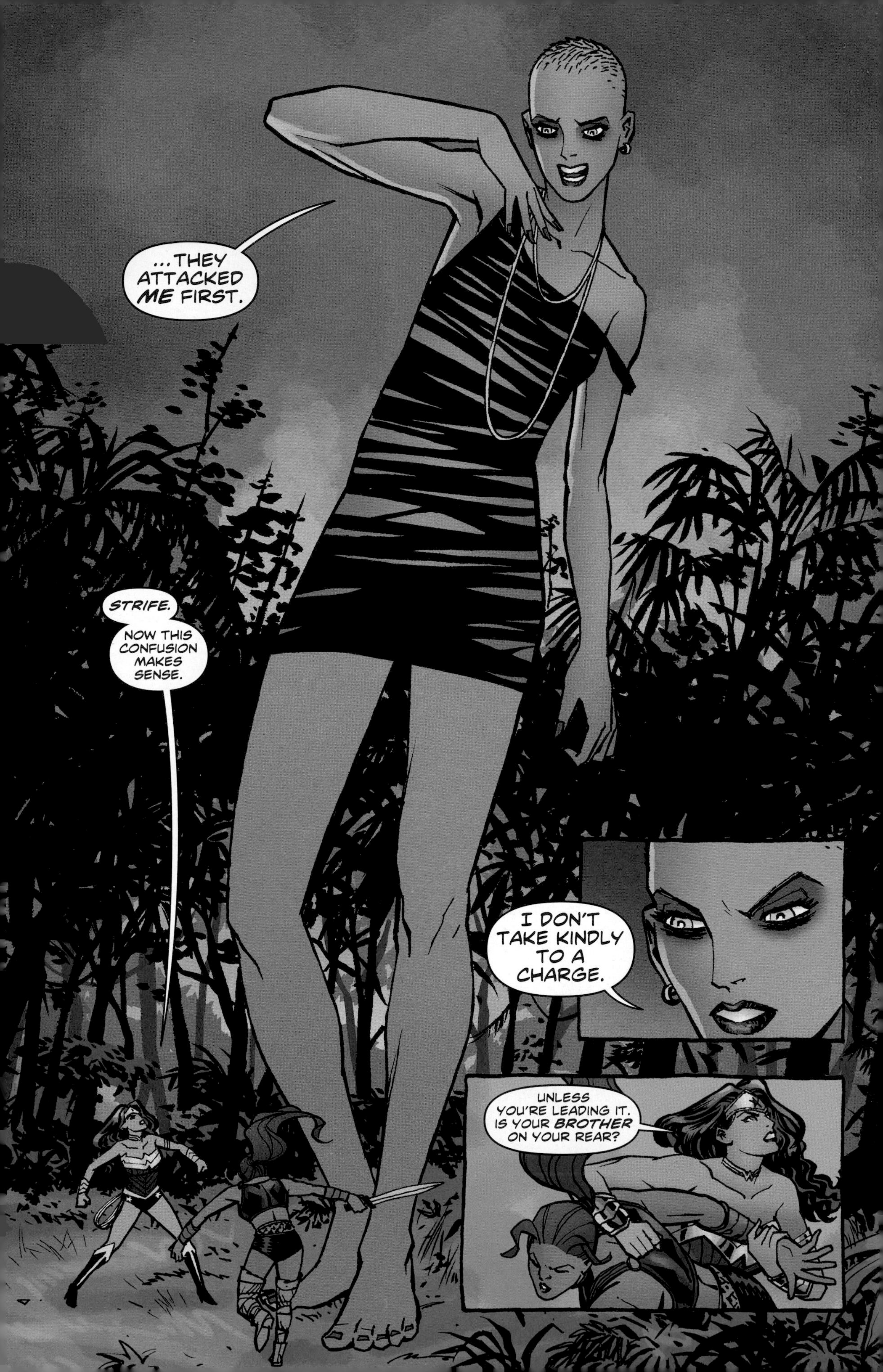
...THEY ATTACKED *ME* FIRST.
STRIFE.
NOW THIS CONFUSION MAKES SENSE.
I DON'T TAKE KINDLY TO A CHARGE.
UNLESS YOU'RE LEADING IT. IS YOUR *BROTHER* ON YOUR REAR?

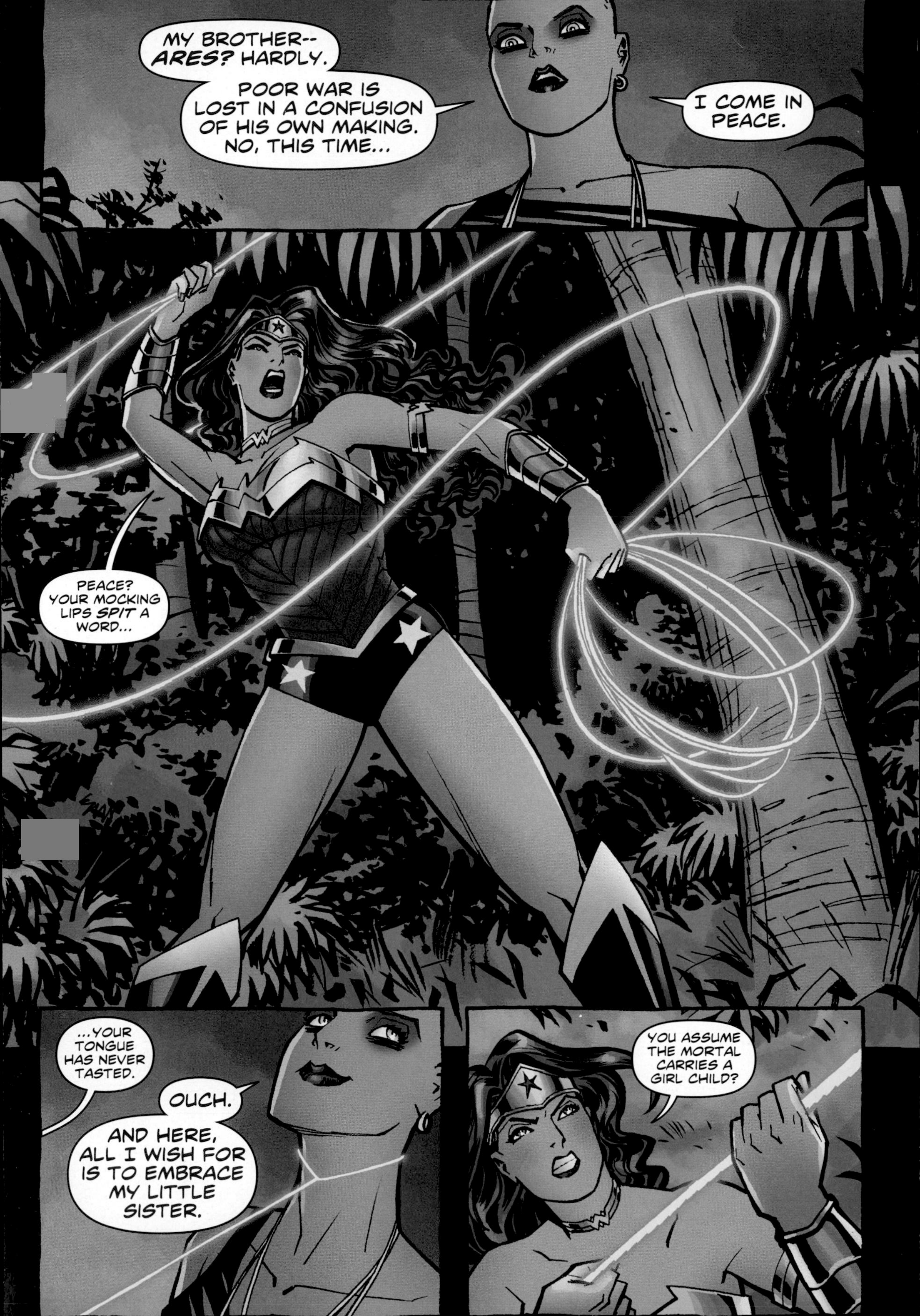
MY BROTHER-- ARES? HARDLY.
POOR WAR IS LOST IN A CONFUSION OF HIS OWN MAKING. NO, THIS TIME...
I COME IN PEACE.
PEACE? YOUR MOCKING LIPS SPIT A WORD...
...YOUR TONGUE HAS NEVER TASTED.
OUCH.
AND HERE, ALL I WISH FOR IS TO EMBRACE MY LITTLE SISTER.
YOU ASSUME THE MORTAL CARRIES A GIRL CHILD?

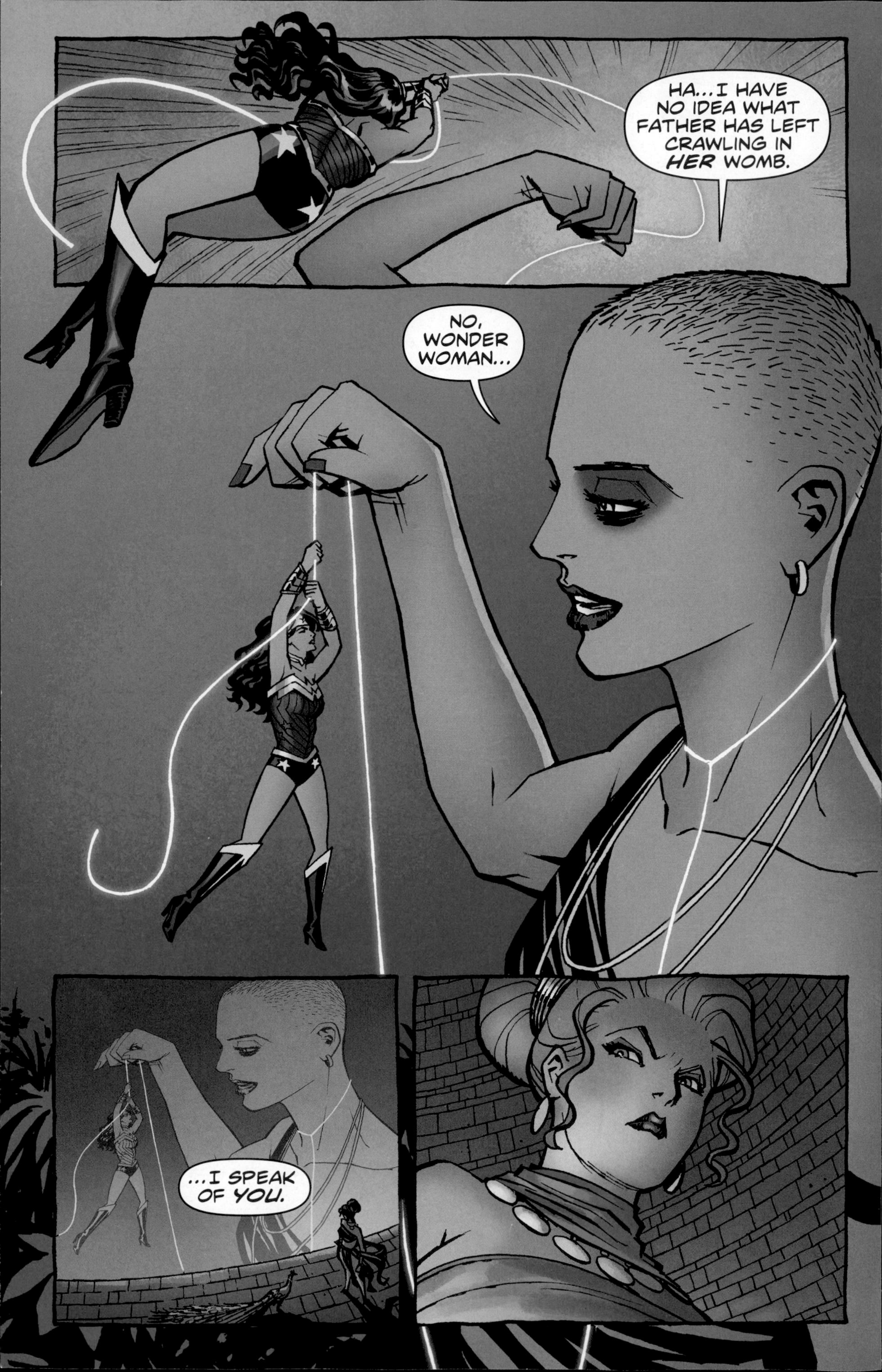
HA...I HAVE NO IDEA WHAT FATHER HAS LEFT CRAWLING IN HER WOMB.
NO, WONDER WOMAN...
...I SPEAK OF YOU.

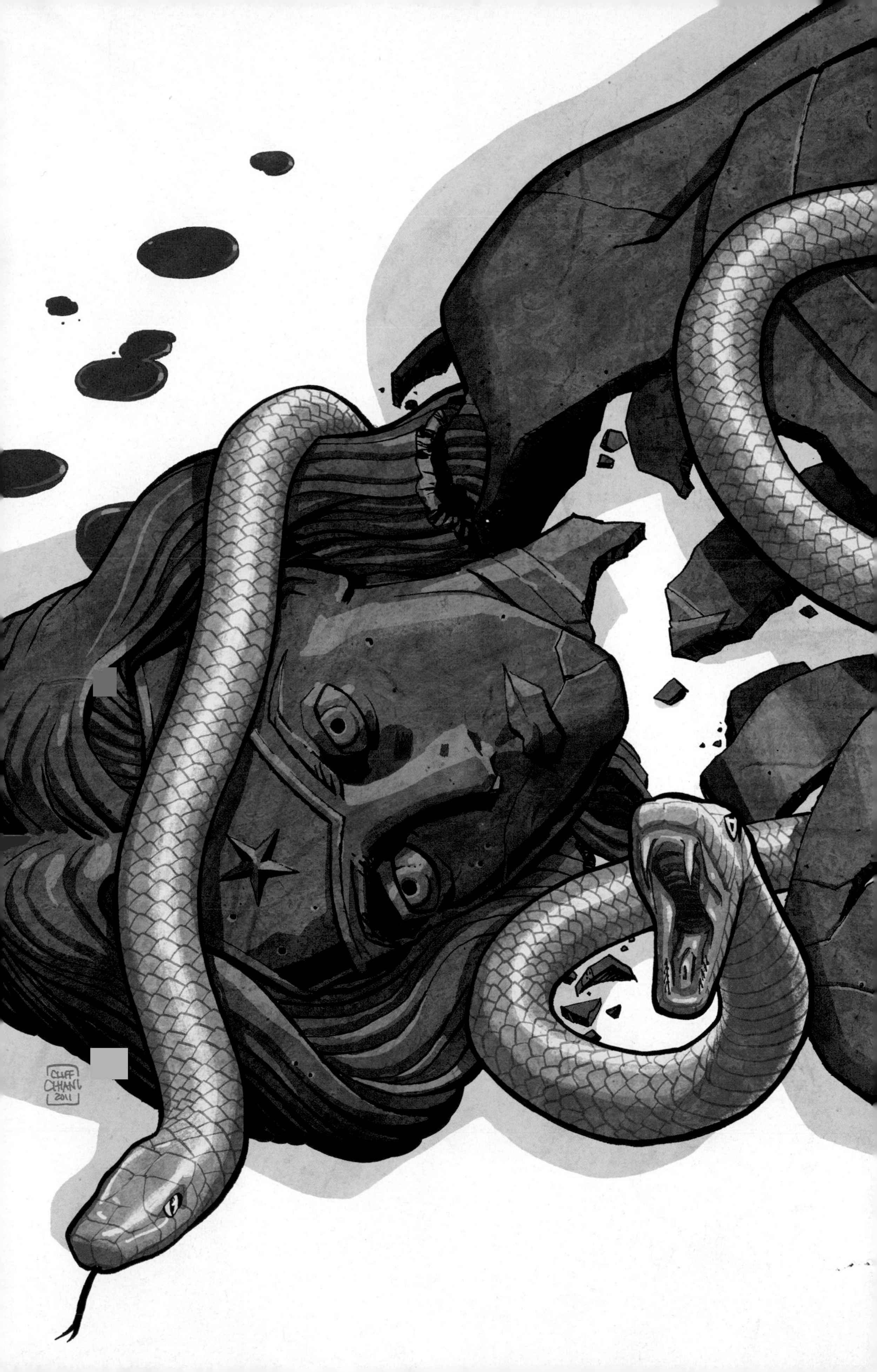
CLIFF
CHIANG
2011

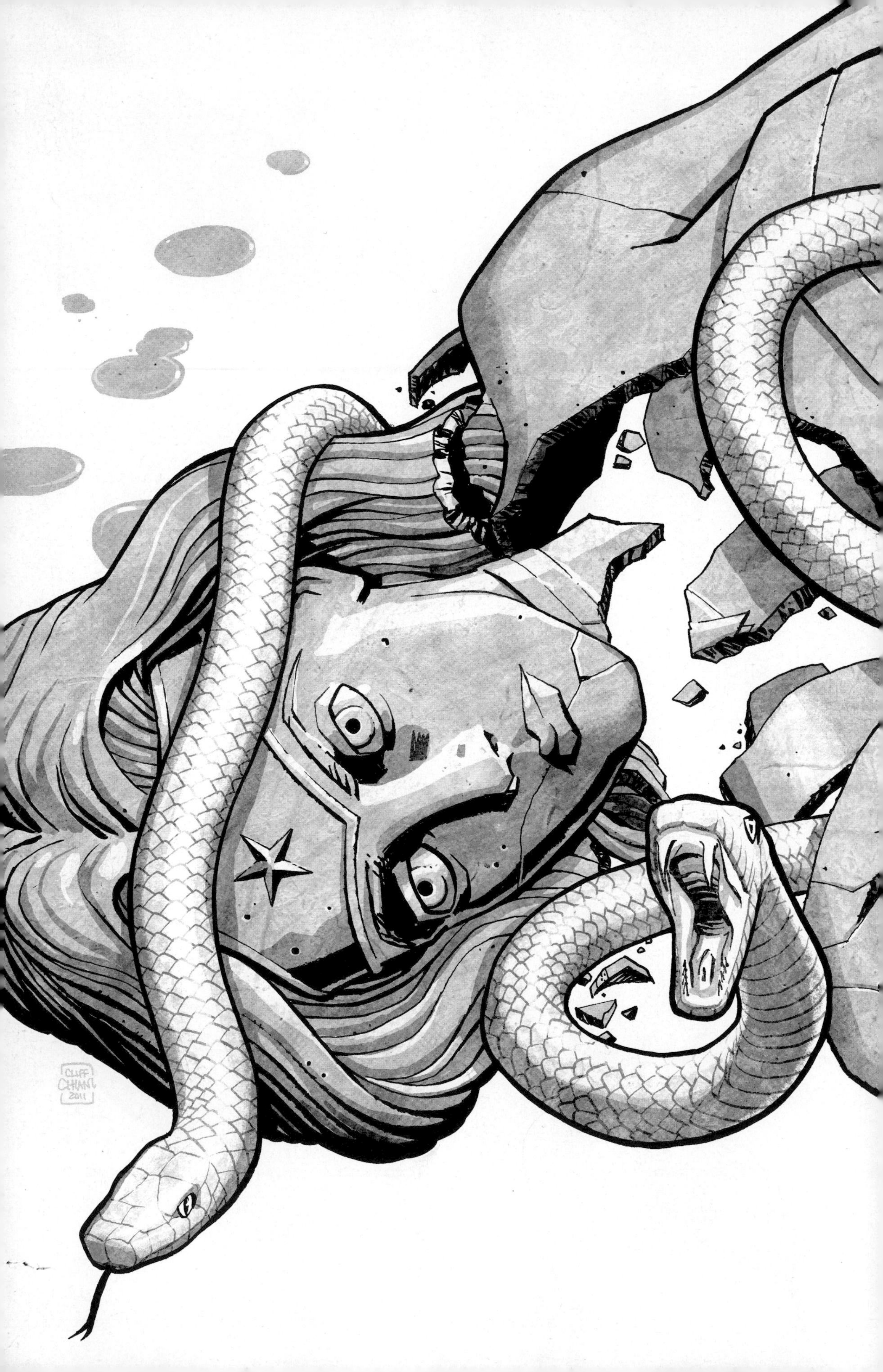
CLIFF CHIANG 2011

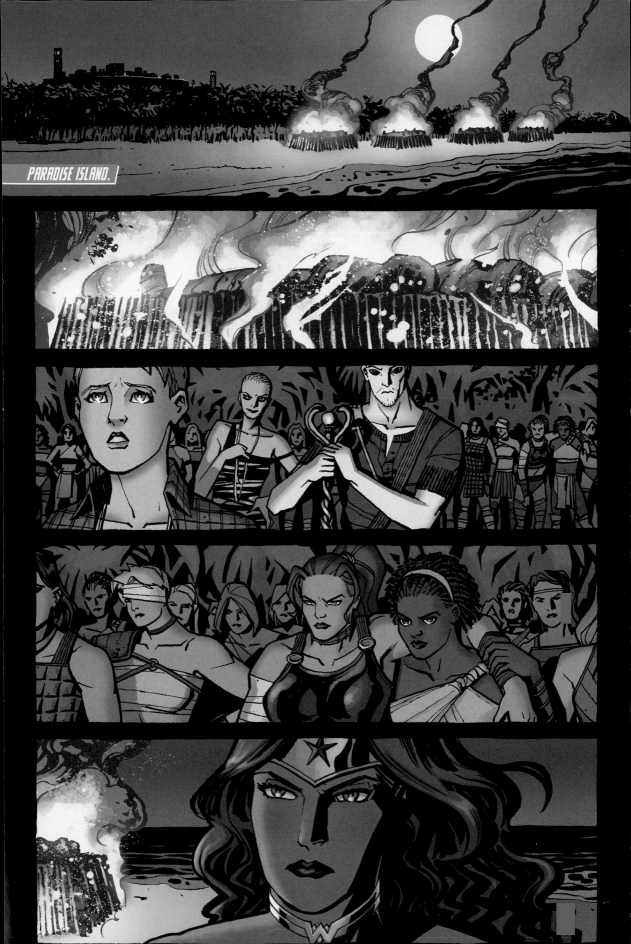

PARADISE ISLAND.

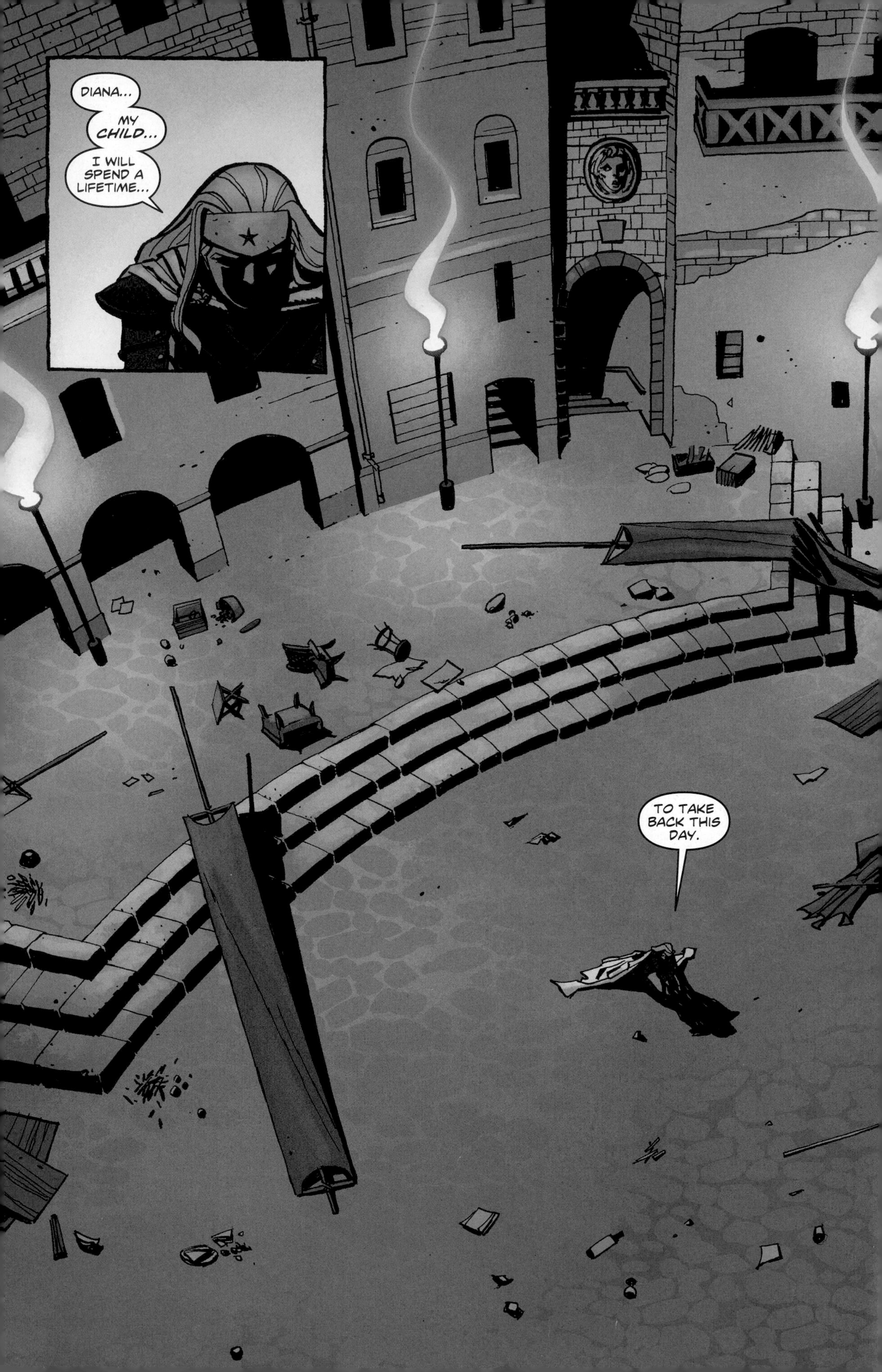
DIANA...
MY CHILD...
I WILL SPEND A LIFETIME...
TO TAKE BACK THIS DAY.

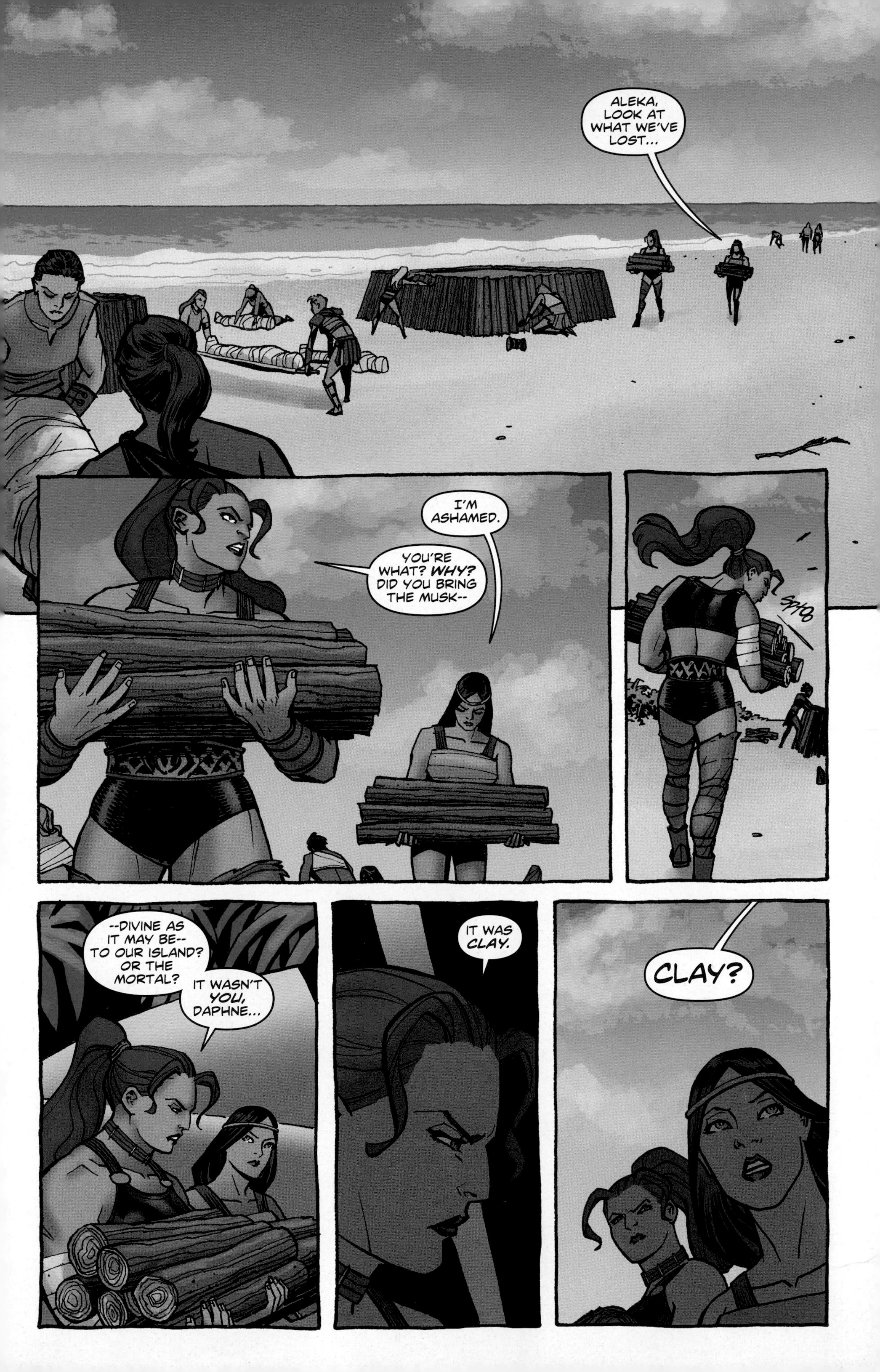
ALEKA, LOOK AT WHAT WE'VE LOST...
I'M ASHAMED.
YOU'RE WHAT? WHY? DID YOU BRING THE MUSK--
SPLOO
--DIVINE AS IT MAY BE-- TO OUR ISLAND? OR THE MORTAL?
IT WASN'T YOU, DAPHNE...
IT WAS CLAY.
CLAY?

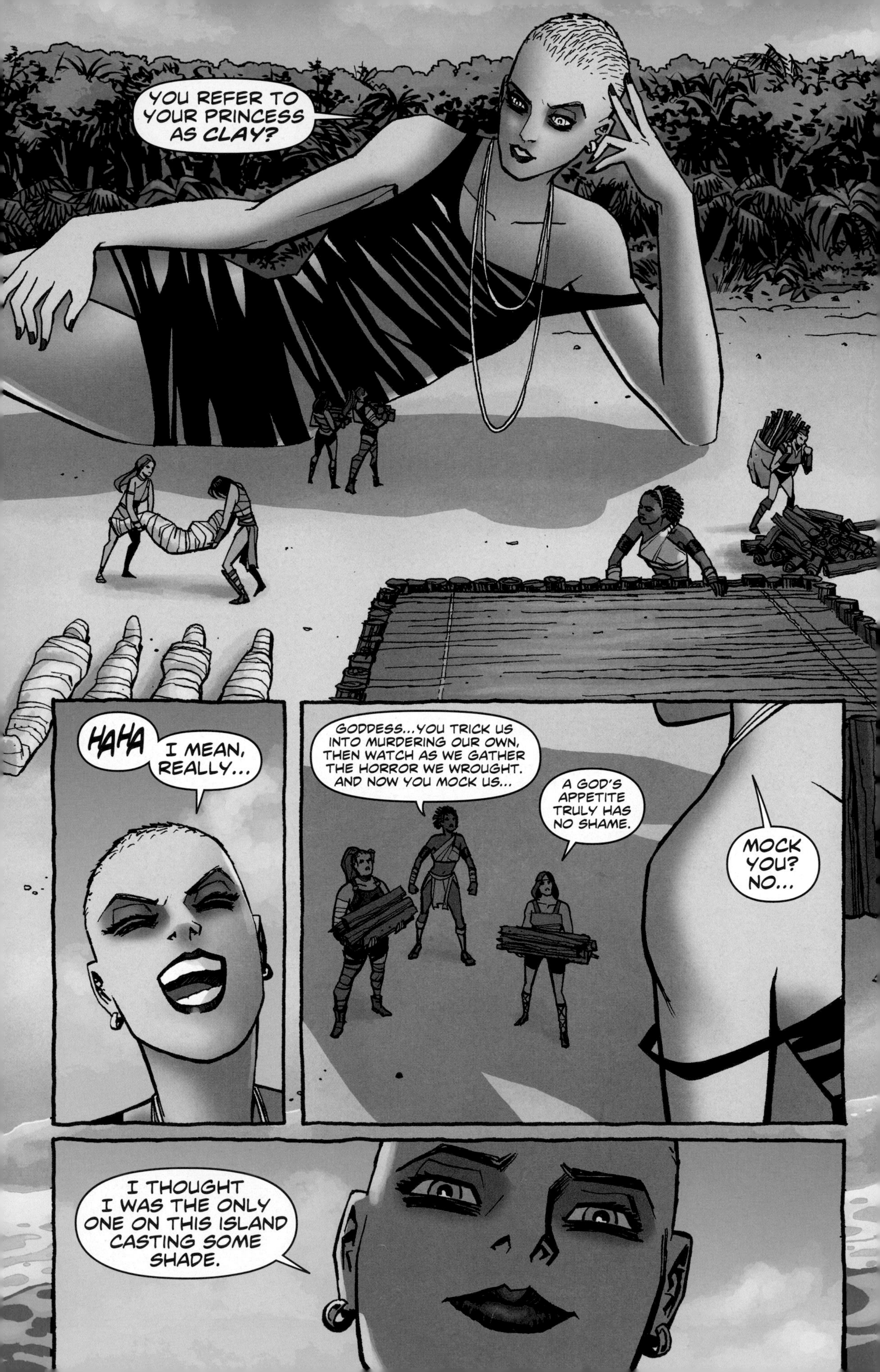
YOU REFER TO YOUR PRINCESS AS CLAY?
HAHA
I MEAN, REALLY...
GODDESS...YOU TRICK US INTO MURDERING OUR OWN, THEN WATCH AS WE GATHER THE HORROR WE WROUGHT. AND NOW YOU MOCK US...
A GOD'S APPETITE TRULY HAS NO SHAME.
MOCK YOU? NO...
I THOUGHT I WAS THE ONLY ONE ON THIS ISLAND CASTING SOME SHADE.

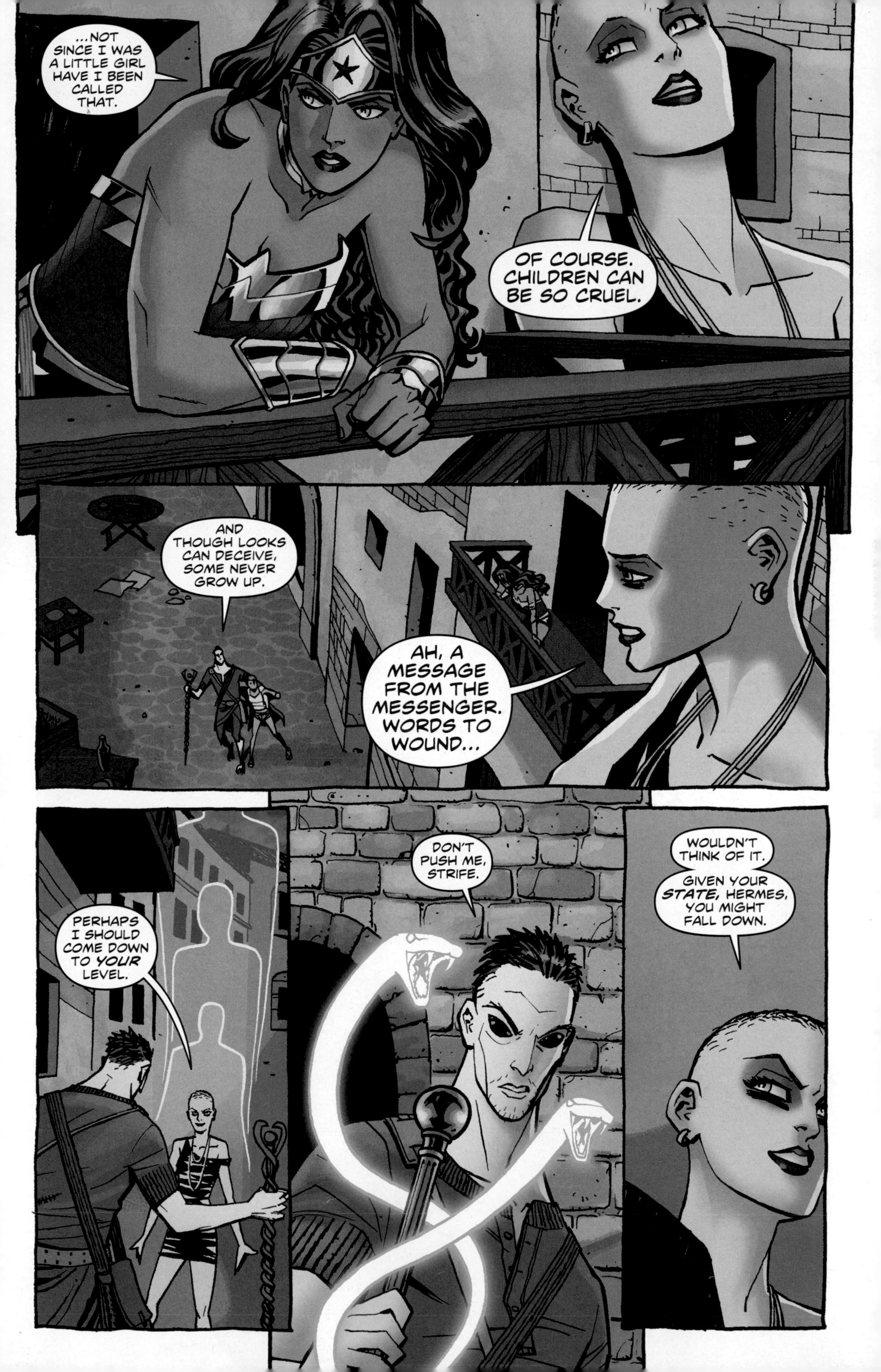
...NOT SINCE I WAS A LITTLE GIRL HAVE I BEEN CALLED THAT.
OF COURSE. CHILDREN CAN BE SO CRUEL.
AND THOUGH LOOKS CAN DECEIVE, SOME NEVER GROW UP.
AH, A MESSAGE FROM THE MESSENGER. WORDS TO WOUND...
PERHAPS I SHOULD COME DOWN TO YOUR LEVEL.
DON'T PUSH ME, STRIFE.
WOULDN'T THINK OF IT.
GIVEN YOUR STATE, HERMES, YOU MIGHT FALL DOWN.

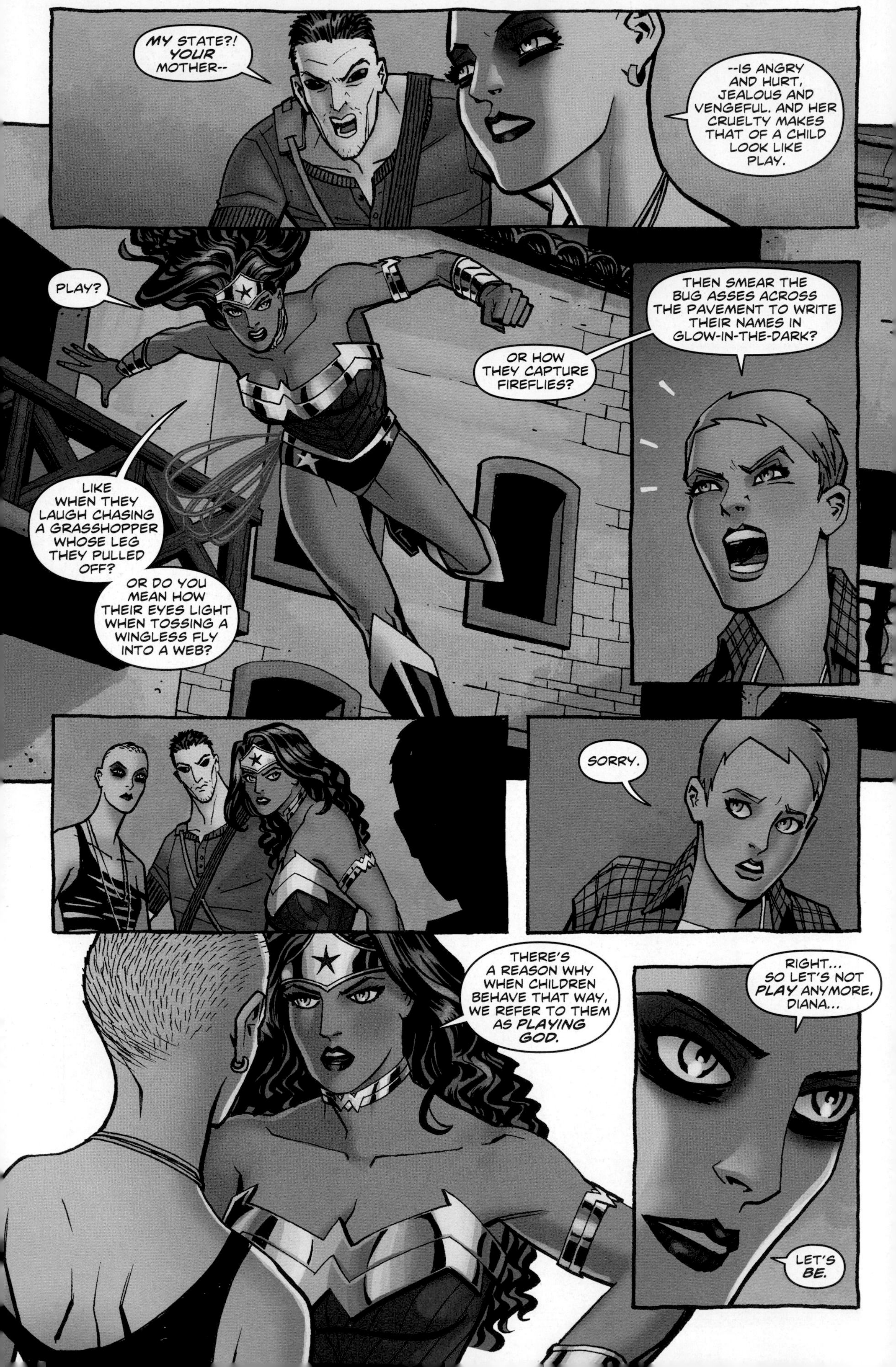

MY STATE?! YOUR MOTHER--
--IS ANGRY AND HURT, JEALOUS AND VENGEFUL. AND HER CRUELTY MAKES THAT OF A CHILD LOOK LIKE PLAY.
PLAY?
LIKE WHEN THEY LAUGH CHASING A GRASSHOPPER WHOSE LEG THEY PULLED OFF?
OR DO YOU MEAN HOW THEIR EYES LIGHT WHEN TOSSING A WINGLESS FLY INTO A WEB?
OR HOW THEY CAPTURE FIREFLIES?
THEN SMEAR THE BUG ASSES ACROSS THE PAVEMENT TO WRITE THEIR NAMES IN GLOW-IN-THE-DARK?
SORRY.
THERE'S A REASON WHY WHEN CHILDREN BEHAVE THAT WAY, WE REFER TO THEM AS PLAYING GOD.
RIGHT... SO LET'S NOT PLAY ANYMORE, DIANA...
LET'S BE.

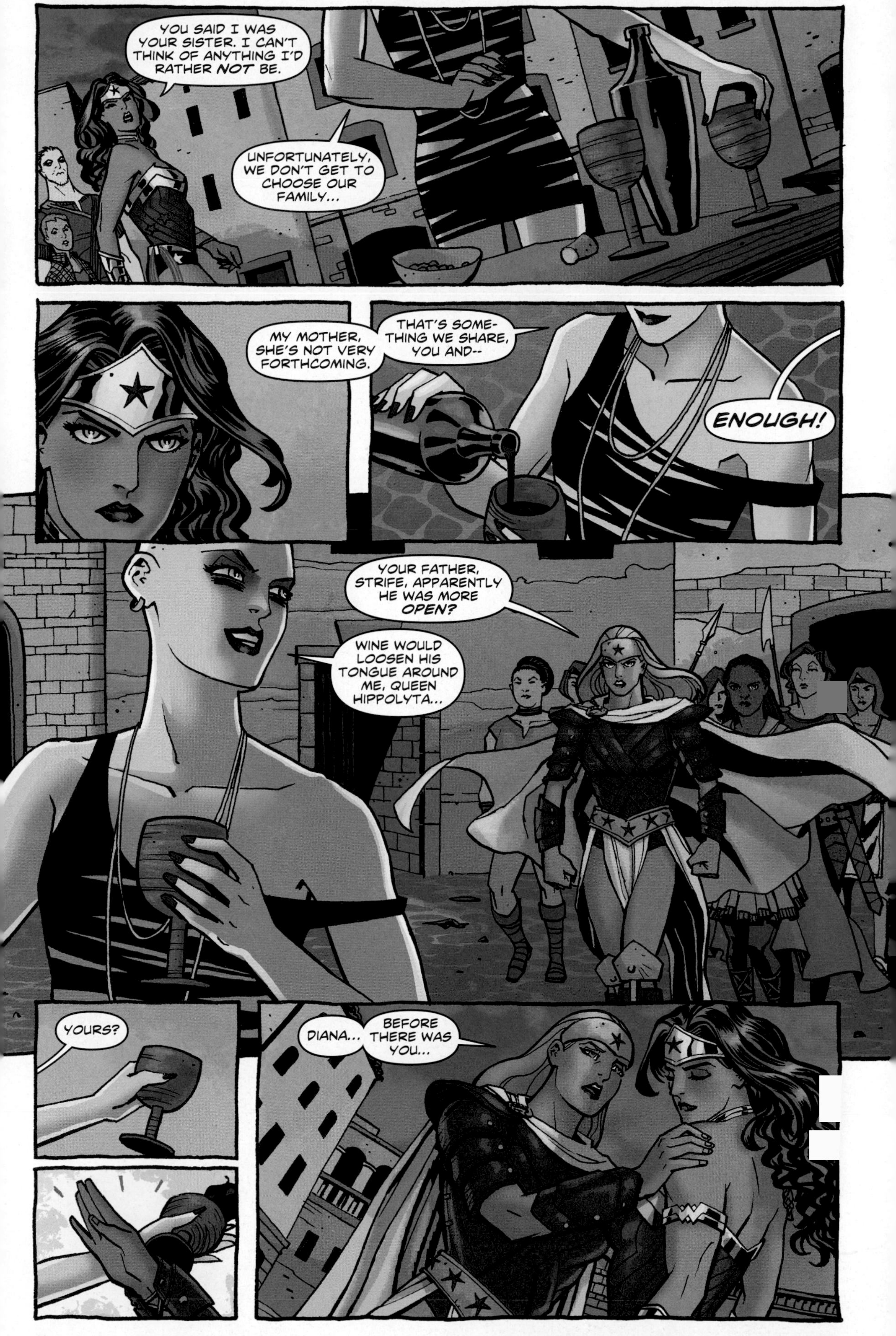
YOU SAID I WAS YOUR SISTER. I CAN'T THINK OF ANYTHING I'D RATHER NOT BE.
UNFORTUNATELY, WE DON'T GET TO CHOOSE OUR FAMILY...
MY MOTHER, SHE'S NOT VERY FORTHCOMING.
THAT'S SOMETHING WE SHARE, YOU AND--
ENOUGH!
YOUR FATHER, STRIFE, APPARENTLY HE WAS MORE OPEN?
WINE WOULD LOOSEN HIS TONGUE AROUND ME, QUEEN HIPPOLYTA...
YOURS?
DIANA... BEFORE THERE WAS YOU...

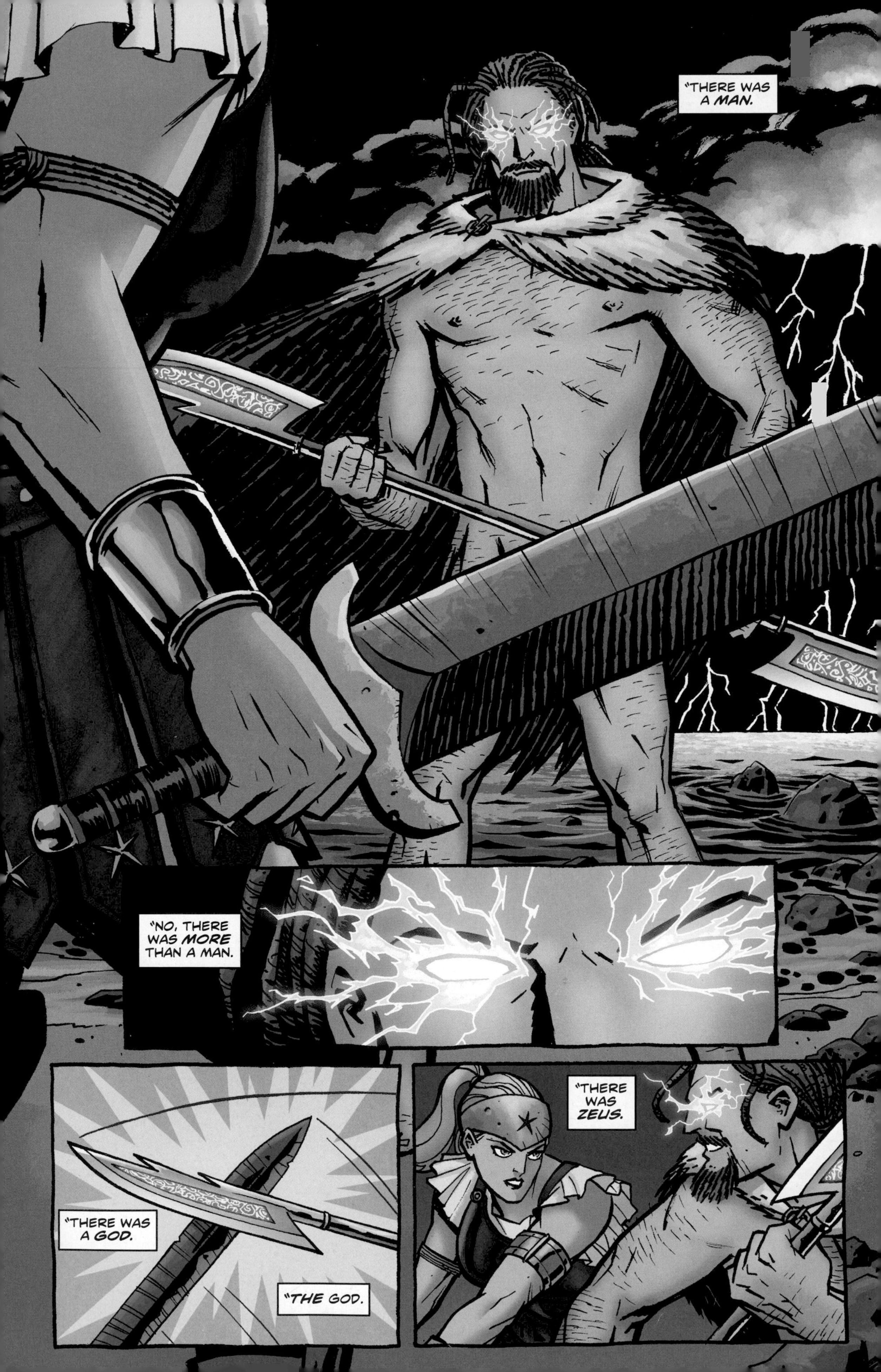
"THERE WAS A MAN.
"NO, THERE WAS MORE THAN A MAN.
"THERE WAS A GOD.
"THE GOD.
"THERE WAS ZEUS.

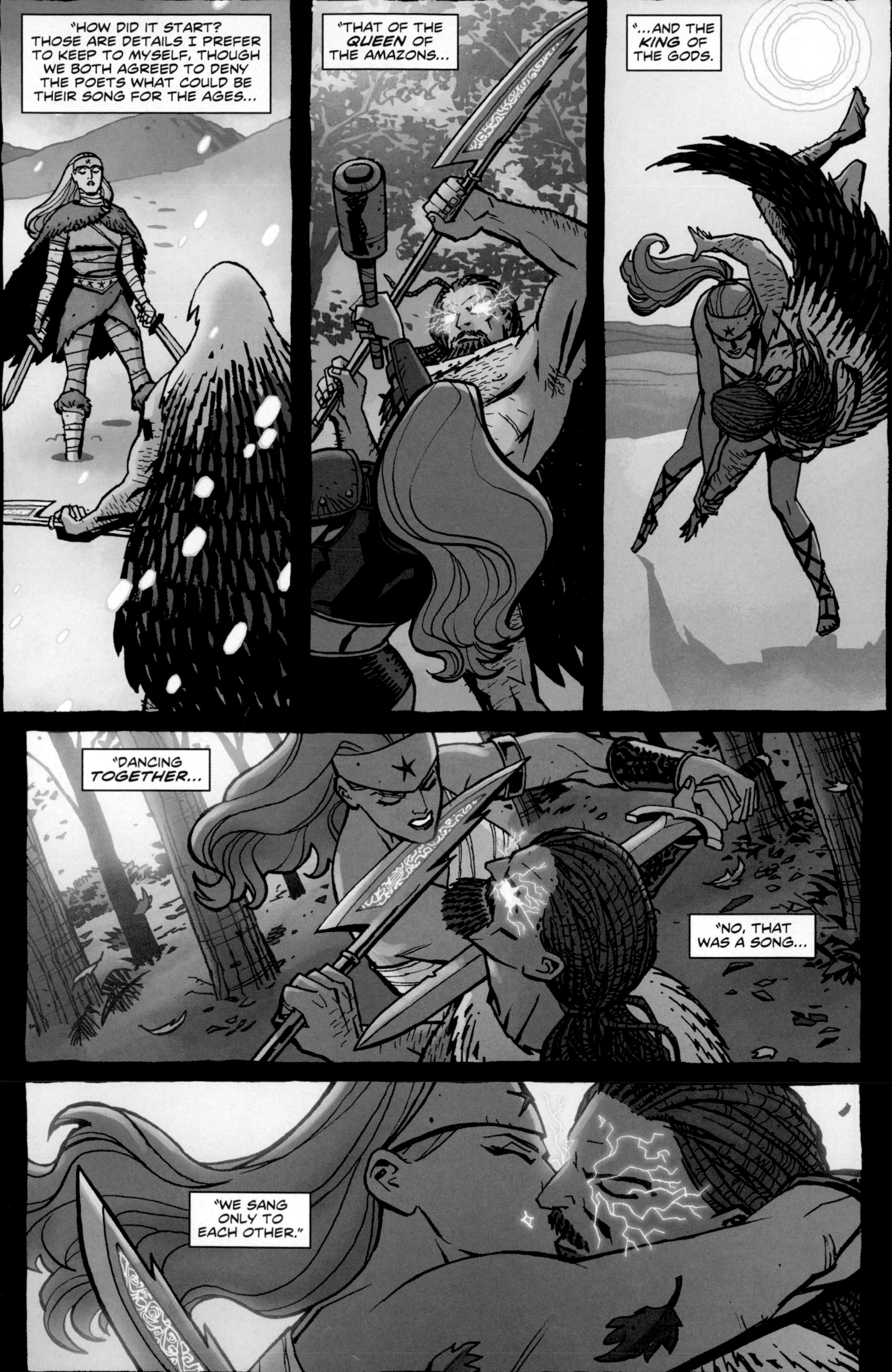
"HOW DID IT START? THOSE ARE DETAILS I PREFER TO KEEP TO MYSELF, THOUGH WE BOTH AGREED TO DENY THE POETS WHAT COULD BE THEIR SONG FOR THE AGES...
"THAT OF THE *QUEEN* OF THE AMAZONS...
"...AND THE *KING* OF THE GODS.
"DANCING *TOGETHER*...
"NO, THAT WAS A SONG...
"WE SANG ONLY TO EACH OTHER."

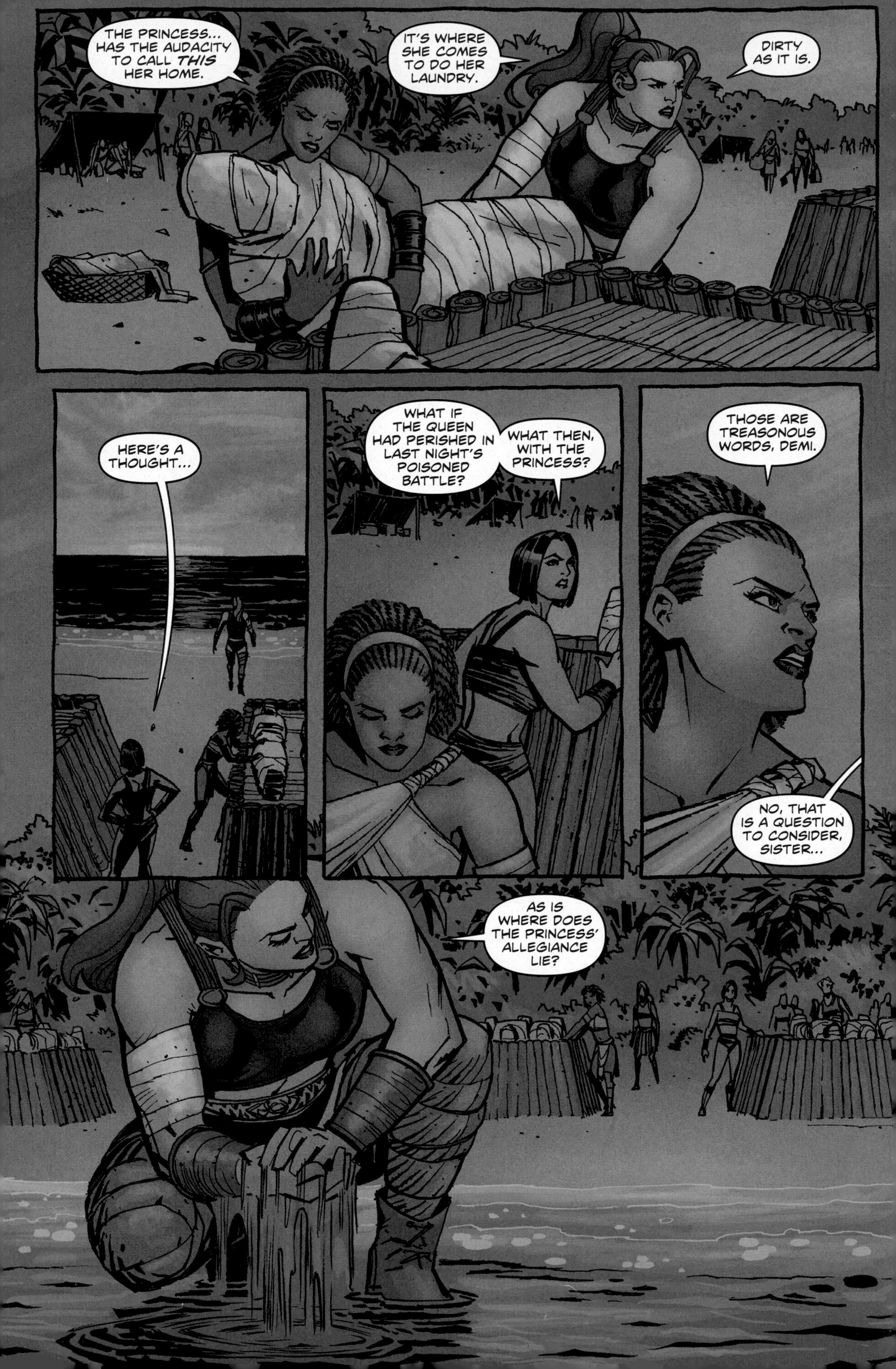
THE PRINCESS... HAS THE AUDACITY TO CALL *THIS* HER HOME.
IT'S WHERE SHE COMES TO DO HER LAUNDRY.
DIRTY AS IT IS.
HERE'S A THOUGHT...
WHAT IF THE QUEEN HAD PERISHED IN LAST NIGHT'S POISONED BATTLE?
WHAT THEN, WITH THE PRINCESS?
THOSE ARE TREASONOUS WORDS, DEMI.
NO, THAT IS A QUESTION TO CONSIDER, SISTER...
AS IS WHERE DOES THE PRINCESS' ALLEGIANCE LIE?

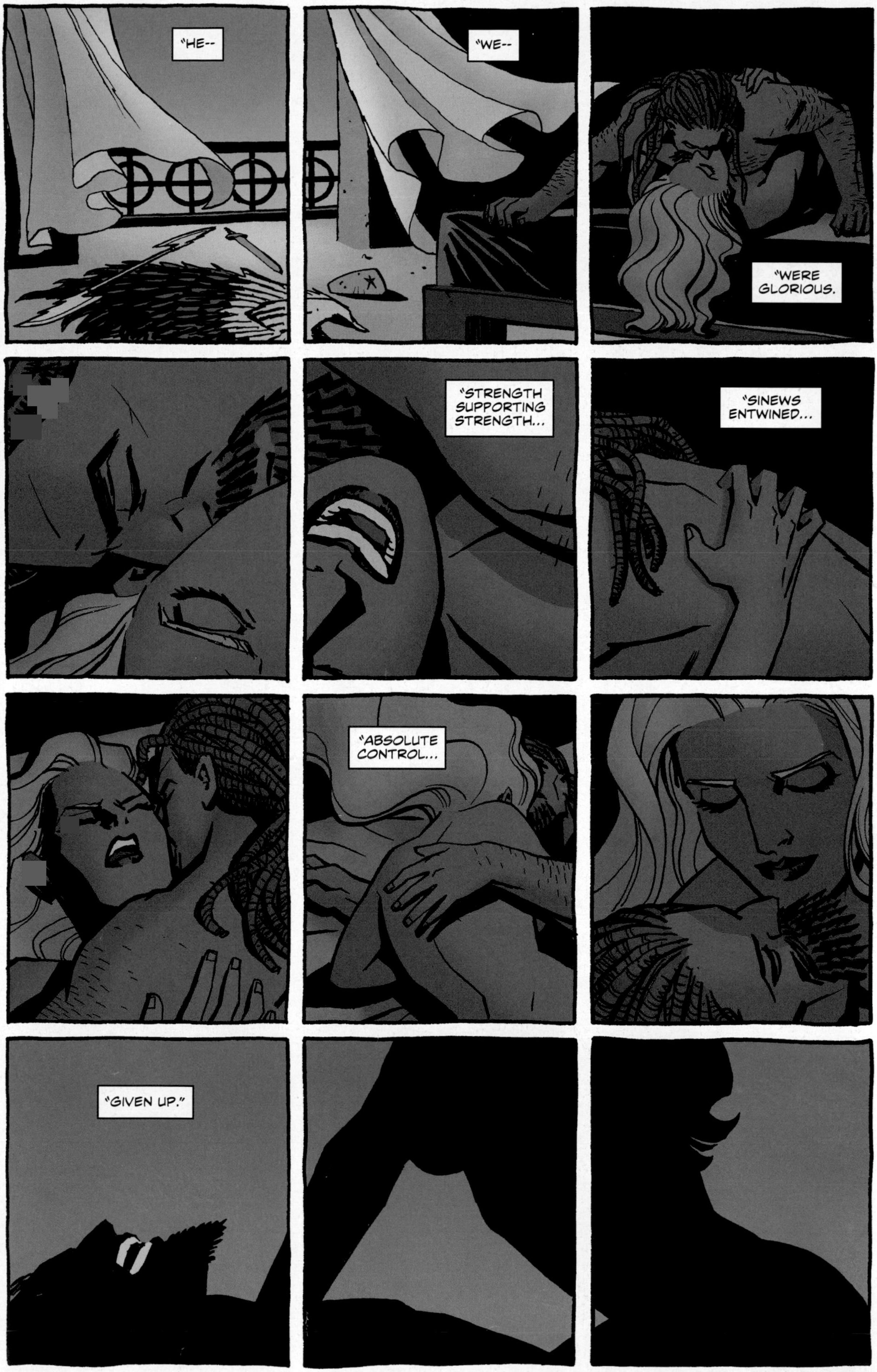
"HE--
"WE--
"WERE GLORIOUS.
"STRENGTH SUPPORTING STRENGTH...
"SINEWS ENTWINED...
"ABSOLUTE CONTROL...
"GIVEN UP."

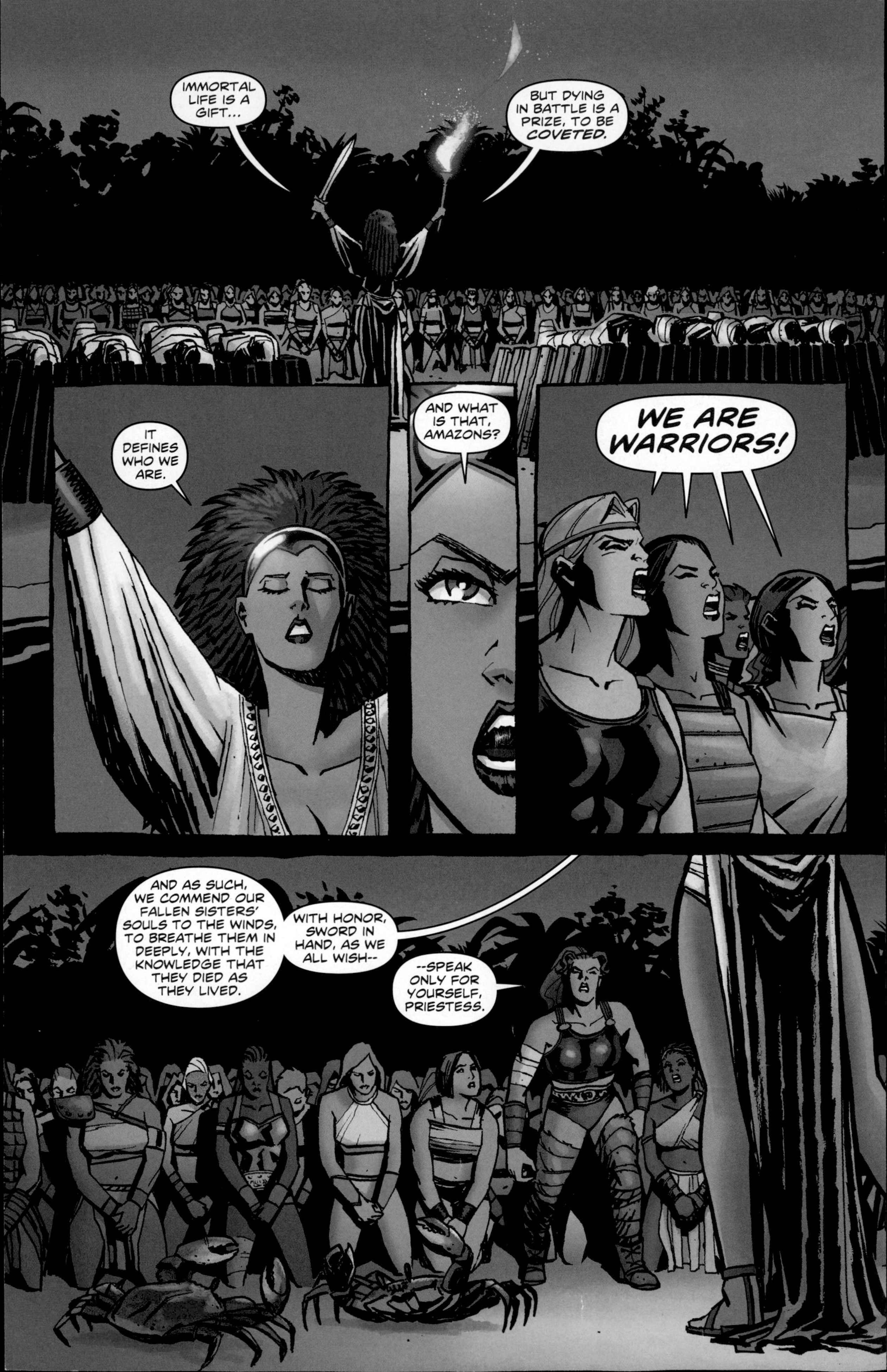
IMMORTAL LIFE IS A GIFT...
BUT DYING IN BATTLE IS A PRIZE, TO BE COVETED.
IT DEFINES WHO WE ARE.
AND WHAT IS THAT, AMAZONS?
WE ARE WARRIORS!
AND AS SUCH, WE COMMEND OUR FALLEN SISTERS' SOULS TO THE WINDS, TO BREATHE THEM IN DEEPLY, WITH THE KNOWLEDGE THAT THEY DIED AS THEY LIVED.
WITH HONOR, SWORD IN HAND, AS WE ALL WISH--
--SPEAK ONLY FOR YOURSELF, PRIESTESS.

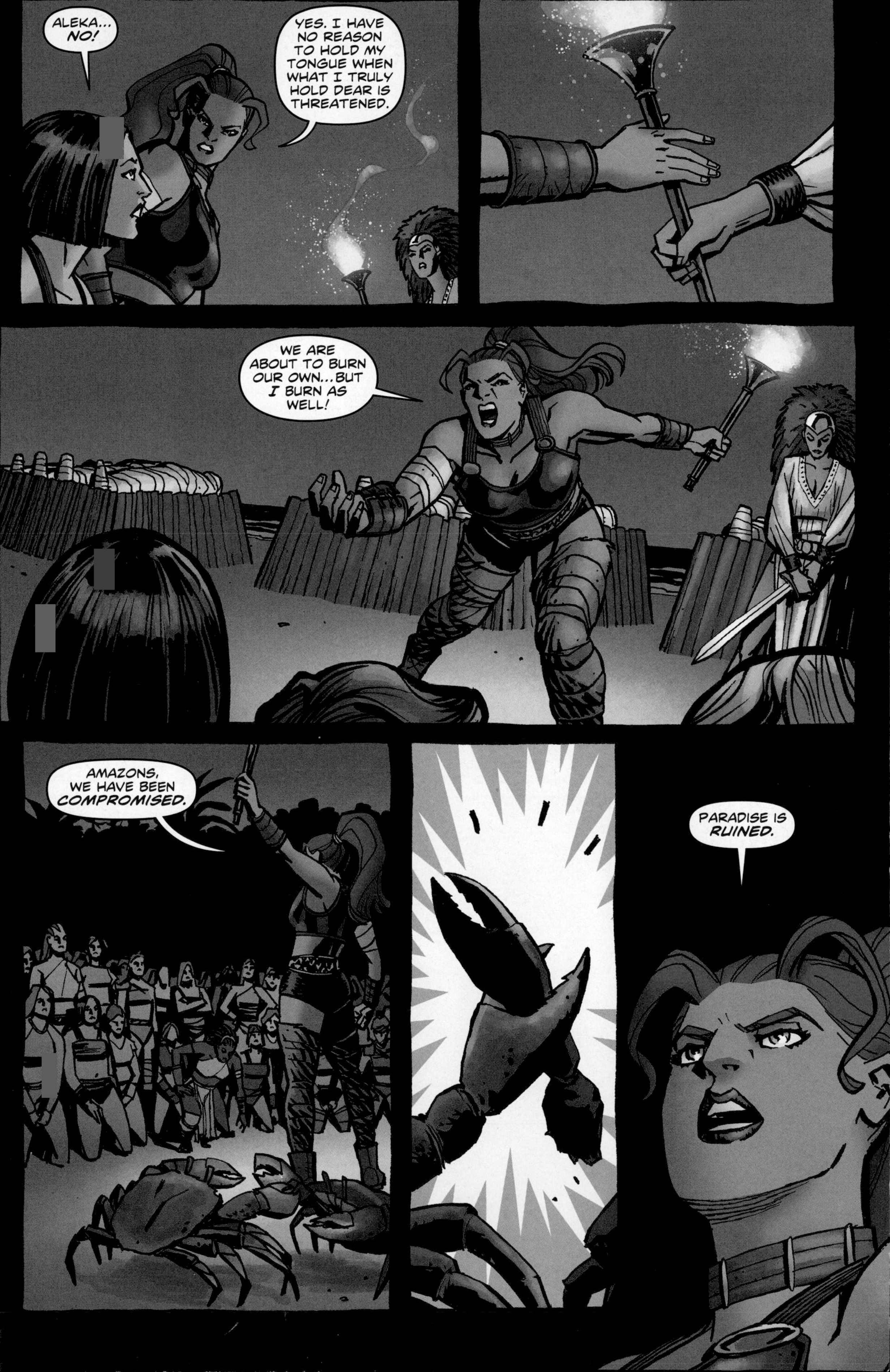
ALEKA... NO!
YES. I HAVE NO REASON TO HOLD MY TONGUE WHEN WHAT I TRULY HOLD DEAR IS THREATENED.
WE ARE ABOUT TO BURN OUR OWN...BUT I BURN AS WELL!
AMAZONS, WE HAVE BEEN COMPROMISED.
PARADISE IS RUINED.

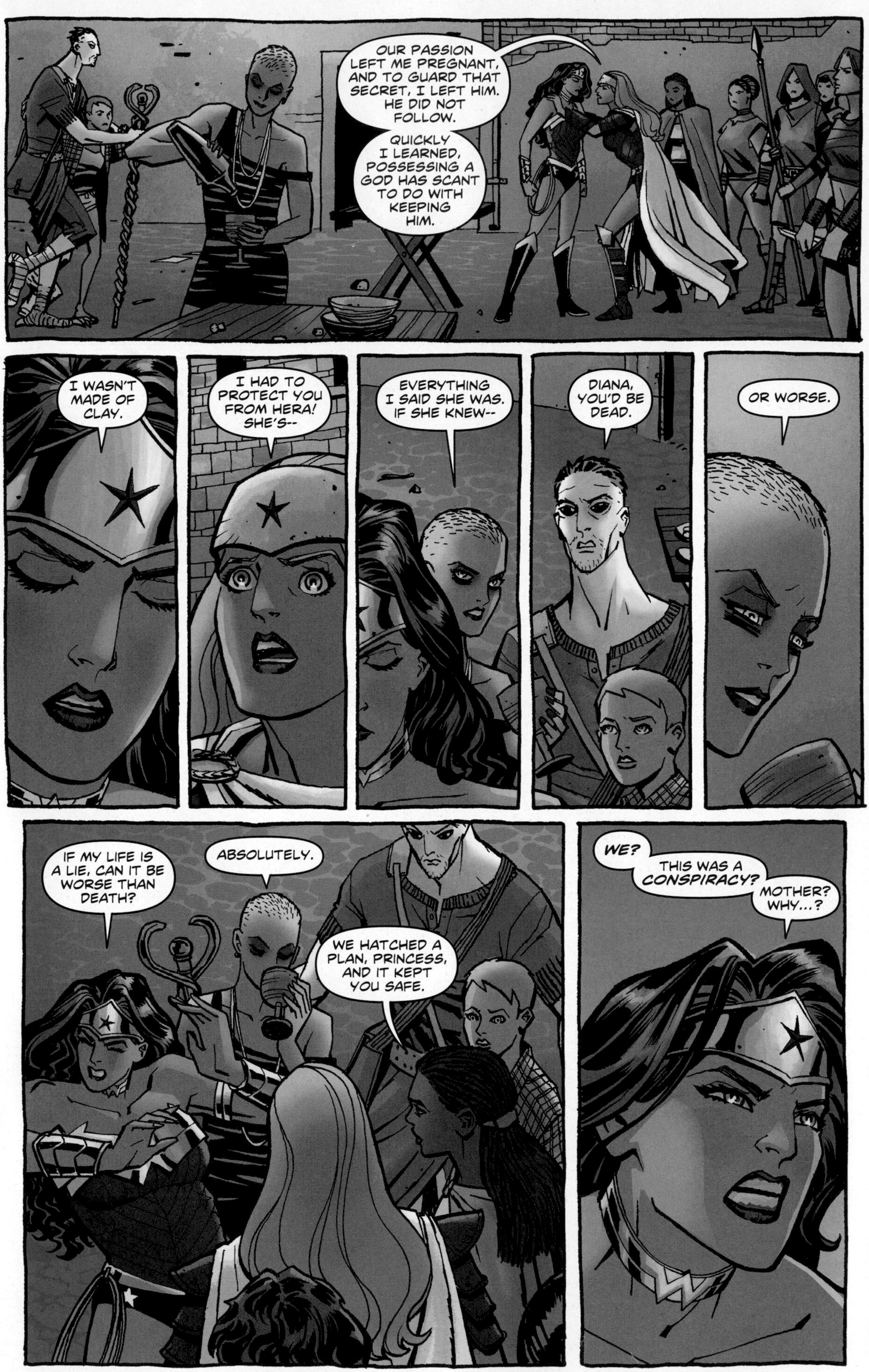
OUR PASSION LEFT ME PREGNANT, AND TO GUARD THAT SECRET, I LEFT HIM. HE DID NOT FOLLOW.
QUICKLY I LEARNED, POSSESSING A GOD HAS SCANT TO DO WITH KEEPING HIM.
I WASN'T MADE OF CLAY.
I HAD TO PROTECT YOU FROM HERA! SHE'S--
EVERYTHING I SAID SHE WAS. IF SHE KNEW--
DIANA, YOU'D BE DEAD.
OR WORSE.
IF MY LIFE IS A LIE, CAN IT BE WORSE THAN DEATH?
ABSOLUTELY.
WE HATCHED A PLAN, PRINCESS, AND IT KEPT YOU SAFE.
WE?
THIS WAS A CONSPIRACY?
MOTHER? WHY...?

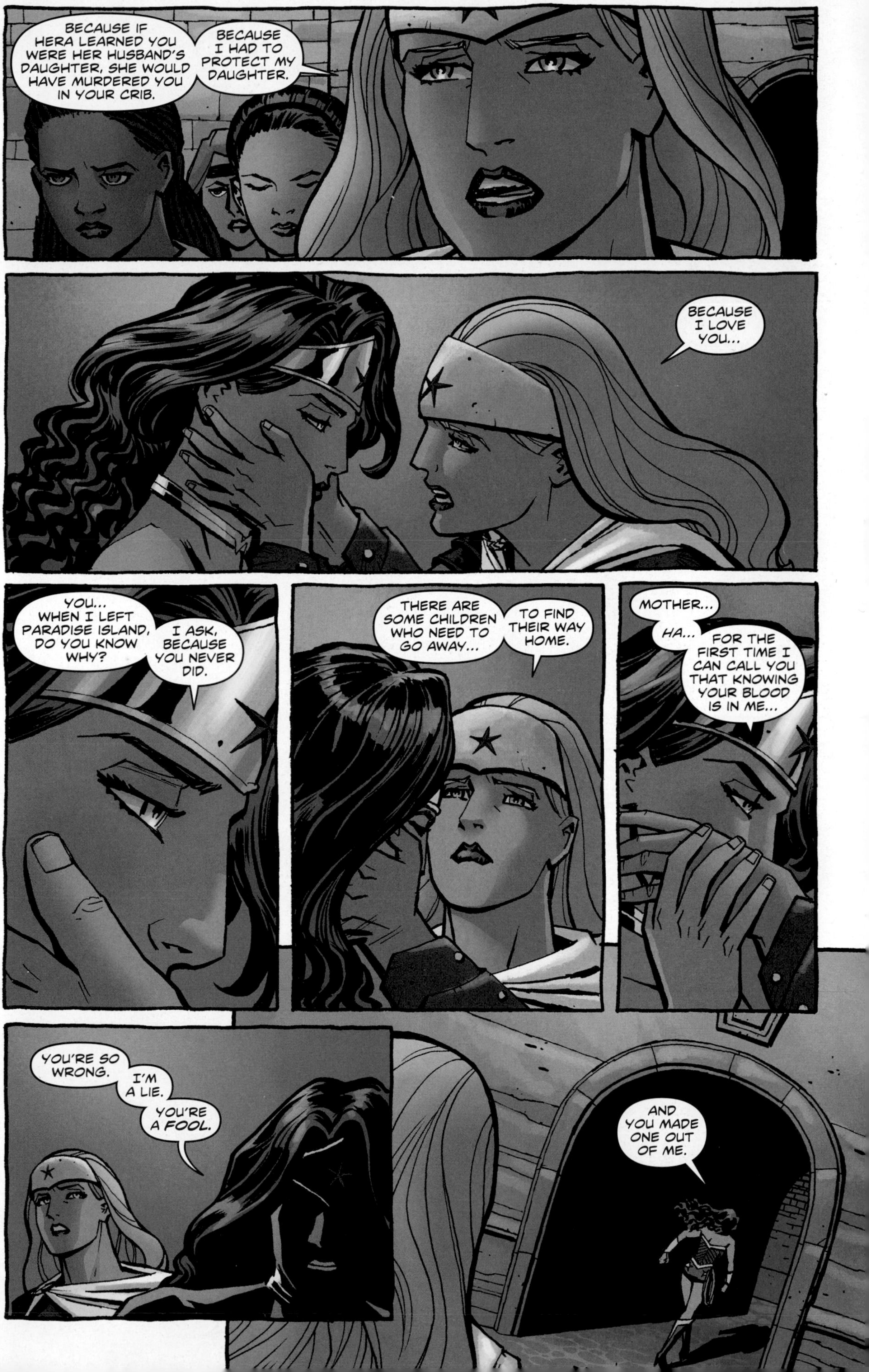
BECAUSE IF HERA LEARNED YOU WERE HER HUSBAND'S DAUGHTER, SHE WOULD HAVE MURDERED YOU IN YOUR CRIB.
BECAUSE I HAD TO PROTECT MY DAUGHTER.
BECAUSE I LOVE YOU...
YOU... WHEN I LEFT PARADISE ISLAND, DO YOU KNOW WHY?
I ASK, BECAUSE YOU NEVER DID.
THERE ARE SOME CHILDREN WHO NEED TO GO AWAY...
TO FIND THEIR WAY HOME.
MOTHER...
HA...
FOR THE FIRST TIME I CAN CALL YOU THAT KNOWING YOUR BLOOD IS IN ME...
YOU'RE SO WRONG.
I'M A LIE.
YOU'RE A FOOL.
AND YOU MADE ONE OUT OF ME.

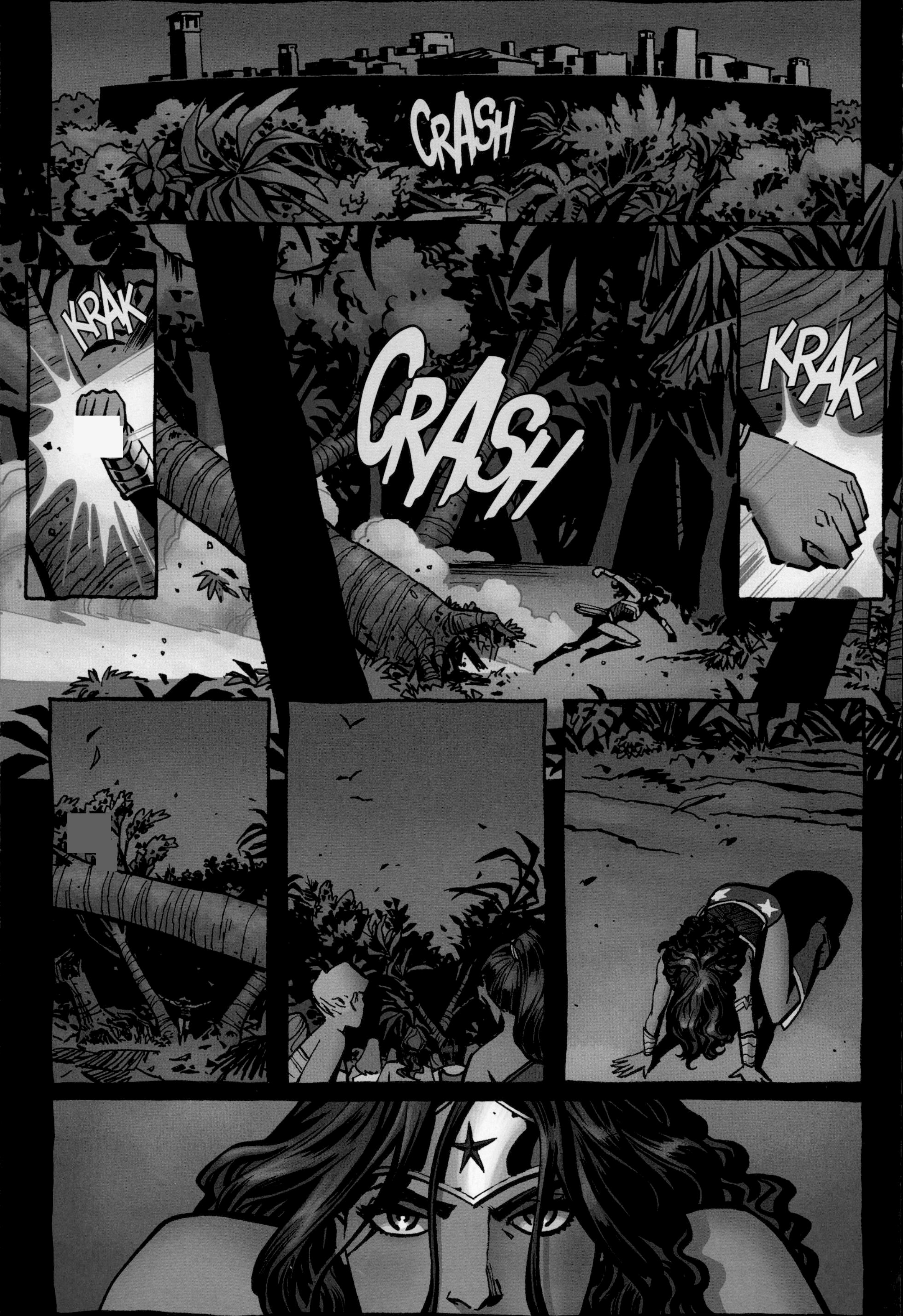
CRASH
KRAK
CRASH
KRAK

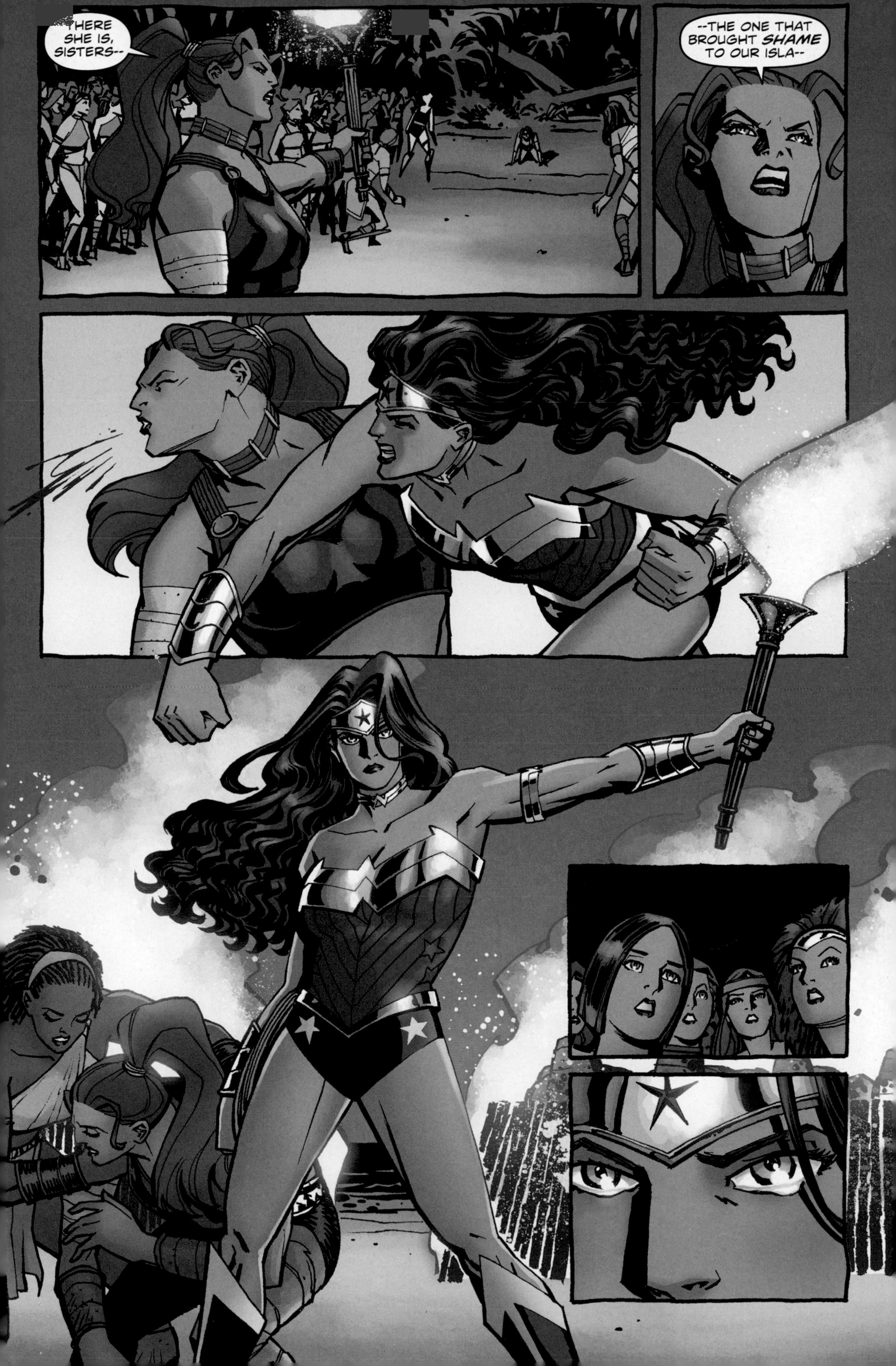
THERE SHE IS, SISTERS--
--THE ONE THAT BROUGHT SHAME TO OUR ISLA--

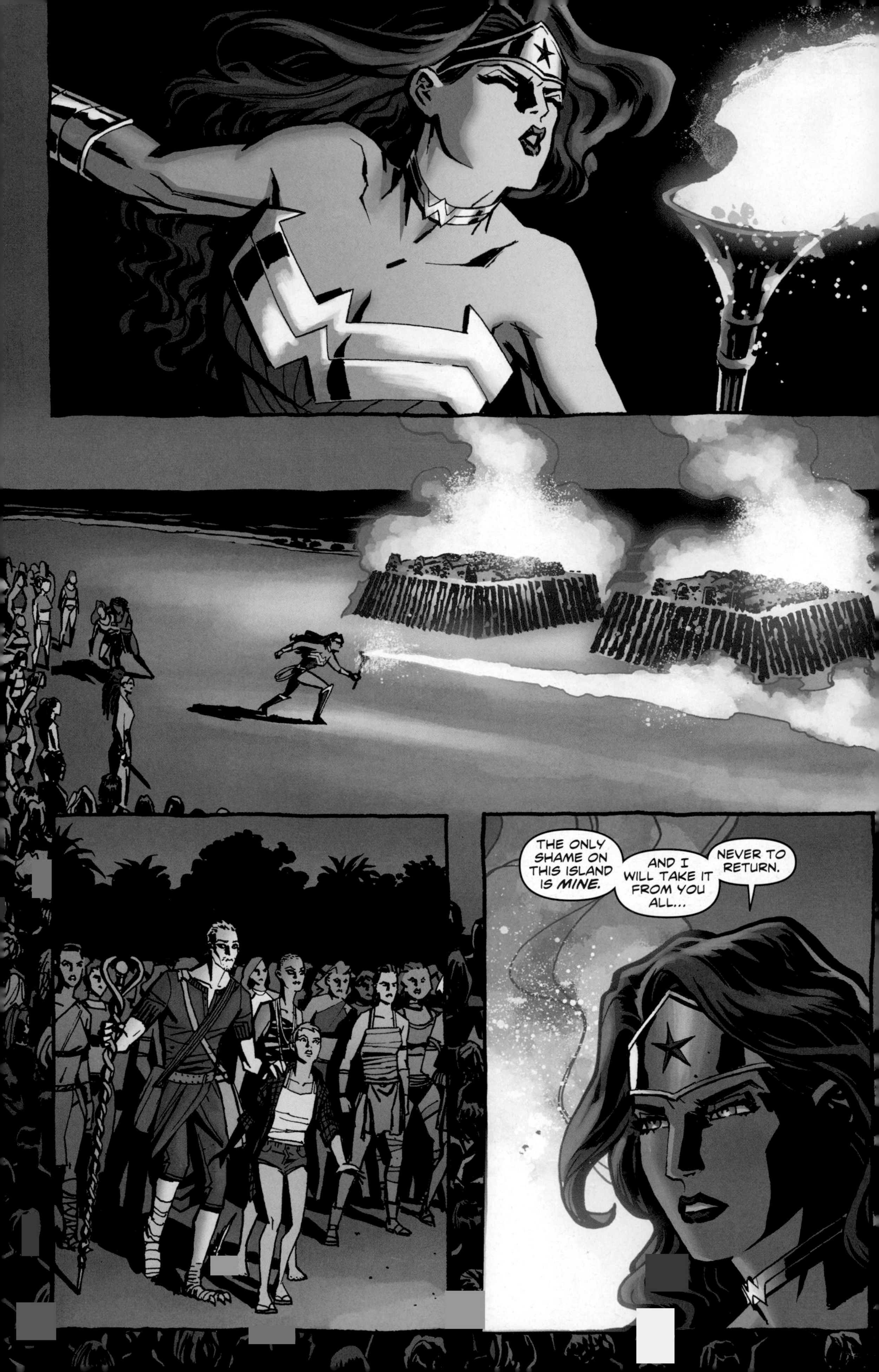
THE ONLY SHAME ON THIS ISLAND IS *MINE.*
AND I WILL TAKE IT FROM YOU ALL...
NEVER TO RETURN.

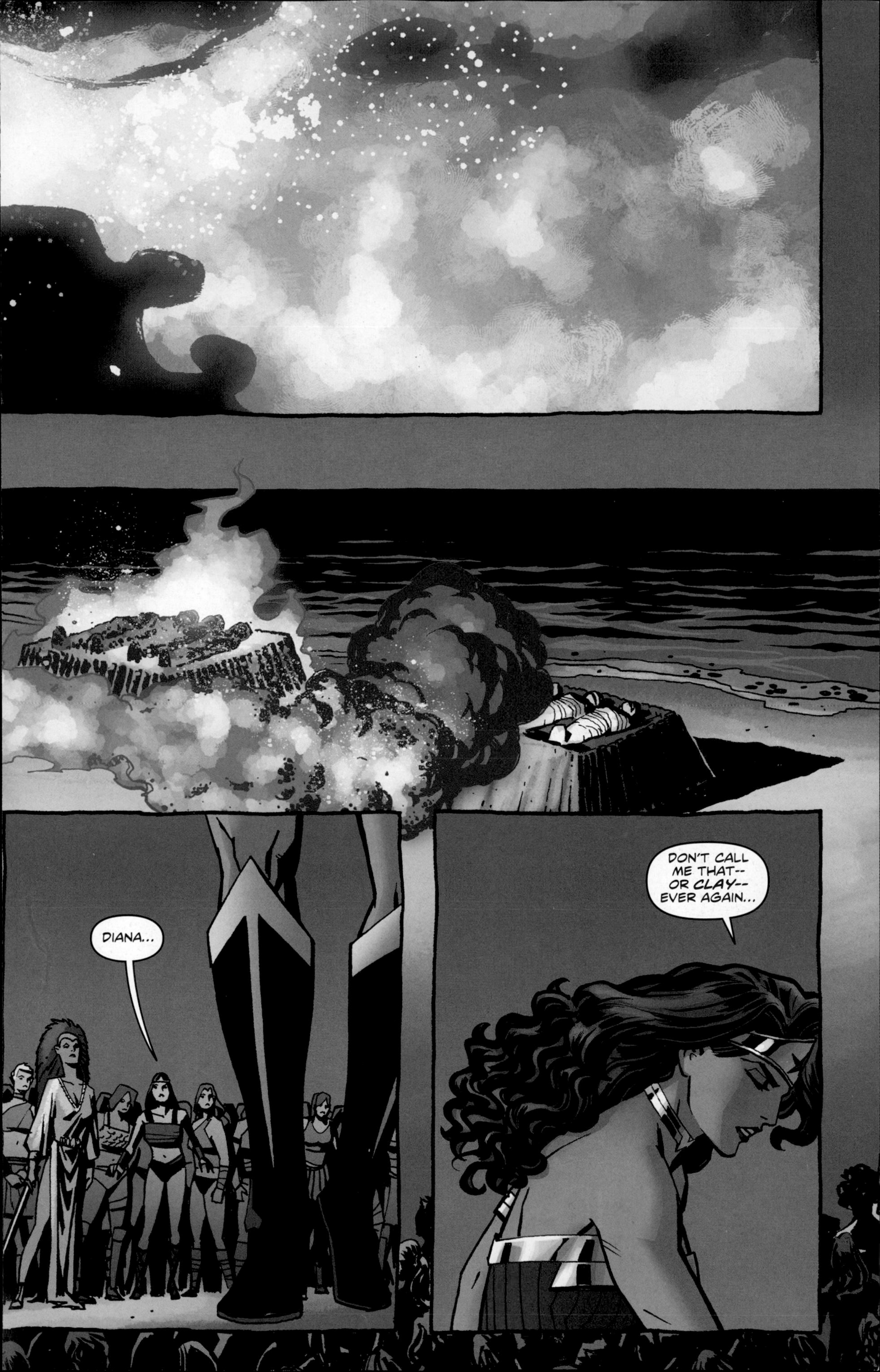
DIANA...
DON'T CALL ME THAT-- OR CLAY-- EVER AGAIN...

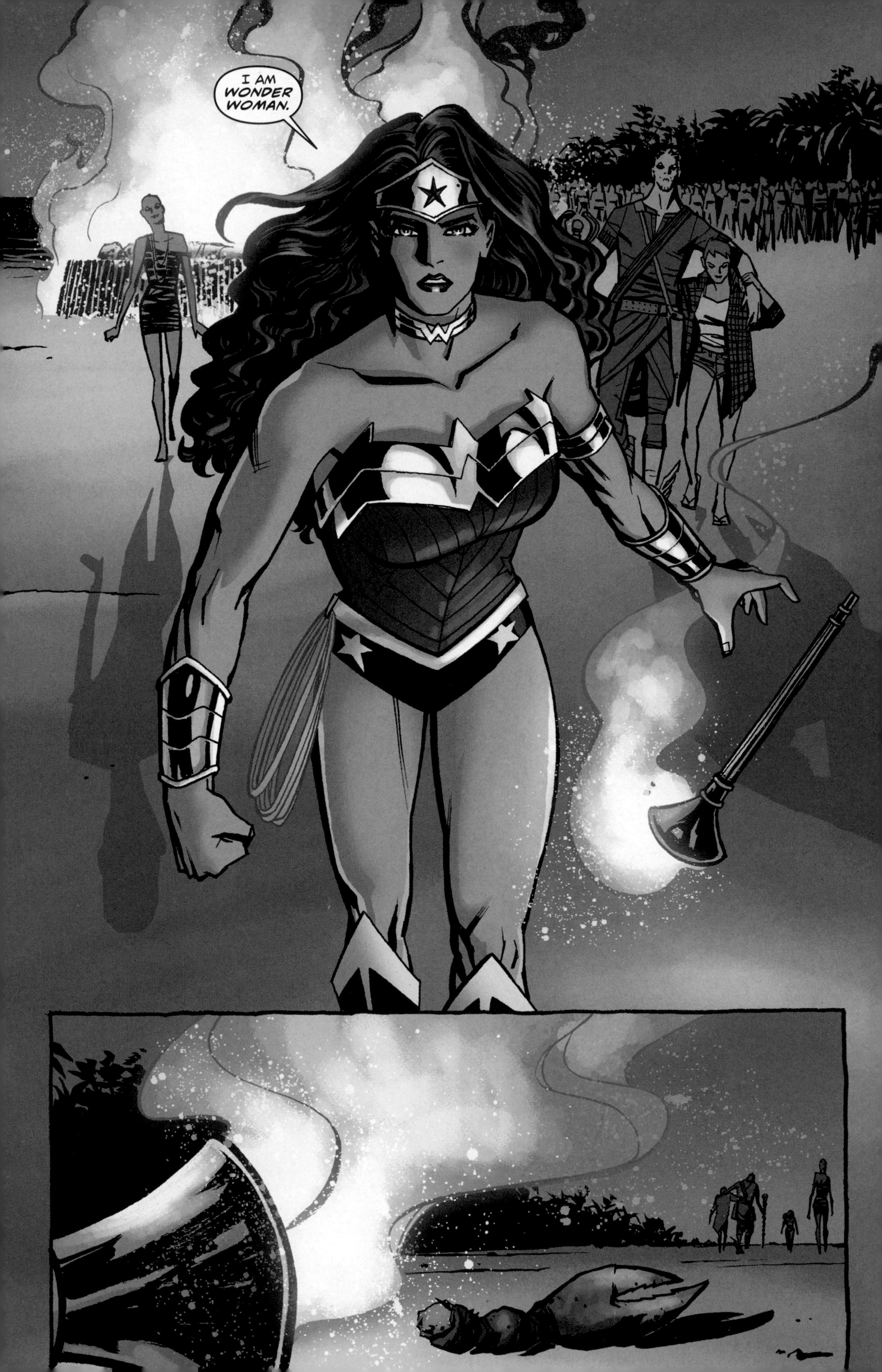
I AM WONDER WOMAN.

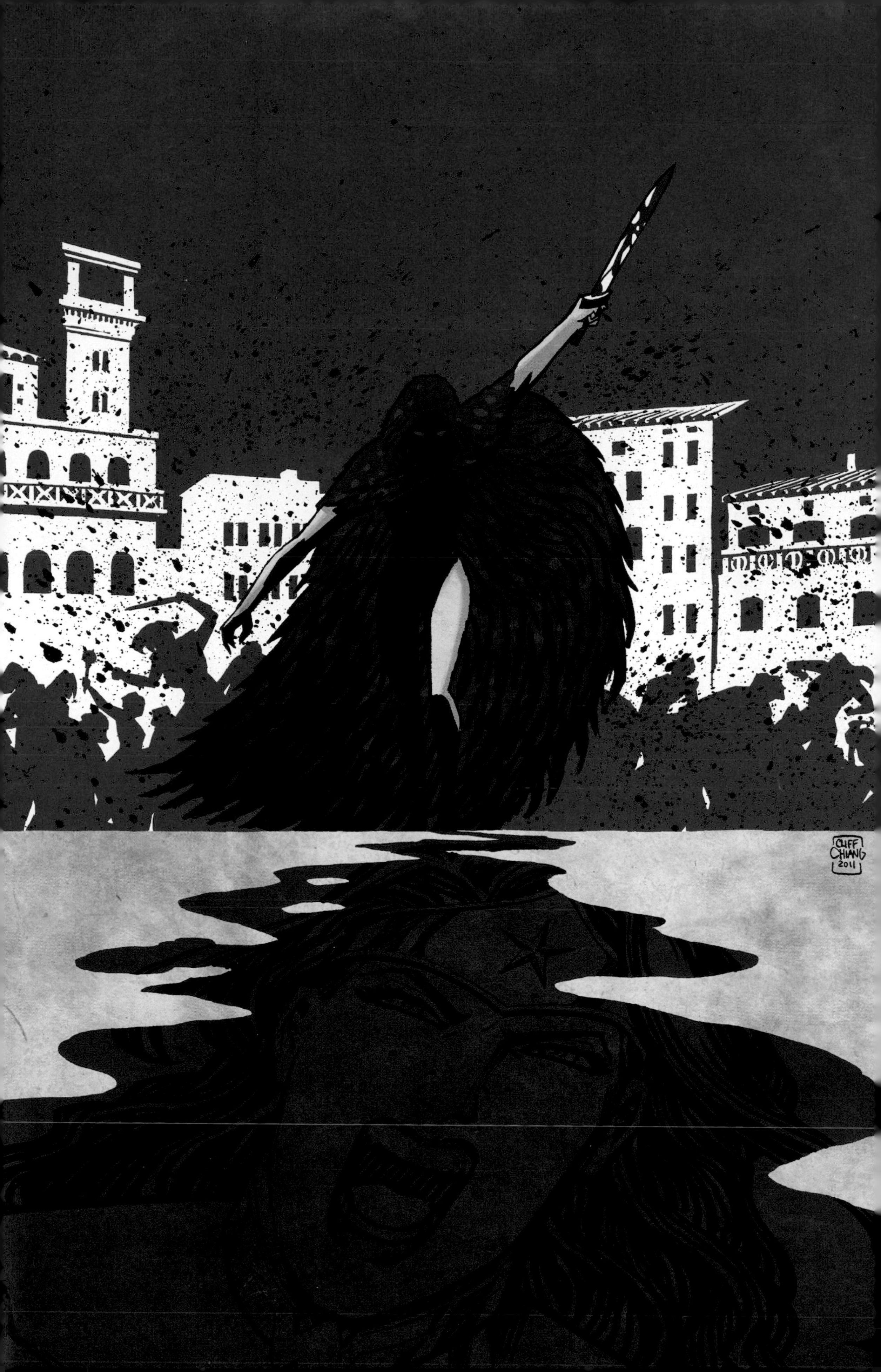
CLIFF CHIANG 2011

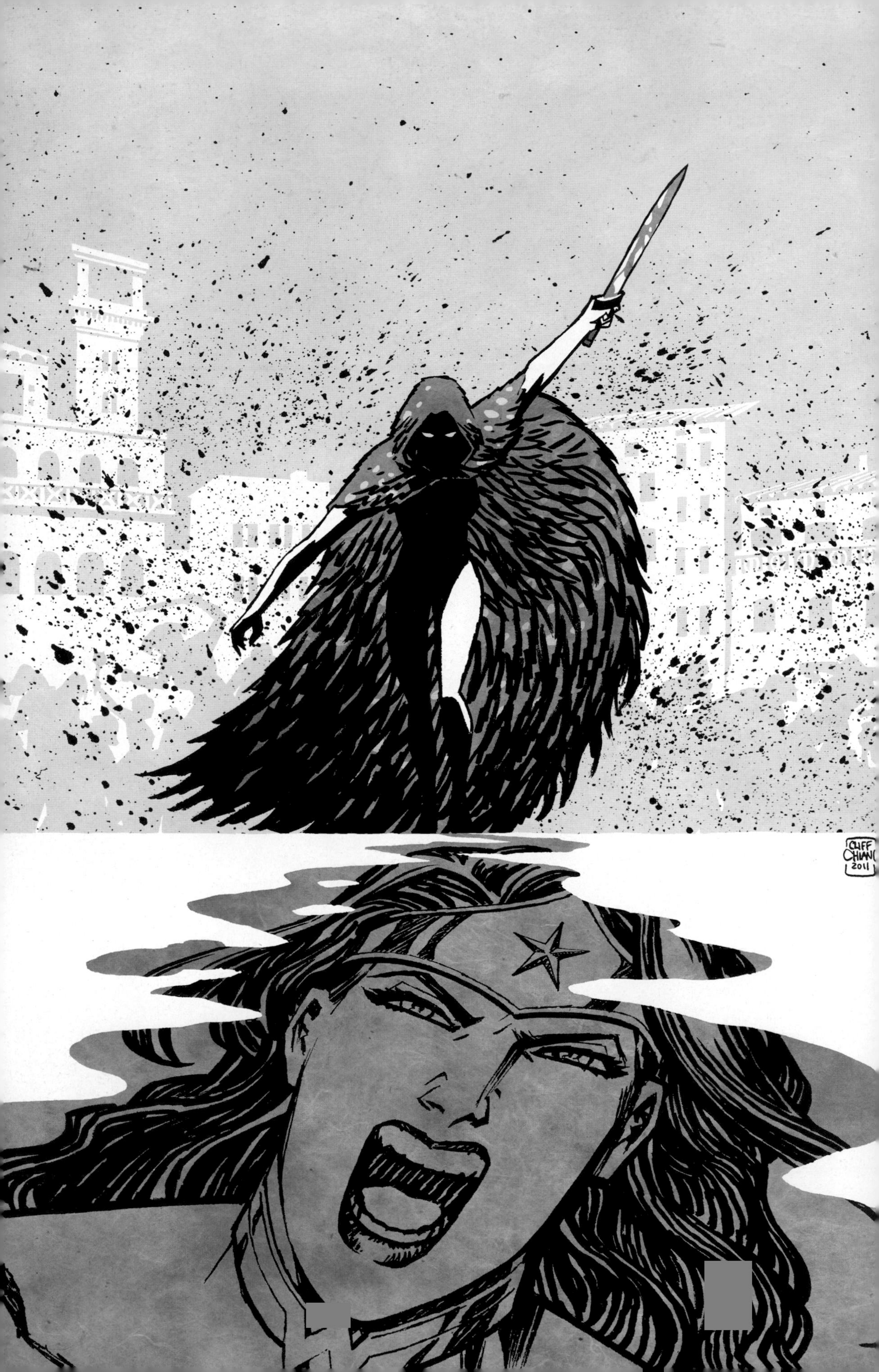
CLIFF CHIANG 2011

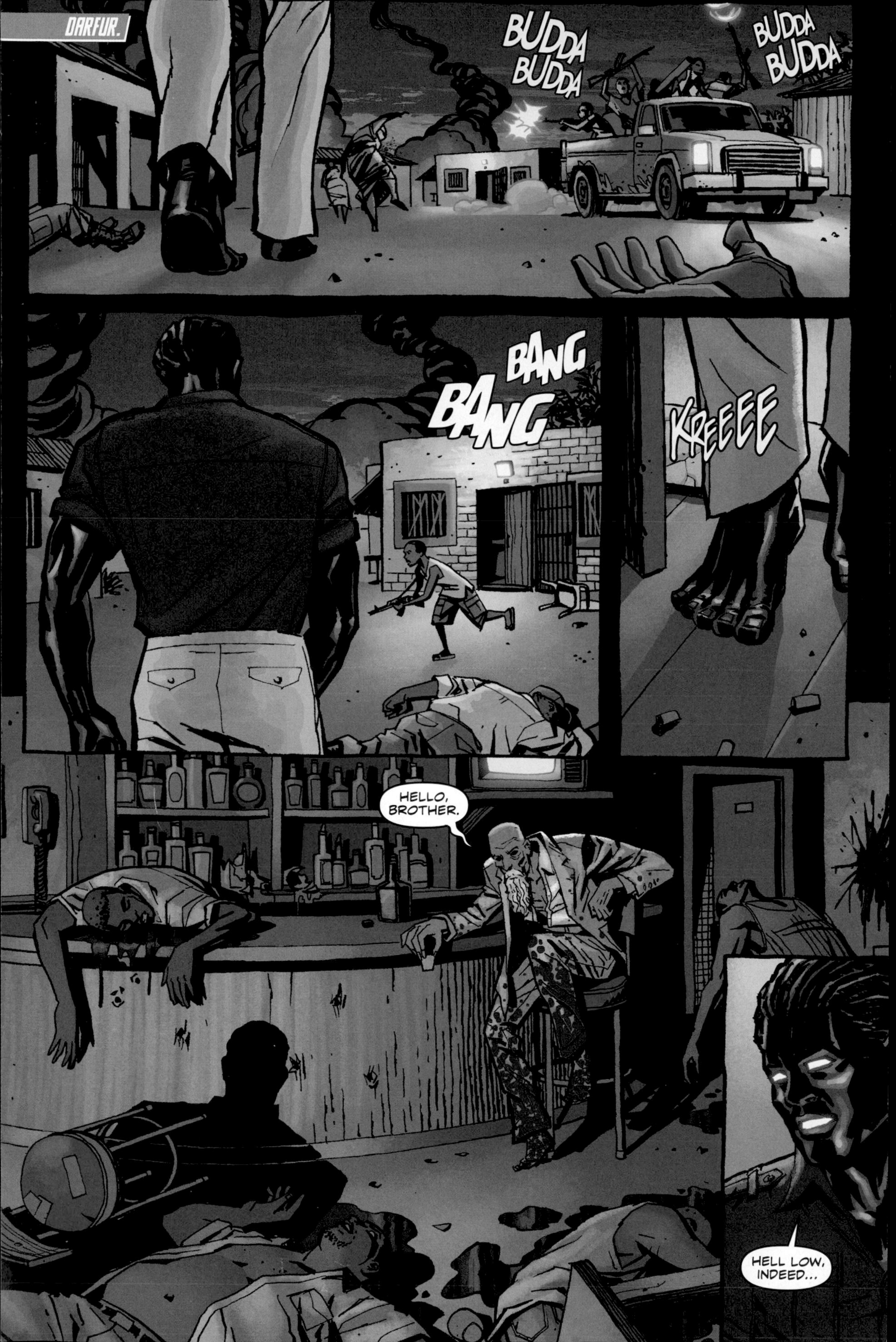
DARFUR.
BUDDA BUDDA
BUDDA BUDDA
BANG
BANG
KREEEE
HELLO, BROTHER.
HELL LOW, INDEED...

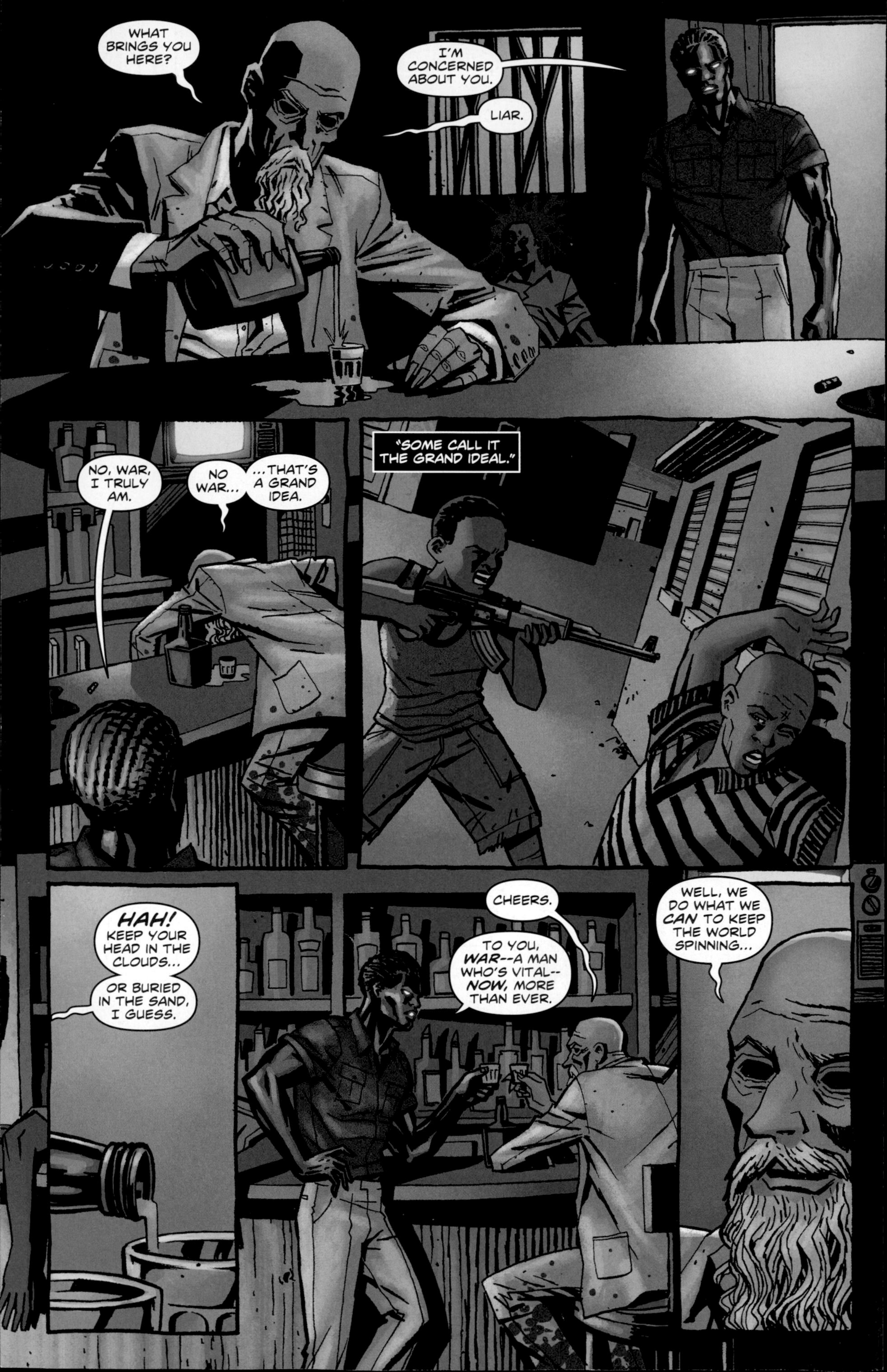
WHAT BRINGS YOU HERE?
I'M CONCERNED ABOUT YOU.
LIAR.
NO, WAR, I TRULY AM.
NO WAR...
...THAT'S A GRAND IDEA.
"SOME CALL IT THE GRAND IDEAL."
HAH! KEEP YOUR HEAD IN THE CLOUDS...
OR BURIED IN THE SAND, I GUESS.
CHEERS.
TO YOU, WAR--A MAN WHO'S VITAL--NOW, MORE THAN EVER.
WELL, WE DO WHAT WE CAN TO KEEP THE WORLD SPINNING...

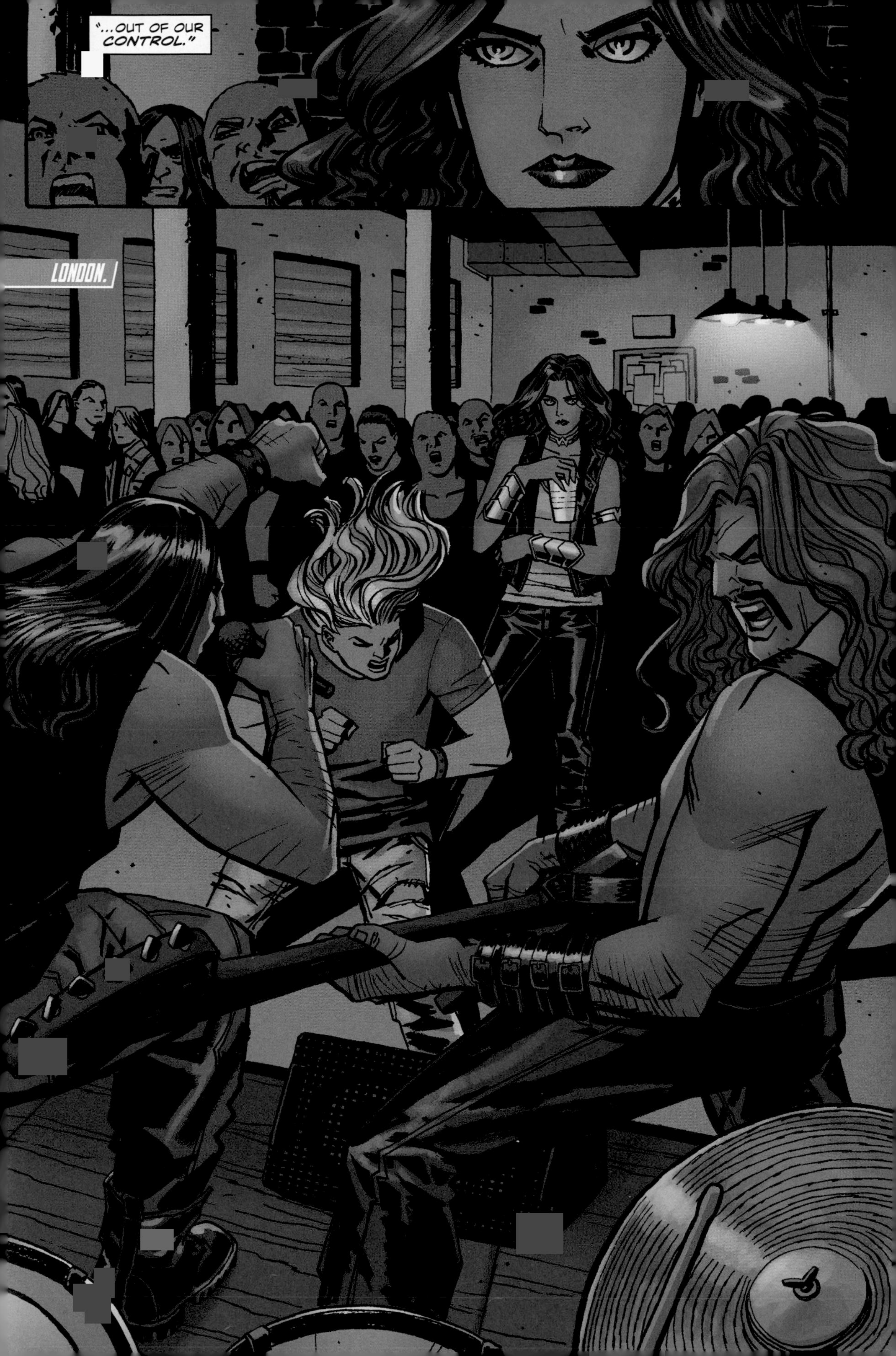
"...OUT OF OUR CONTROL."
LONDON.

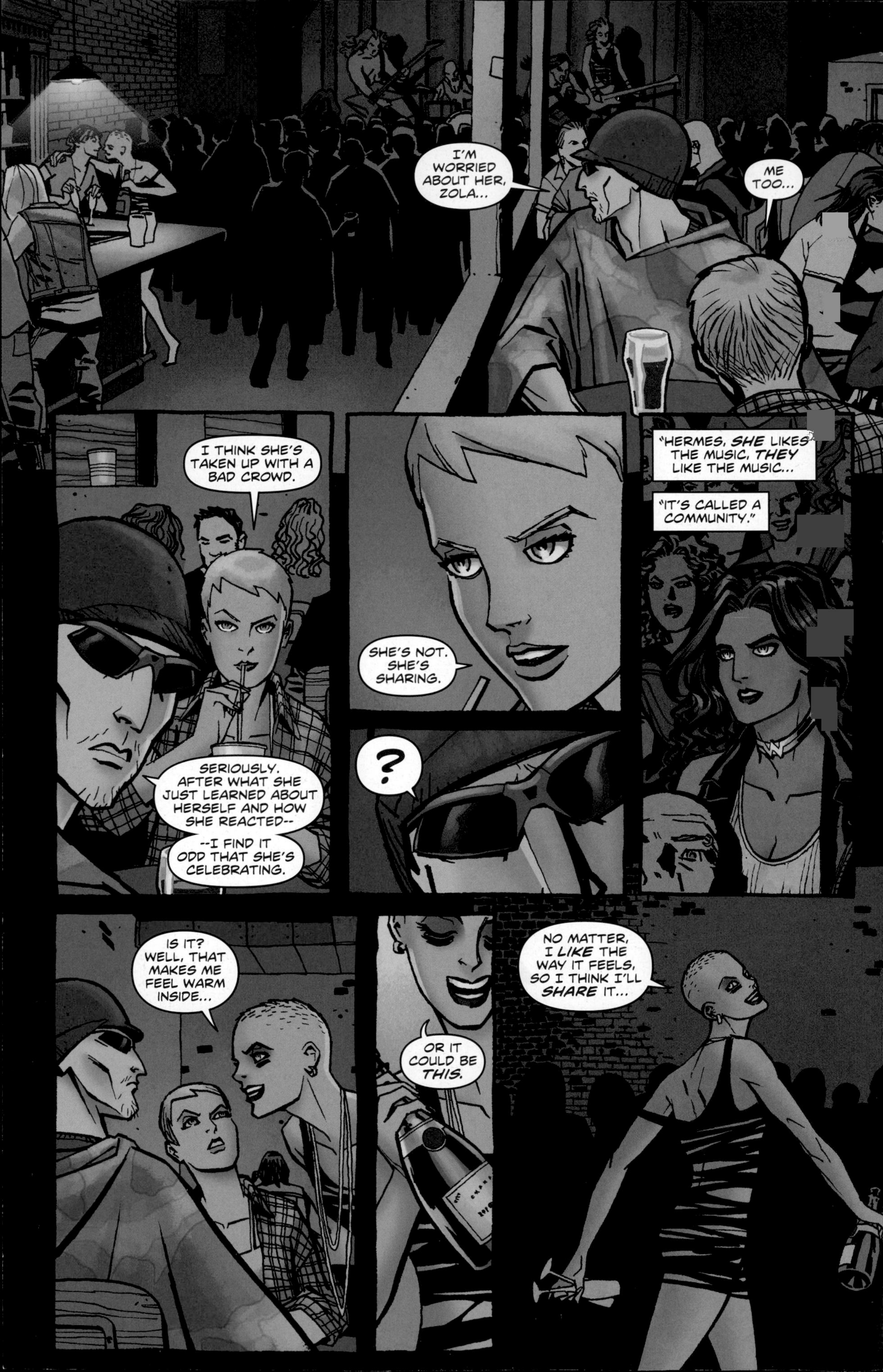

I'M WORRIED ABOUT HER, ZOLA...
ME TOO...
I THINK SHE'S TAKEN UP WITH A BAD CROWD.
SHE'S NOT. SHE'S SHARING.
"HERMES, SHE LIKES THE MUSIC, THEY LIKE THE MUSIC...
"IT'S CALLED A COMMUNITY."
SERIOUSLY. AFTER WHAT SHE JUST LEARNED ABOUT HERSELF AND HOW SHE REACTED--
--I FIND IT ODD THAT SHE'S CELEBRATING.
?
IS IT? WELL, THAT MAKES ME FEEL WARM INSIDE...
OR IT COULD BE THIS.
NO MATTER, I LIKE THE WAY IT FEELS, SO I THINK I'LL SHARE IT...

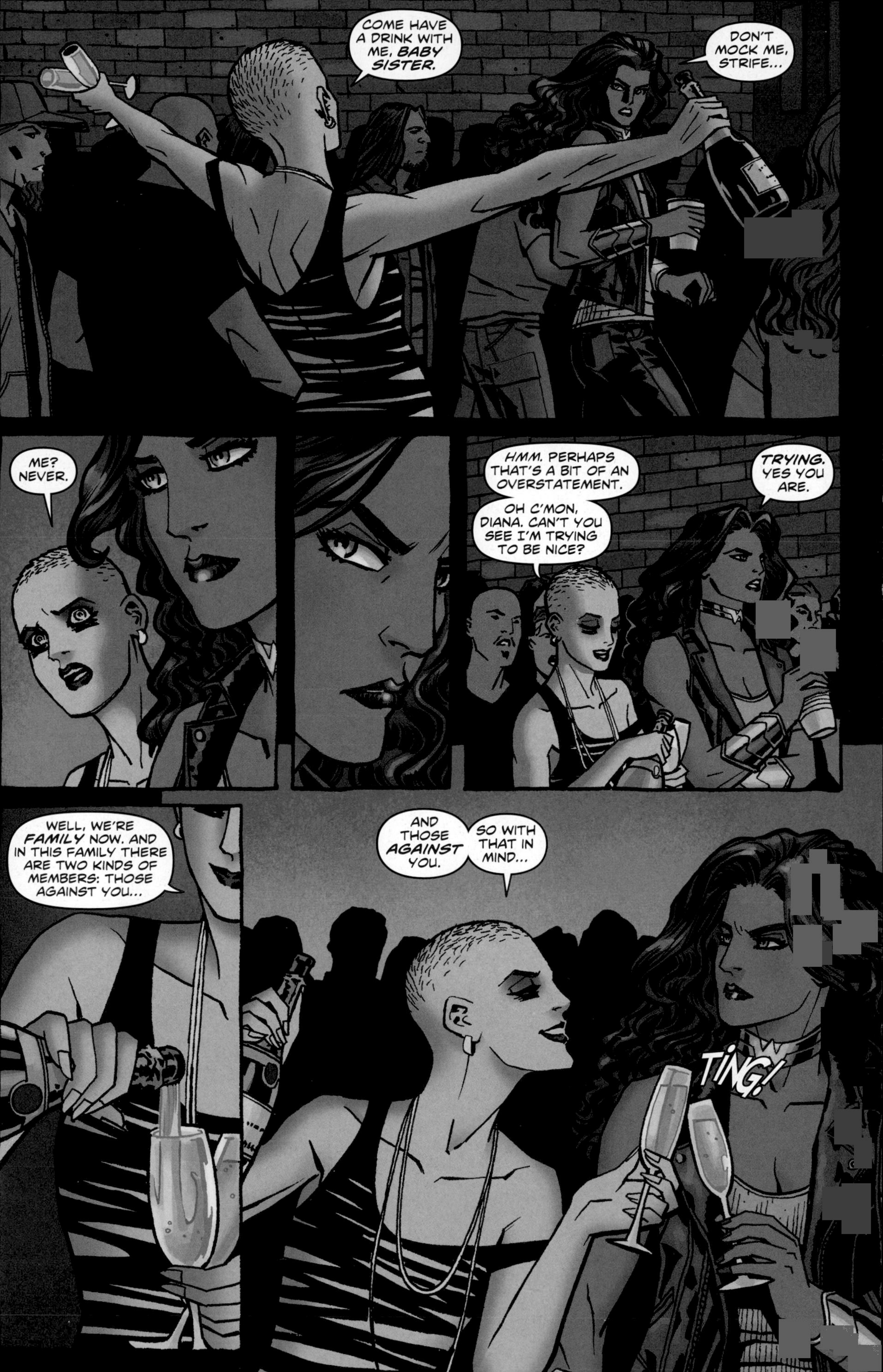
COME HAVE A DRINK WITH ME, *BABY SISTER.*
DON'T MOCK ME, STRIFE...
ME? NEVER.
HMM. PERHAPS THAT'S A BIT OF AN OVERSTATEMENT.
OH C'MON, DIANA. CAN'T YOU SEE I'M TRYING TO BE NICE?
TRYING. YES YOU ARE.
WELL, WE'RE *FAMILY* NOW. AND IN THIS FAMILY THERE ARE TWO KINDS OF MEMBERS: THOSE AGAINST YOU...
AND THOSE *AGAINST* YOU.
SO WITH THAT IN MIND...
TING!

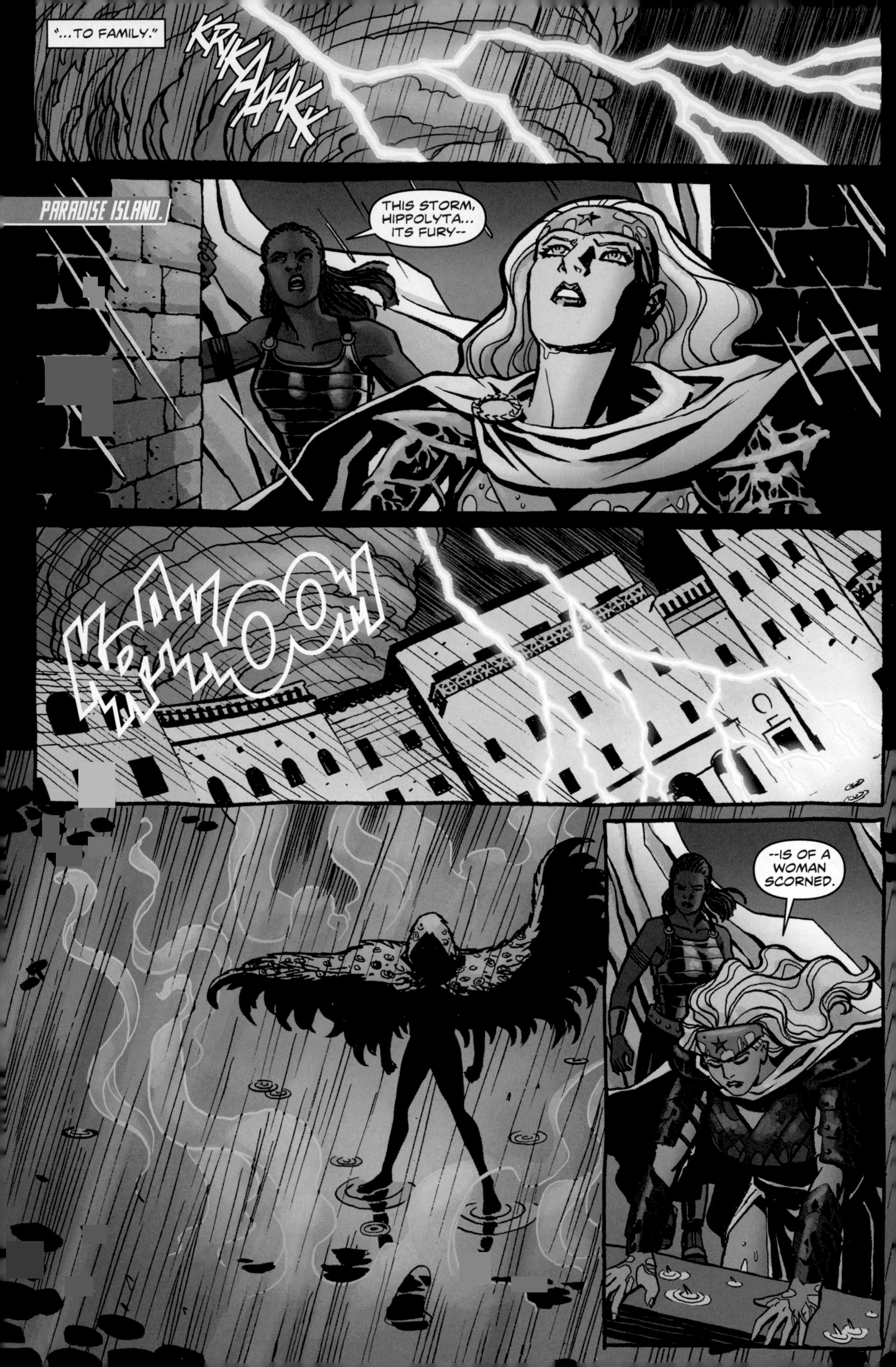
"...TO FAMILY."
KRIKAAAKK
PARADISE ISLAND.
THIS STORM, HIPPOLYTA... ITS FURY--
--IS OF A WOMAN SCORNED.

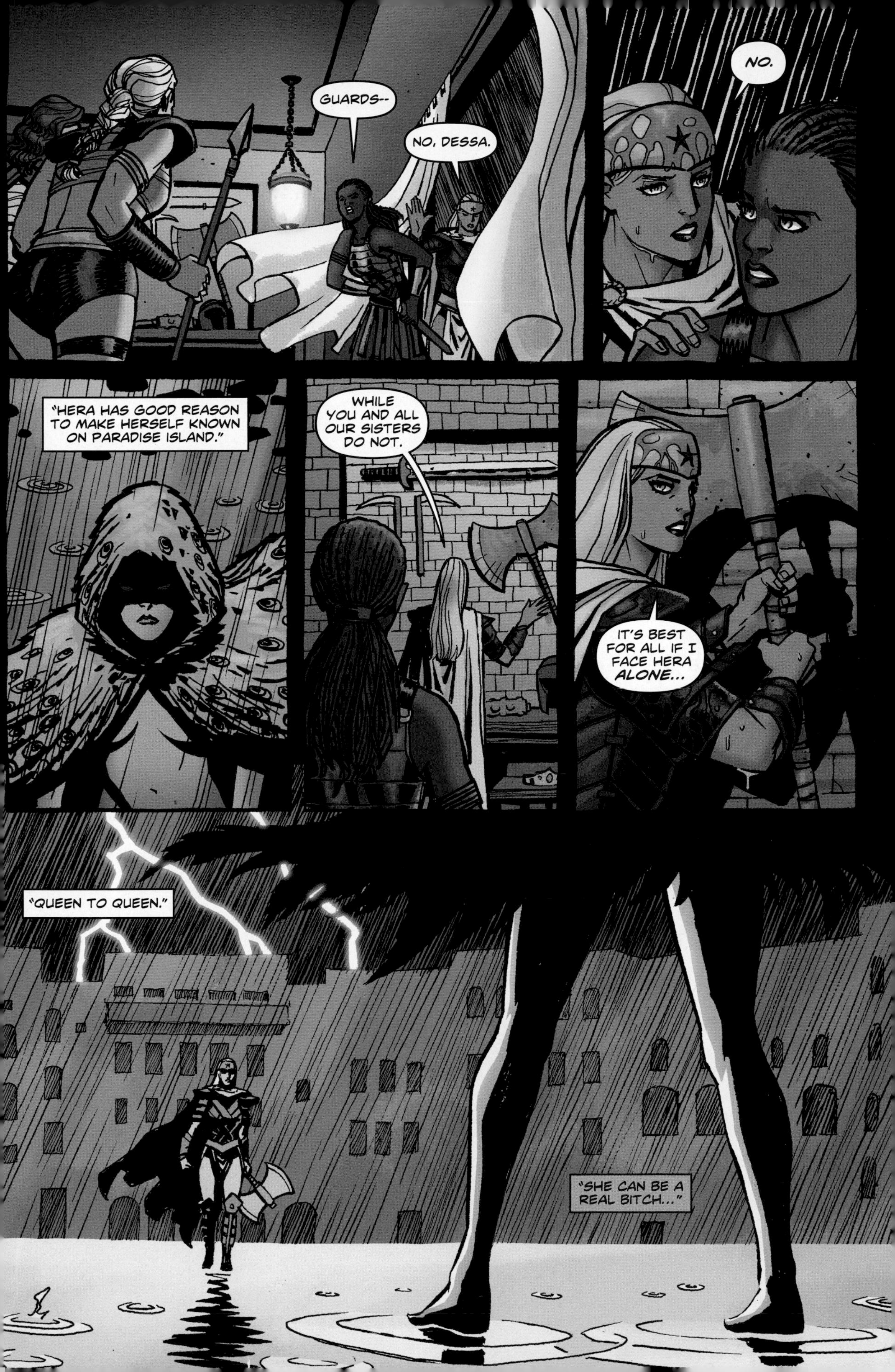
GUARDS--
NO, DESSA.
NO.
"HERA HAS GOOD REASON TO MAKE HERSELF KNOWN ON PARADISE ISLAND."
WHILE YOU AND ALL OUR SISTERS DO NOT.
IT'S BEST FOR ALL IF I FACE HERA *ALONE...*
"QUEEN TO QUEEN."
"SHE CAN BE A REAL BITCH..."

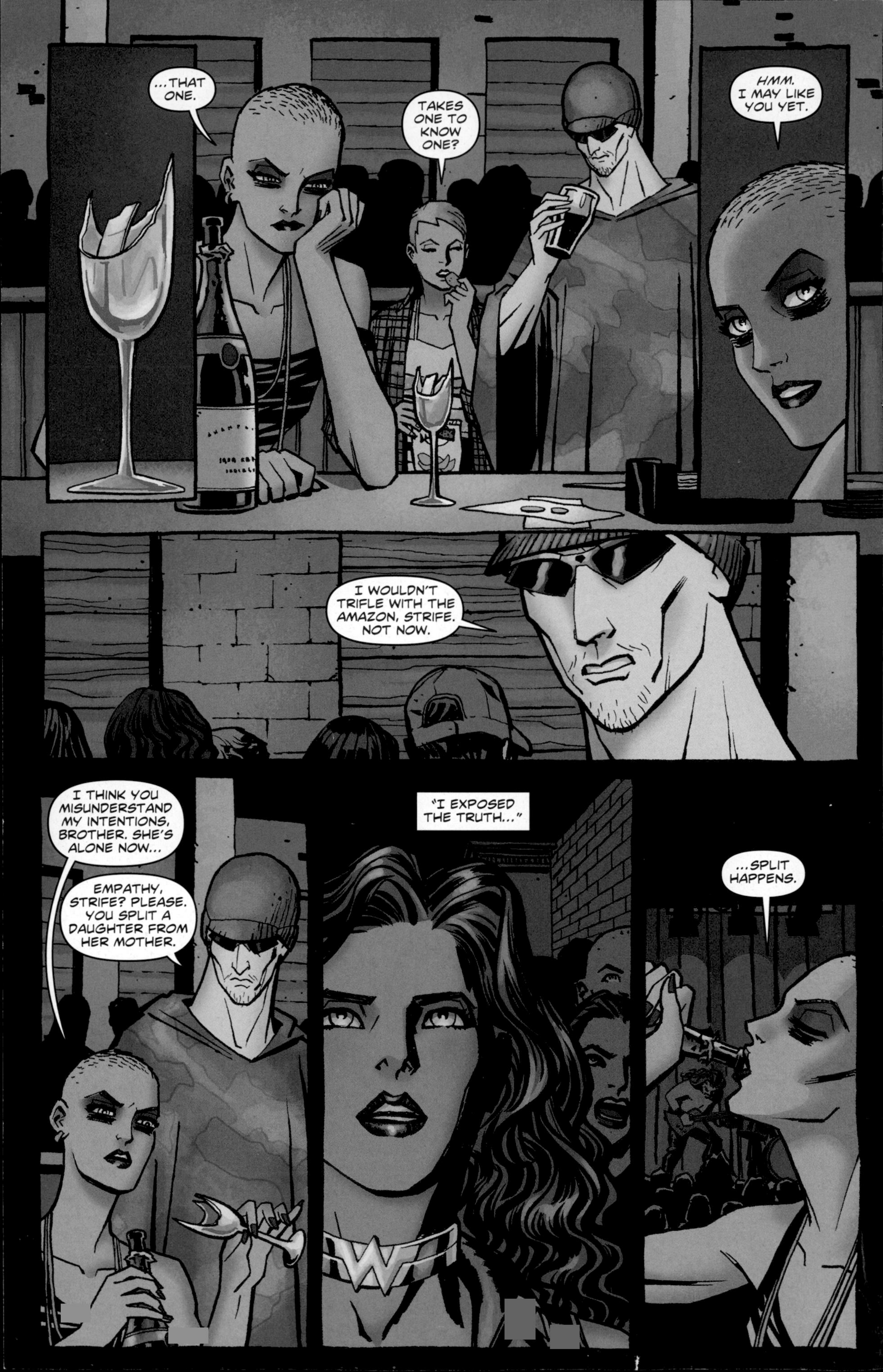
...THAT ONE.
TAKES ONE TO KNOW ONE?
HMM. I MAY LIKE YOU YET.
I WOULDN'T TRIFLE WITH THE AMAZON, STRIFE. NOT NOW.
I THINK YOU MISUNDERSTAND MY INTENTIONS, BROTHER. SHE'S ALONE NOW...
EMPATHY, STRIFE? PLEASE. YOU SPLIT A DAUGHTER FROM HER MOTHER.
"I EXPOSED THE TRUTH..."
...SPLIT HAPPENS.

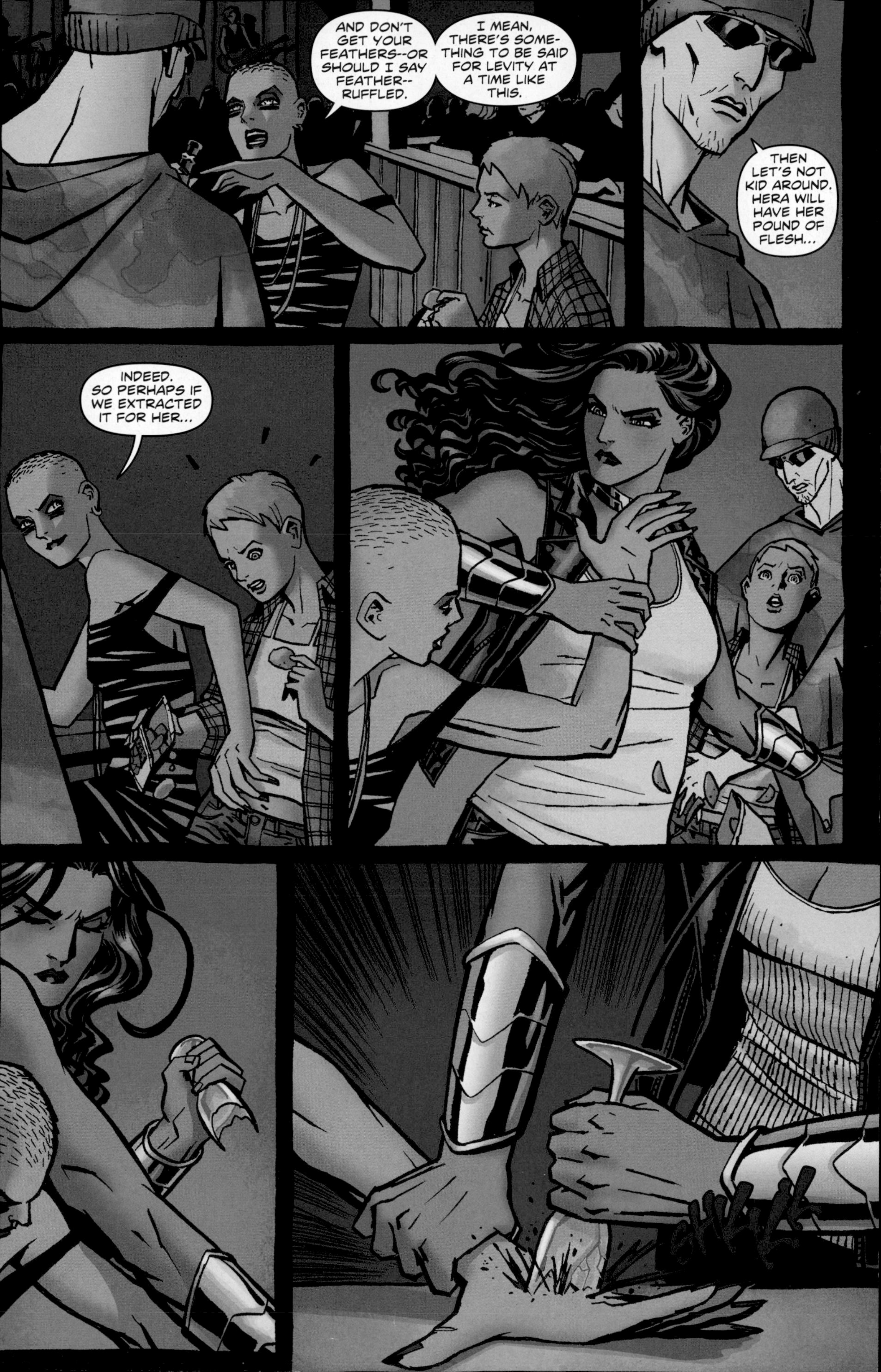
AND DON'T GET YOUR FEATHERS--OR SHOULD I SAY FEATHER--RUFFLED.
I MEAN, THERE'S SOMETHING TO BE SAID FOR LEVITY AT A TIME LIKE THIS.
THEN LET'S NOT KID AROUND. HERA WILL HAVE HER POUND OF FLESH...
INDEED. SO PERHAPS IF WE EXTRACTED IT FOR HER...

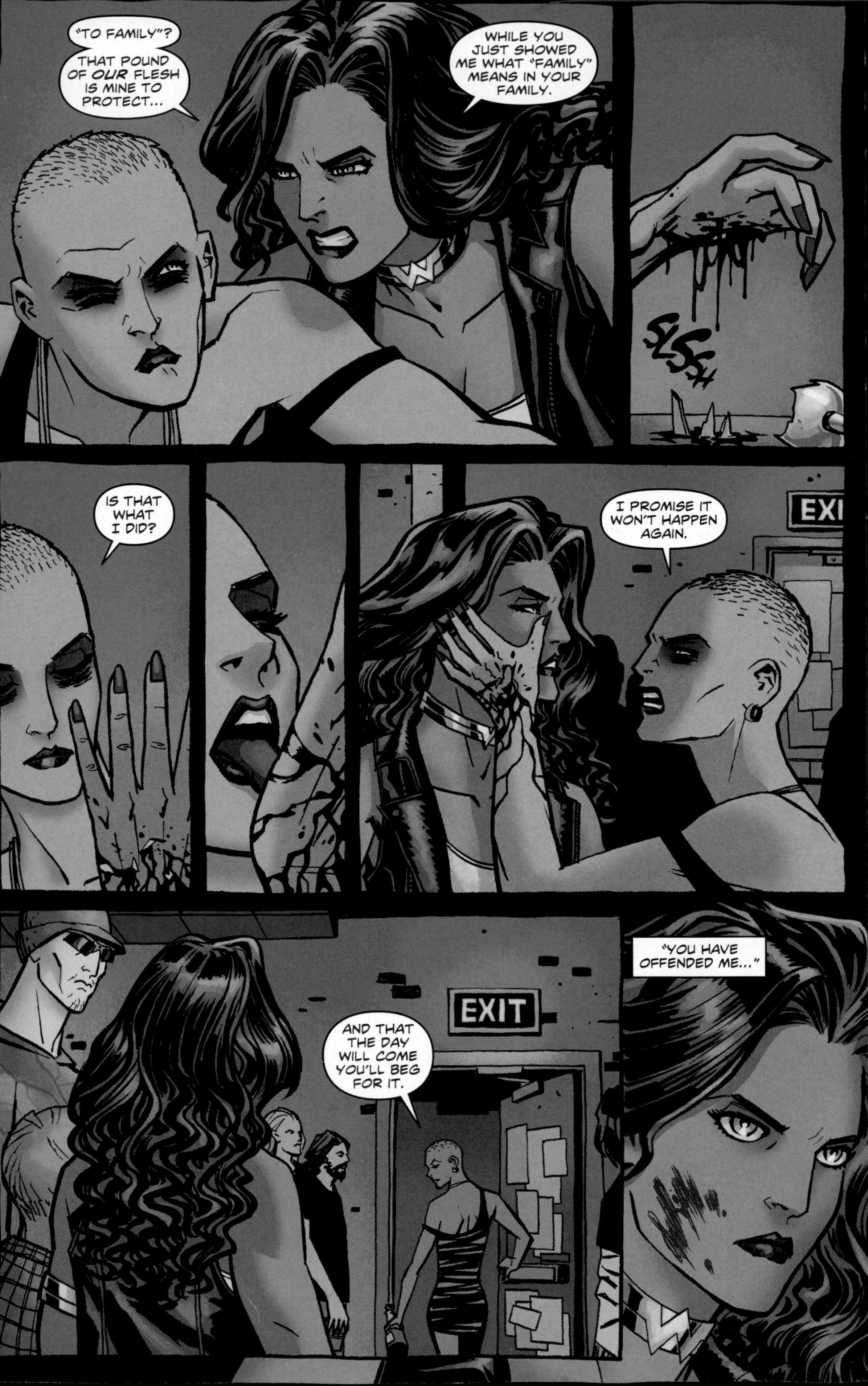
"TO FAMILY"? THAT POUND OF OUR FLESH IS MINE TO PROTECT...
WHILE YOU JUST SHOWED ME WHAT "FAMILY" MEANS IN YOUR FAMILY.
SLSSH
IS THAT WHAT I DID?
I PROMISE IT WON'T HAPPEN AGAIN.
EXIT
EXIT
AND THAT THE DAY WILL COME YOU'LL BEG FOR IT.
"YOU HAVE OFFENDED ME..."

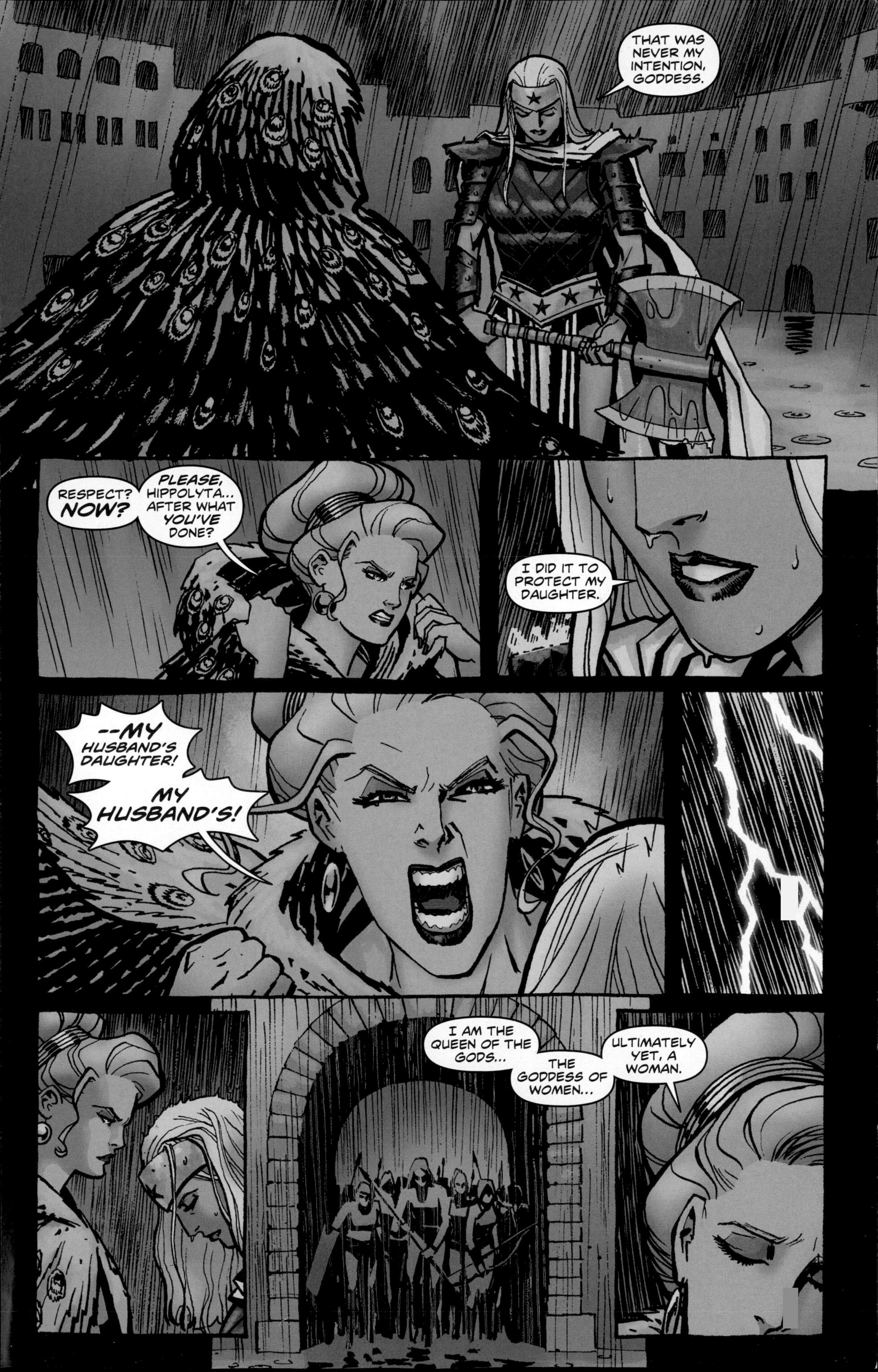
THAT WAS NEVER MY INTENTION, GODDESS.
RESPECT? NOW?
PLEASE, HIPPOLYTA... AFTER WHAT YOU'VE DONE?
I DID IT TO PROTECT MY DAUGHTER.
--MY HUSBAND'S DAUGHTER!
MY HUSBAND'S!
I AM THE QUEEN OF THE GODS...
THE GODDESS OF WOMEN...
ULTIMATELY YET, A WOMAN.

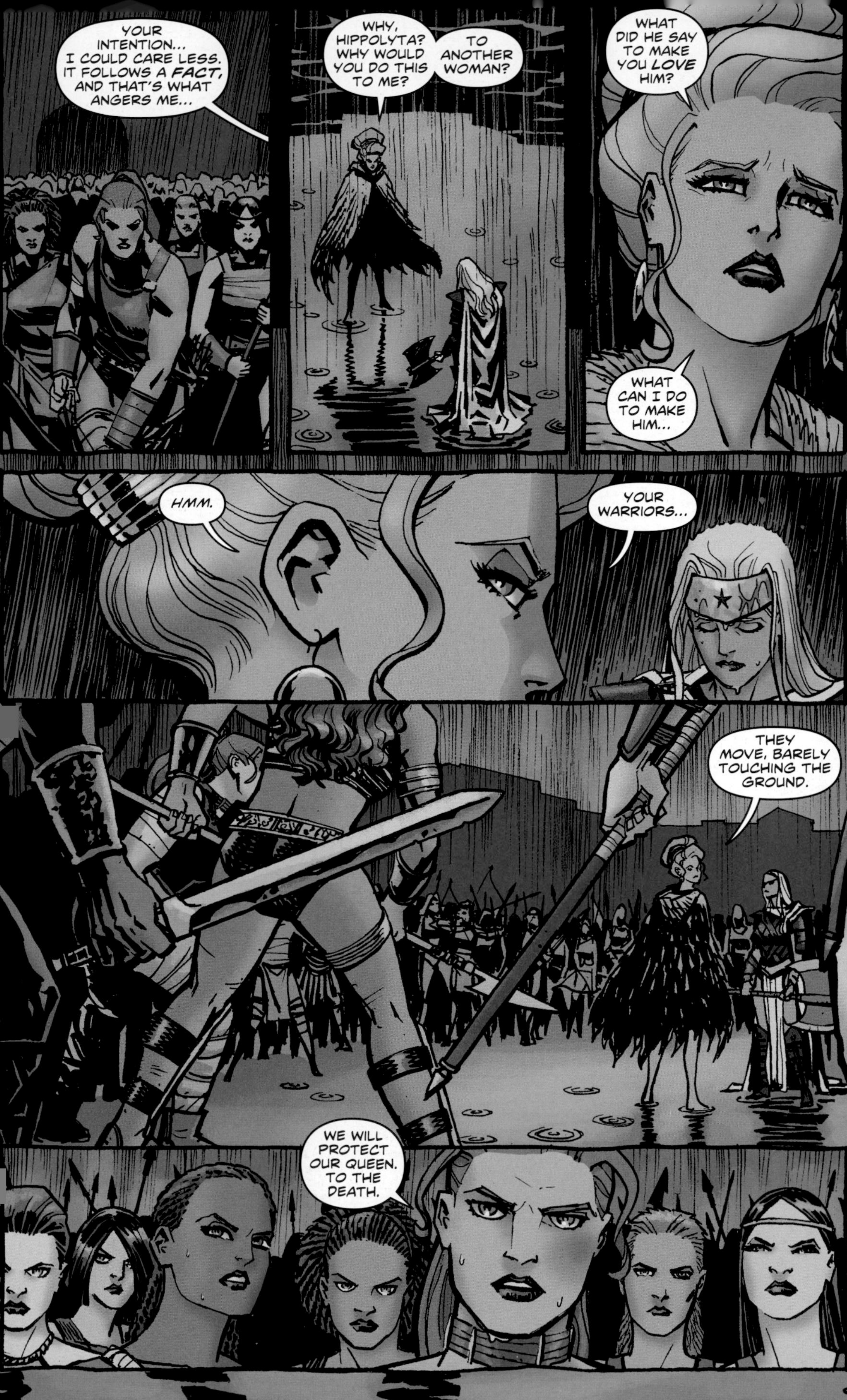
YOUR INTENTION... I COULD CARE LESS. IT FOLLOWS A *FACT*, AND THAT'S WHAT ANGERS ME...
WHY, HIPPOLYTA? WHY WOULD YOU DO THIS TO ME?
TO ANOTHER WOMAN?
WHAT DID HE SAY TO MAKE YOU *LOVE* HIM?
WHAT CAN I DO TO MAKE HIM...
HMM.
YOUR WARRIORS...
THEY MOVE, BARELY TOUCHING THE GROUND.
WE WILL PROTECT OUR QUEEN. TO THE DEATH.

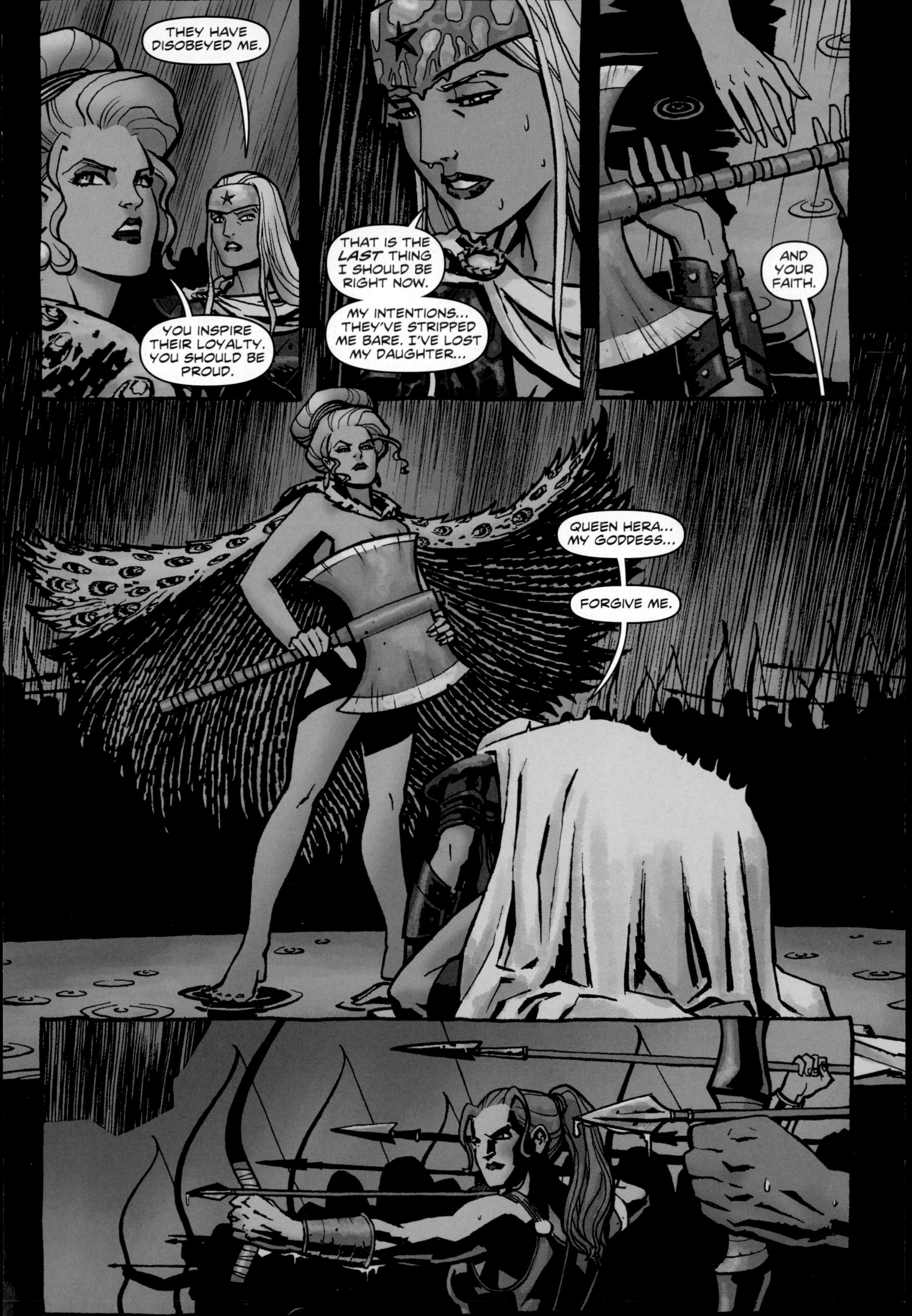
THEY HAVE DISOBEYED ME.
YOU INSPIRE THEIR LOYALTY. YOU SHOULD BE PROUD.
THAT IS THE LAST THING I SHOULD BE RIGHT NOW.
MY INTENTIONS... THEY'VE STRIPPED ME BARE. I'VE LOST MY DAUGHTER...
AND YOUR FAITH.
QUEEN HERA... MY GODDESS...
FORGIVE ME.

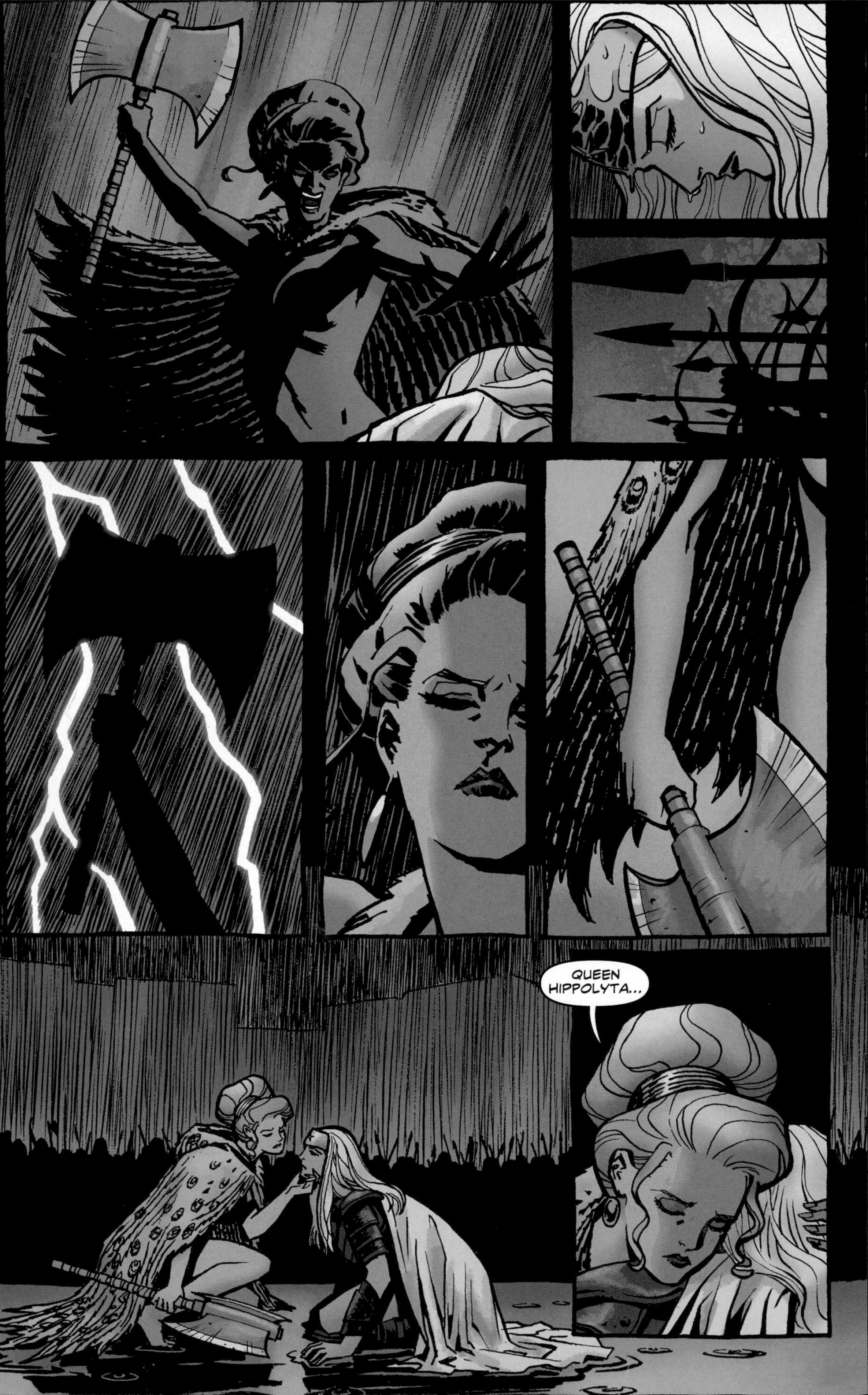
QUEEN HIPPOLYTA...

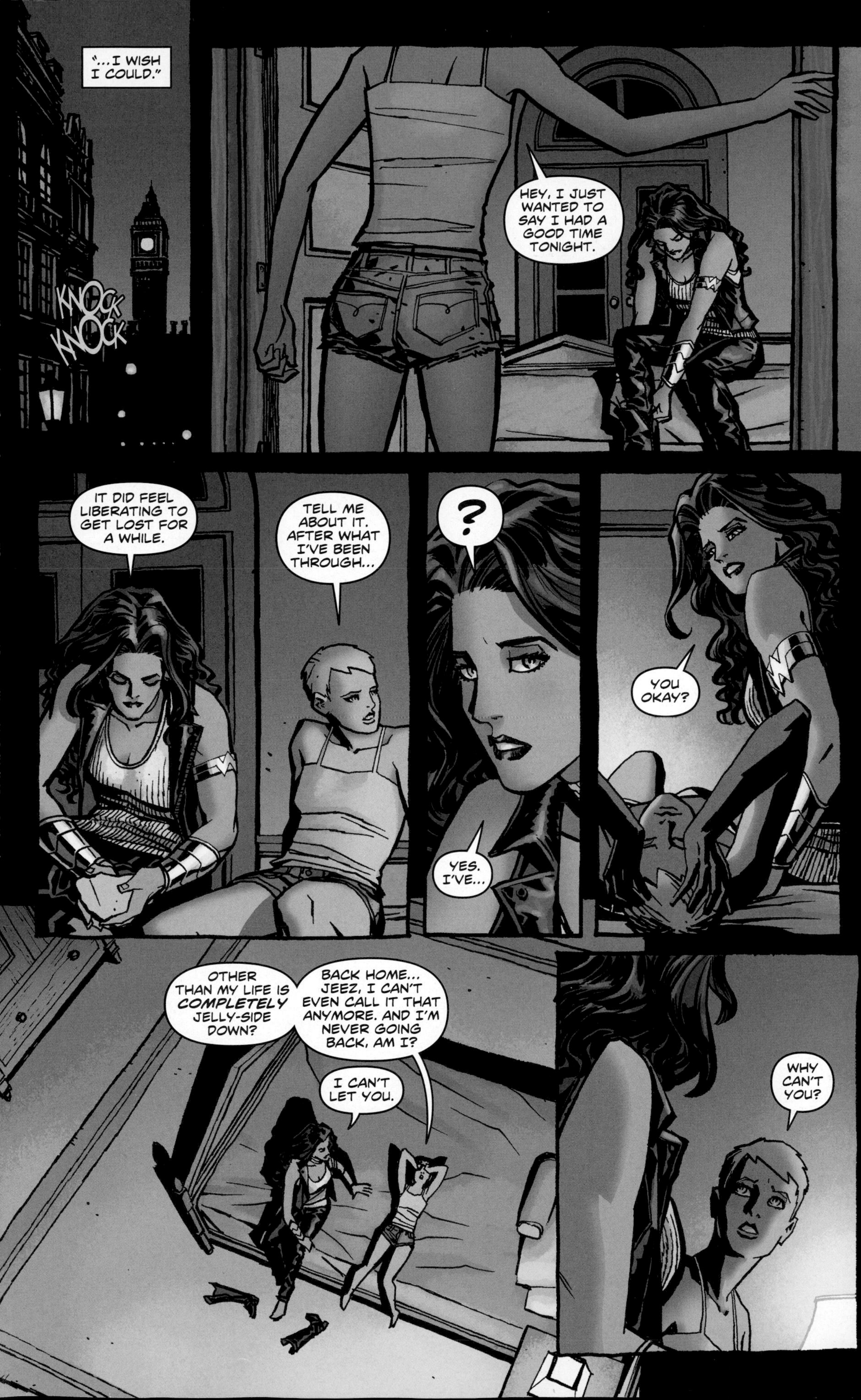
"...I WISH I COULD."
KNOCK KNOCK
HEY, I JUST WANTED TO SAY I HAD A GOOD TIME TONIGHT.
IT DID FEEL LIBERATING TO GET LOST FOR A WHILE.
TELL ME ABOUT IT. AFTER WHAT I'VE BEEN THROUGH...
?
YES. I'VE...
YOU OKAY?
OTHER THAN MY LIFE IS *COMPLETELY* JELLY-SIDE DOWN?
BACK HOME... JEEZ, I CAN'T EVEN CALL IT THAT ANYMORE. AND I'M NEVER GOING BACK, AM I?
I CAN'T LET YOU.
WHY CAN'T YOU?

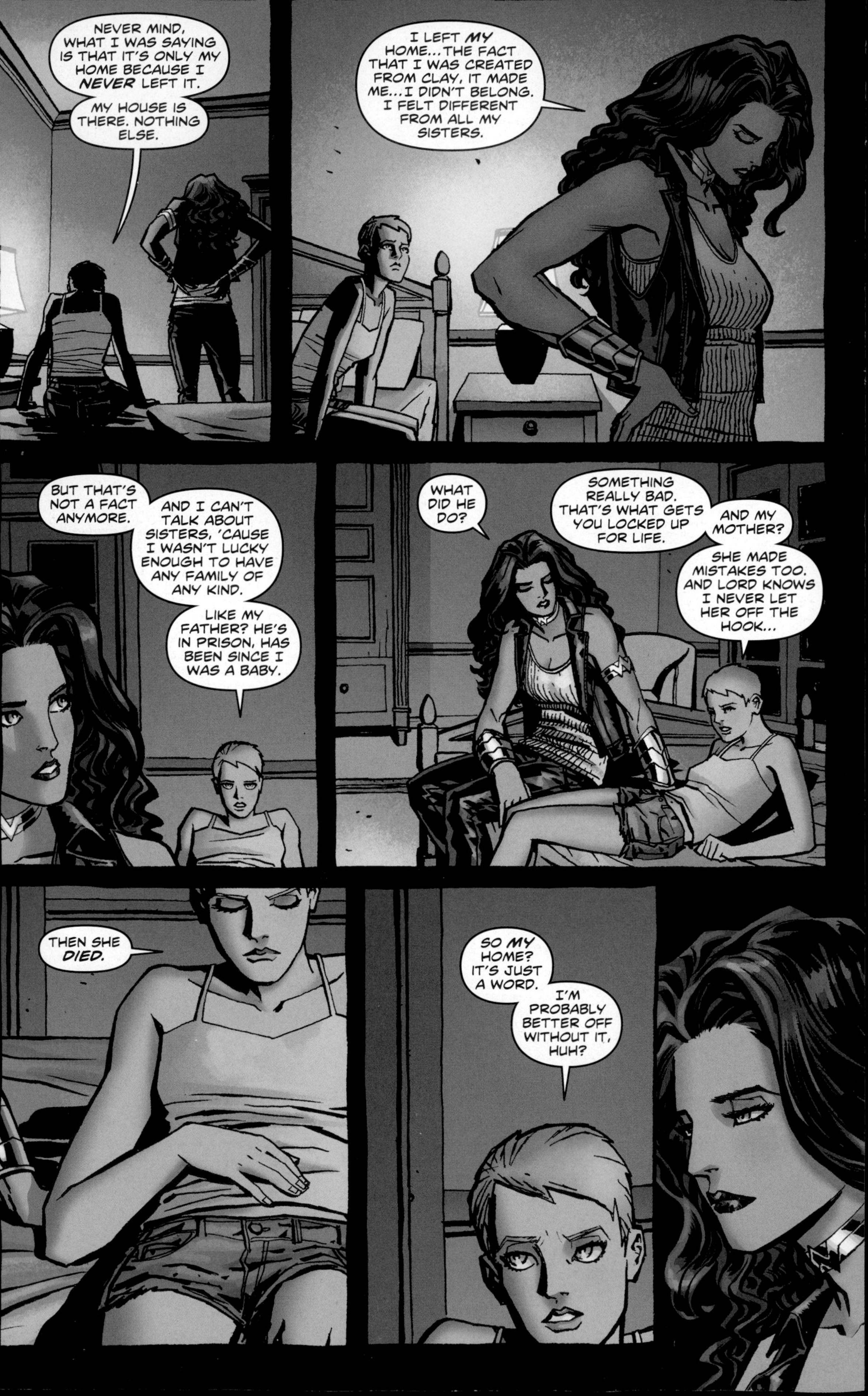
NEVER MIND, WHAT I WAS SAYING IS THAT IT'S ONLY MY HOME BECAUSE I NEVER LEFT IT.
MY HOUSE IS THERE. NOTHING ELSE.
I LEFT MY HOME... THE FACT THAT I WAS CREATED FROM CLAY, IT MADE ME... I DIDN'T BELONG. I FELT DIFFERENT FROM ALL MY SISTERS.
BUT THAT'S NOT A FACT ANYMORE.
AND I CAN'T TALK ABOUT SISTERS, 'CAUSE I WASN'T LUCKY ENOUGH TO HAVE ANY FAMILY OF ANY KIND.
LIKE MY FATHER? HE'S IN PRISON, HAS BEEN SINCE I WAS A BABY.
WHAT DID HE DO?
SOMETHING REALLY BAD. THAT'S WHAT GETS YOU LOCKED UP FOR LIFE.
AND MY MOTHER?
SHE MADE MISTAKES TOO. AND LORD KNOWS I NEVER LET HER OFF THE HOOK...
THEN SHE DIED.
SO MY HOME? IT'S JUST A WORD.
I'M PROBABLY BETTER OFF WITHOUT IT, HUH?

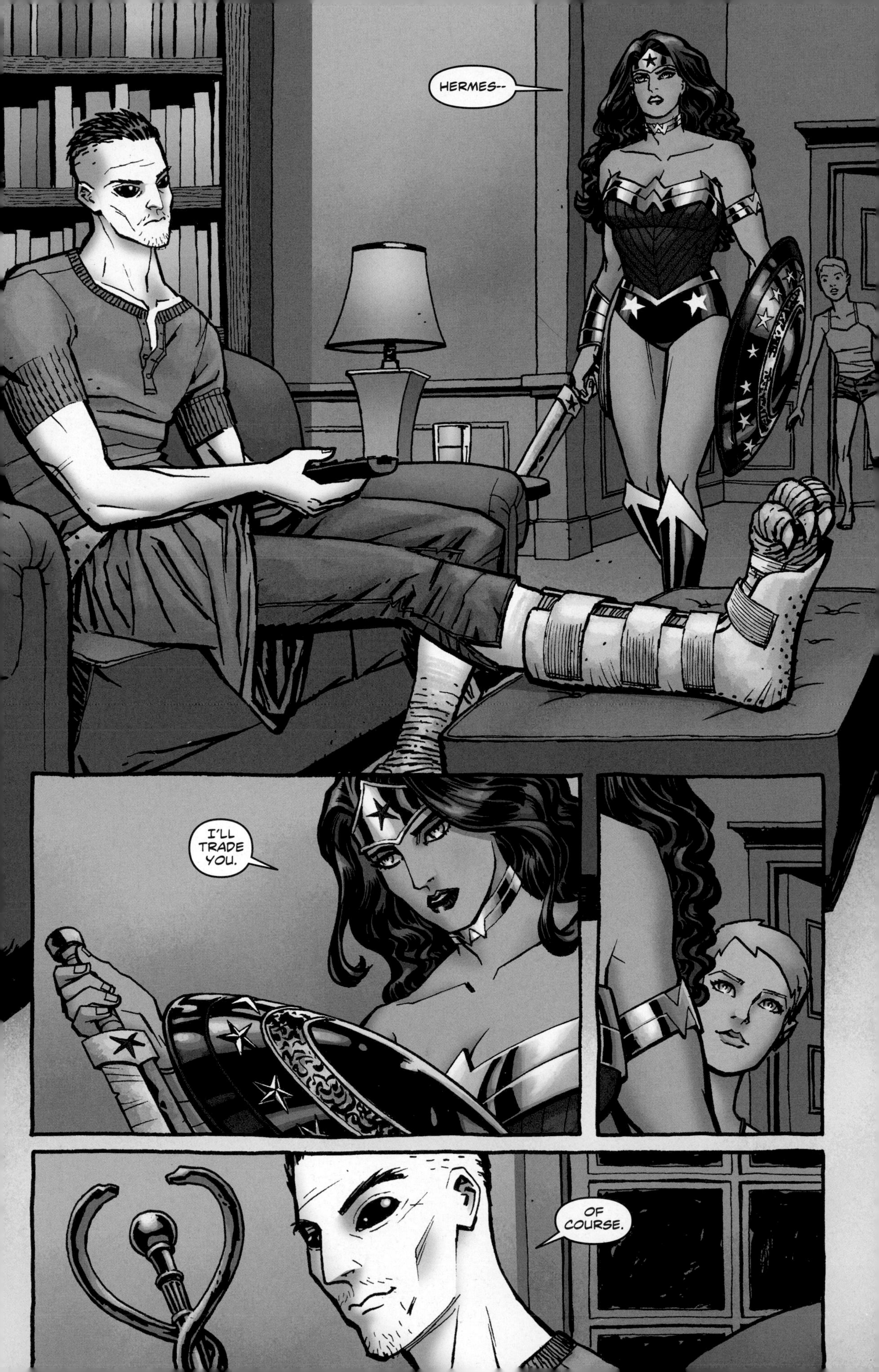
HERMES--
I'LL TRADE YOU.
OF COURSE.

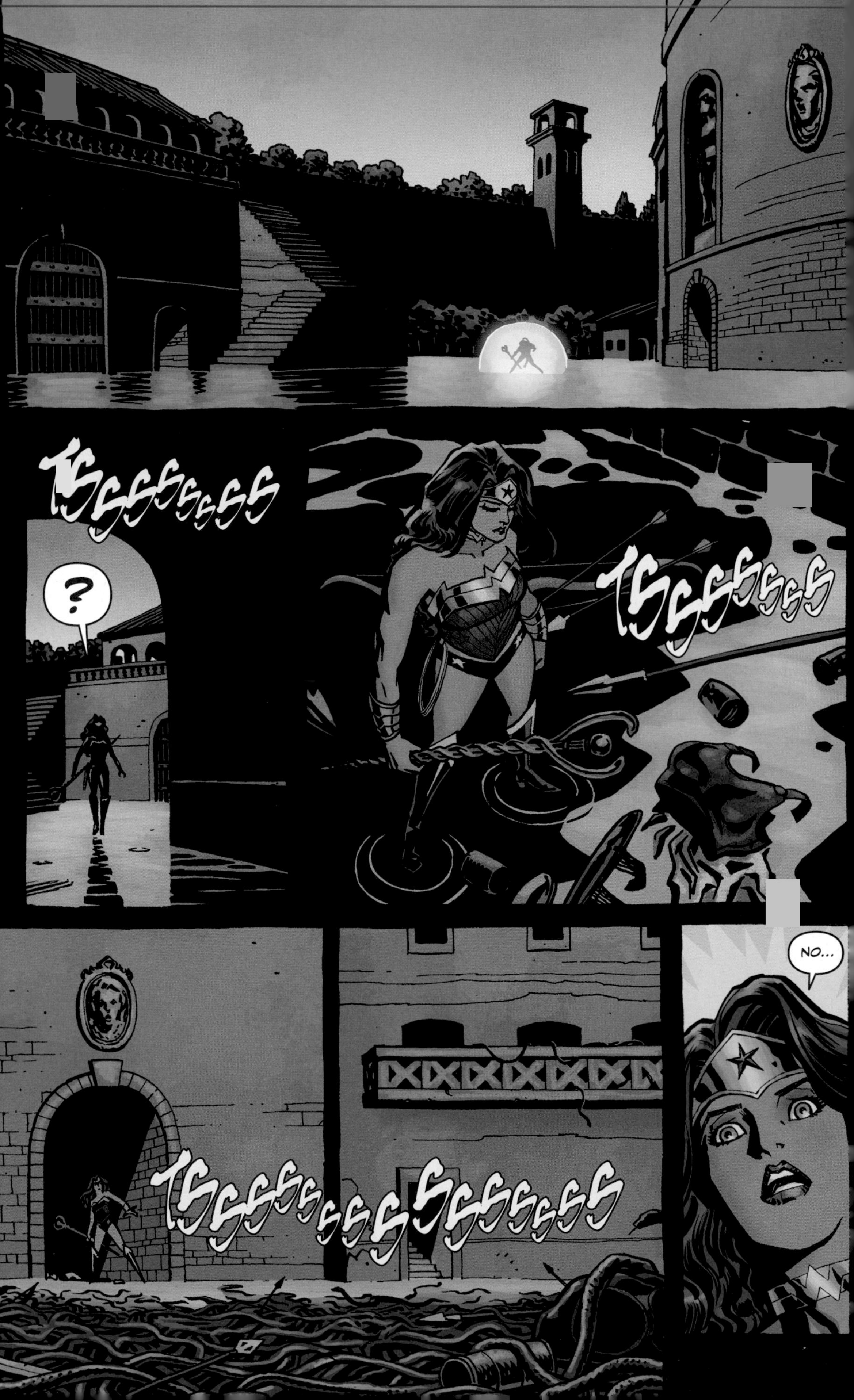

TSSSSSSSSS
?
TSSSSSSSS
TSSSSSSSSSSSSSSSSS
NO...

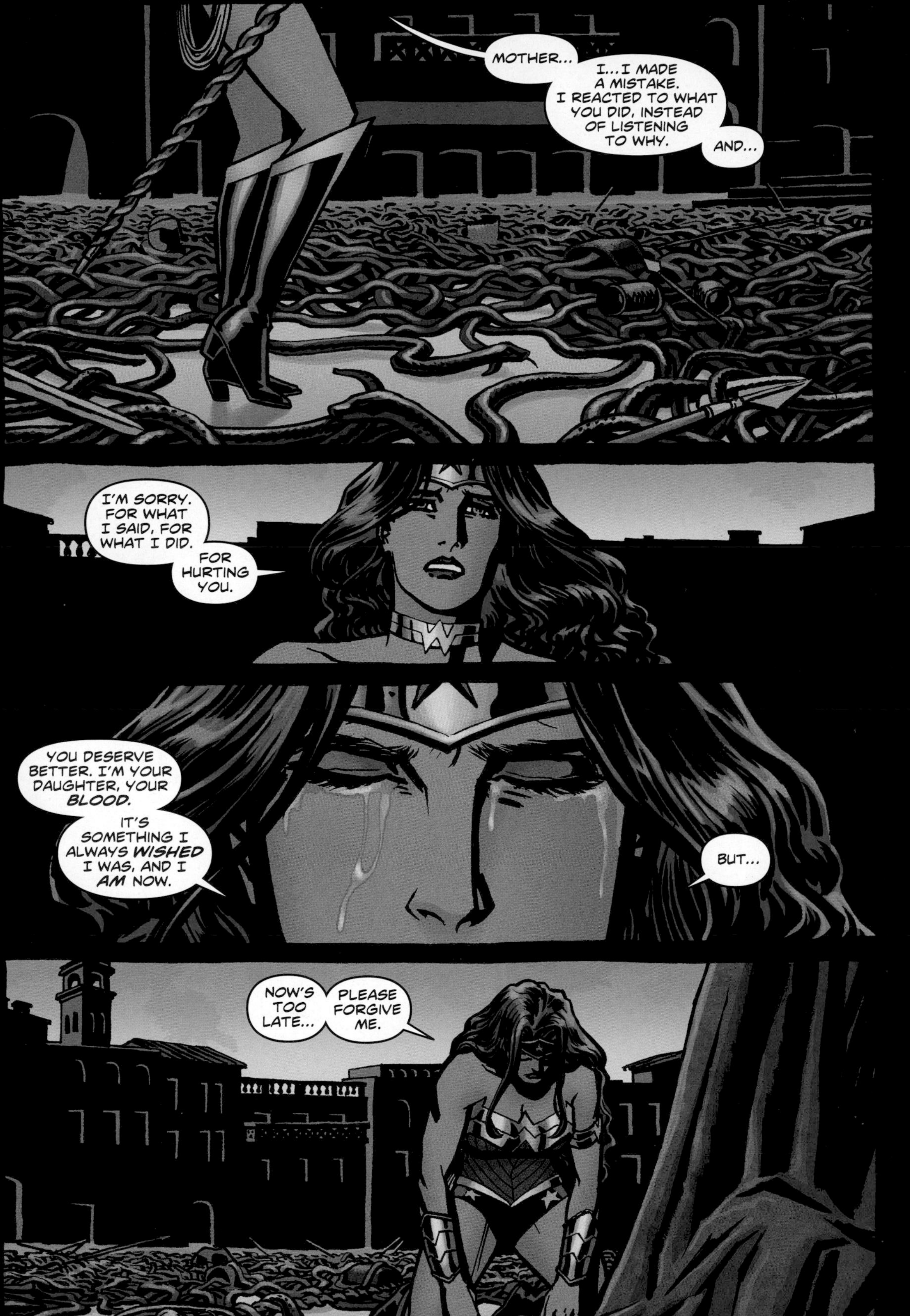
MOTHER...
I...I MADE A MISTAKE. I REACTED TO WHAT YOU DID, INSTEAD OF LISTENING TO WHY.
AND...
I'M SORRY. FOR WHAT I SAID, FOR WHAT I DID.
FOR HURTING YOU.
YOU DESERVE BETTER. I'M YOUR DAUGHTER, YOUR **BLOOD.**
IT'S SOMETHING I ALWAYS **WISHED** I WAS, AND I **AM** NOW.
BUT...
NOW'S TOO LATE...
PLEASE FORGIVE ME.

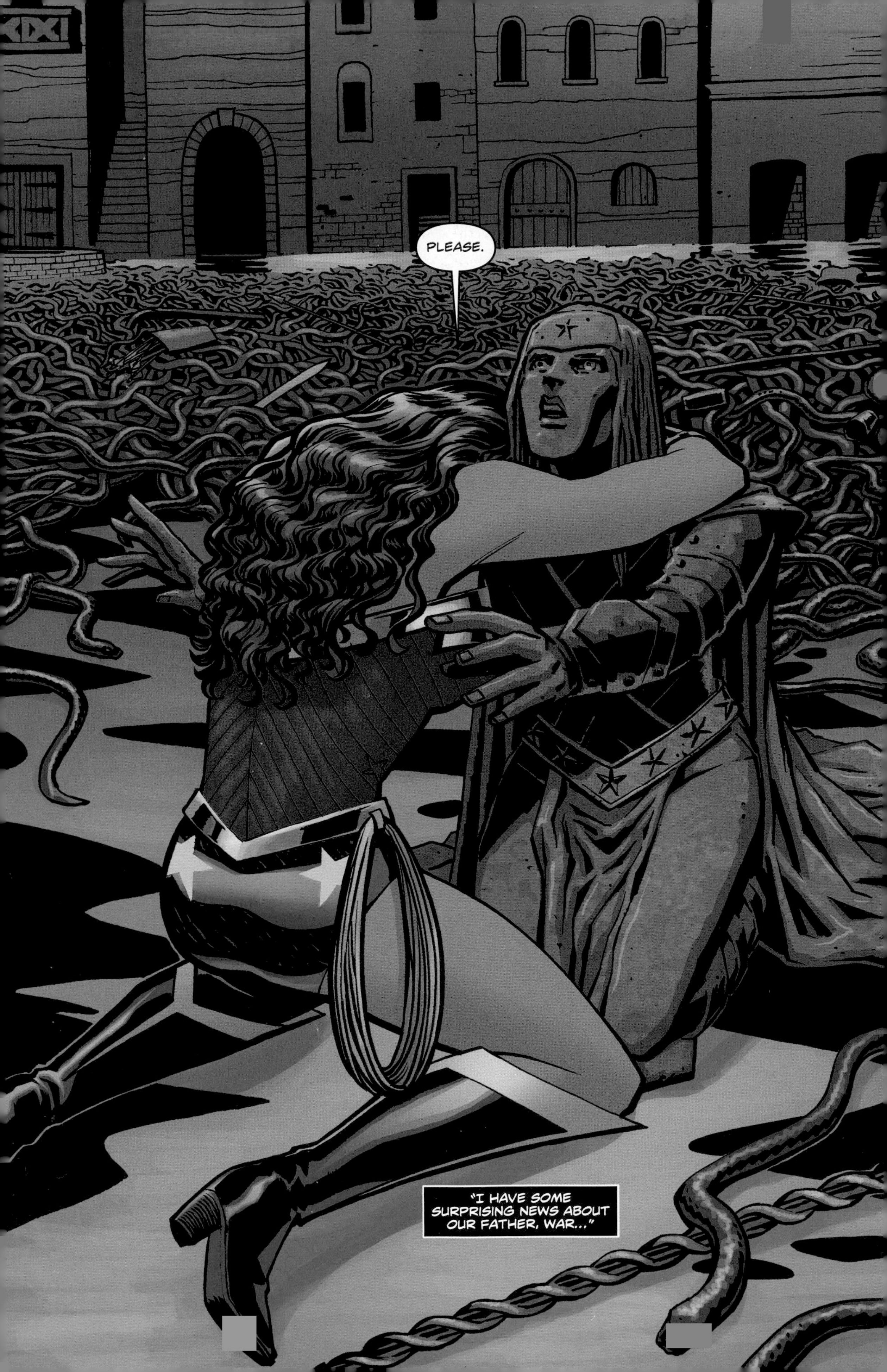
PLEASE.
"I HAVE SOME SURPRISING NEWS ABOUT OUR FATHER, WAR..."

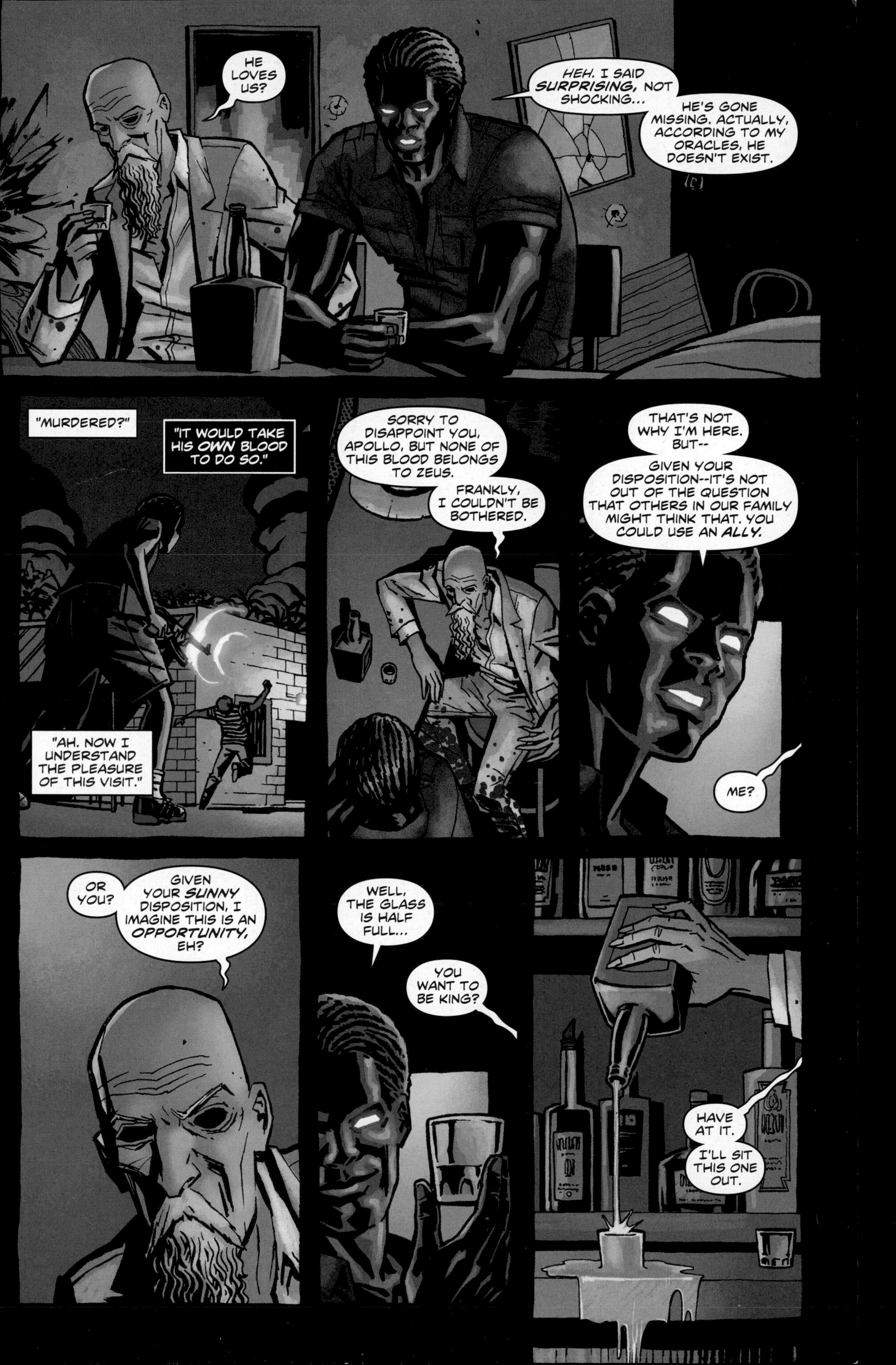

HE LOVES US?
HEH. I SAID SURPRISING, NOT SHOCKING...
HE'S GONE MISSING. ACTUALLY, ACCORDING TO MY ORACLES, HE DOESN'T EXIST.
"MURDERED?"
"IT WOULD TAKE HIS OWN BLOOD TO DO SO."
"AH. NOW I UNDERSTAND THE PLEASURE OF THIS VISIT."
SORRY TO DISAPPOINT YOU, APOLLO, BUT NONE OF THIS BLOOD BELONGS TO ZEUS.
FRANKLY, I COULDN'T BE BOTHERED.
THAT'S NOT WHY I'M HERE. BUT--
GIVEN YOUR DISPOSITION--IT'S NOT OUT OF THE QUESTION THAT OTHERS IN OUR FAMILY MIGHT THINK THAT. YOU COULD USE AN ALLY.
ME?
OR YOU?
GIVEN YOUR SUNNY DISPOSITION, I IMAGINE THIS IS AN OPPORTUNITY, EH?
WELL, THE GLASS IS HALF FULL...
YOU WANT TO BE KING?
HAVE AT IT.
I'LL SIT THIS ONE OUT.

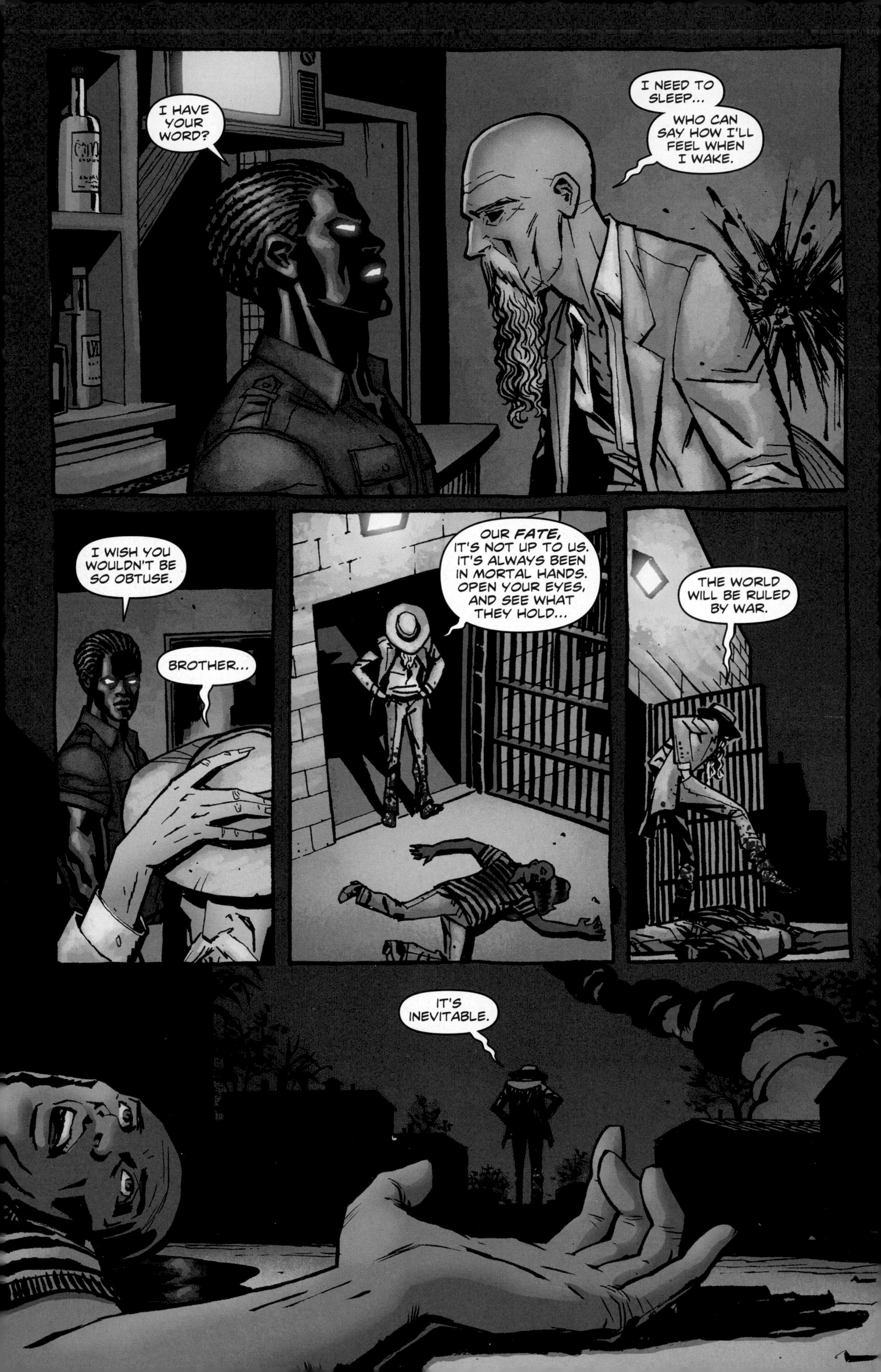
I HAVE YOUR WORD?
I NEED TO SLEEP...
WHO CAN SAY HOW I'LL FEEL WHEN I WAKE.
I WISH YOU WOULDN'T BE SO OBTUSE.
BROTHER...
OUR *FATE,* IT'S NOT UP TO US. IT'S ALWAYS BEEN IN MORTAL HANDS. OPEN YOUR EYES, AND SEE WHAT THEY HOLD...
THE WORLD WILL BE RULED BY WAR.
IT'S INEVITABLE.

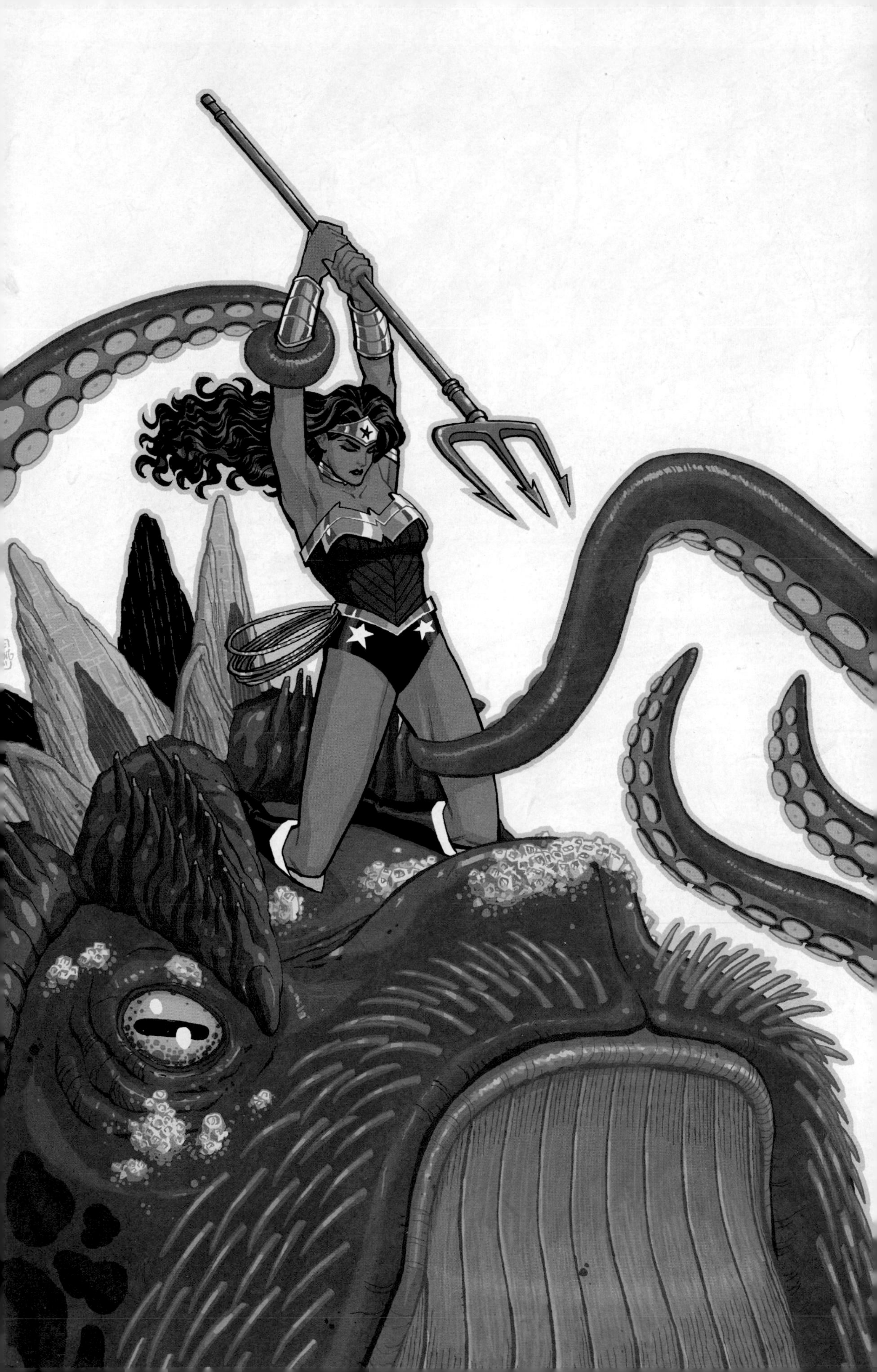

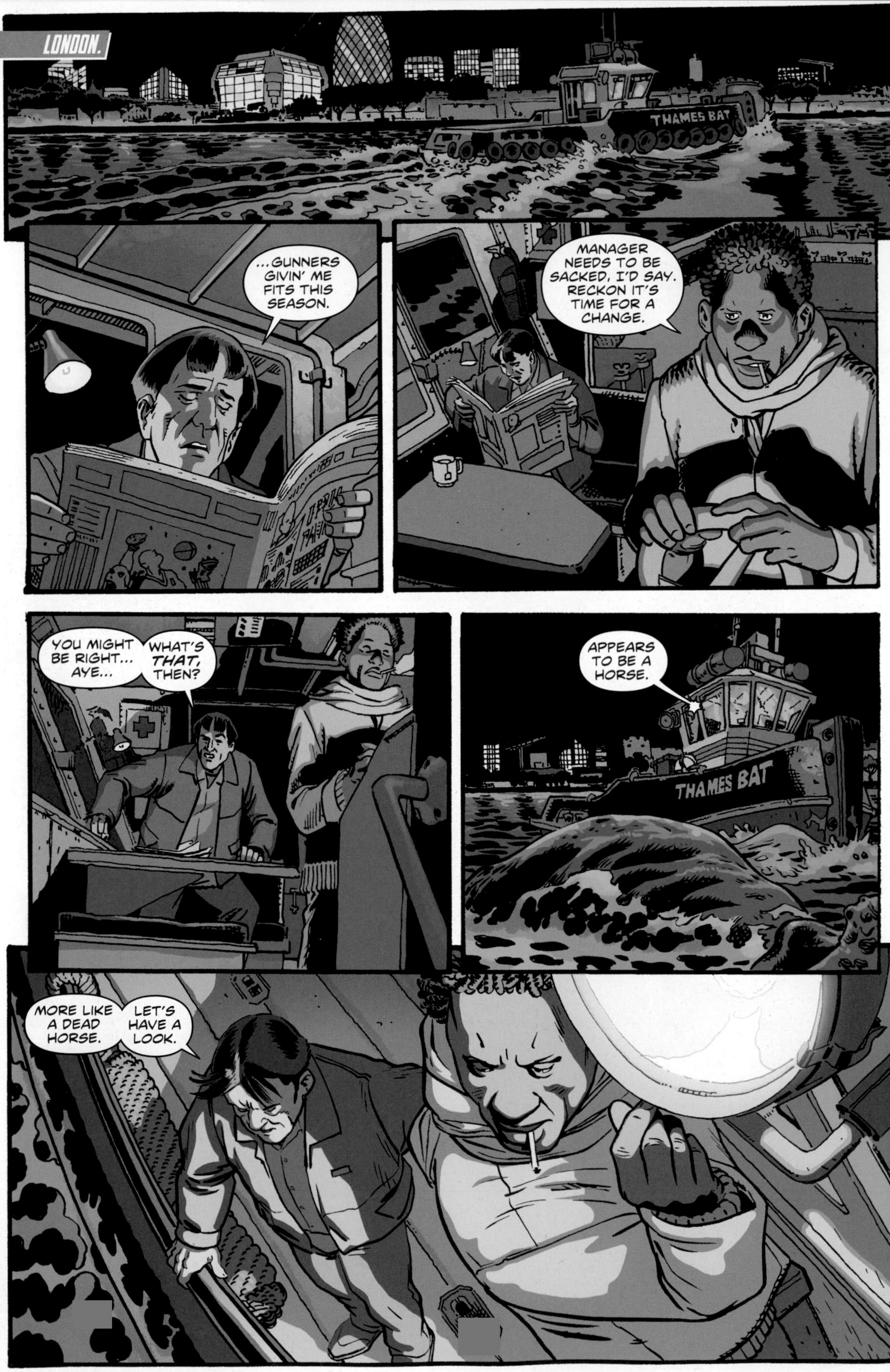
LONDON.
THAMES BAT
...GUNNERS GIVIN' ME FITS THIS SEASON.
MANAGER NEEDS TO BE SACKED, I'D SAY. RECKON IT'S TIME FOR A CHANGE.
YOU MIGHT BE RIGHT... AYE...
WHAT'S *THAT,* THEN?
APPEARS TO BE A HORSE.
THAMES BAT
MORE LIKE A DEAD HORSE.
LET'S HAVE A LOOK.

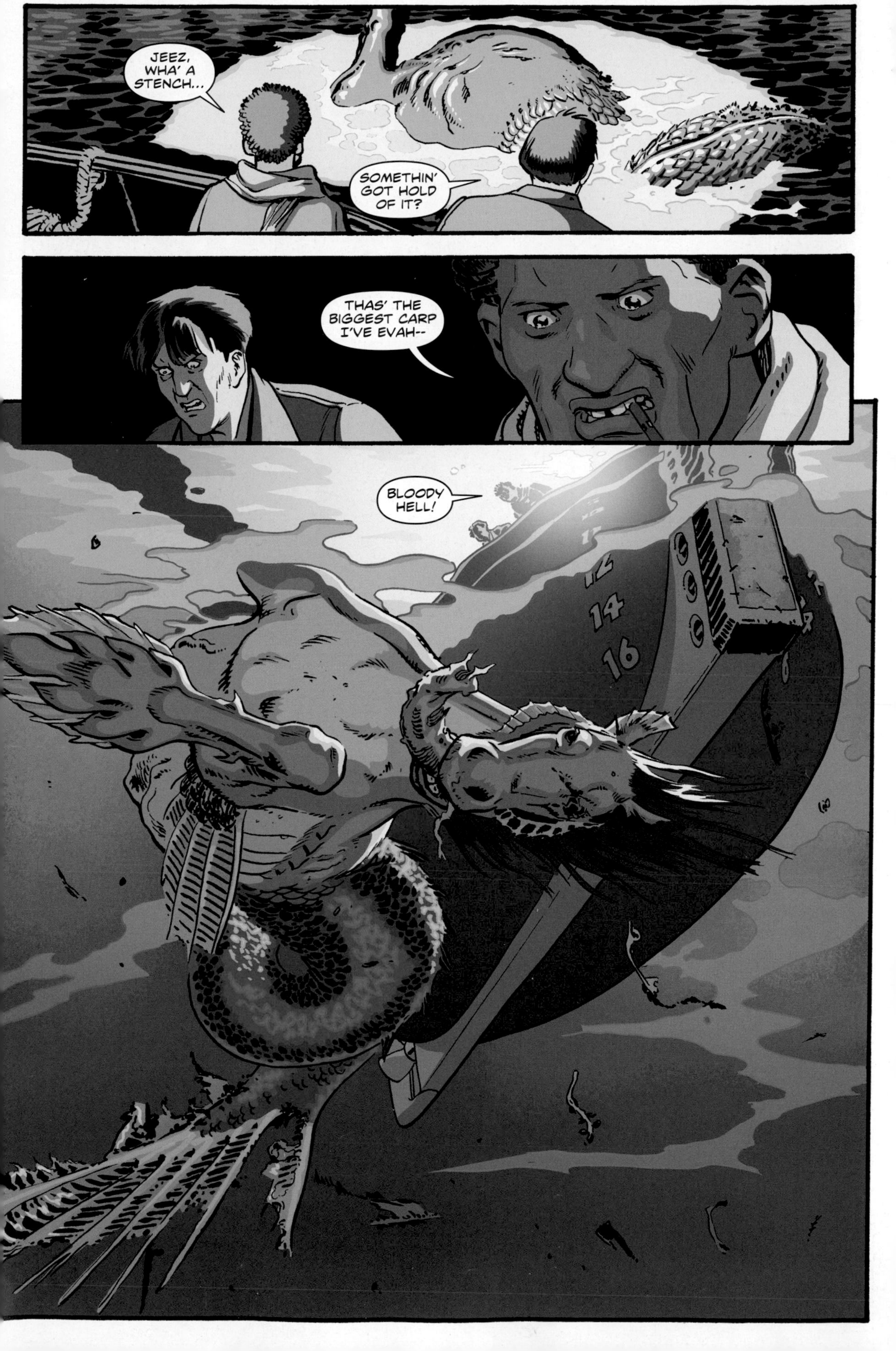
JEEZ, WHA' A STENCH...
SOMETHIN' GOT HOLD OF IT?
THAS' THE BIGGEST CARP I'VE EVAH--
BLOODY HELL!
12
14
16

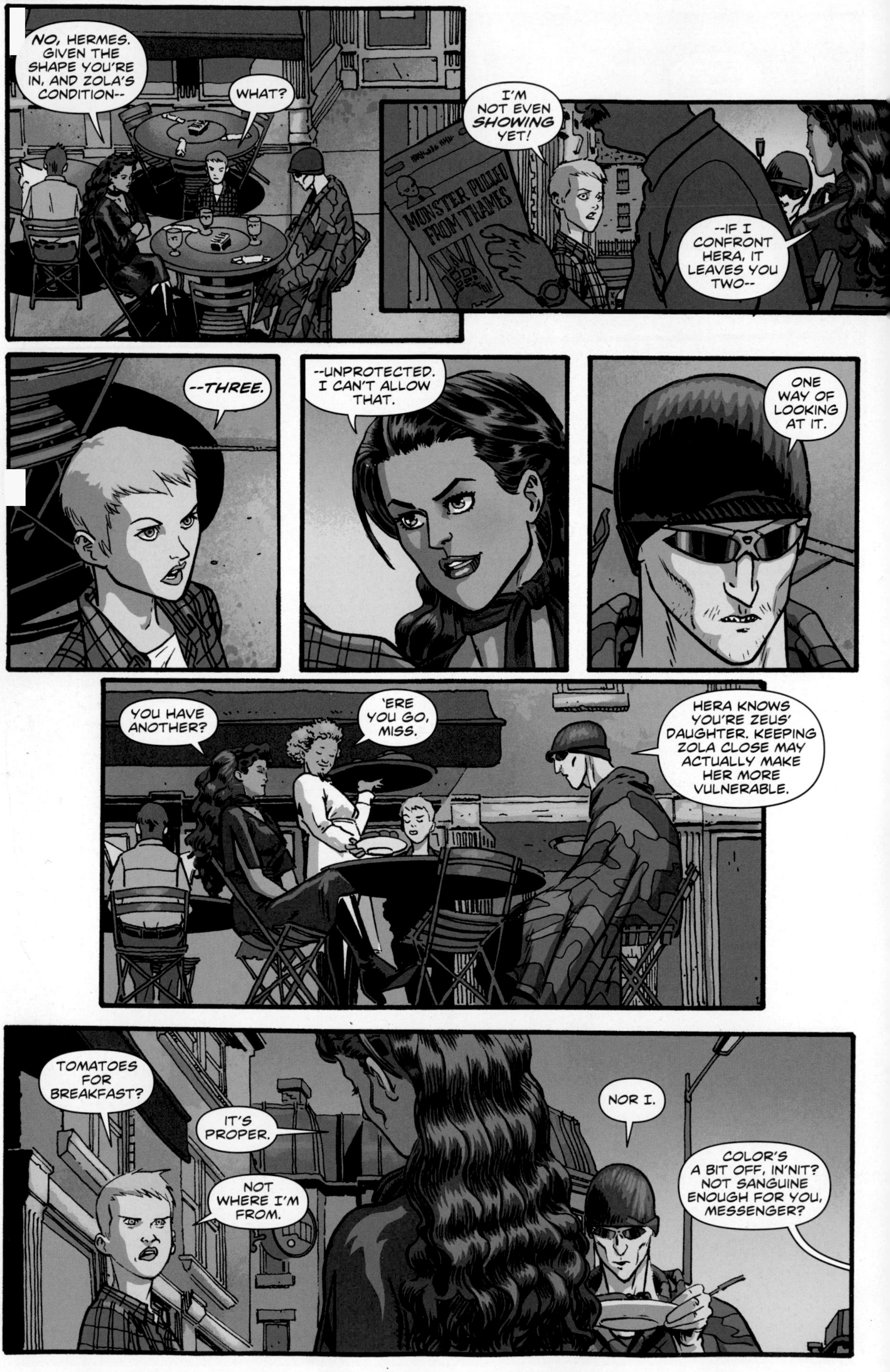
NO, HERMES. GIVEN THE SHAPE YOU'RE IN, AND ZOLA'S CONDITION--
WHAT?
I'M NOT EVEN SHOWING YET!
MONSTER PULLED FROM THAMES
--IF I CONFRONT HERA, IT LEAVES YOU TWO--
--THREE.
--UNPROTECTED. I CAN'T ALLOW THAT.
ONE WAY OF LOOKING AT IT.
YOU HAVE ANOTHER?
'ERE YOU GO, MISS.
HERA KNOWS YOU'RE ZEUS' DAUGHTER. KEEPING ZOLA CLOSE MAY ACTUALLY MAKE HER MORE VULNERABLE.
TOMATOES FOR BREAKFAST?
IT'S PROPER.
NOT WHERE I'M FROM.
NOR I.
COLOR'S A BIT OFF, IN'NIT? NOT SANGUINE ENOUGH FOR YOU, MESSENGER?

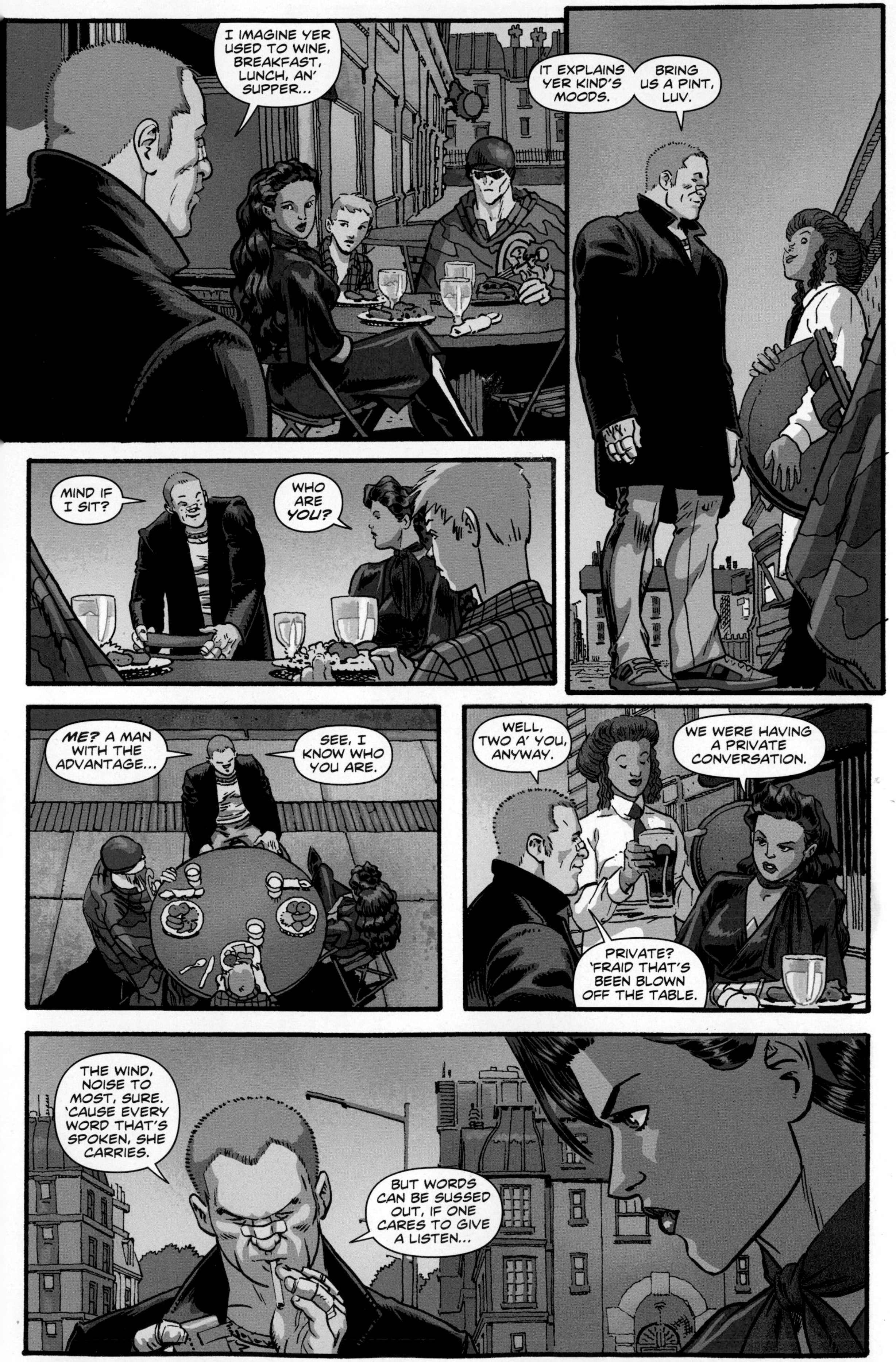
I IMAGINE YER USED TO WINE, BREAKFAST, LUNCH, AN' SUPPER...
IT EXPLAINS YER KIND'S MOODS.
BRING US A PINT, LUV.
MIND IF I SIT?
WHO ARE *YOU*?
ME? A MAN WITH THE ADVANTAGE...
SEE, I KNOW WHO YOU ARE.
WELL, TWO A' YOU, ANYWAY.
WE WERE HAVING A PRIVATE CONVERSATION.
PRIVATE? 'FRAID THAT'S BEEN BLOWN OFF THE TABLE.
THE WIND, NOISE TO MOST, SURE. 'CAUSE EVERY WORD THAT'S SPOKEN, SHE CARRIES.
BUT WORDS CAN BE SUSSED OUT, IF ONE CARES TO GIVE A LISTEN...

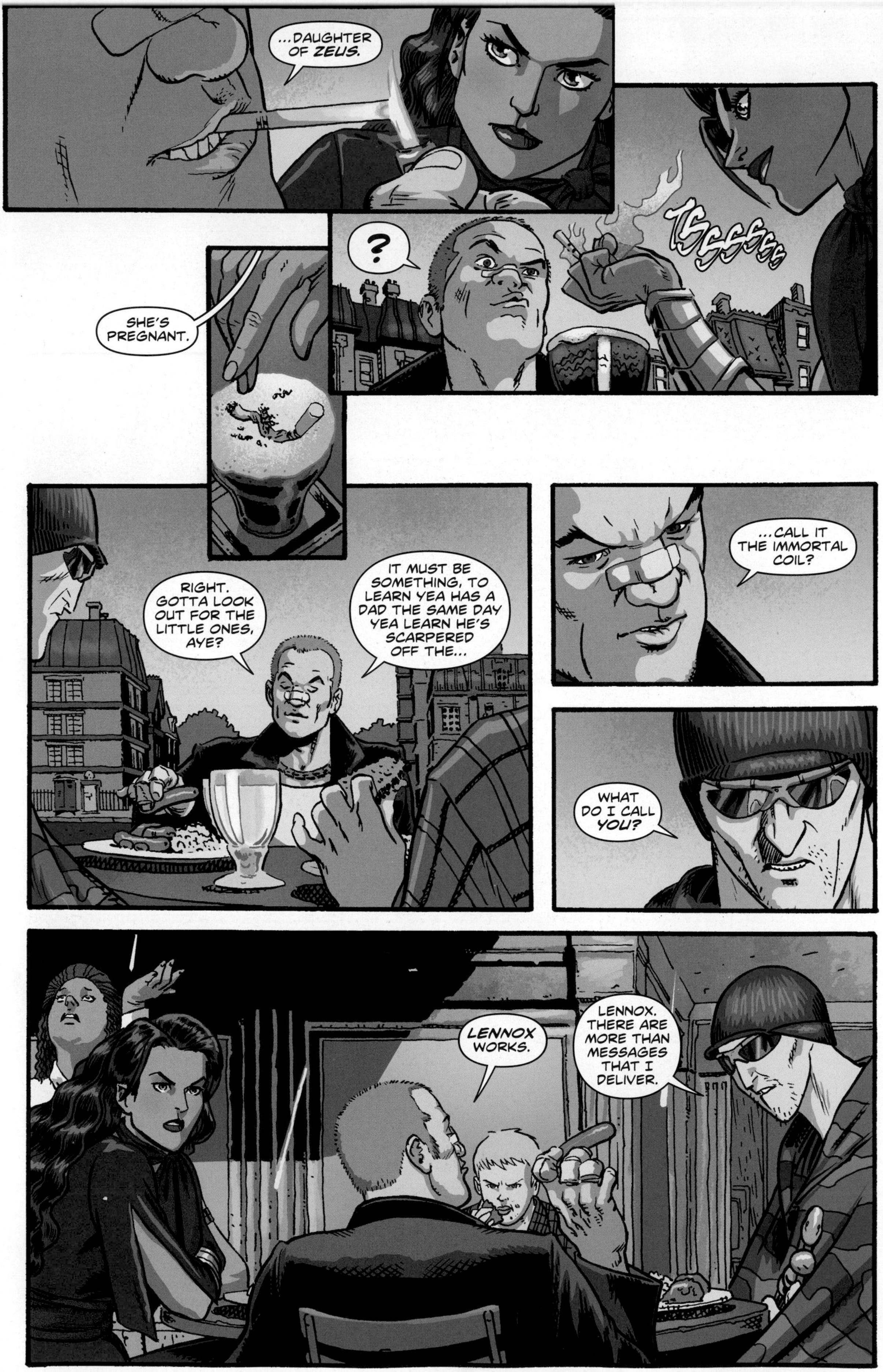
...DAUGHTER OF ZEUS.
?
TSSSSSSS
SHE'S PREGNANT.
RIGHT. GOTTA LOOK OUT FOR THE LITTLE ONES, AYE?
IT MUST BE SOMETHING, TO LEARN YEA HAS A DAD THE SAME DAY YEA LEARN HE'S SCARPERED OFF THE...
...CALL IT THE IMMORTAL COIL?
WHAT DO I CALL YOU?
LENNOX WORKS.
LENNOX. THERE ARE MORE THAN MESSAGES THAT I DELIVER.

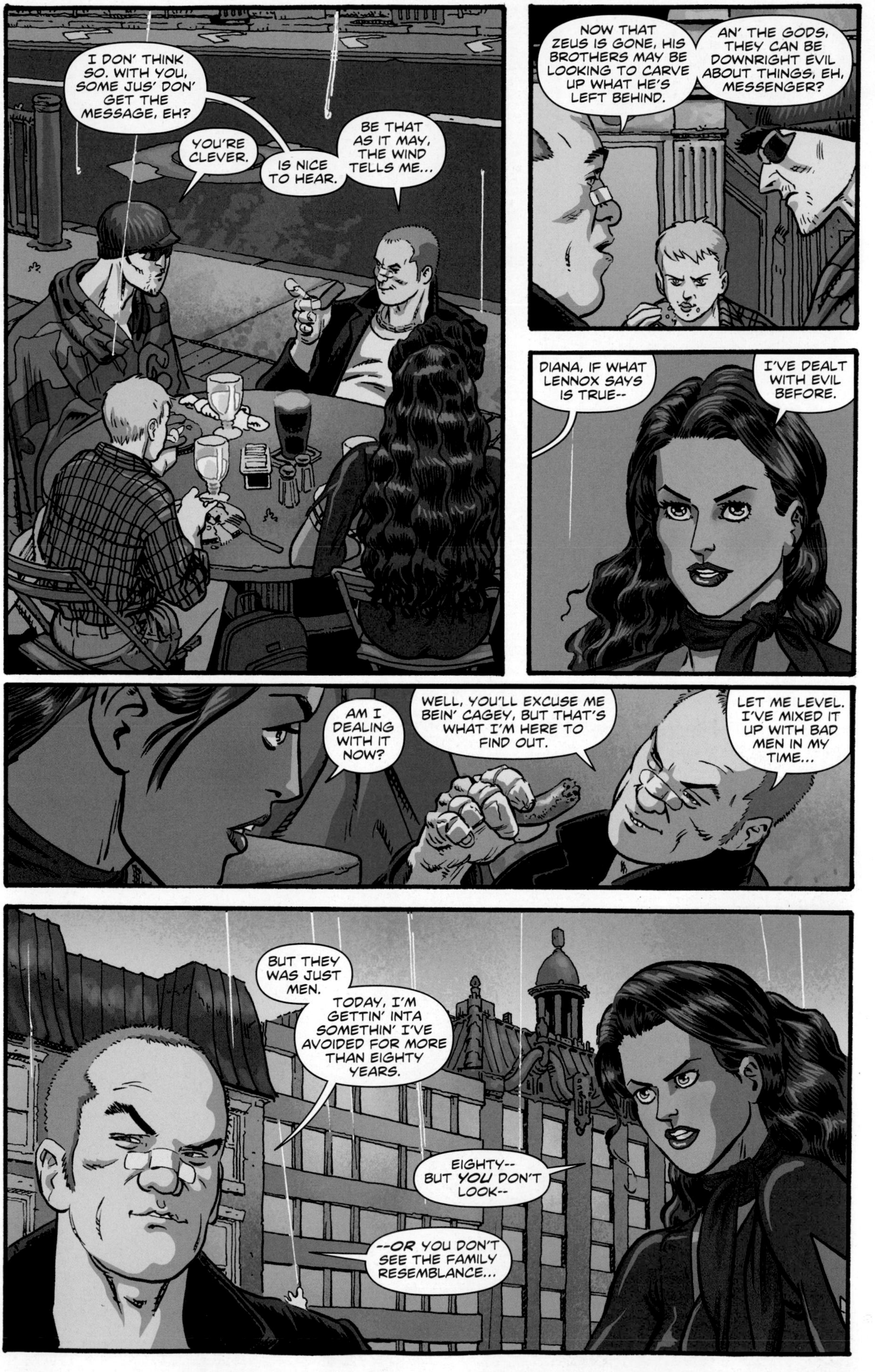
I DON' THINK SO. WITH YOU, SOME JUS' DON' GET THE MESSAGE, EH?
YOU'RE CLEVER.
IS NICE TO HEAR.
BE THAT AS IT MAY, THE WIND TELLS ME...
NOW THAT ZEUS IS GONE, HIS BROTHERS MAY BE LOOKING TO CARVE UP WHAT HE'S LEFT BEHIND.
AN' THE GODS, THEY CAN BE DOWNRIGHT EVIL ABOUT THINGS, EH, MESSENGER?
DIANA, IF WHAT LENNOX SAYS IS TRUE--
I'VE DEALT WITH EVIL BEFORE.
AM I DEALING WITH IT NOW?
WELL, YOU'LL EXCUSE ME BEIN' CAGEY, BUT THAT'S WHAT I'M HERE TO FIND OUT.
LET ME LEVEL. I'VE MIXED IT UP WITH BAD MEN IN MY TIME...
BUT THEY WAS JUST MEN.
TODAY, I'M GETTIN' INTA SOMETHIN' I'VE AVOIDED FOR MORE THAN EIGHTY YEARS.
EIGHTY-- BUT *YOU* DON'T LOOK--
--*OR* YOU DON'T SEE THE FAMILY RESEMBLANCE...

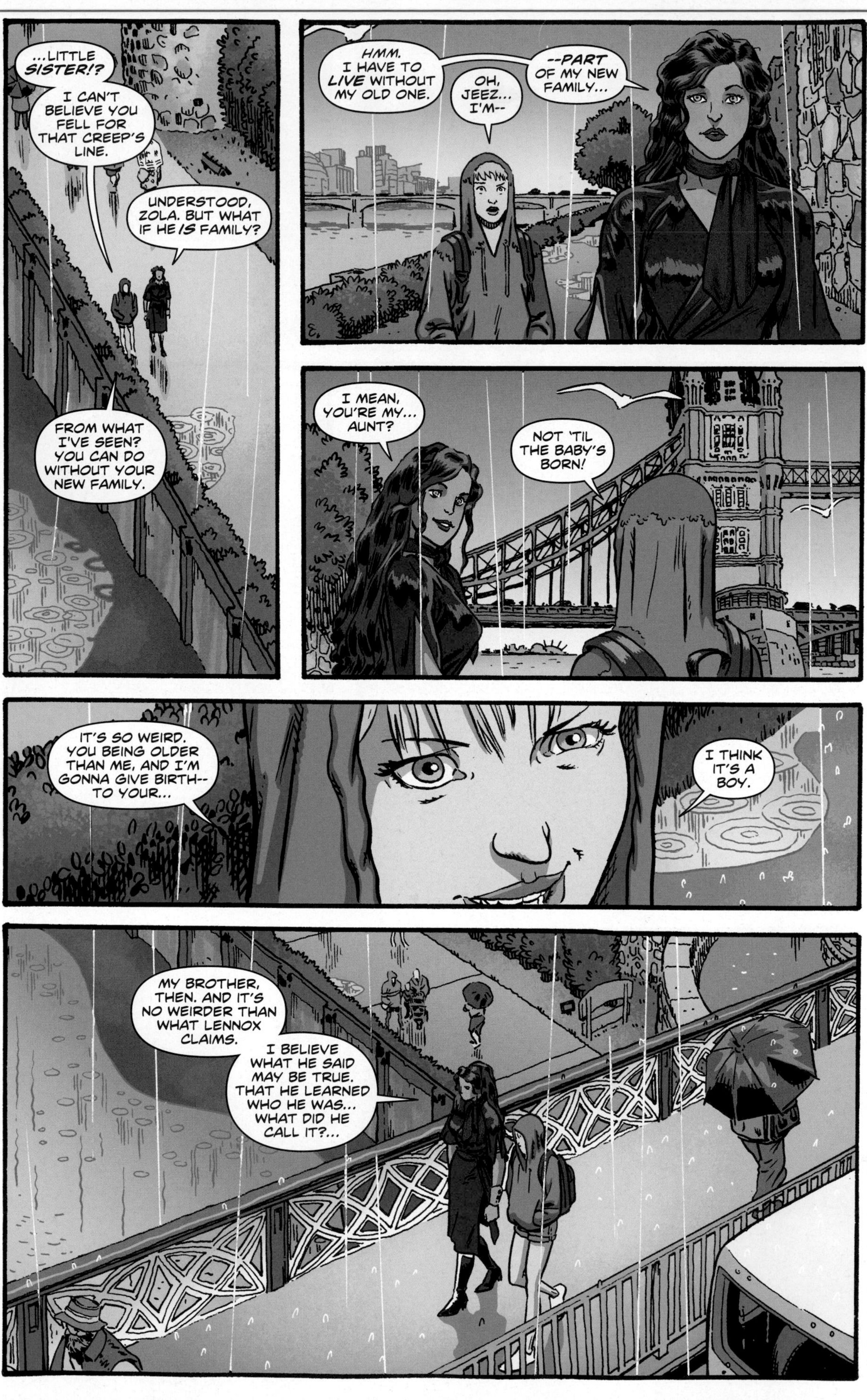
...LITTLE SISTER!?
I CAN'T BELIEVE YOU FELL FOR THAT CREEP'S LINE.
UNDERSTOOD, ZOLA. BUT WHAT IF HE IS FAMILY?
FROM WHAT I'VE SEEN? YOU CAN DO WITHOUT YOUR NEW FAMILY.
HMM. I HAVE TO LIVE WITHOUT MY OLD ONE.
OH, JEEZ... I'M--
--PART OF MY NEW FAMILY...
I MEAN, YOU'RE MY... AUNT?
NOT 'TIL THE BABY'S BORN!
IT'S SO WEIRD. YOU BEING OLDER THAN ME, AND I'M GONNA GIVE BIRTH-- TO YOUR...
I THINK IT'S A BOY.
MY BROTHER, THEN. AND IT'S NO WEIRDER THAN WHAT LENNOX CLAIMS.
I BELIEVE WHAT HE SAID MAY BE TRUE. THAT HE LEARNED WHO HE WAS... WHAT DID HE CALL IT?...

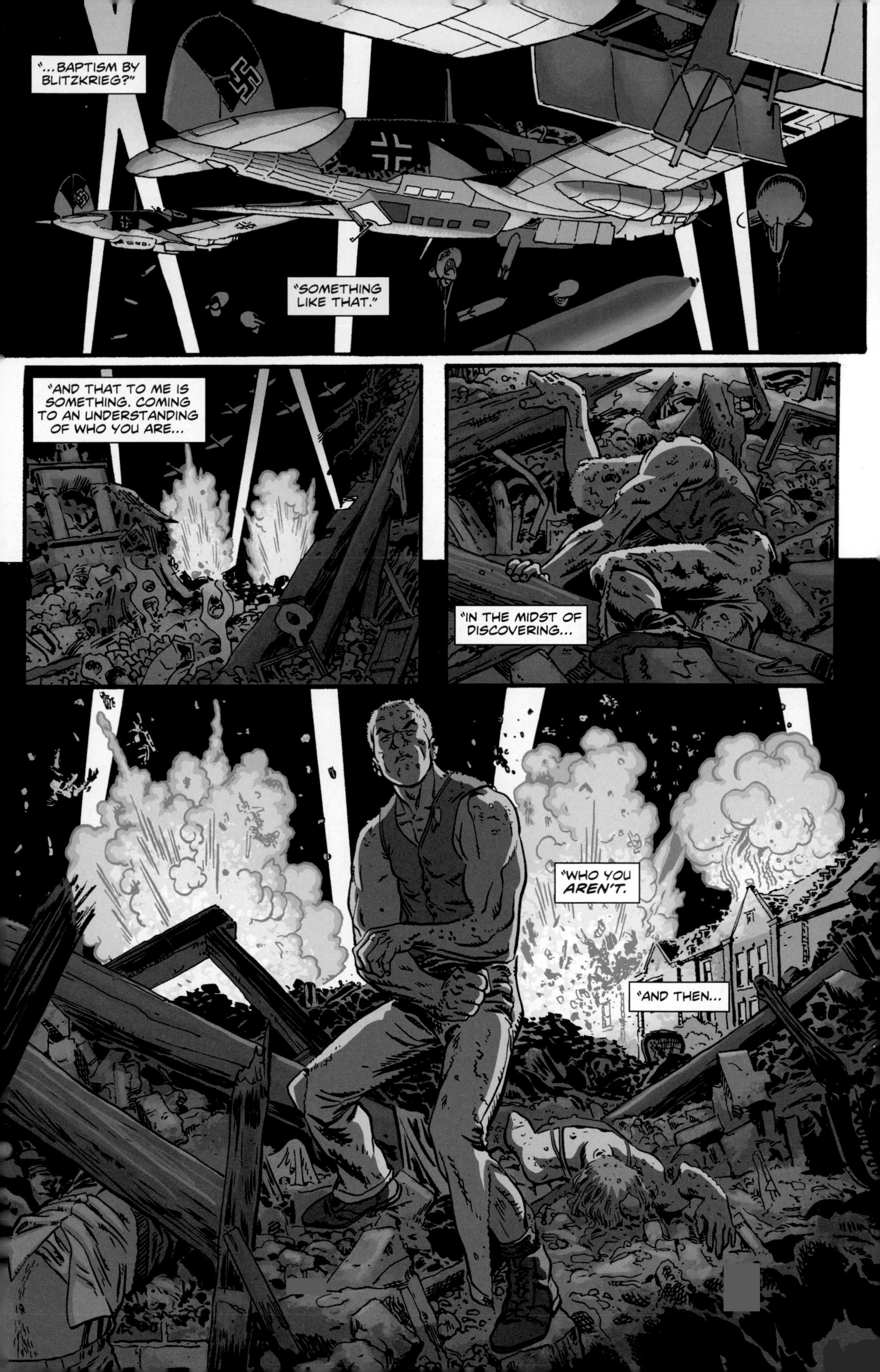
"...BAPTISM BY BLITZKRIEG?"
"SOMETHING LIKE THAT."
"AND THAT TO ME IS SOMETHING. COMING TO AN UNDERSTANDING OF WHO YOU ARE...
"IN THE MIDST OF DISCOVERING...
"WHO YOU AREN'T.
"AND THEN...

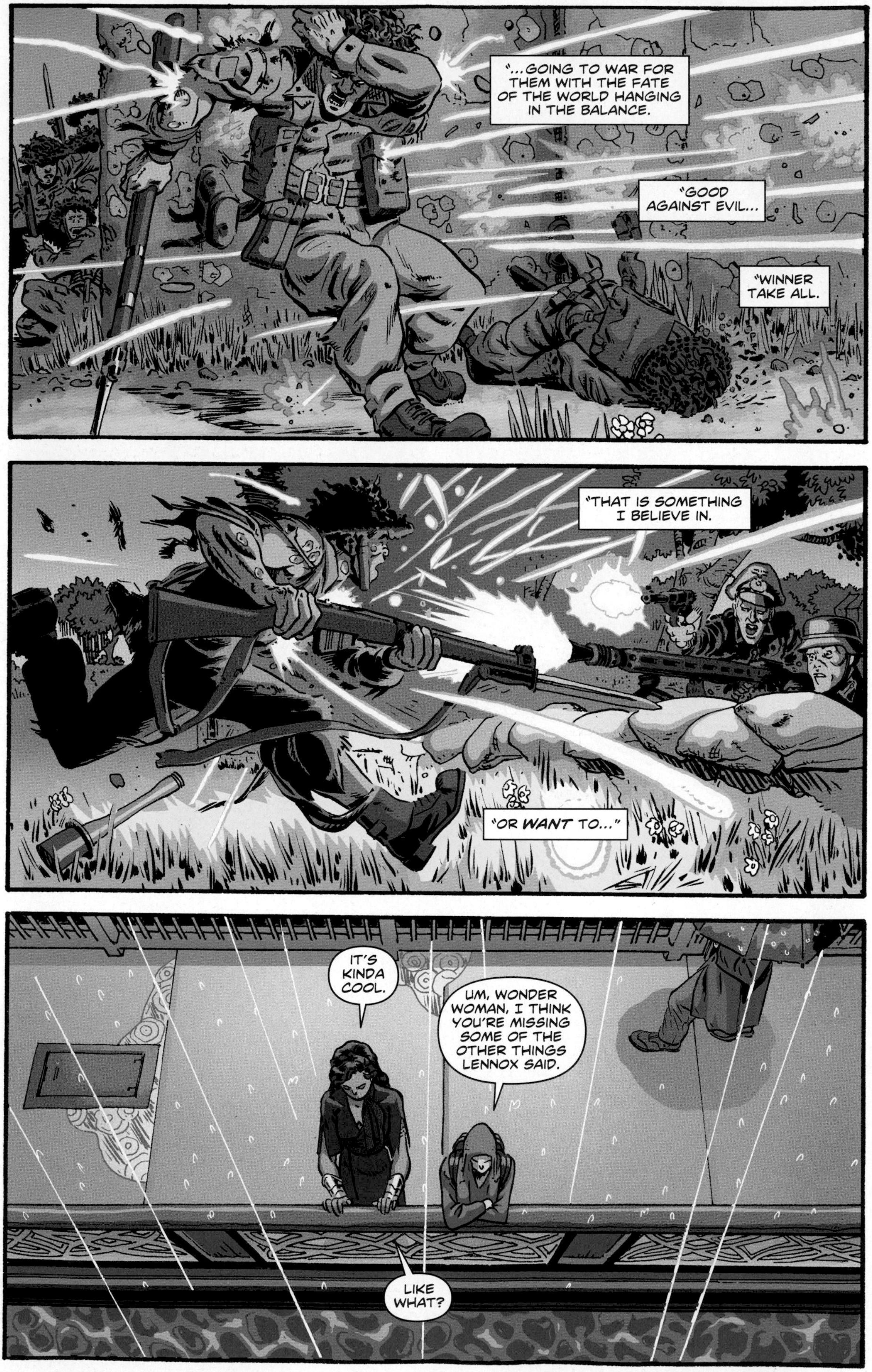
"...GOING TO WAR FOR THEM WITH THE FATE OF THE WORLD HANGING IN THE BALANCE.
"GOOD AGAINST EVIL...
"WINNER TAKE ALL.
"THAT IS SOMETHING I BELIEVE IN.
"OR *WANT* TO..."
IT'S KINDA COOL.
UM, WONDER WOMAN, I THINK YOU'RE MISSING SOME OF THE OTHER THINGS LENNOX SAID.
LIKE WHAT?

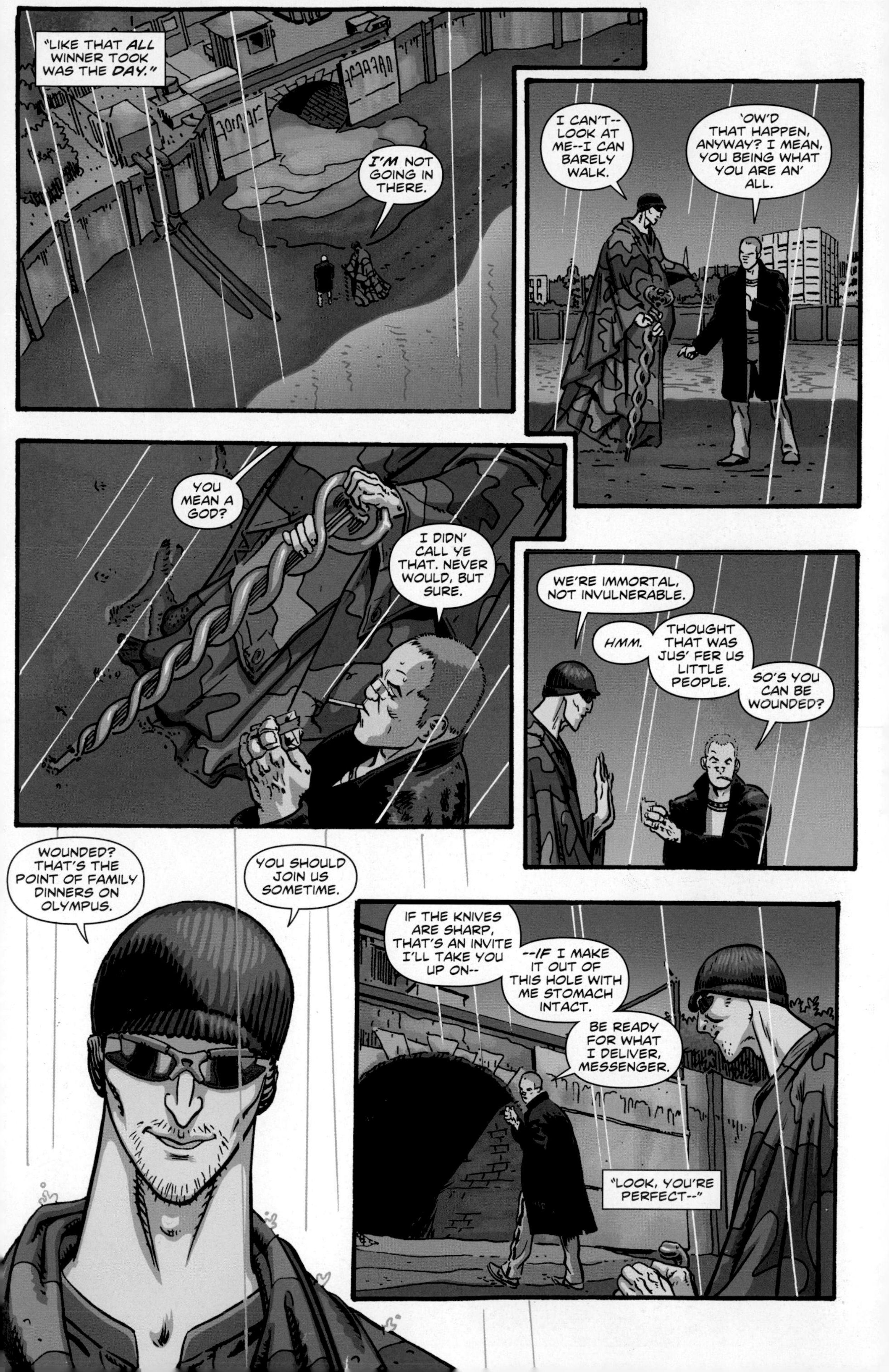
"LIKE THAT *ALL* WINNER TOOK WAS THE *DAY*."
I'M NOT GOING IN THERE.
I CAN'T-- LOOK AT ME--I CAN BARELY WALK.
'OW'D THAT HAPPEN, ANYWAY? I MEAN, YOU BEING WHAT YOU ARE AN' ALL.
YOU MEAN A GOD?
I DIDN' CALL YE THAT. NEVER WOULD, BUT SURE.
WE'RE IMMORTAL, NOT INVULNERABLE.
HMM.
THOUGHT THAT WAS JUS' FER US LITTLE PEOPLE.
SO'S YOU CAN BE WOUNDED?
WOUNDED? THAT'S THE POINT OF FAMILY DINNERS ON OLYMPUS.
YOU SHOULD JOIN US SOMETIME.
IF THE KNIVES ARE SHARP, THAT'S AN INVITE I'LL TAKE YOU UP ON--
--*IF* I MAKE IT OUT OF THIS HOLE WITH ME STOMACH INTACT.
BE READY FOR WHAT I DELIVER, MESSENGER.
"LOOK, YOU'RE PERFECT--"

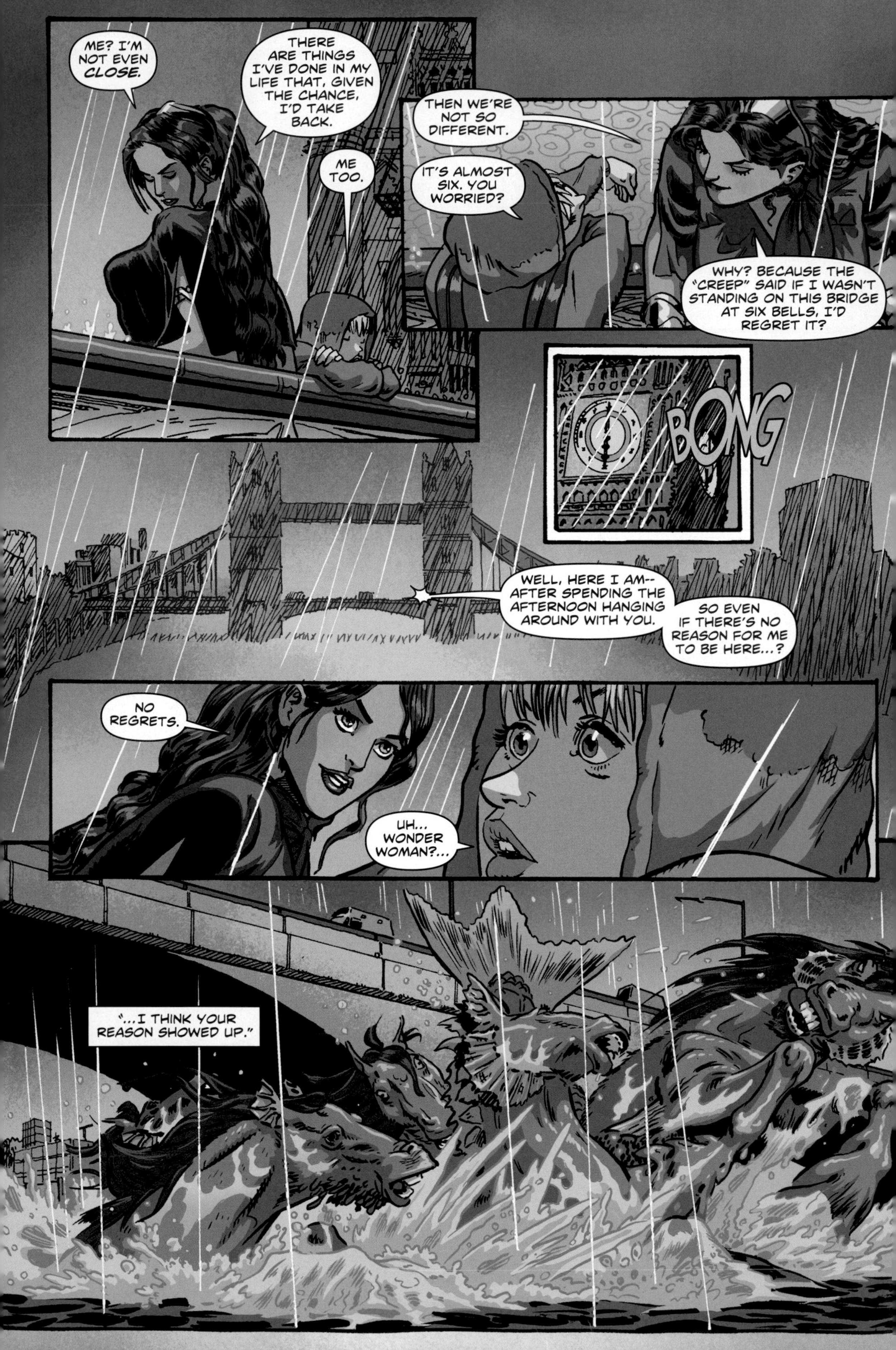
ME? I'M NOT EVEN CLOSE.
THERE ARE THINGS I'VE DONE IN MY LIFE THAT, GIVEN THE CHANCE, I'D TAKE BACK.
ME TOO.
THEN WE'RE NOT SO DIFFERENT.
IT'S ALMOST SIX. YOU WORRIED?
WHY? BECAUSE THE "CREEP" SAID IF I WASN'T STANDING ON THIS BRIDGE AT SIX BELLS, I'D REGRET IT?
BONG
WELL, HERE I AM-- AFTER SPENDING THE AFTERNOON HANGING AROUND WITH YOU.
SO EVEN IF THERE'S NO REASON FOR ME TO BE HERE...?
NO REGRETS.
UH... WONDER WOMAN?...
"...I THINK YOUR REASON SHOWED UP."

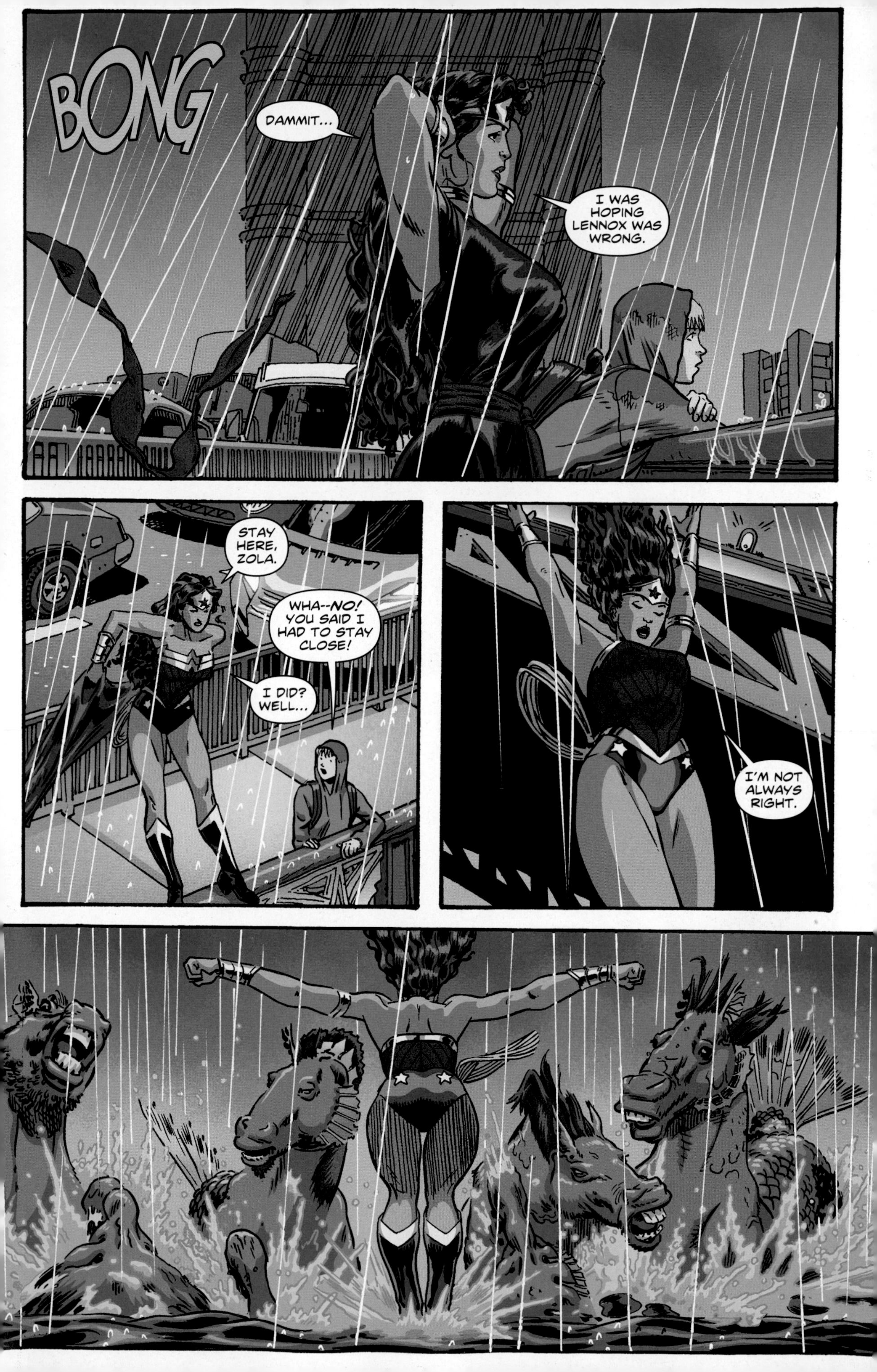
BONG
DAMMIT...
I WAS HOPING LENNOX WAS WRONG.
STAY HERE, ZOLA.
WHA--NO! YOU SAID I HAD TO STAY CLOSE!
I DID? WELL...
I'M NOT ALWAYS RIGHT.

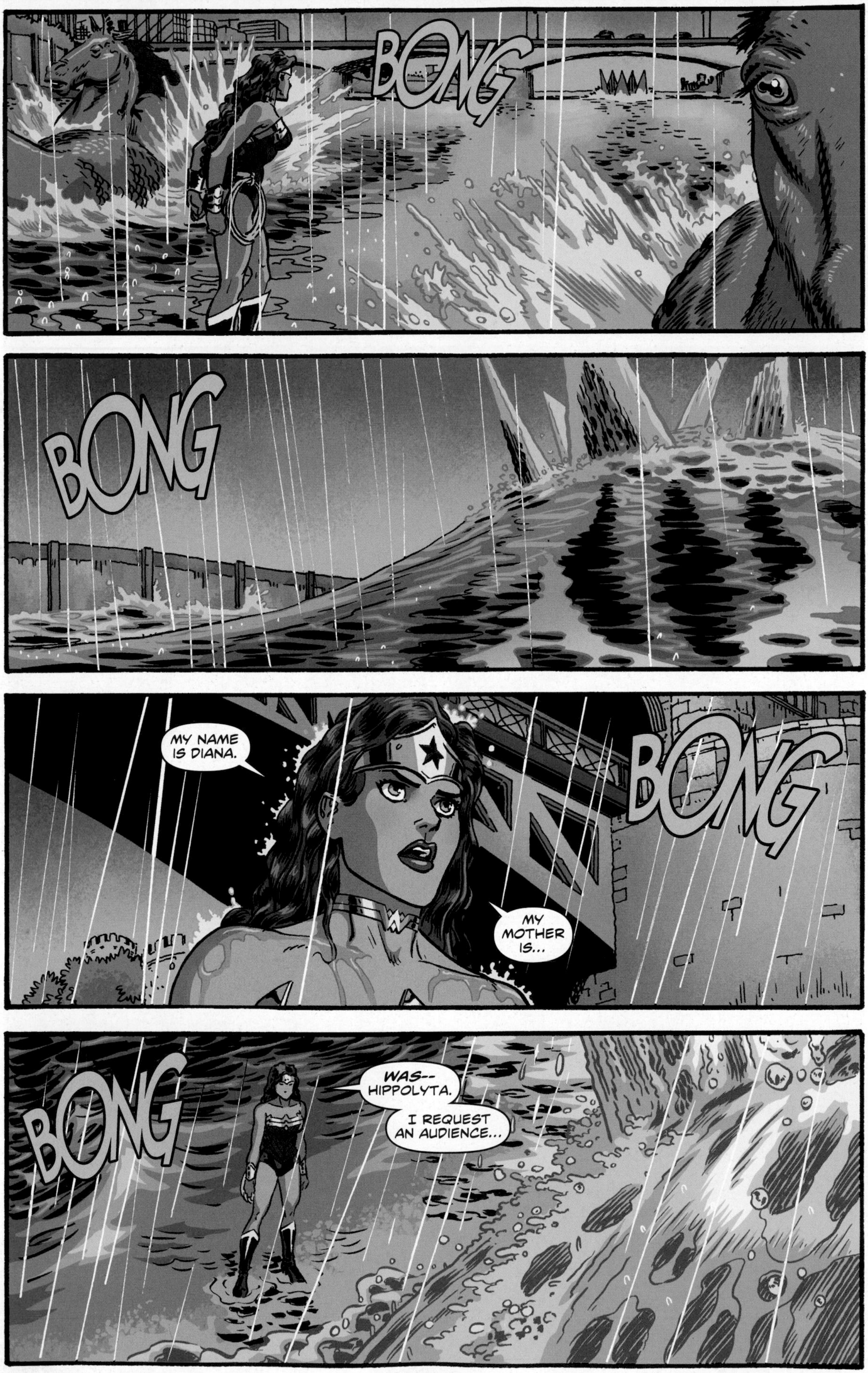
BONG
BONG
MY NAME IS DIANA.
BONG
MY MOTHER IS...
BONG
WAS-- HIPPOLYTA.
I REQUEST AN AUDIENCE...

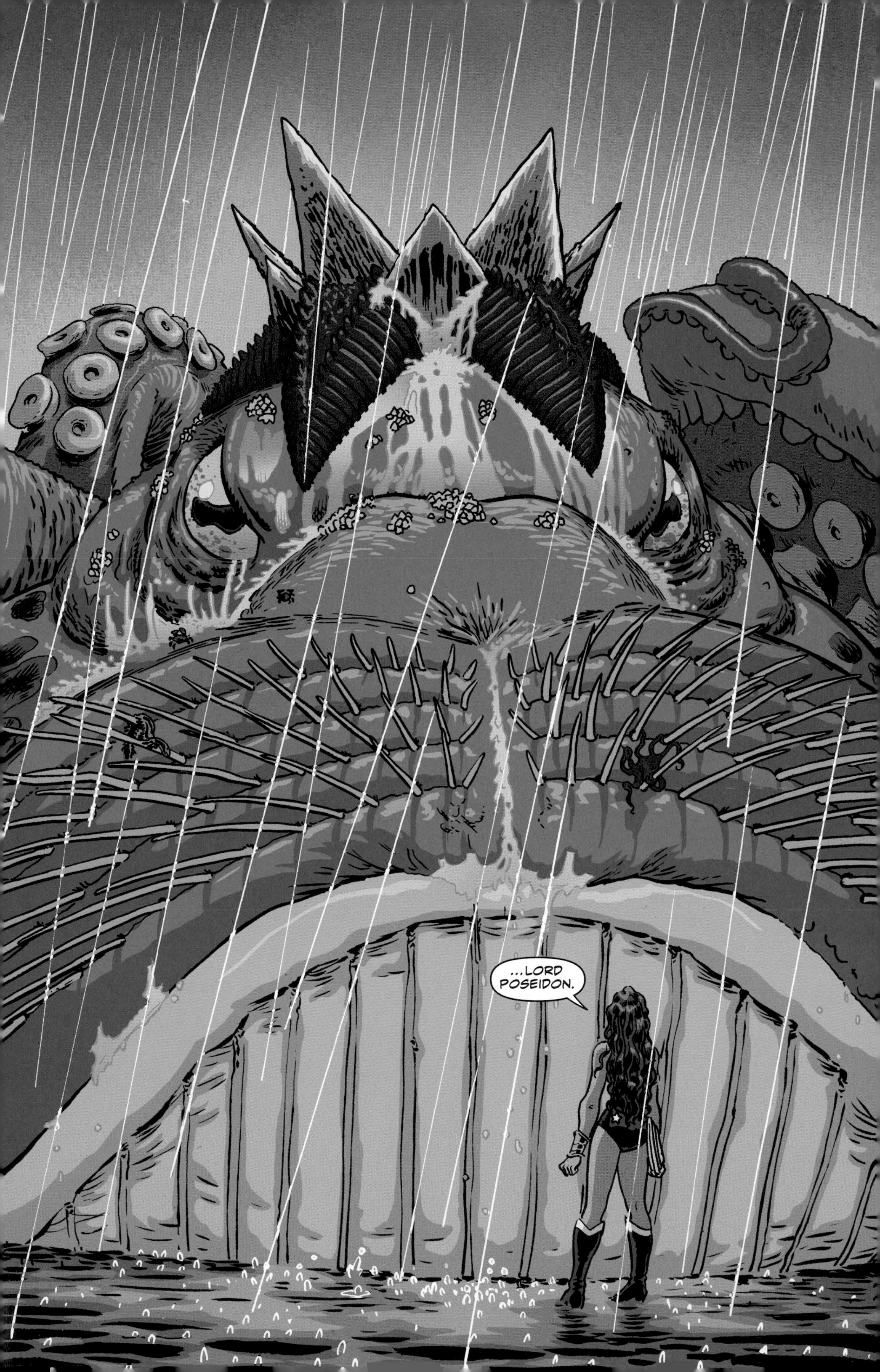
...LORD POSEIDON.

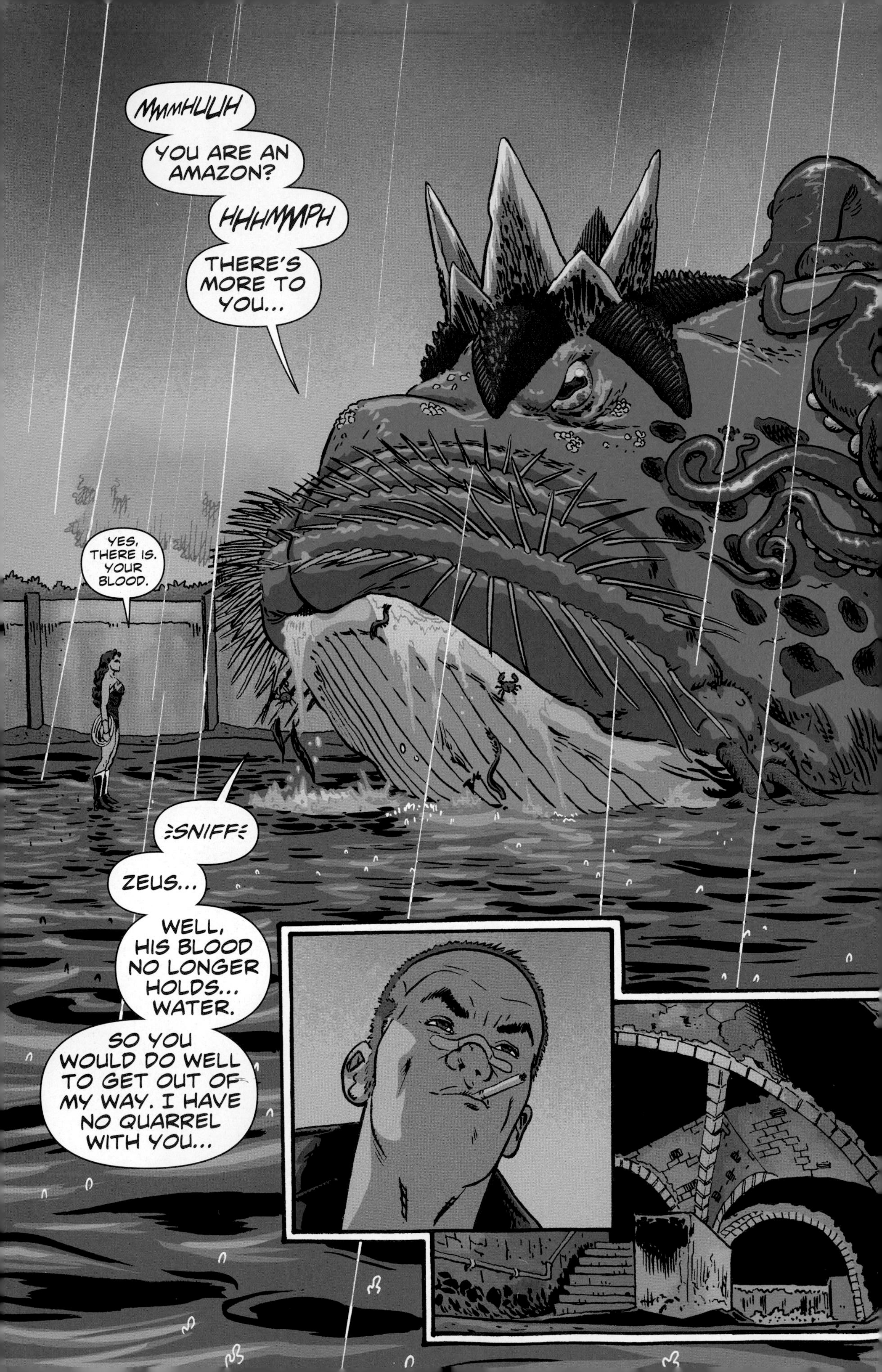
MMMHUUH
YOU ARE AN AMAZON?
HHHMMPH
THERE'S MORE TO YOU...
YES, THERE IS. YOUR BLOOD.
SNIFF
ZEUS...
WELL, HIS BLOOD NO LONGER HOLDS... WATER.
SO YOU WOULD DO WELL TO GET OUT OF MY WAY. I HAVE NO QUARREL WITH YOU...

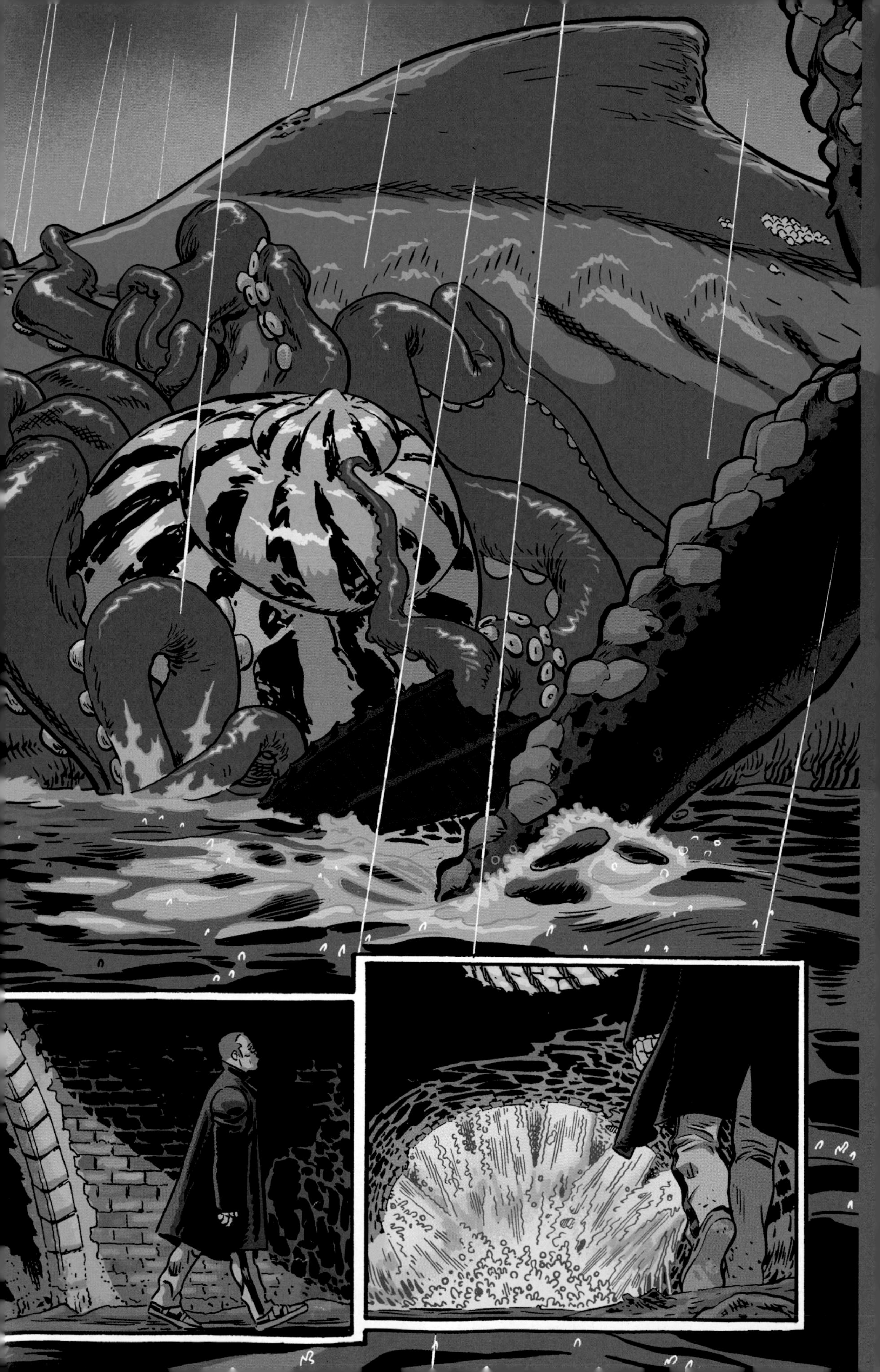

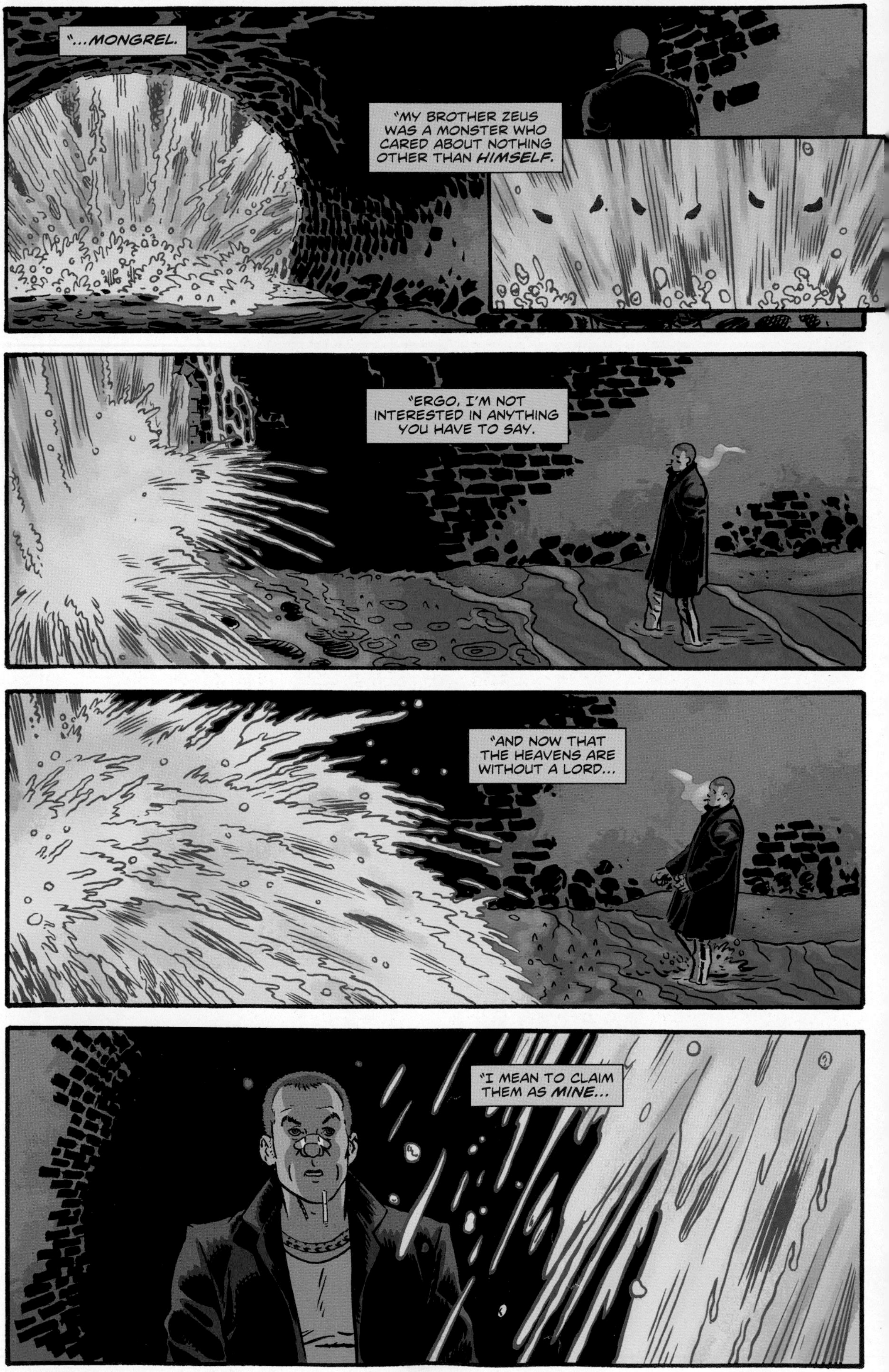
"...MONGREL.
"MY BROTHER ZEUS WAS A MONSTER WHO CARED ABOUT NOTHING OTHER THAN HIMSELF.
"ERGO, I'M NOT INTERESTED IN ANYTHING YOU HAVE TO SAY.
"AND NOW THAT THE HEAVENS ARE WITHOUT A LORD...
"I MEAN TO CLAIM THEM AS MINE...

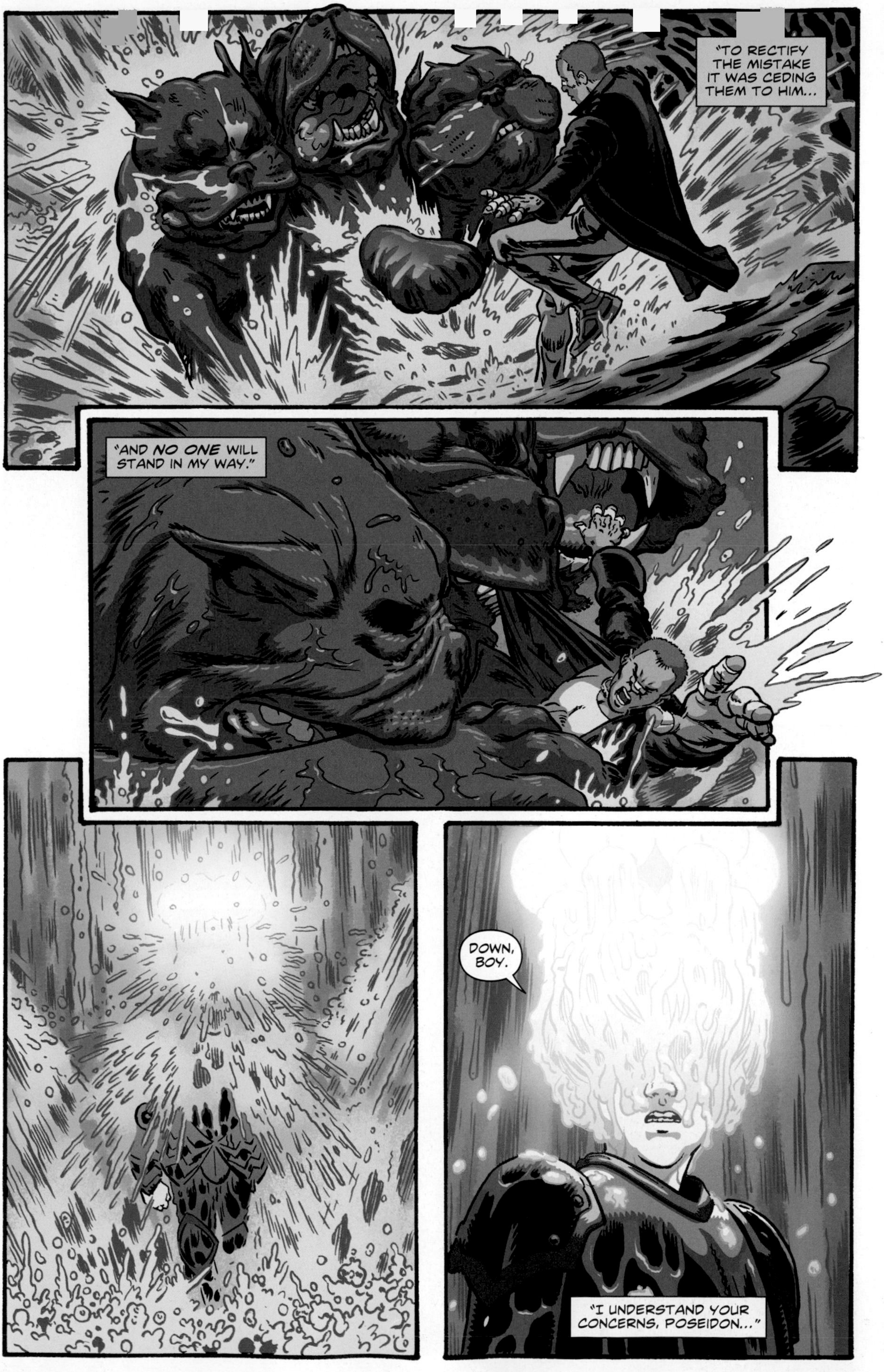
"TO RECTIFY THE MISTAKE IT WAS CEDING THEM TO HIM...
"AND NO ONE WILL STAND IN MY WAY."
DOWN, BOY.
"I UNDERSTAND YOUR CONCERNS, POSEIDON..."

...BUT I AM AFRAID *HERA* CLAIMS THE HEAVENS AS *HERS.*

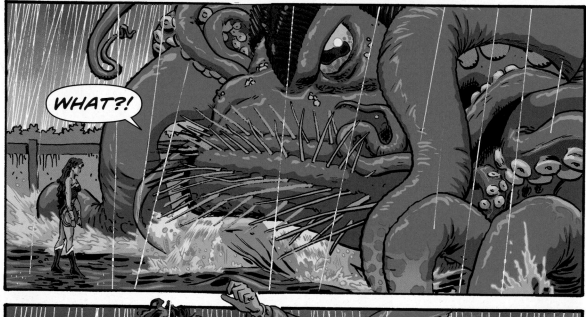

WHAT?!

SHE DARES?!?

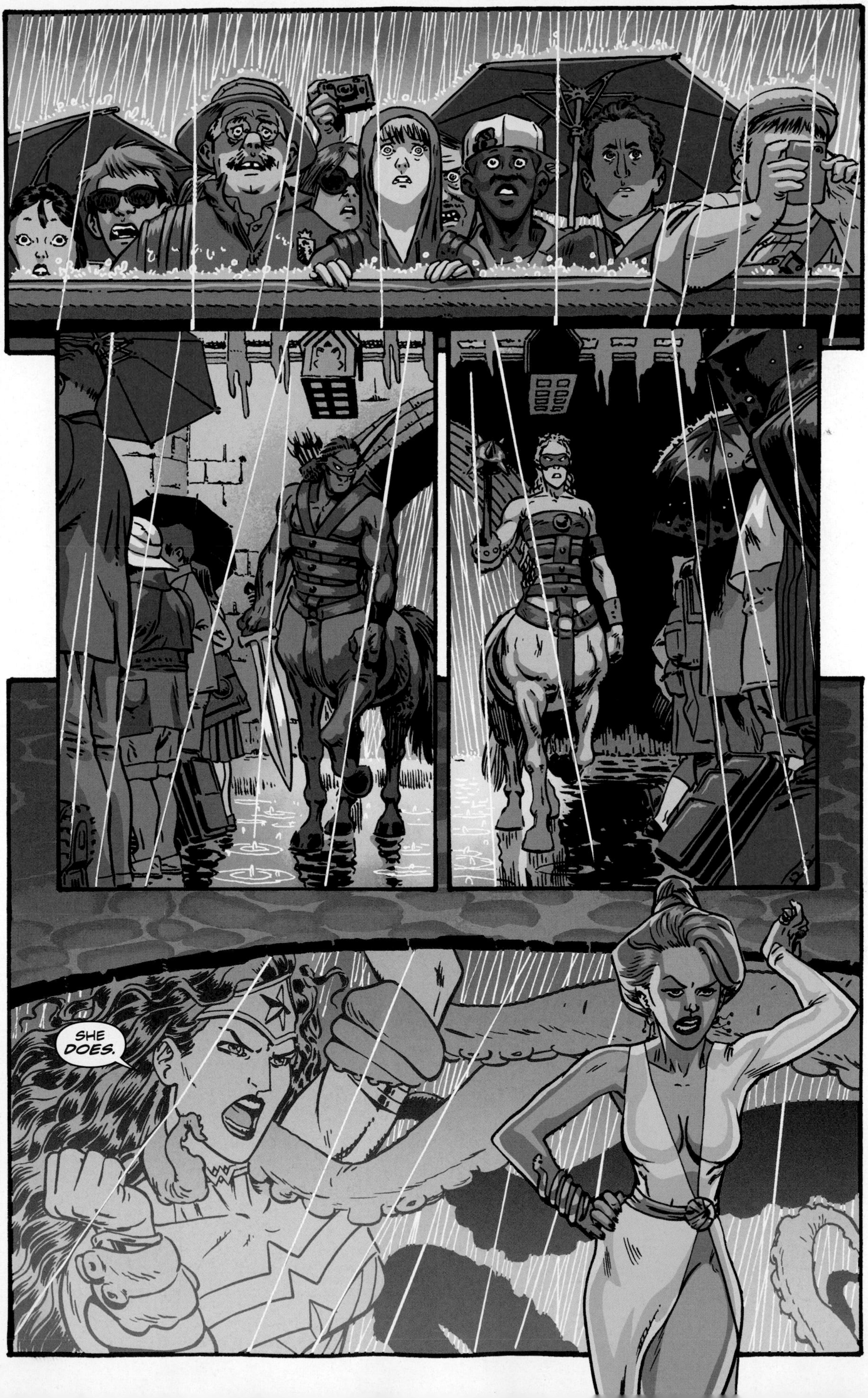
SHE DOES.

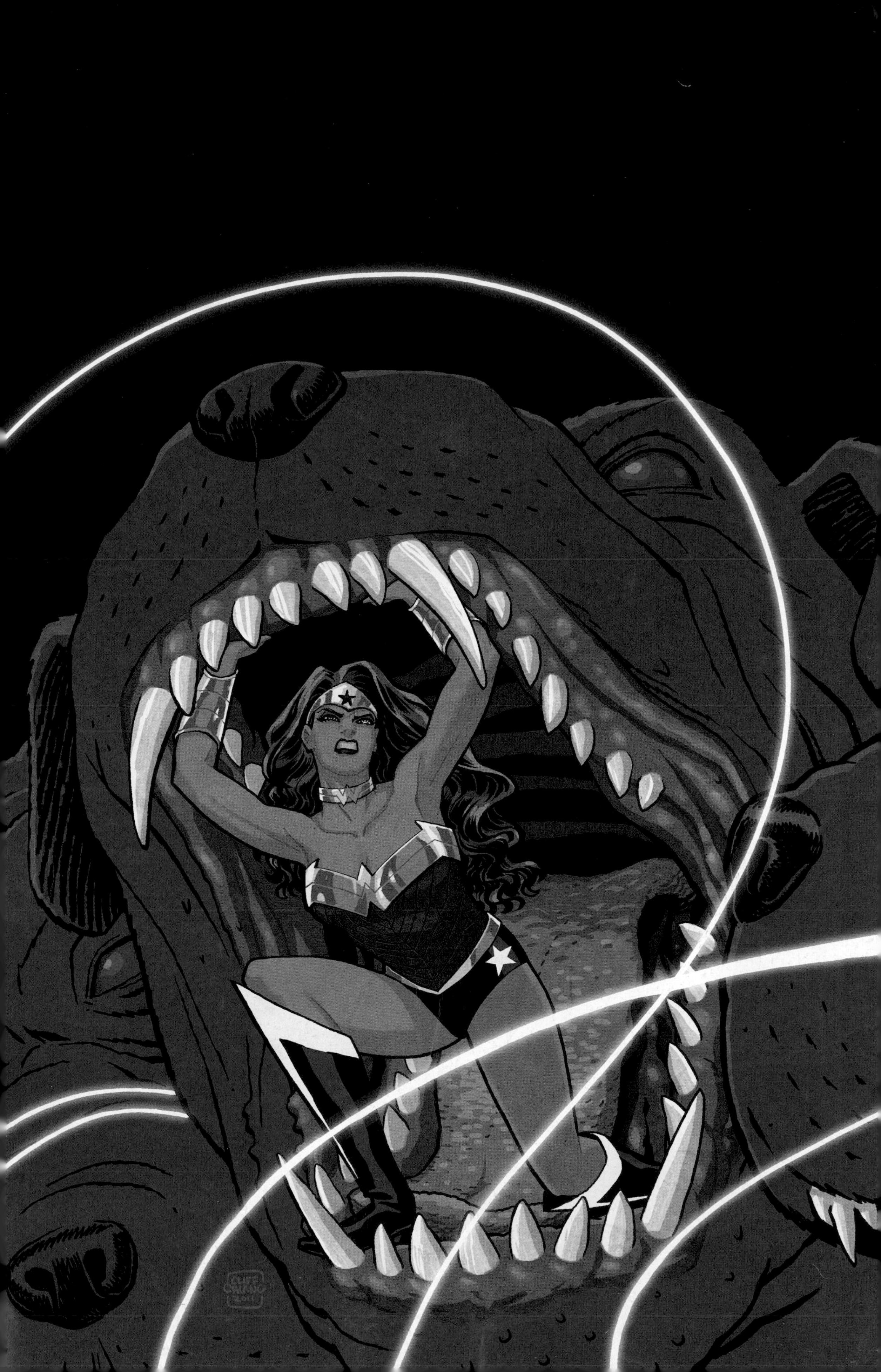

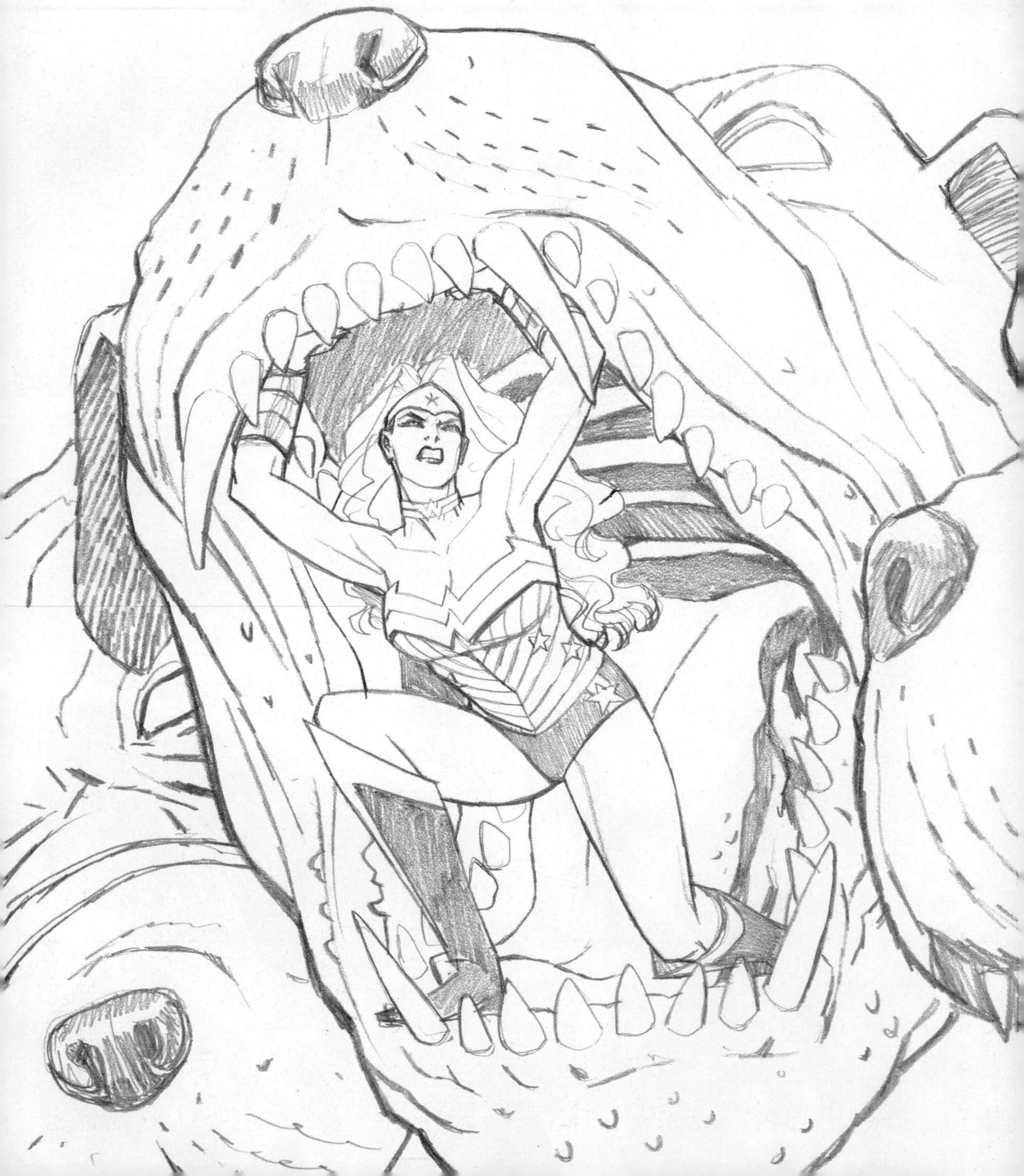

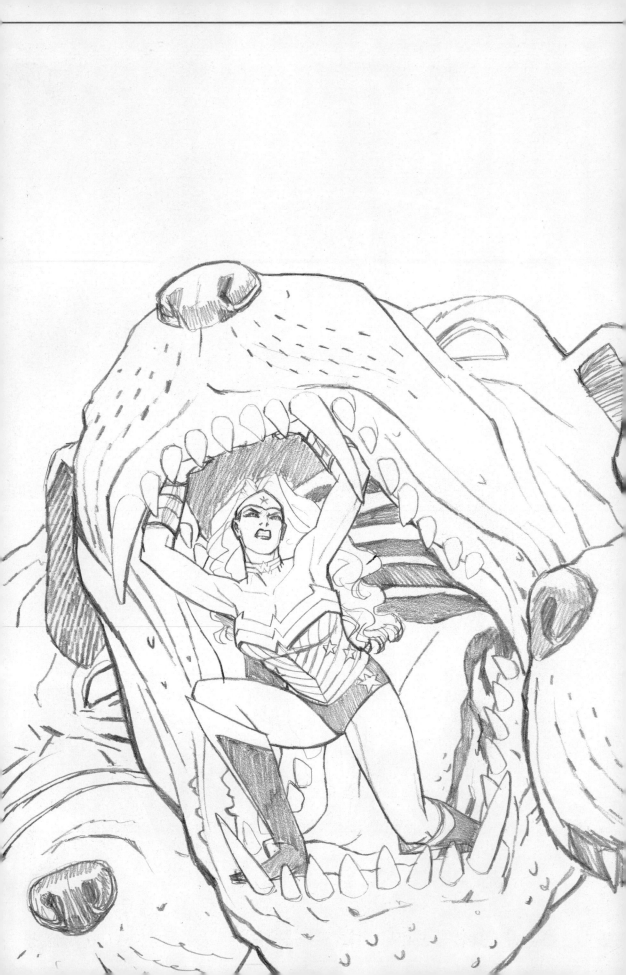

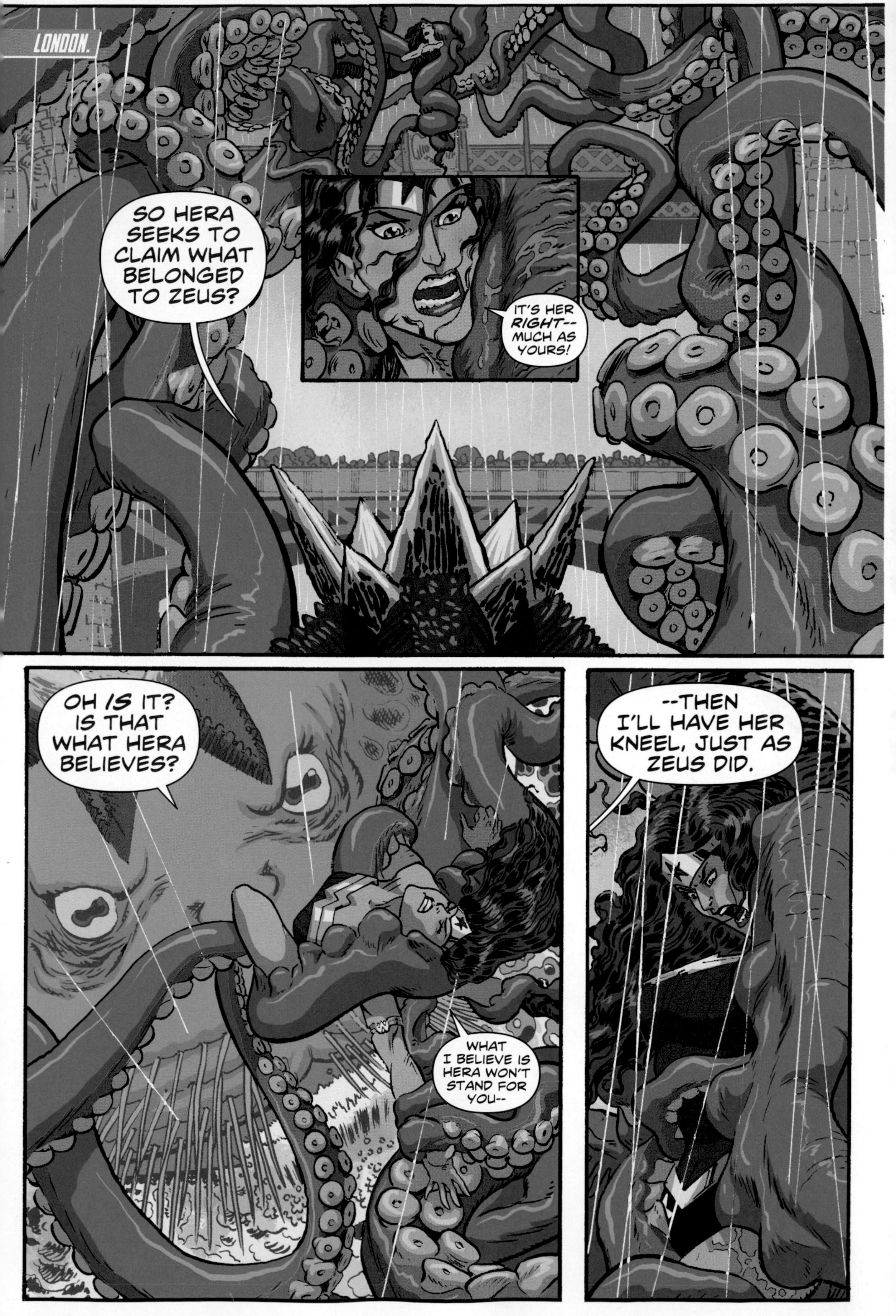
LONDON.
SO HERA SEEKS TO CLAIM WHAT BELONGED TO ZEUS?
IT'S HER RIGHT-- MUCH AS YOURS!
OH IS IT? IS THAT WHAT HERA BELIEVES?
WHAT I BELIEVE IS HERA WON'T STAND FOR YOU--
--THEN I'LL HAVE HER KNEEL, JUST AS ZEUS DID.

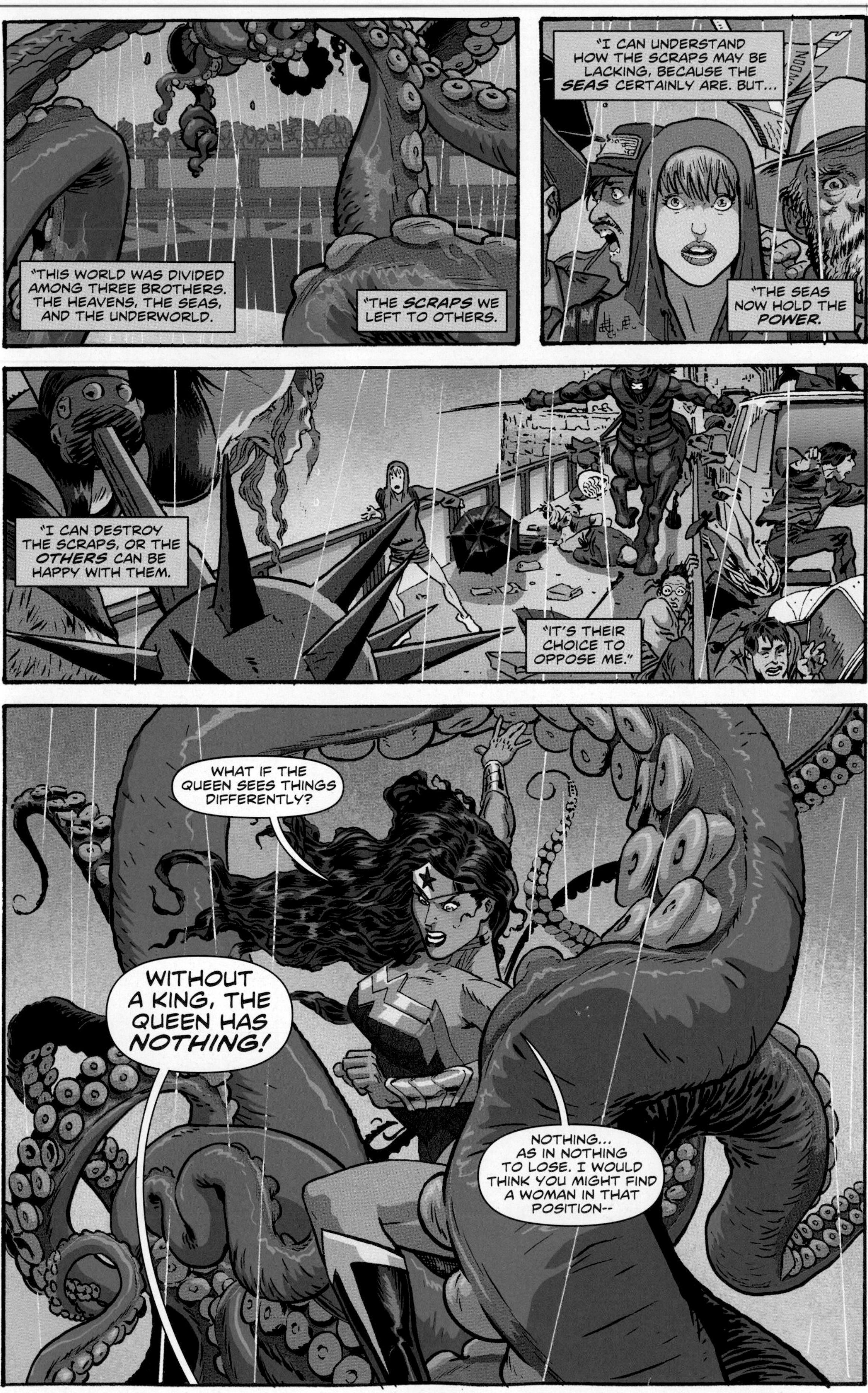
"THIS WORLD WAS DIVIDED AMONG THREE BROTHERS. THE HEAVENS, THE SEAS, AND THE UNDERWORLD.
"THE *SCRAPS* WE LEFT TO OTHERS.
"I CAN UNDERSTAND HOW THE SCRAPS MAY BE LACKING, BECAUSE THE *SEAS* CERTAINLY ARE. BUT...
"THE SEAS NOW HOLD THE *POWER*.
"I CAN DESTROY THE SCRAPS, OR THE *OTHERS* CAN BE HAPPY WITH THEM.
"IT'S THEIR CHOICE TO OPPOSE ME."
WHAT IF THE QUEEN SEES THINGS DIFFERENTLY?
WITHOUT A KING, THE QUEEN HAS *NOTHING!*
NOTHING... AS IN NOTHING TO LOSE. I WOULD THINK YOU MIGHT FIND A WOMAN IN THAT POSITION--

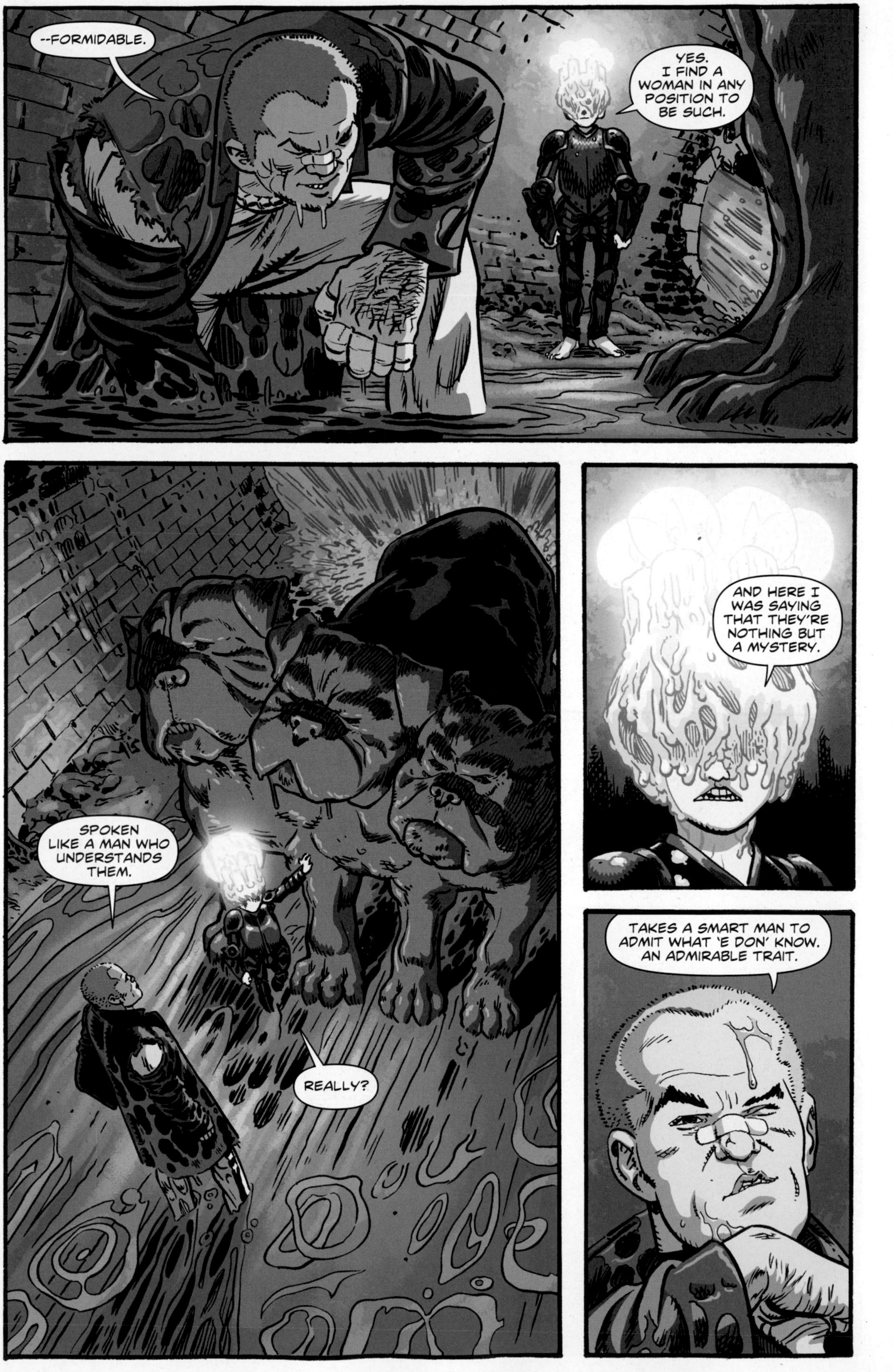
--FORMIDABLE.
YES. I FIND A WOMAN IN ANY POSITION TO BE SUCH.
SPOKEN LIKE A MAN WHO UNDERSTANDS THEM.
REALLY?
AND HERE I WAS SAYING THAT THEY'RE NOTHING BUT A MYSTERY.
TAKES A SMART MAN TO ADMIT WHAT 'E DON' KNOW. AN ADMIRABLE TRAIT.

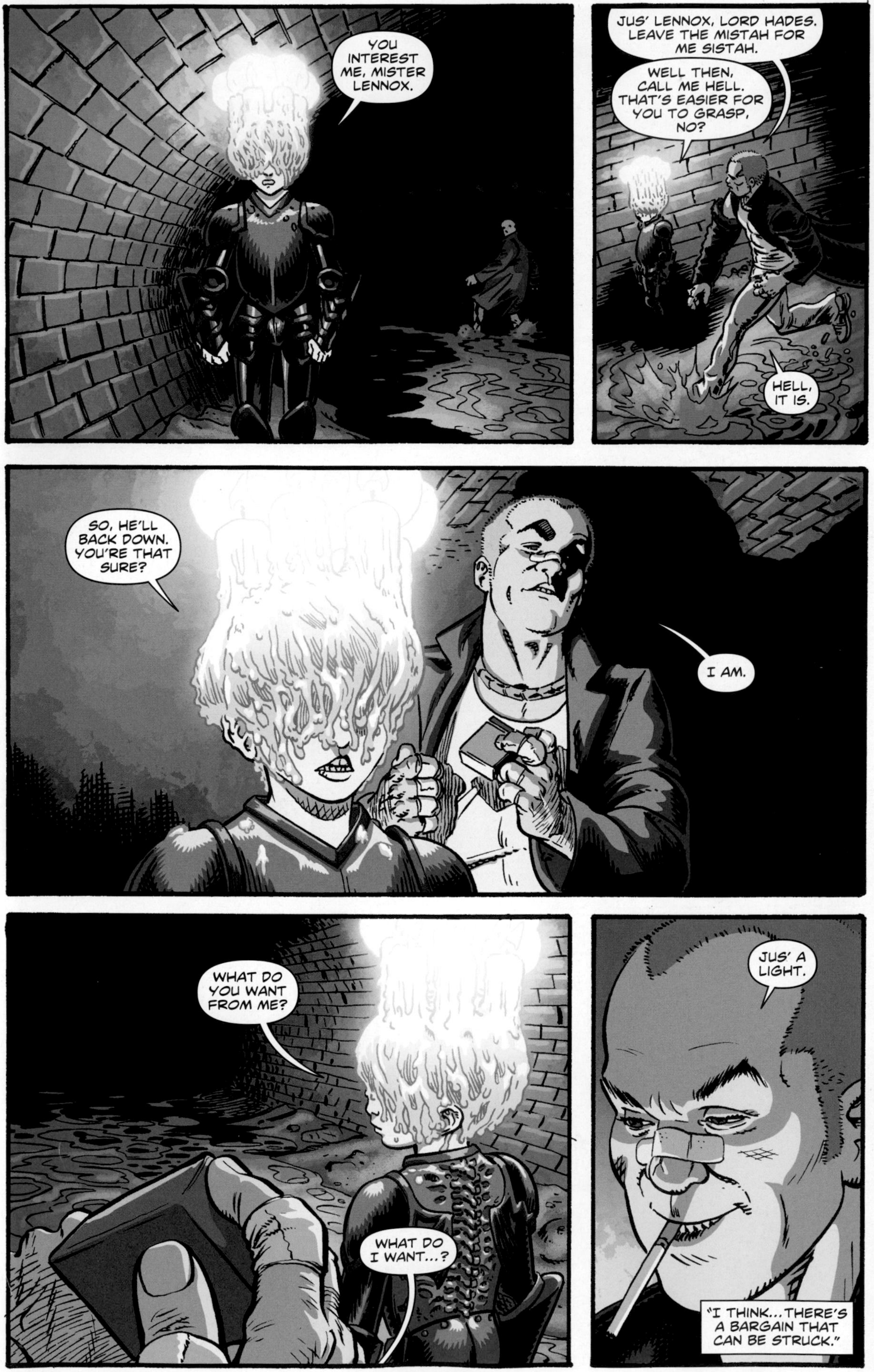
YOU INTEREST ME, MISTER LENNOX.
JUS' LENNOX, LORD HADES. LEAVE THE MISTAH FOR ME SISTAH.
WELL THEN, CALL ME HELL. THAT'S EASIER FOR YOU TO GRASP, NO?
HELL, IT IS.
SO, HE'LL BACK DOWN. YOU'RE THAT SURE?
I AM.
WHAT DO YOU WANT FROM ME?
WHAT DO I WANT...?
JUS' A LIGHT.
"I THINK... THERE'S A BARGAIN THAT CAN BE STRUCK."

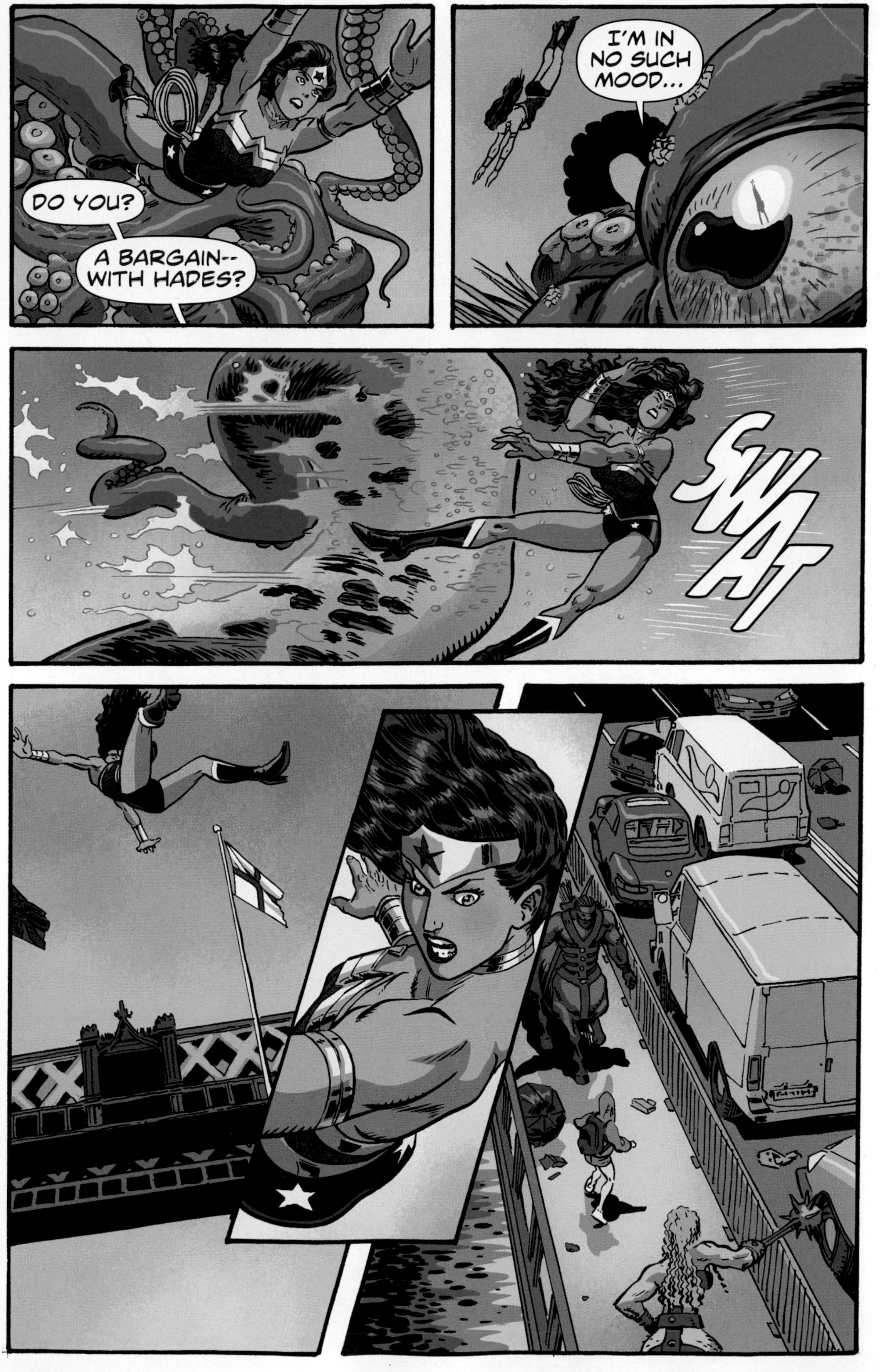
DO YOU?
A BARGAIN-- WITH HADES?
I'M IN NO SUCH MOOD...
SWAT

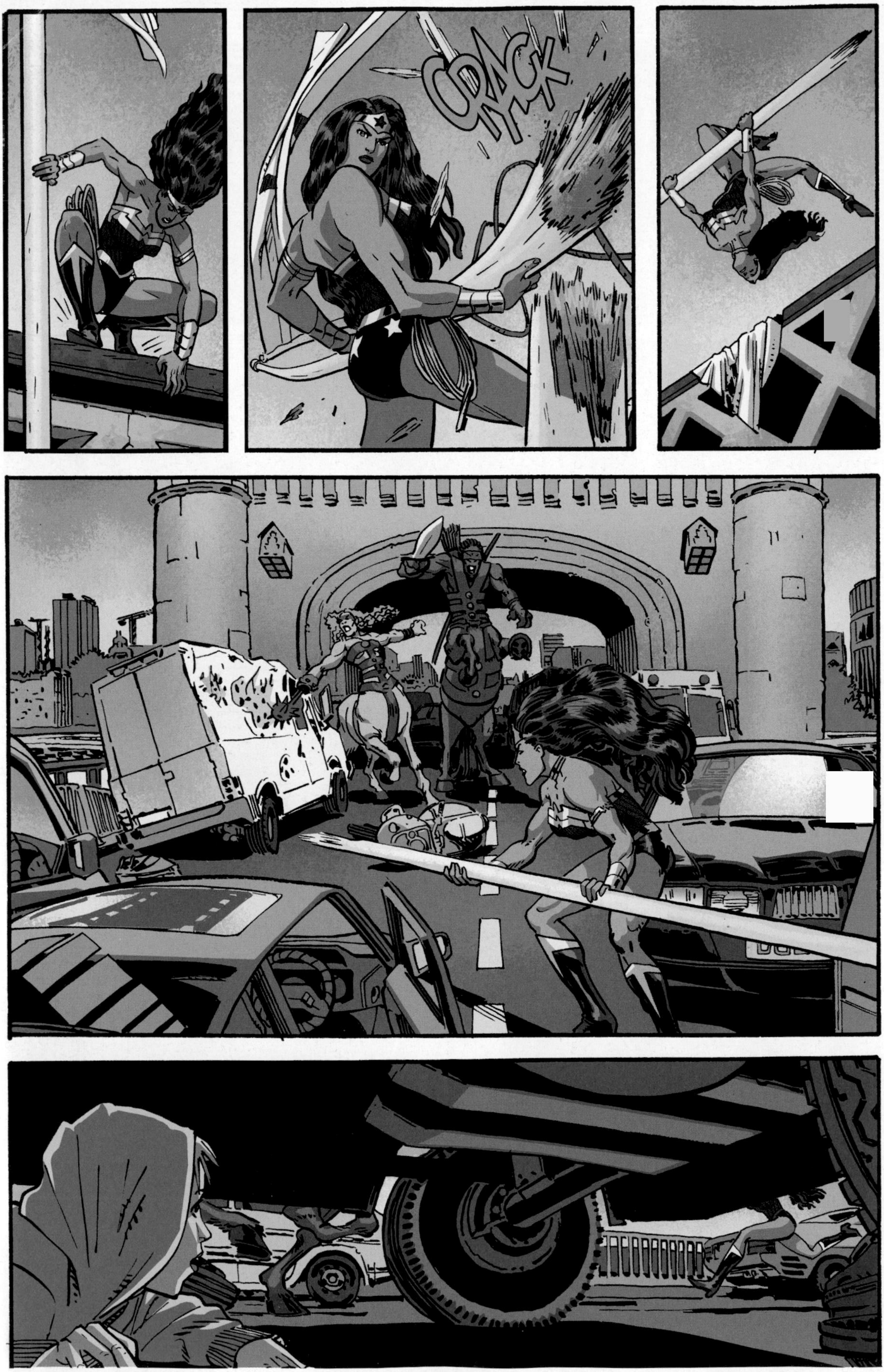
CRACK

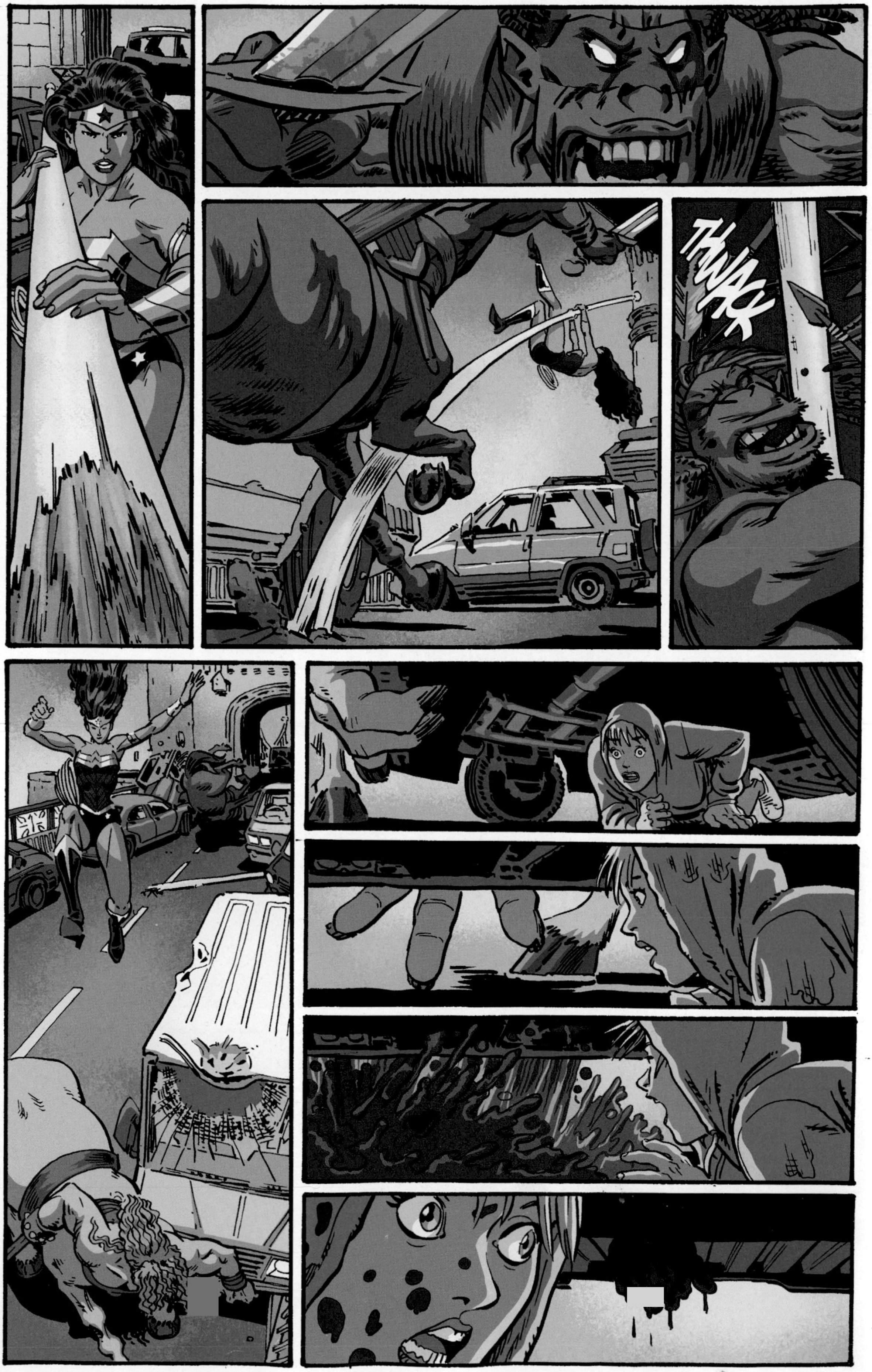
THWACK

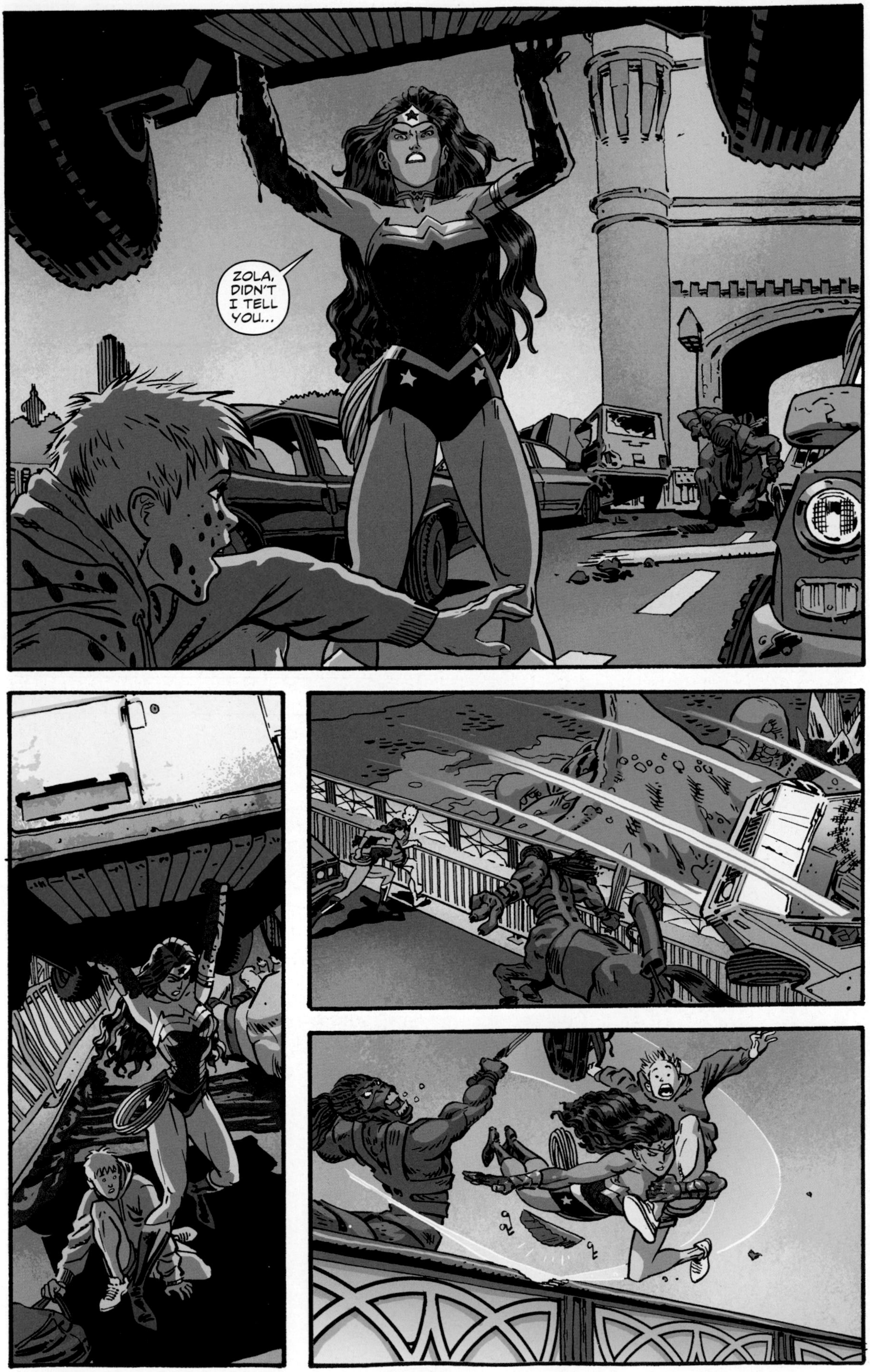
ZOLA, DIDN'T I TELL YOU...

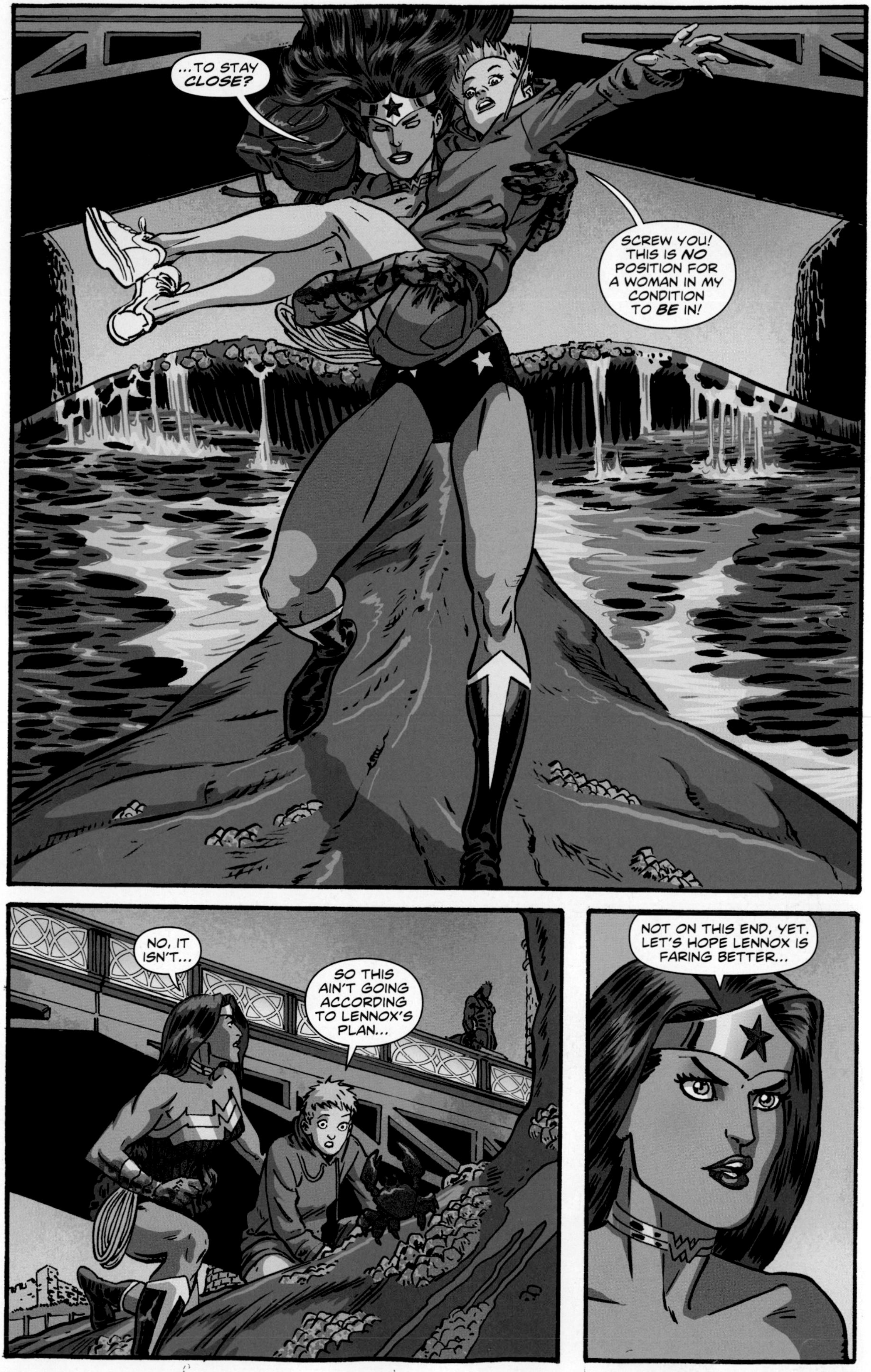
...TO STAY CLOSE?
SCREW YOU! THIS IS NO POSITION FOR A WOMAN IN MY CONDITION TO BE IN!
NO, IT ISN'T...
SO THIS AIN'T GOING ACCORDING TO LENNOX'S PLAN...
NOT ON THIS END, YET. LET'S HOPE LENNOX IS FARING BETTER...

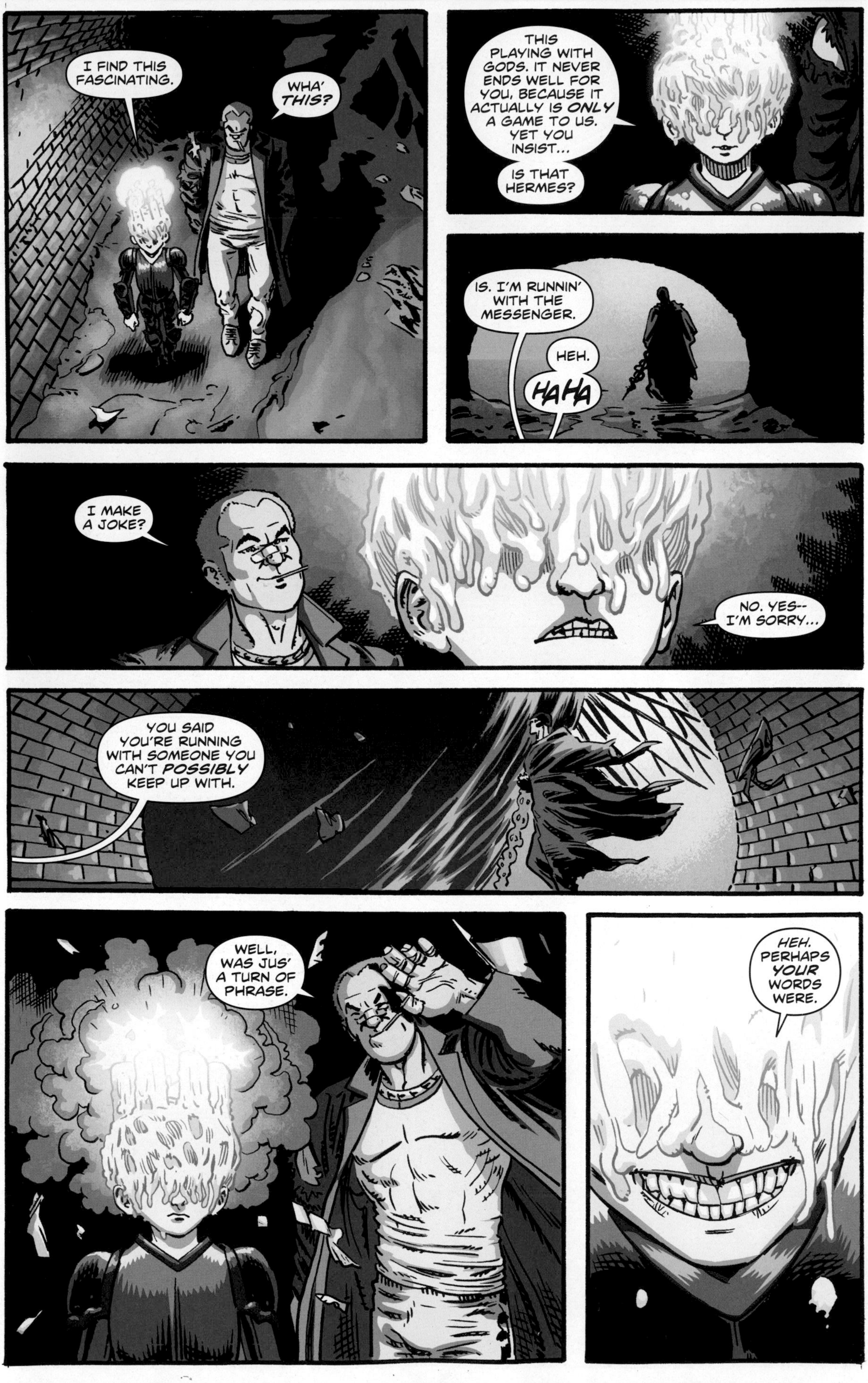
I FIND THIS FASCINATING.
WHA' THIS?
THIS PLAYING WITH GODS. IT NEVER ENDS WELL FOR YOU, BECAUSE IT ACTUALLY IS ONLY A GAME TO US. YET YOU INSIST...
IS THAT HERMES?
IS. I'M RUNNIN' WITH THE MESSENGER.
HEH.
HA HA
I MAKE A JOKE?
NO. YES-- I'M SORRY...
YOU SAID YOU'RE RUNNING WITH SOMEONE YOU CAN'T POSSIBLY KEEP UP WITH.
WELL, WAS JUS' A TURN OF PHRASE.
HEH. PERHAPS YOUR WORDS WERE.

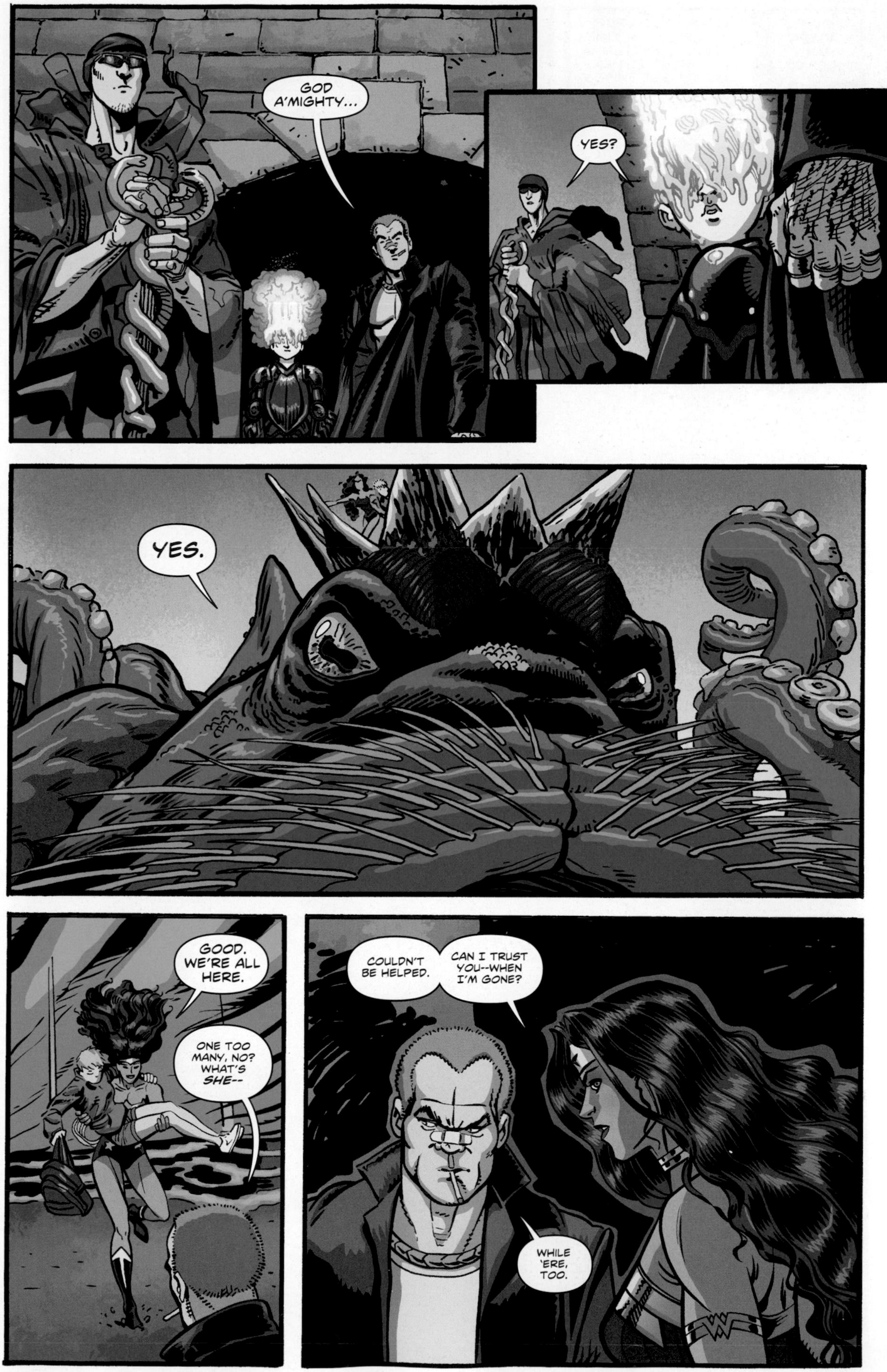
GOD A'MIGHTY...
YES?
YES.
GOOD. WE'RE ALL HERE.
ONE TOO MANY, NO? WHAT'S SHE--
COULDN'T BE HELPED.
CAN I TRUST YOU--WHEN I'M GONE?
WHILE 'ERE, TOO.

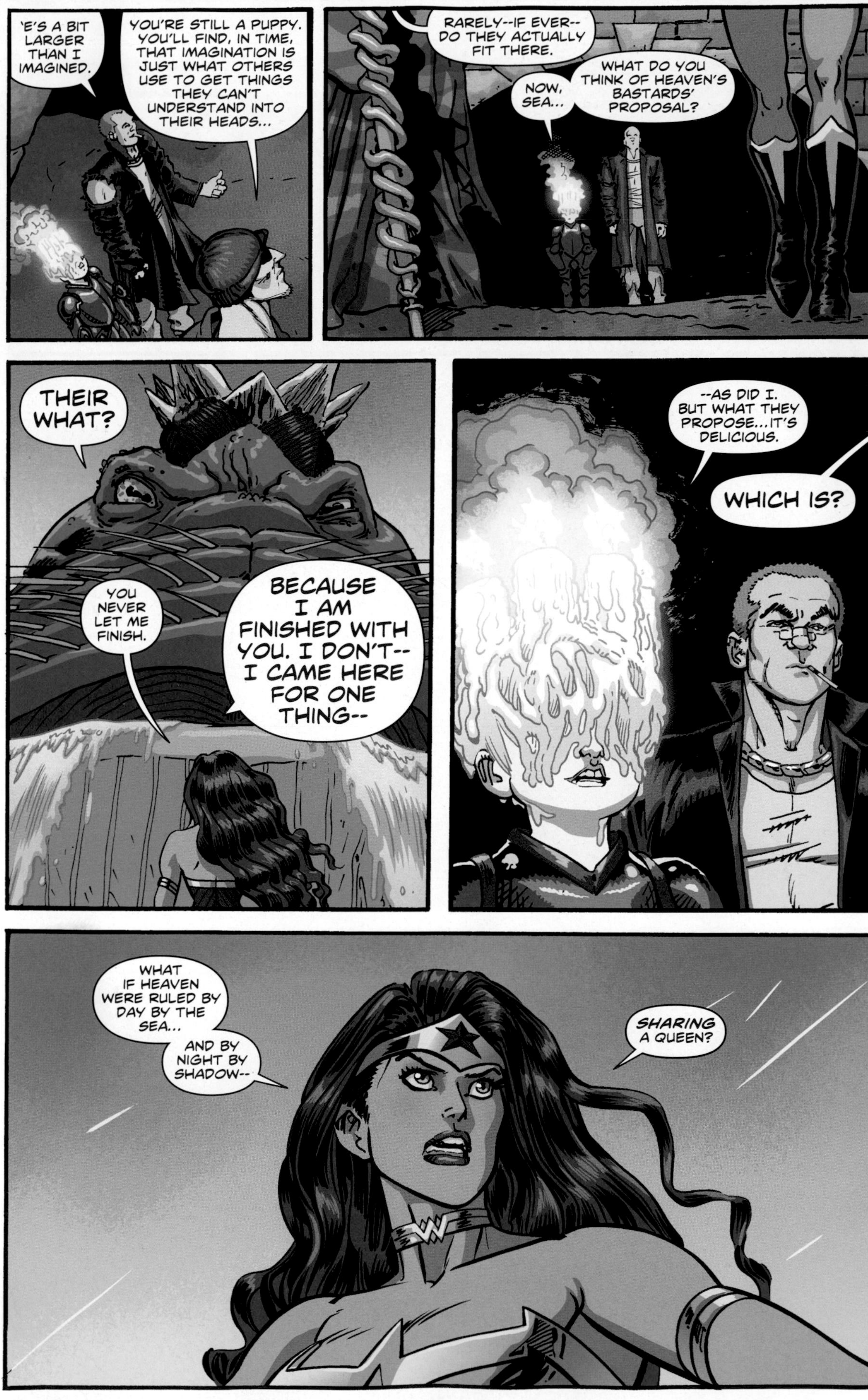
'E'S A BIT LARGER THAN I IMAGINED.
YOU'RE STILL A PUPPY. YOU'LL FIND, IN TIME, THAT IMAGINATION IS JUST WHAT OTHERS USE TO GET THINGS THEY CAN'T UNDERSTAND INTO THEIR HEADS...
RARELY--IF EVER--DO THEY ACTUALLY FIT THERE.
NOW, SEA...
WHAT DO YOU THINK OF HEAVEN'S BASTARDS' PROPOSAL?
THEIR WHAT?
YOU NEVER LET ME FINISH.
BECAUSE I AM FINISHED WITH YOU. I DON'T--I CAME HERE FOR ONE THING--
--AS DID I. BUT WHAT THEY PROPOSE...IT'S DELICIOUS.
WHICH IS?
WHAT IF HEAVEN WERE RULED BY DAY BY THE SEA...
AND BY NIGHT BY SHADOW--
SHARING A QUEEN?

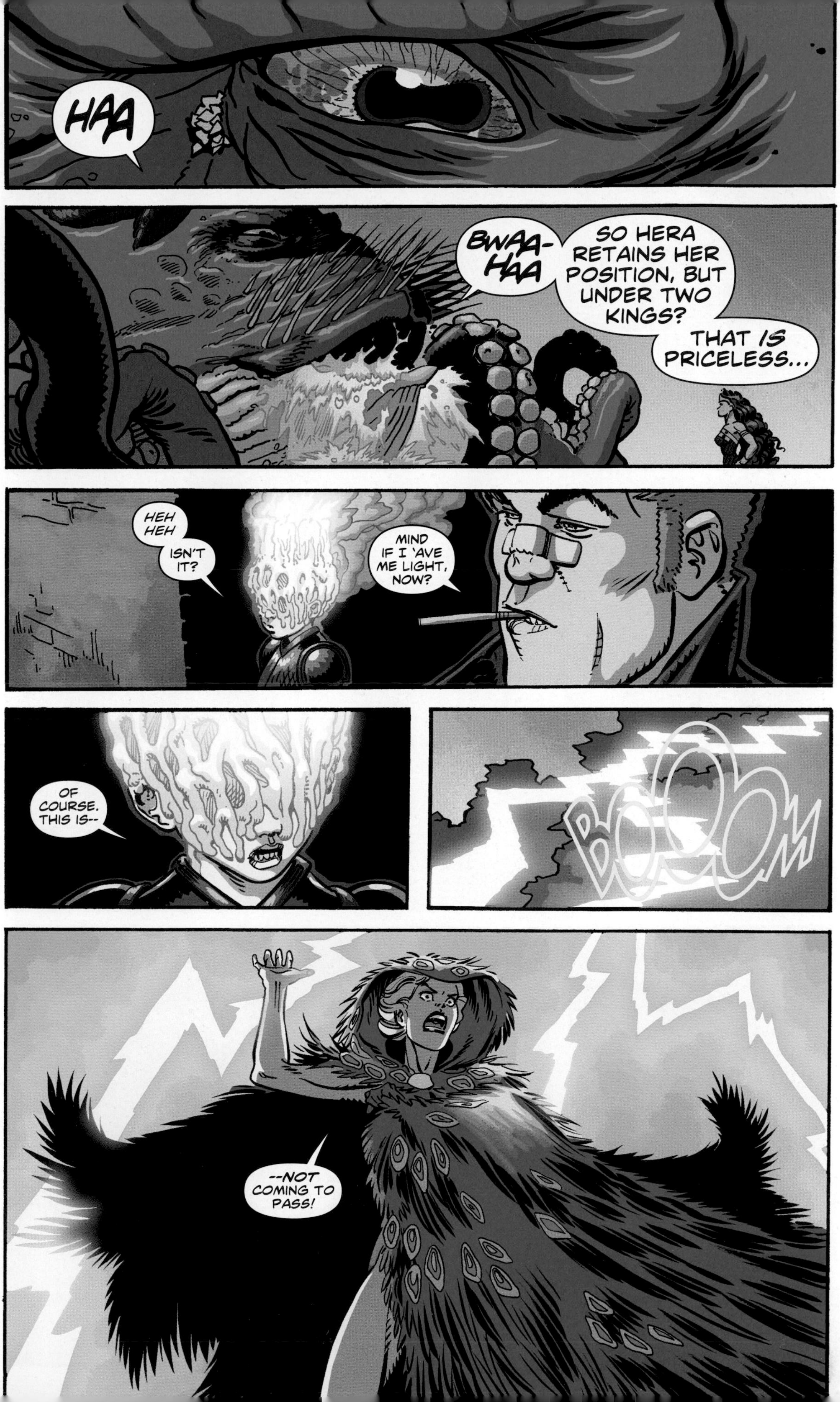
HAA
BWAA-HAA
SO HERA RETAINS HER POSITION, BUT UNDER TWO KINGS?
THAT *IS* PRICELESS...
HEH HEH
ISN'T IT?
MIND IF I 'AVE ME LIGHT, NOW?
OF COURSE. THIS IS--
BOOOOM
--NOT COMING TO PASS!

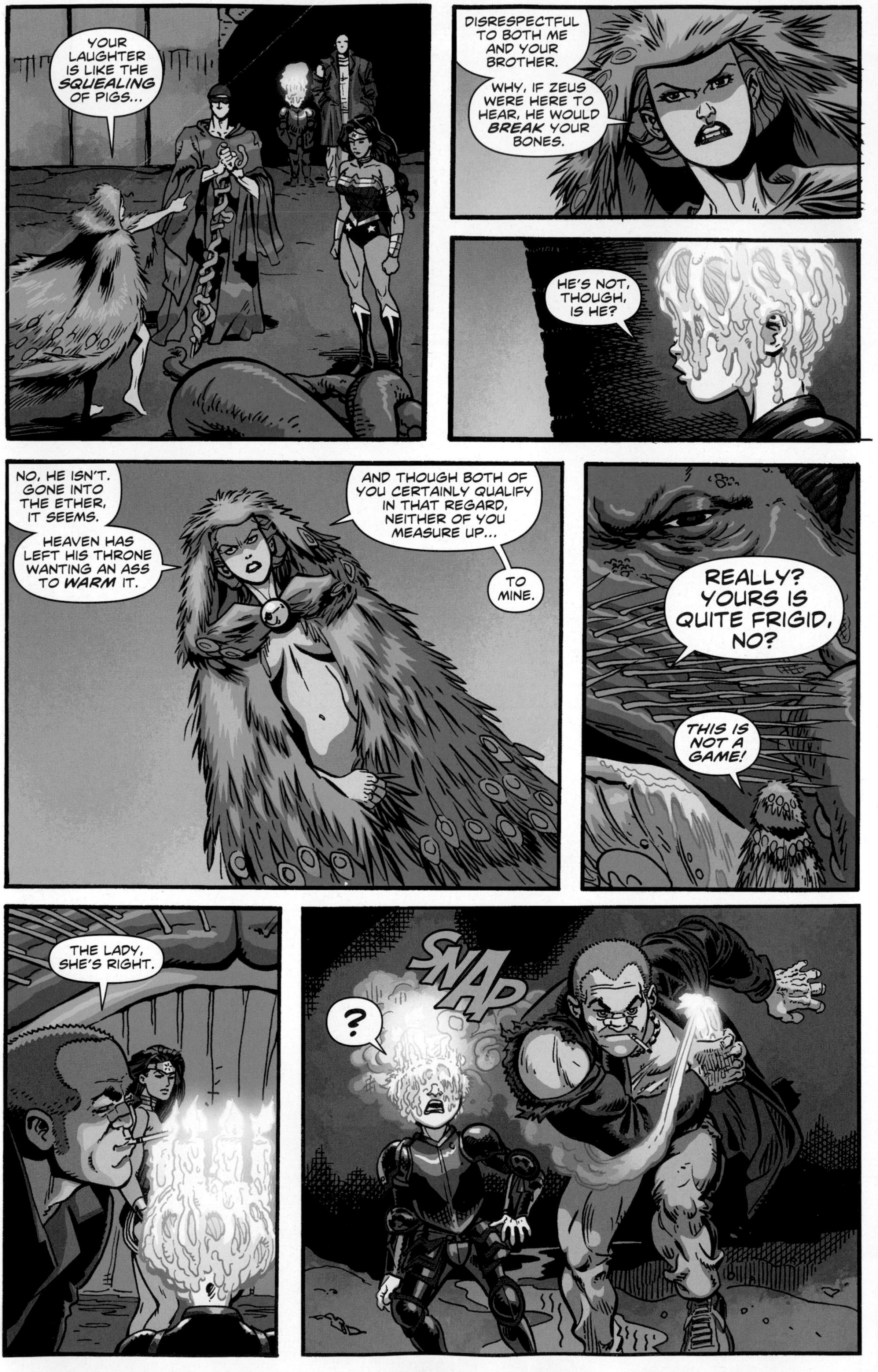
YOUR LAUGHTER IS LIKE THE SQUEALING OF PIGS...
DISRESPECTFUL TO BOTH ME AND YOUR BROTHER.
WHY, IF ZEUS WERE HERE TO HEAR, HE WOULD BREAK YOUR BONES.
HE'S NOT, THOUGH, IS HE?
NO, HE ISN'T. GONE INTO THE ETHER, IT SEEMS.
HEAVEN HAS LEFT HIS THRONE WANTING AN ASS TO WARM IT.
AND THOUGH BOTH OF YOU CERTAINLY QUALIFY IN THAT REGARD, NEITHER OF YOU MEASURE UP...
TO MINE.
REALLY? YOURS IS QUITE FRIGID, NO?
THIS IS NOT A GAME!
THE LADY, SHE'S RIGHT.
SNAP
?

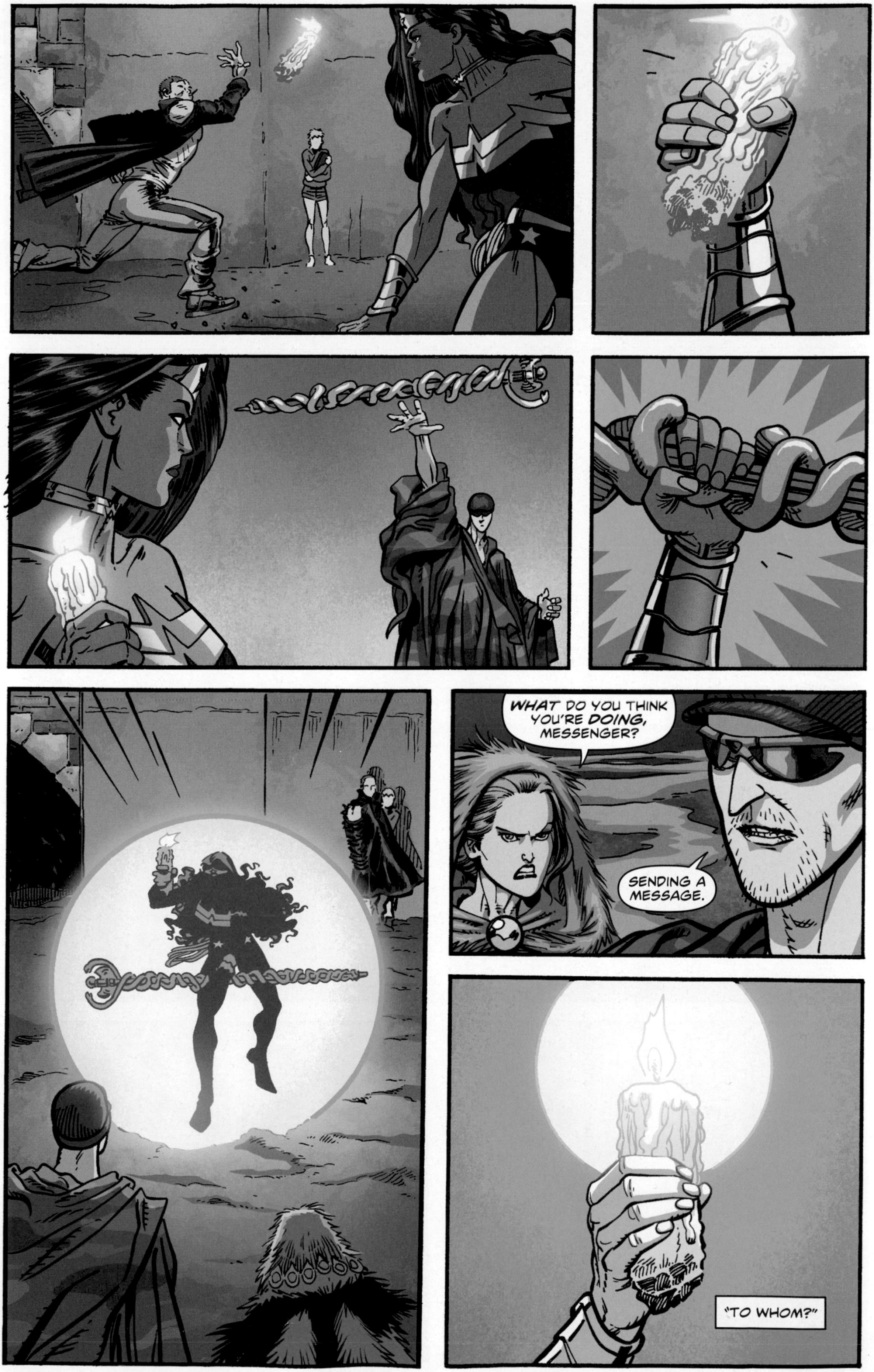
WHAT DO YOU THINK YOU'RE DOING, MESSENGER?
SENDING A MESSAGE.
"TO WHOM?"

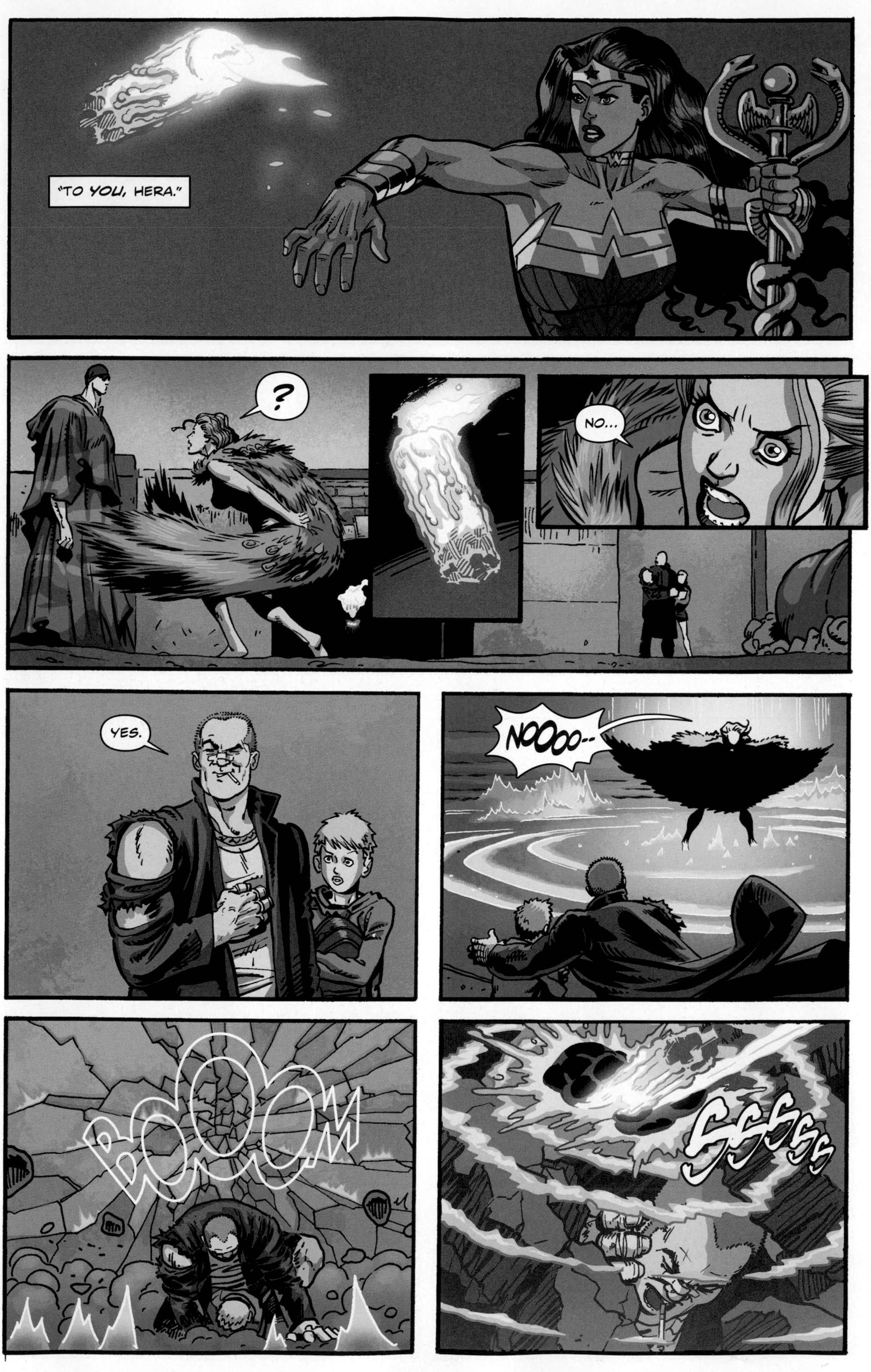

"TO YOU, HERA."
?
NO...
YES.
NOOOO--
BOOOM
SSSSS

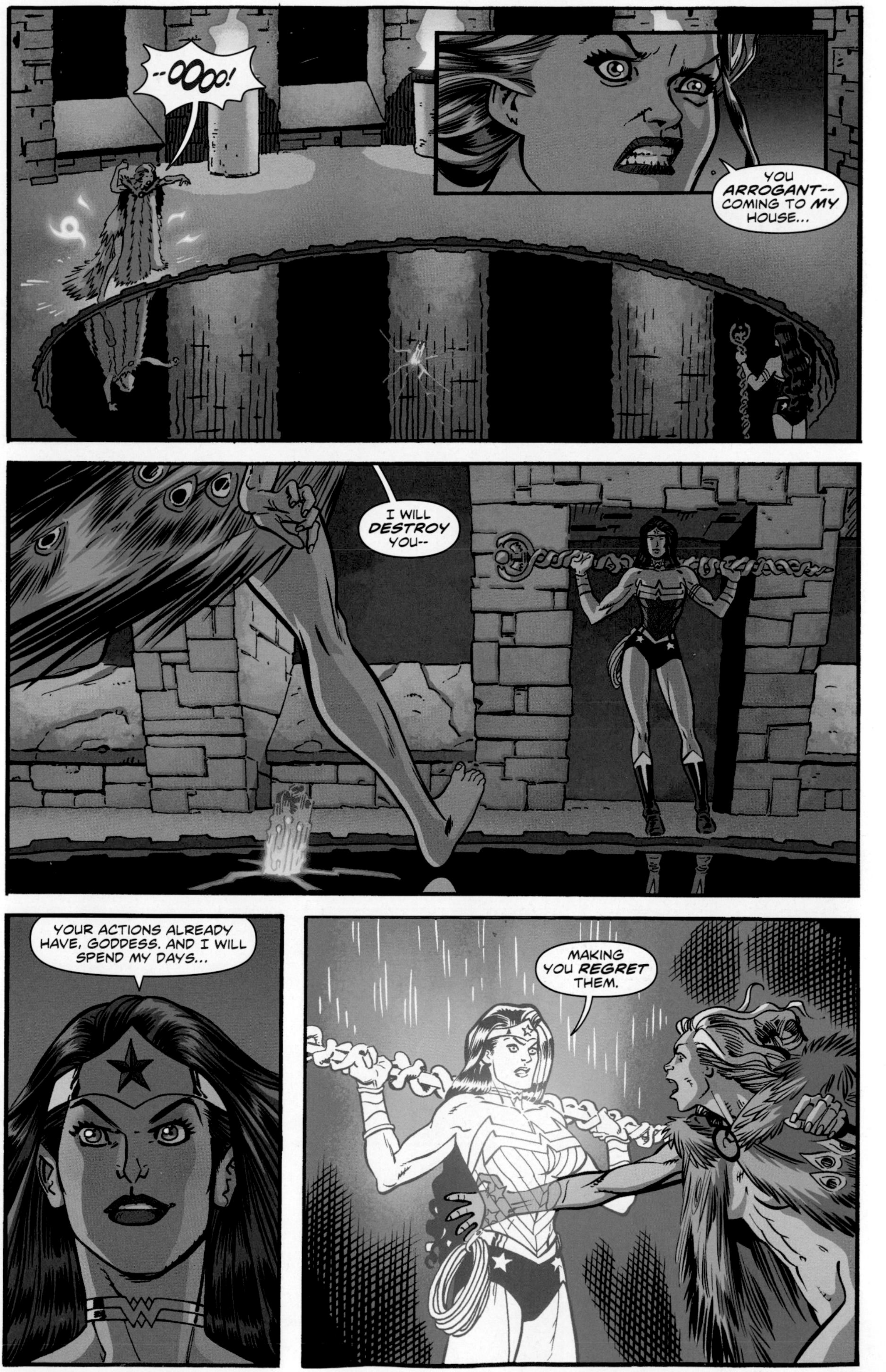
--OOOO!
YOU ARROGANT-- COMING TO MY HOUSE...
I WILL DESTROY YOU--
YOUR ACTIONS ALREADY HAVE, GODDESS. AND I WILL SPEND MY DAYS...
MAKING YOU REGRET THEM.

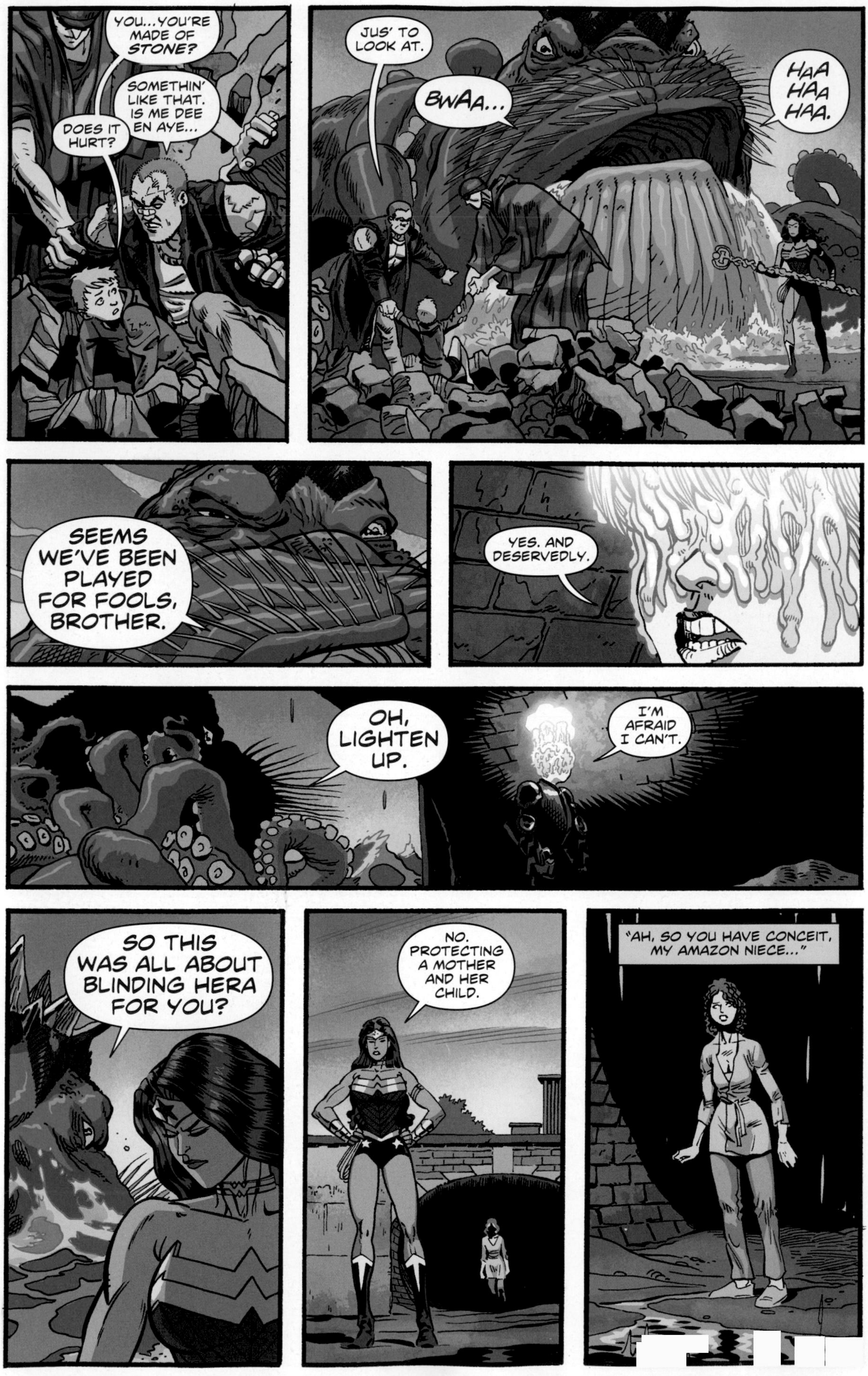
YOU...YOU'RE MADE OF STONE?
SOMETHIN' LIKE THAT. IS ME DEE EN AYE...
DOES IT HURT?
JUS' TO LOOK AT.
BWAA...
HAA HAA HAA.
SEEMS WE'VE BEEN PLAYED FOR FOOLS, BROTHER.
YES. AND DESERVEDLY.
OH, LIGHTEN UP.
I'M AFRAID I CAN'T.
SO THIS WAS ALL ABOUT BLINDING HERA FOR YOU?
NO. PROTECTING A MOTHER AND HER CHILD.
"AH, SO YOU HAVE CONCEIT, MY AMAZON NIECE..."

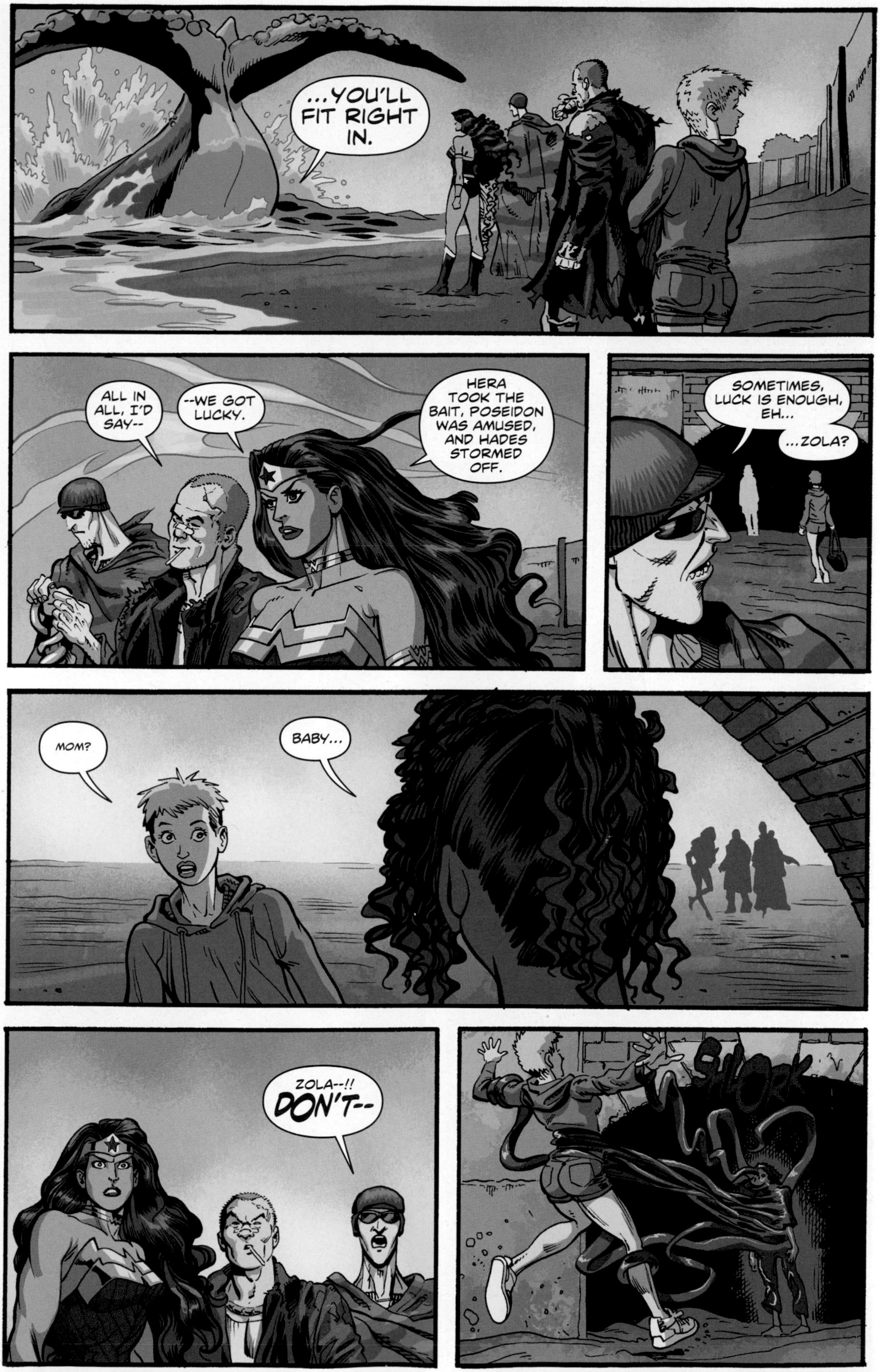
...YOU'LL FIT RIGHT IN.
ALL IN ALL, I'D SAY--
--WE GOT LUCKY.
HERA TOOK THE BAIT, POSEIDON WAS AMUSED, AND HADES STORMED OFF.
SOMETIMES, LUCK IS ENOUGH, EH...
...ZOLA?
MOM?
BABY...
ZOLA--!! DON'T--
SHLORK

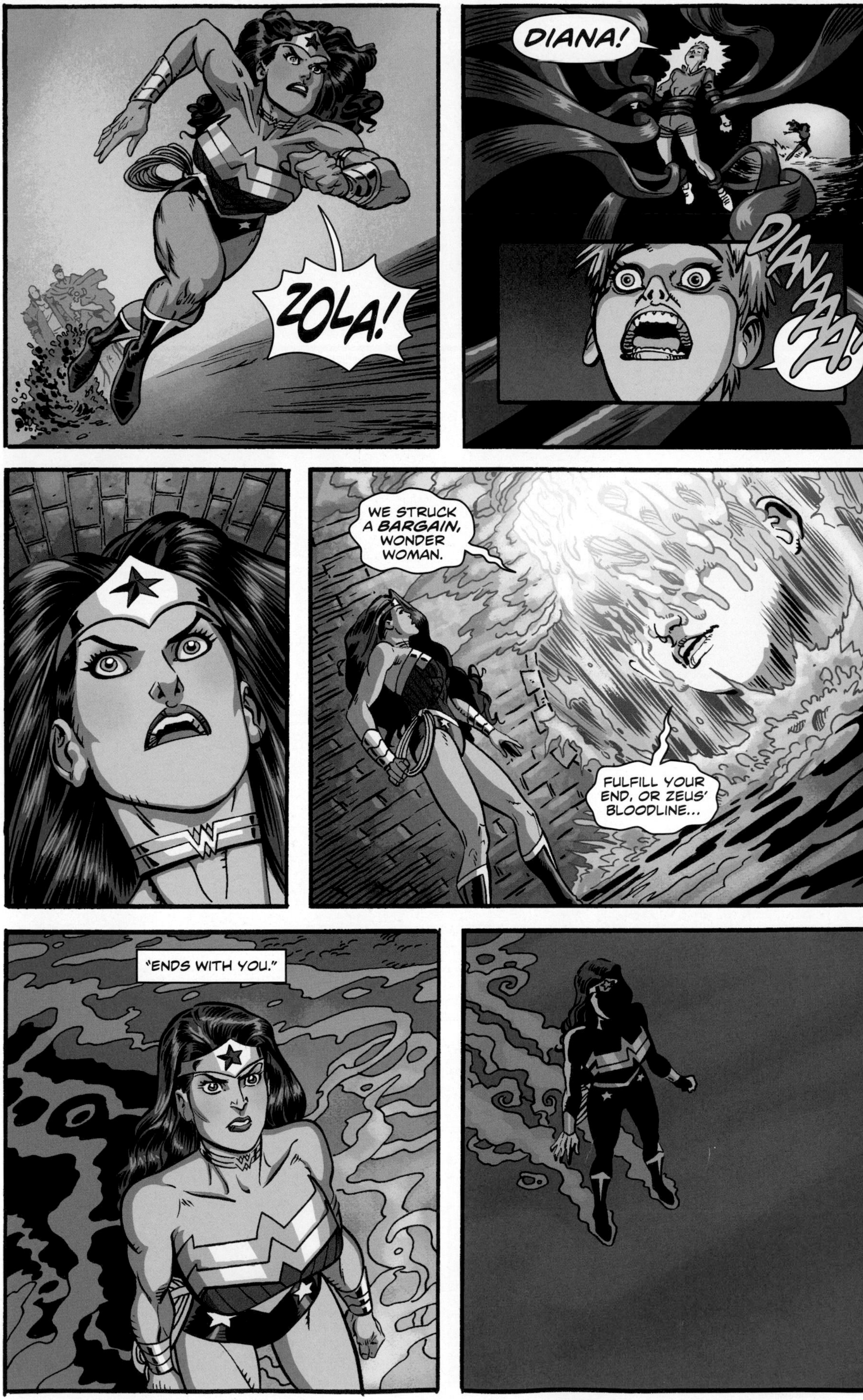
ZOLA!
DIANA!
DIANAAAA!
WE STRUCK A *BARGAIN*, WONDER WOMAN.
FULFILL YOUR END, OR ZEUS' BLOODLINE...
"ENDS WITH YOU."

WONDER WOMAN

CHARACTER DESIGNS BY CLIFF CHIANG

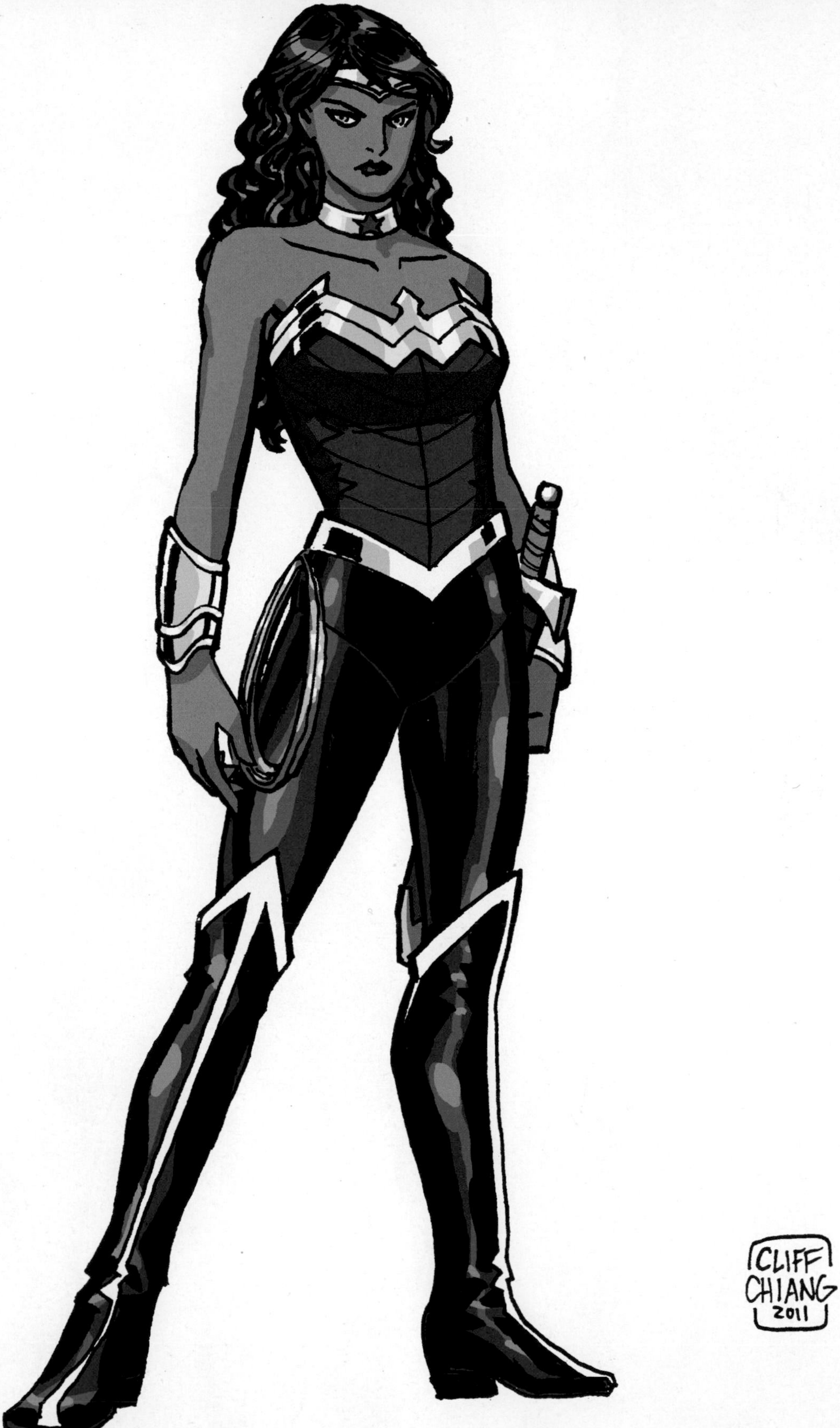
CLIFF CHIANG 2011

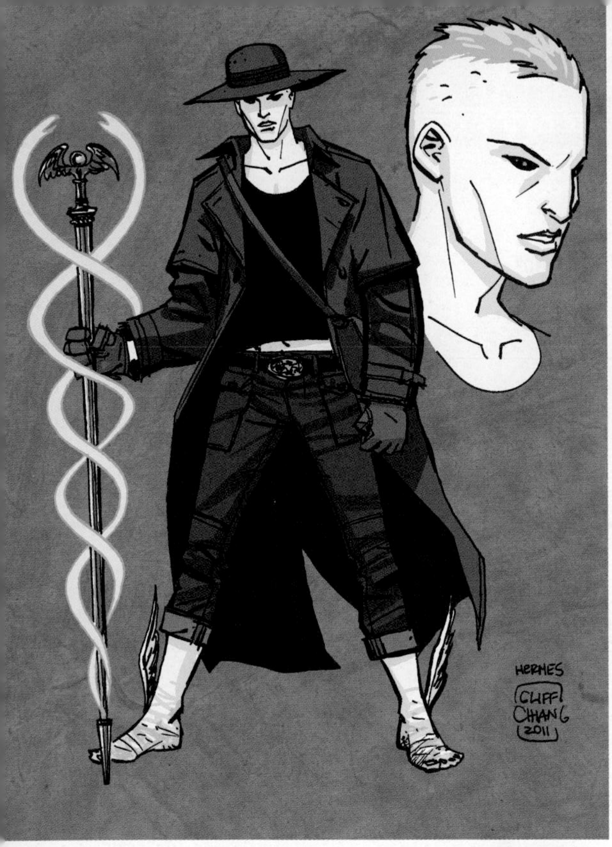
HERMES
CLIFF CHIANG 2011

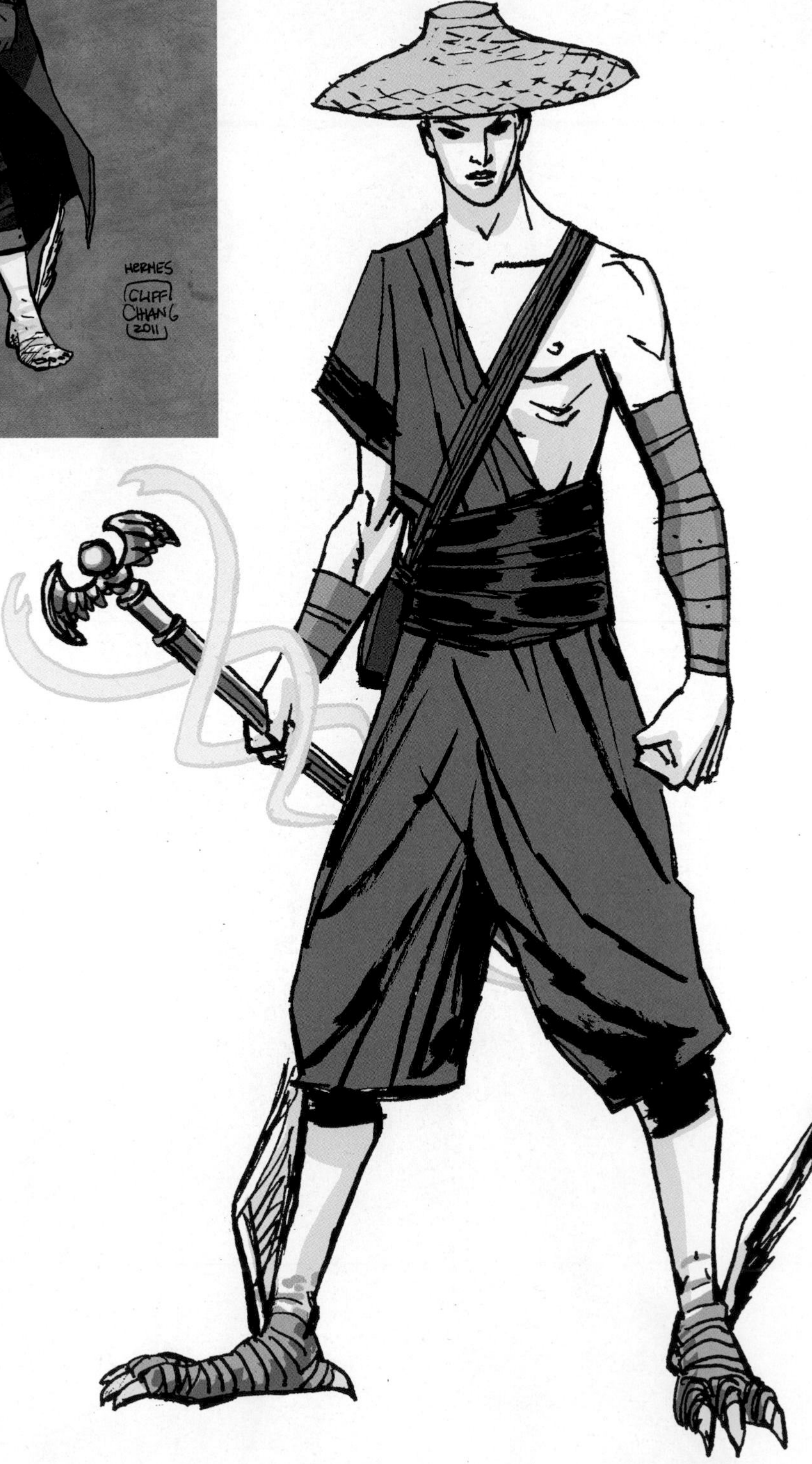

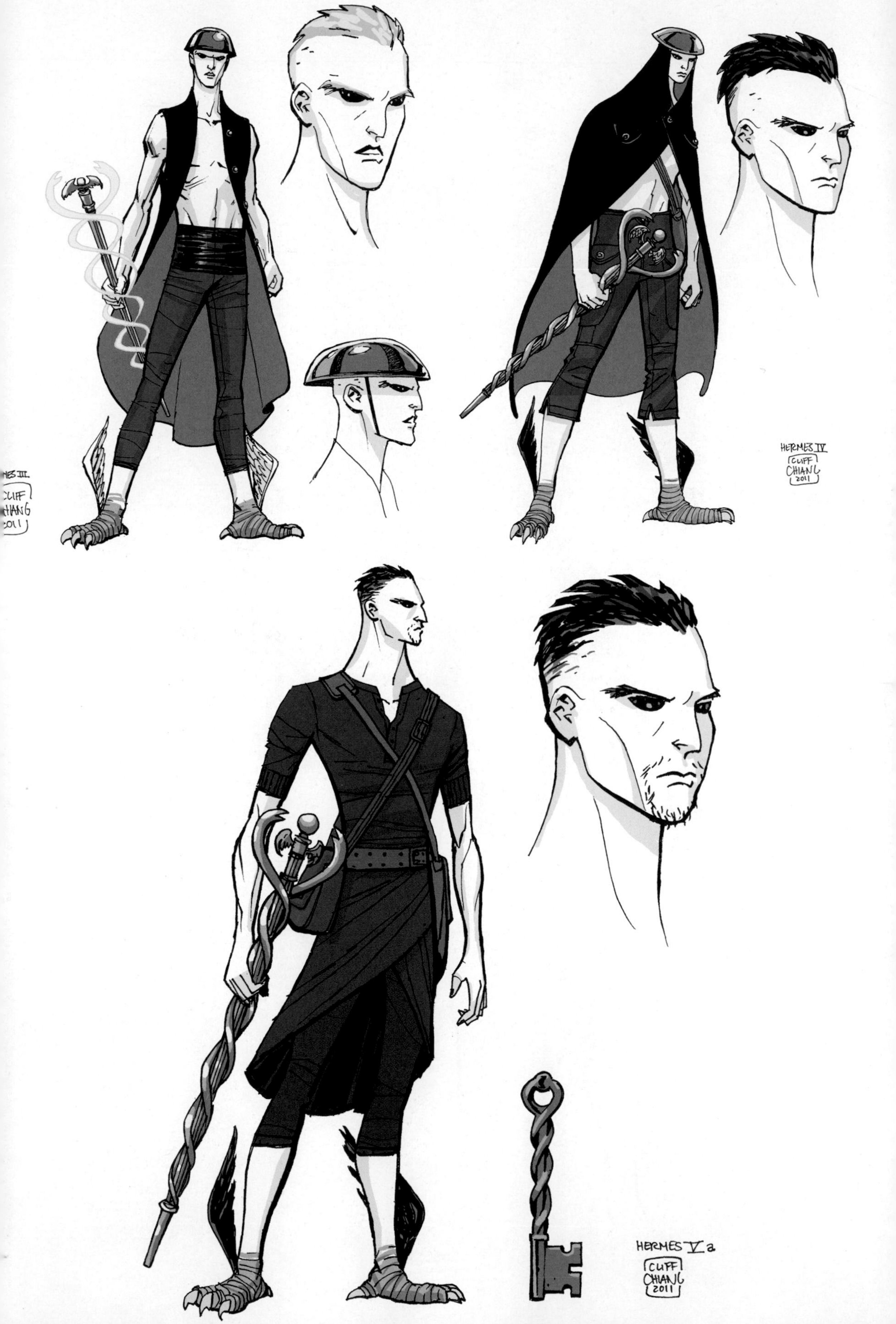
MES III.
CLIFF
HIANG
2011
HERMES IV
CLIFF
CHIANG
2011
HERMES V a
CLIFF
CHIANG
2011

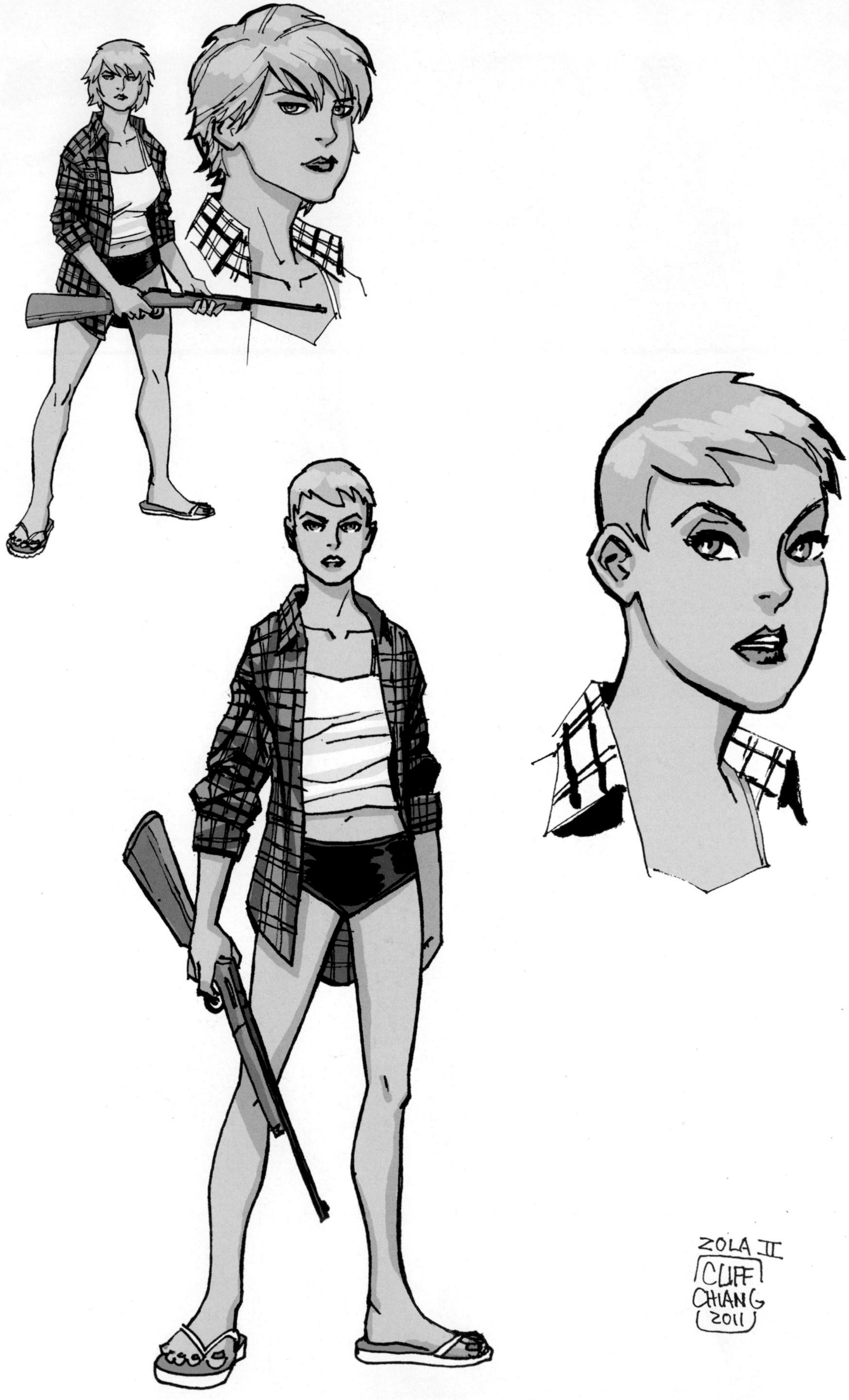
ZOLA II
CLIFF
CHIANG
2011

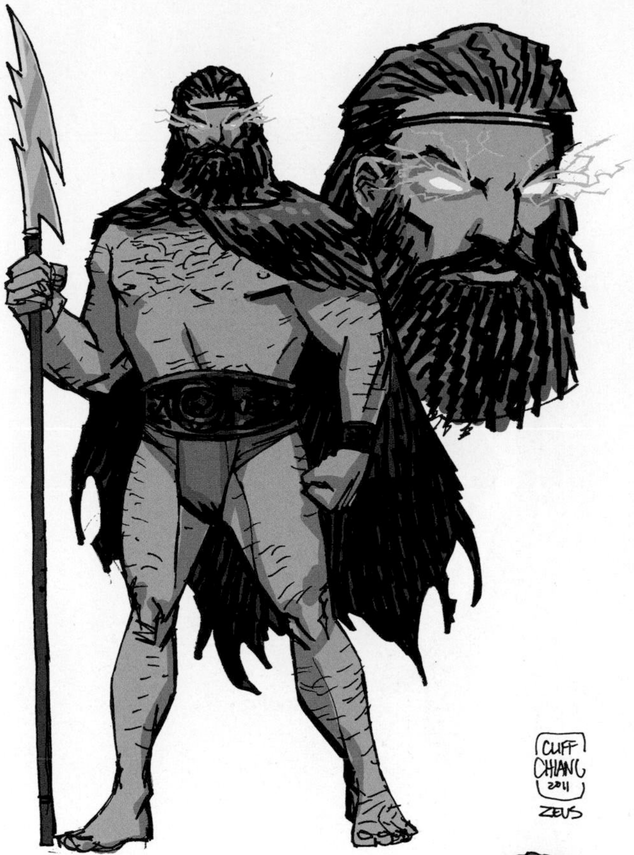
CLIFF CHIANG 2011
ZEUS

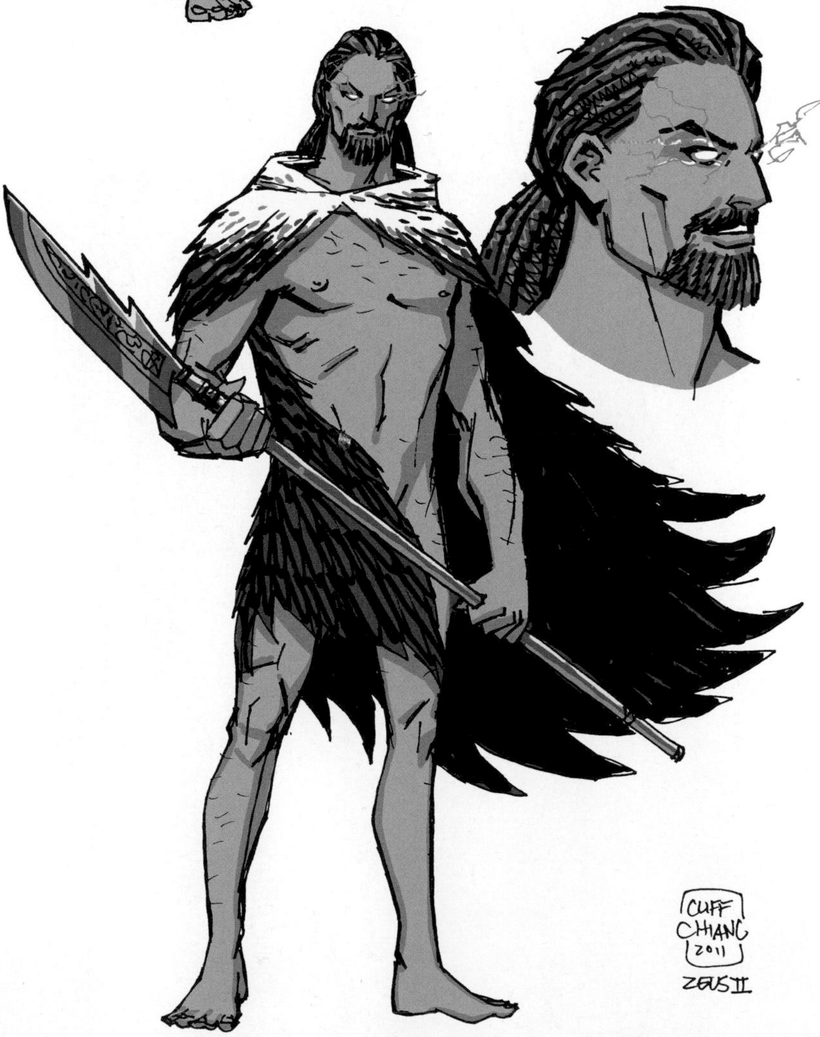
CLIFF CHIANG 2011
ZEUS II

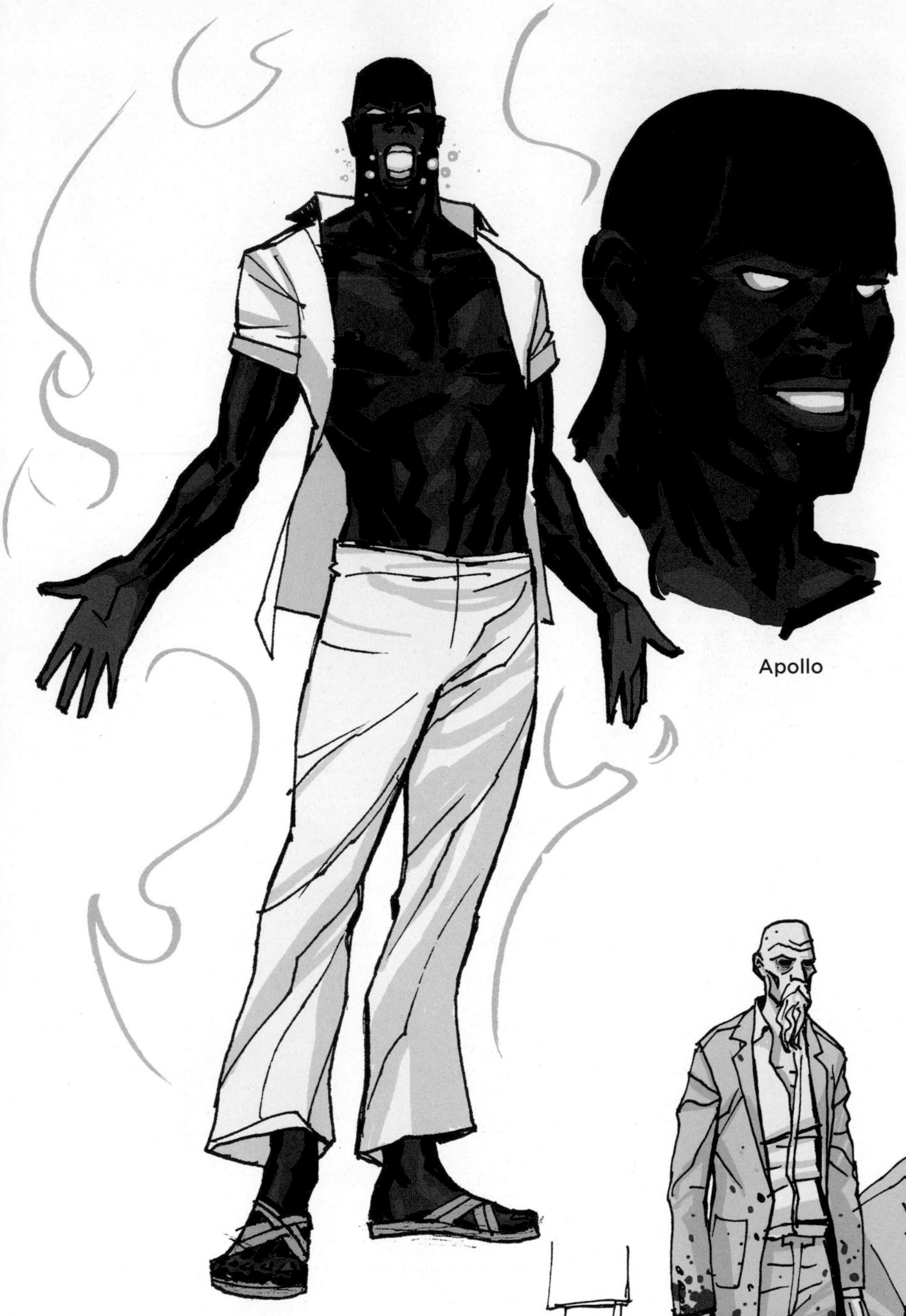

Apollo

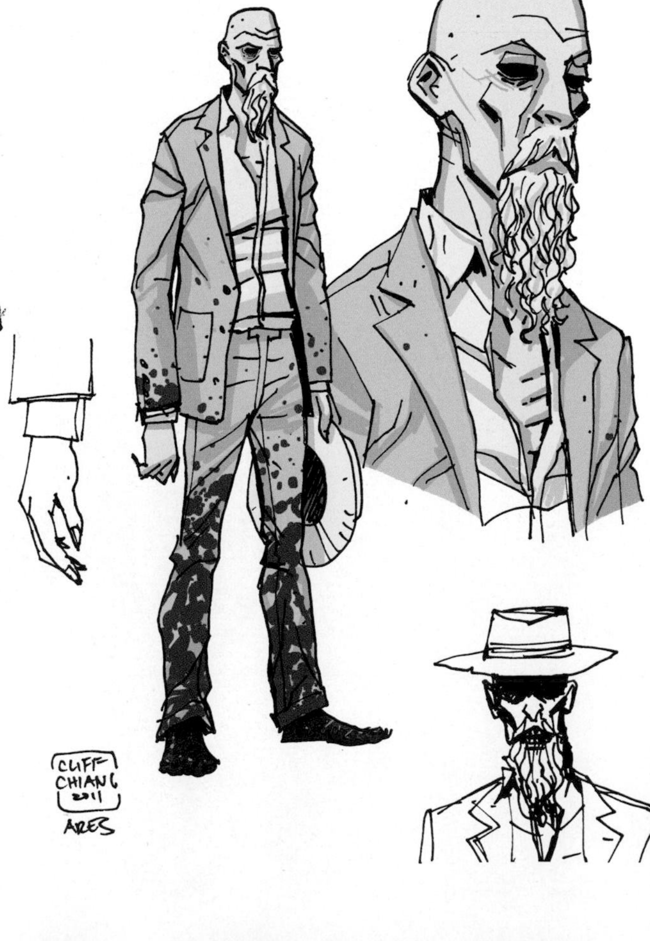
CLIFF CHIANG 2011
ARES

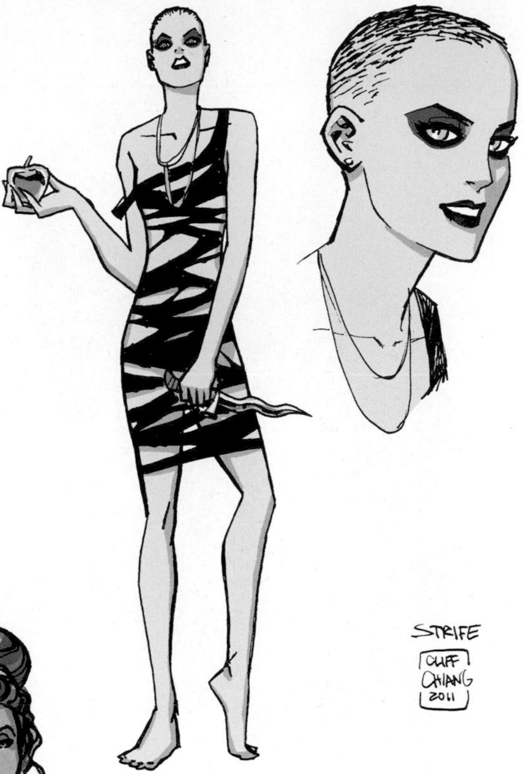
STRIFE
CLIFF CHIANG 2011

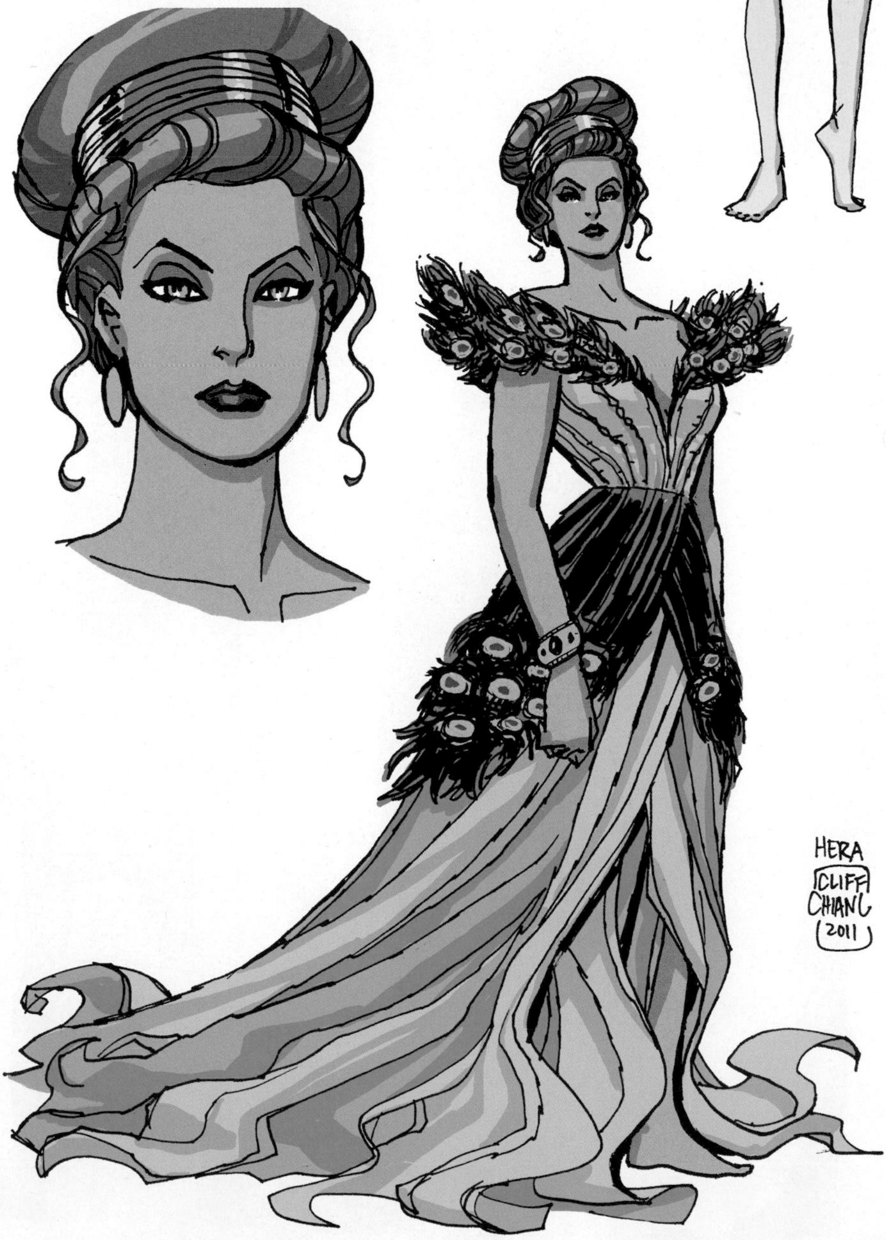
HERA
CLIFF CHIANG 2011

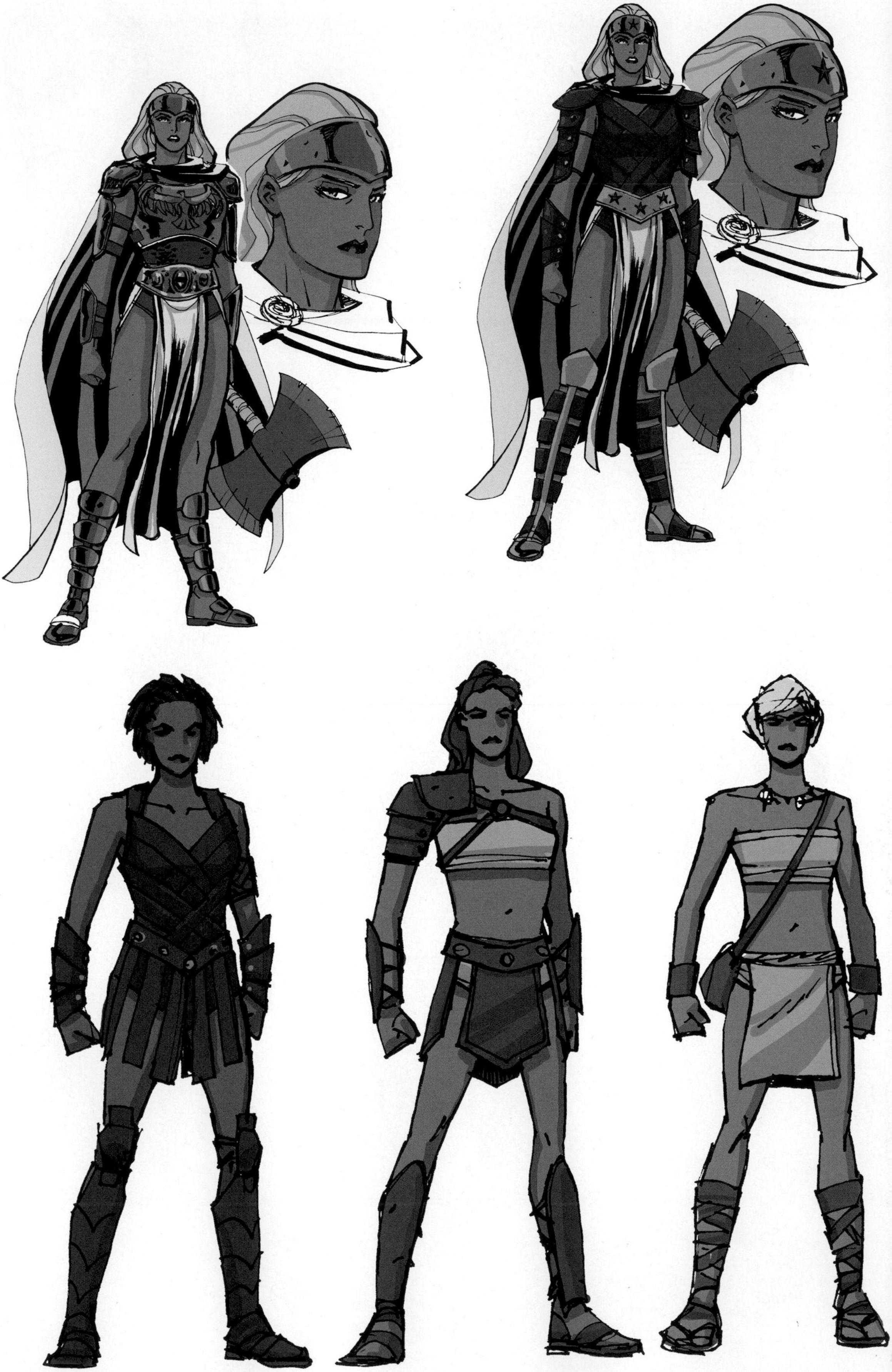

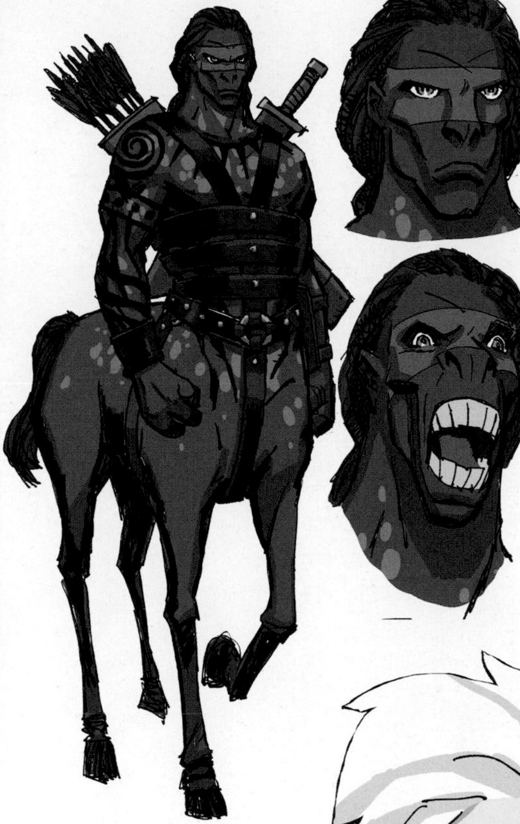

Designs for Hippolyta, the Amazons and the male and female centaurs.

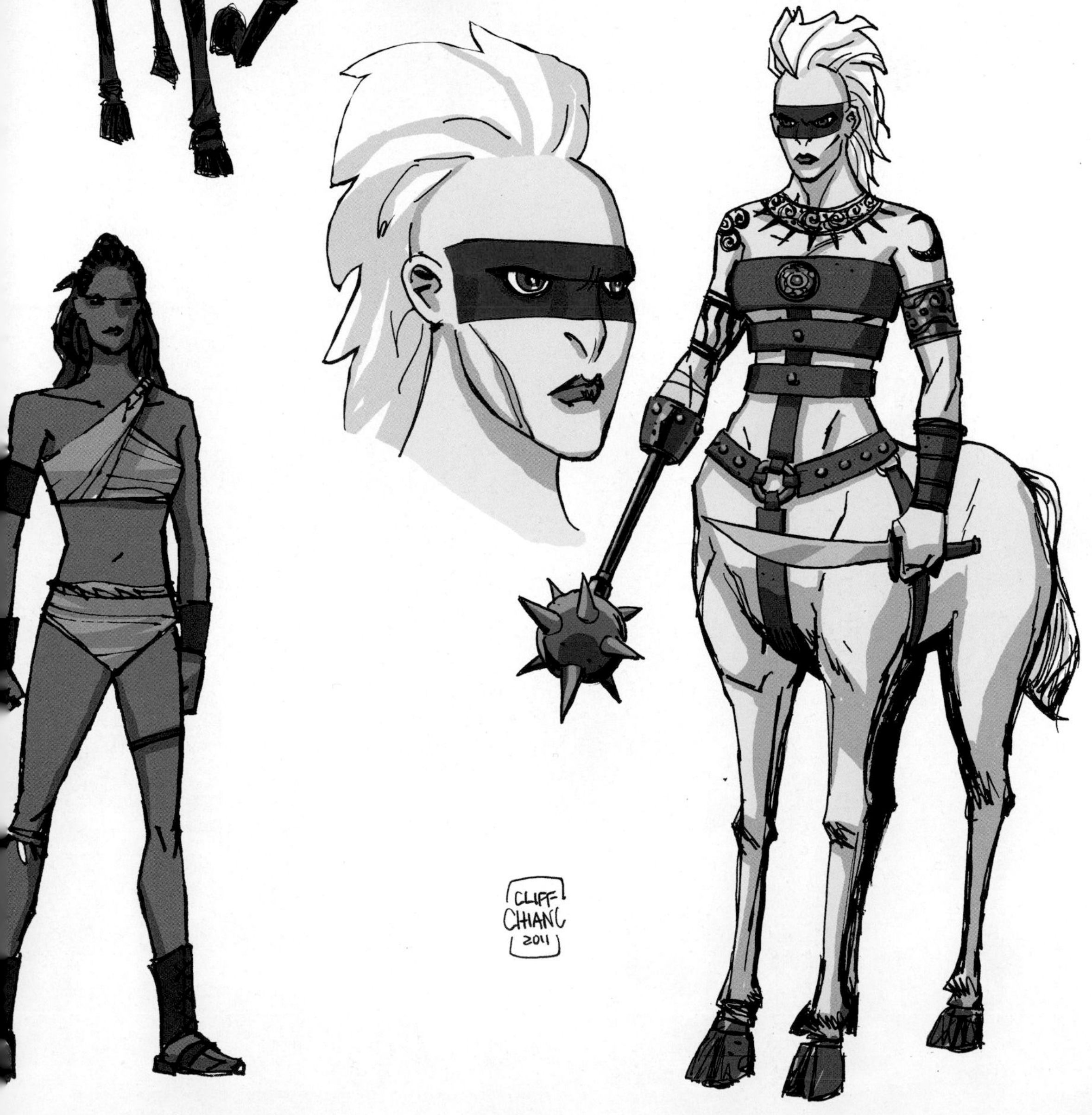
CLIFF CHIANG 2011

WONDER WOMAN
COVER SKETCHES BY CLIFF CHIANG

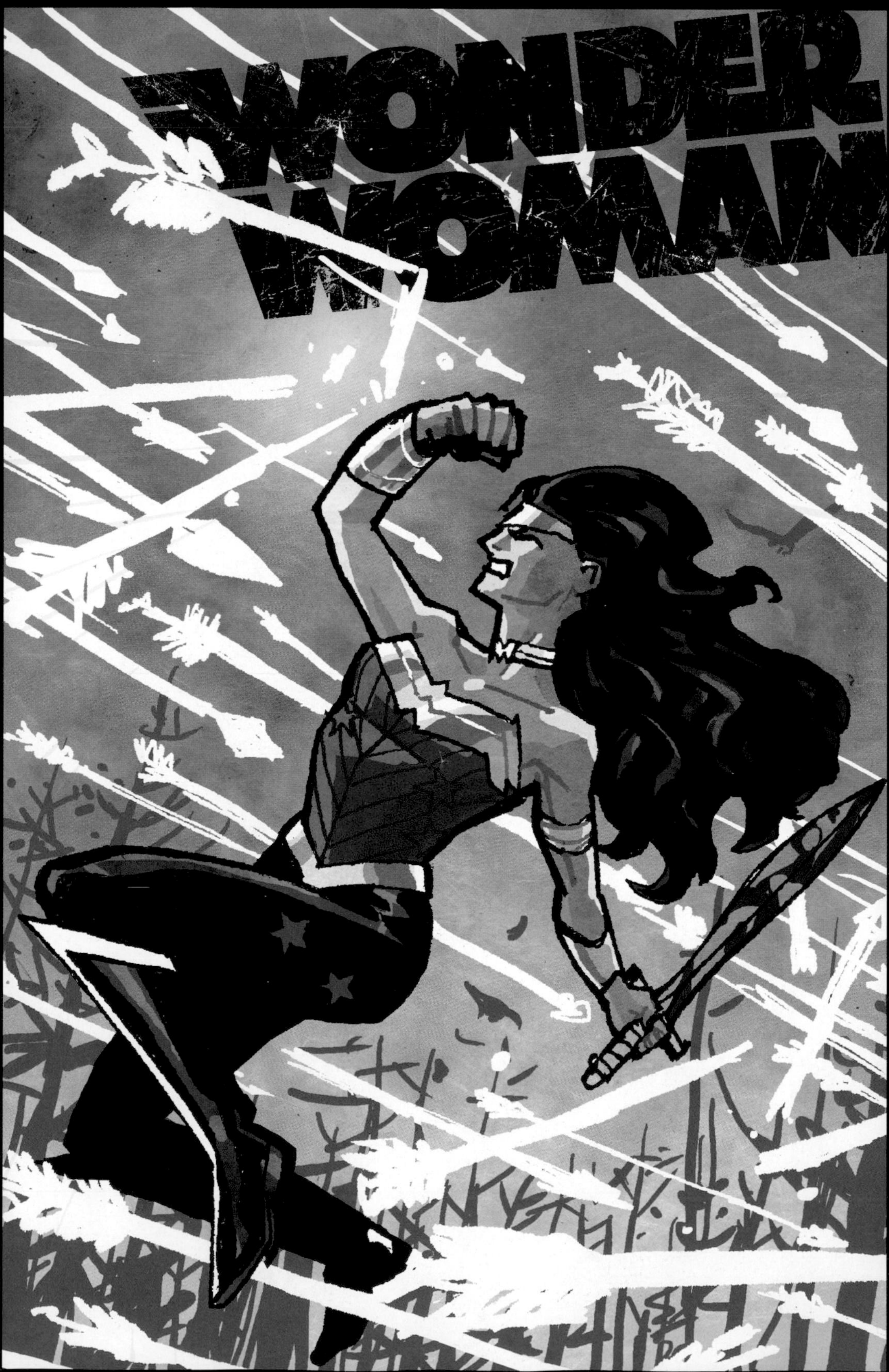
WONDER WOMAN

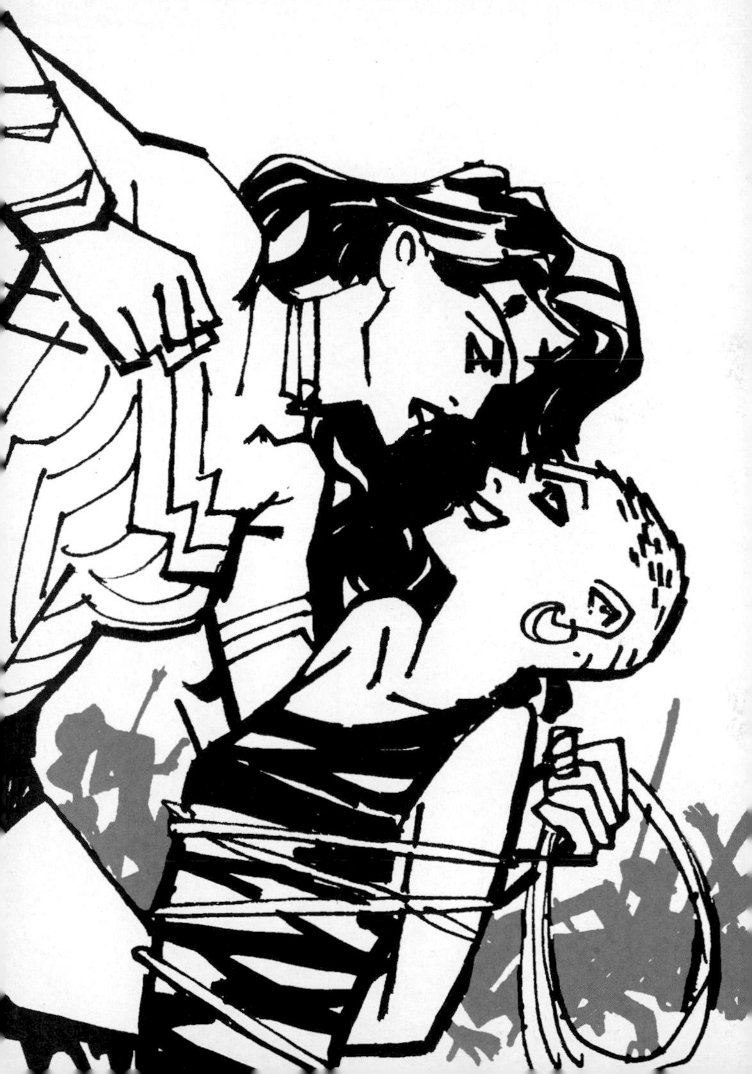

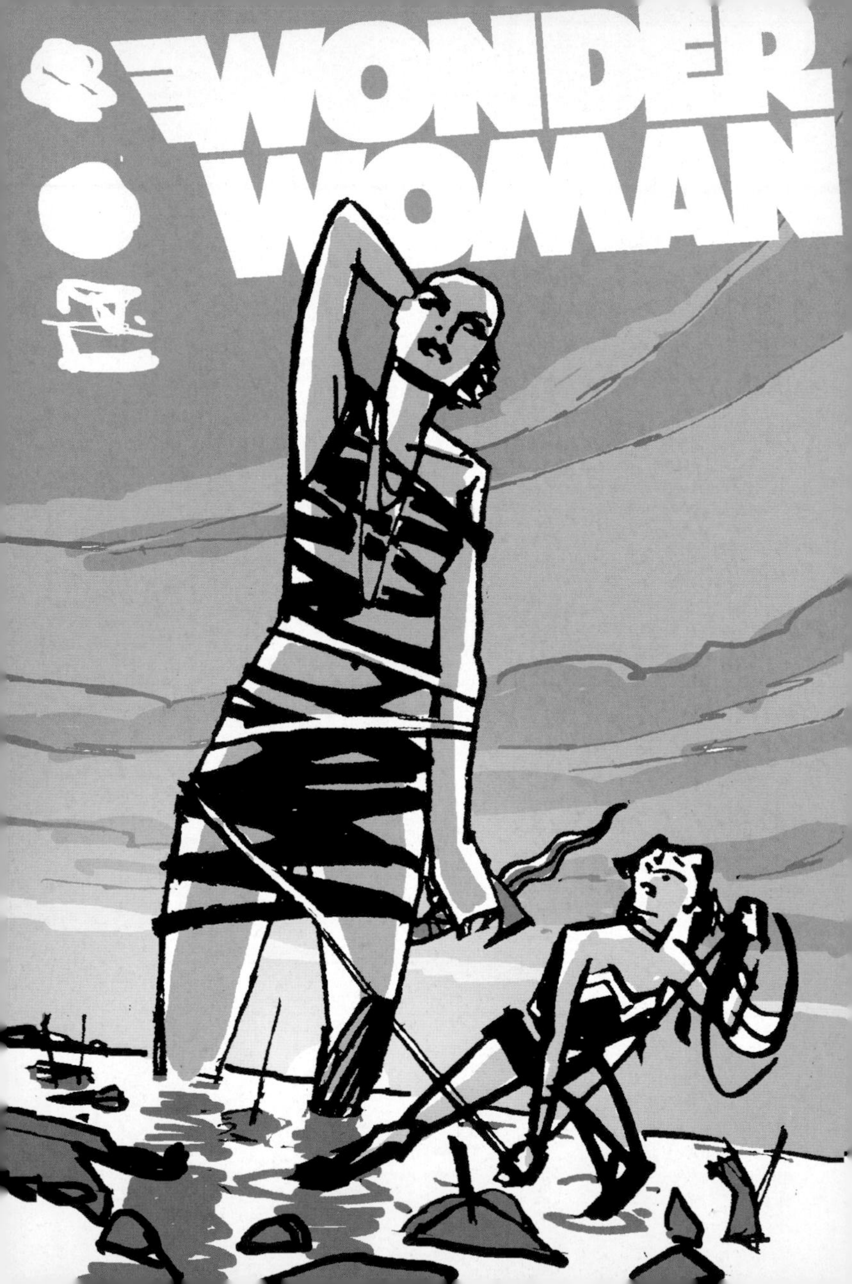
WONDER
WOMAN

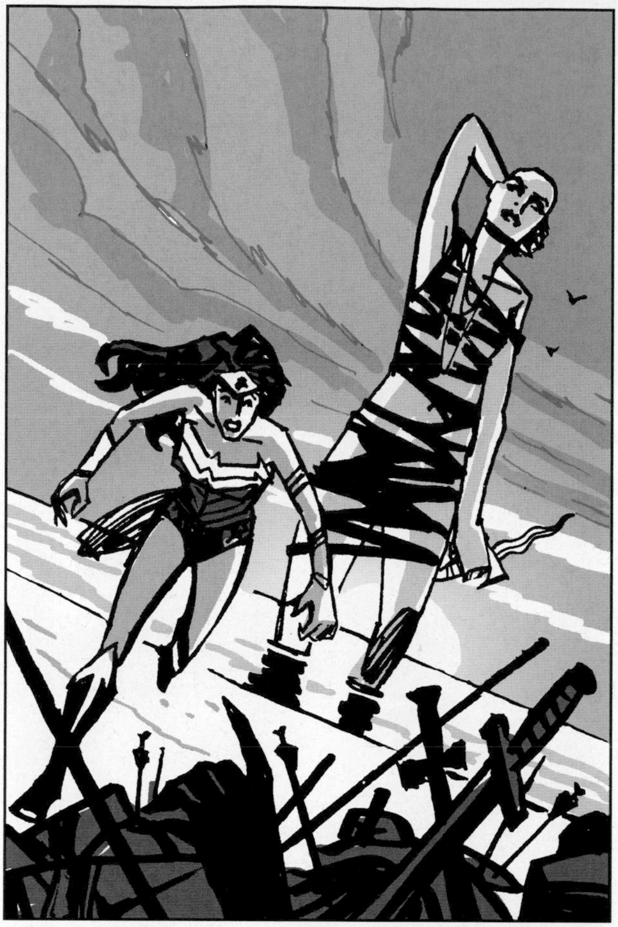

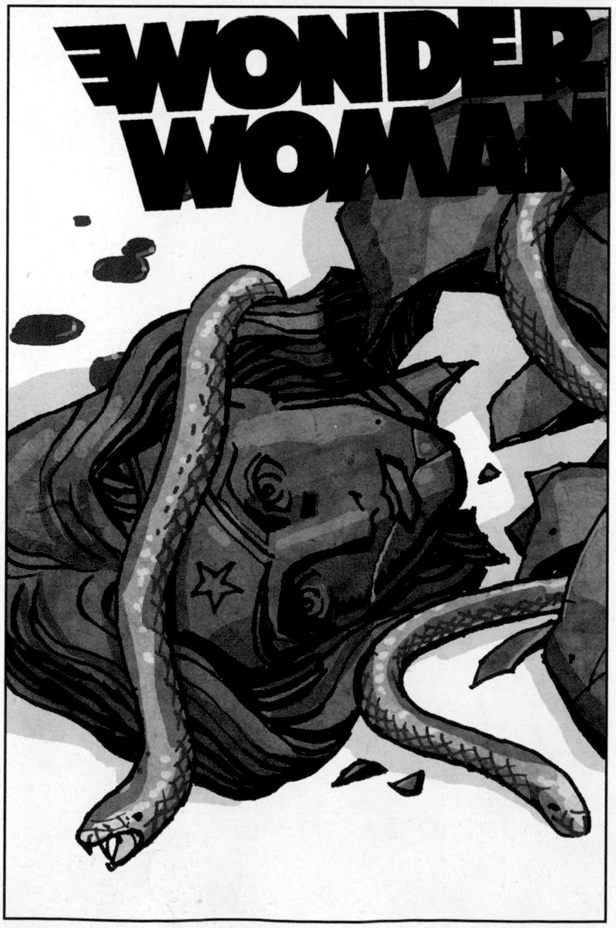
WONDER
WOMAN

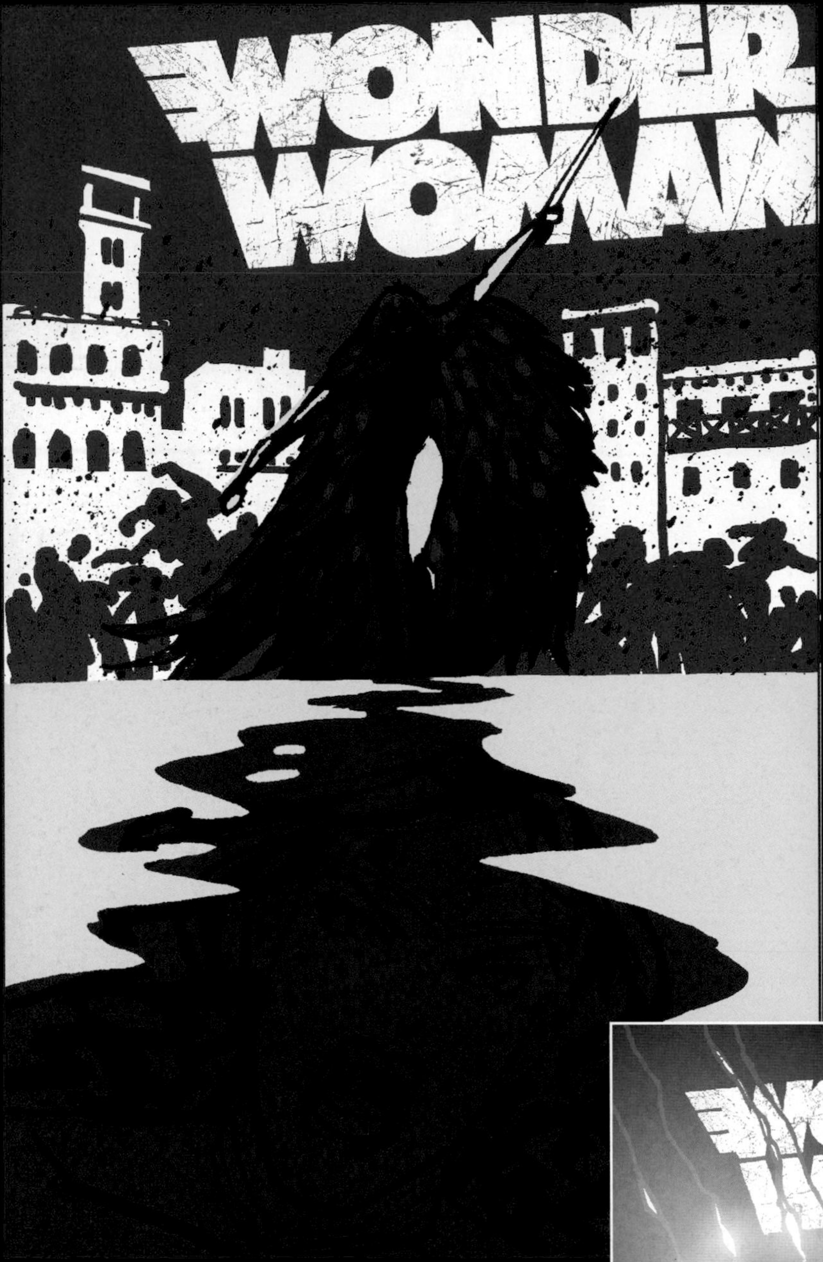
WONDER WOMAN

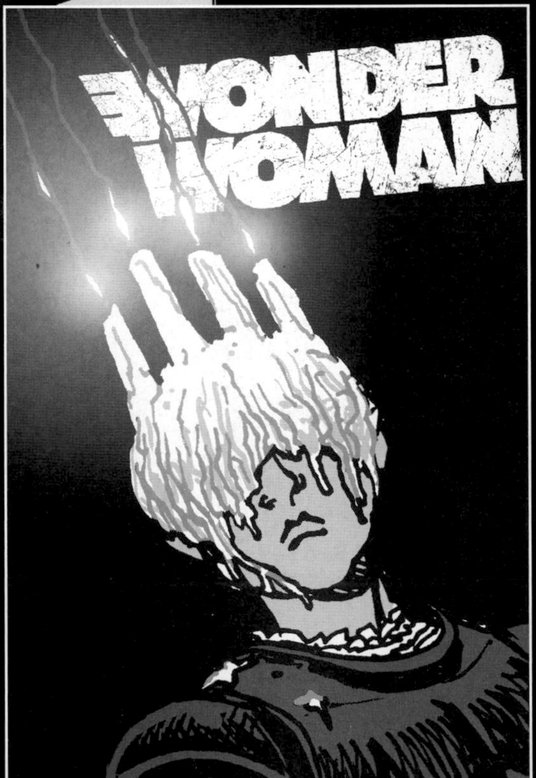
WONDER WOMAN

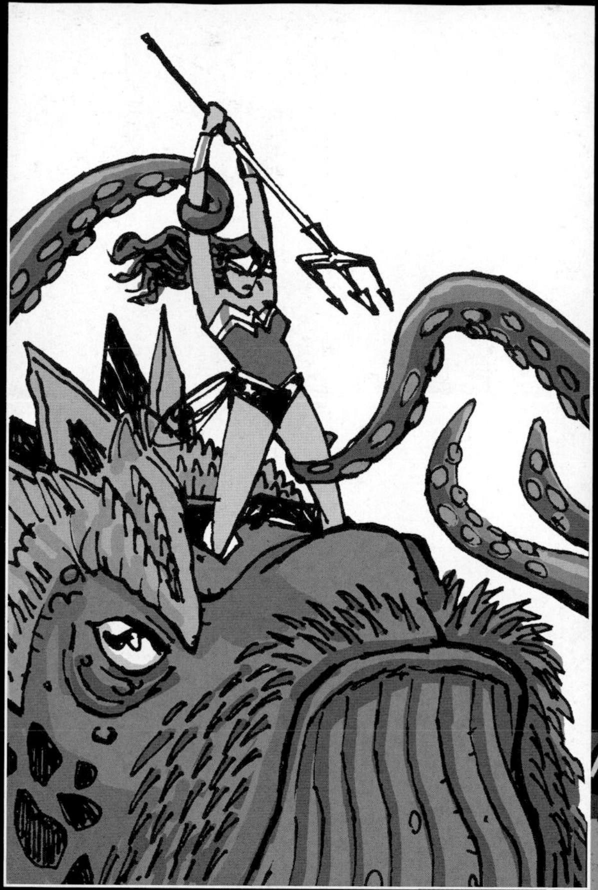

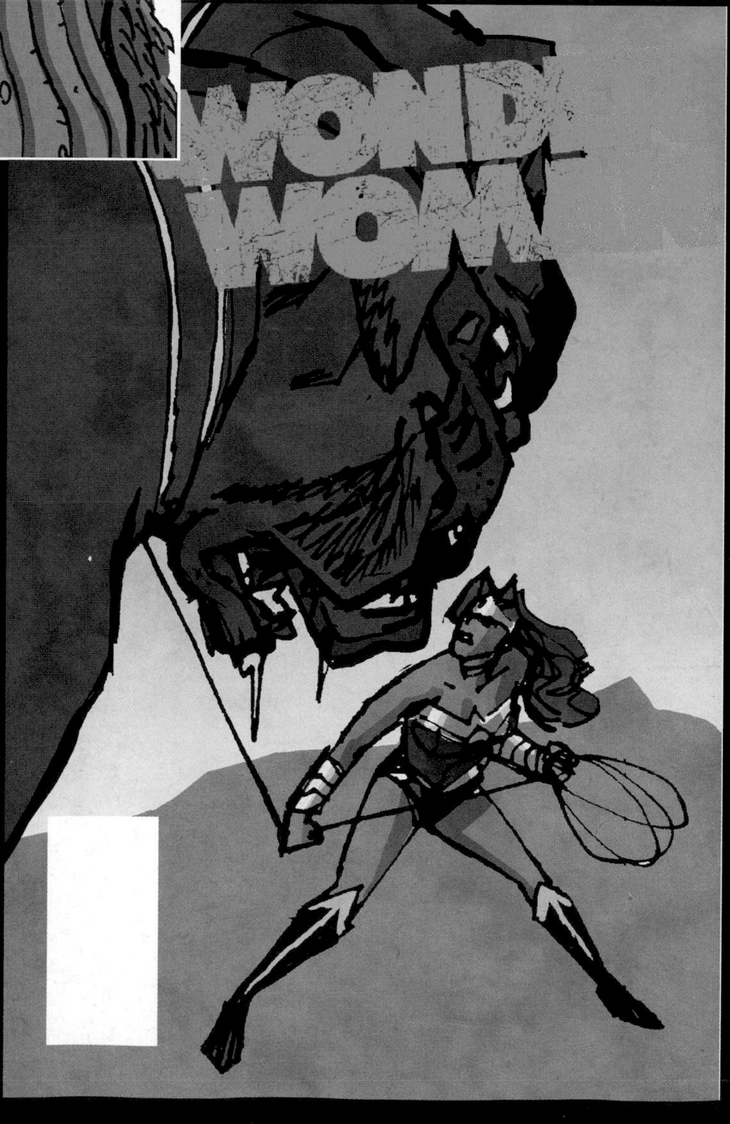
WOND
WOM